The
Royal Shakespeare Company

A HISTORY OF TEN DECADES

SALLY BEAUMAN

Oxford New York Toronto Melbourne
OXFORD UNIVERSITY PRESS
1982

Oxford University Press, Walton Street, Oxford OX2 6DP

London Glasgow New York Toronto
Delhi Bombay Calcutta Madras Karachi
Kuala Lumpur Singapore Hong Kong Tokyo
Nairobi Dar es Salaam Cape Town
Melbourne Auckland
and associates in
Beirut Berlin Ibadan Mexico City Nicosia

Library of Congress Cataloging in Publication Data
Beauman, Sally.
The Royal Shakespeare Company.
Includes index.
1. Royal Shakespeare Company. 2. Shakespeare,
William, 1564–1616—Stage history. I. Title
PN2596.S82R683 792'.09424'89 81–16969
ISBN 0-19-212209-6 AACR2

Set by King's English Typesetters Ltd
Printed in Great Britain
at the University Press, Oxford
by Eric Buckley
Printer to the University

For Alan

Acknowledgements

This book has been influenced by many conversations, over a period of years, with people working for the Royal Shakespeare Company, including actors, administrators, designers, directors, stage staff and writers – to all of whom I am very grateful.

Once I began work on the book I was particularly helped by the following people, and my deepest thanks go to them: Harry Andrews; Dame Peggy Ashcroft; John Barton; Reginald Bosley; Nicholas Bridges-Adams; David Brierley; Peter Brook; Nancy Burman; Glen Byam Shaw; Lord Chandos (for permission to quote from his grandfather's letters); Ron Daniels; Patrick Donnell; Fabia Drake; Dennis Flower; Sir John Gielgud; Sir Peter Hall; Terry Hands; Peter Harlock; Mrs John Hitching (Luise Randle Ayrton); Ian Holm; Alan Howard; Rachel Kempson; the late John Laurie; Sir Emile Littler; Mrs David Lloyd (who lent me her mother's 1920s diaries); Keith Michell; Trevor Nunn; Lord Olivier; Richard Pasco; Anthony Quayle; Ian Richardson; Norman Rodway; James Sargent; Paul Scofield; Sebastian Shaw; Janet Suzman; J. C. Trewin; Gwynne Whitby; and William Wilkinson.

My thanks also go to the Governors of the RSC; to Douglas Matthews and the staff of the London Library; to Eileen Robinson and Mary White and the staff of the Shakespeare Birthplace Trust Library, Stratford-upon-Avon; to The Society of Authors on behalf of the Bernard Shaw Estate and the Granville-Barker Estate for permission to quote from letters; to the Special Collections Division, University of Calgary Libraries for permission to quote from the Bridges-Adams papers; and to the Phoenix Trust for their generous financial assistance.

I have in all cases attempted to trace copyright holders, and where I have failed I apologize for any apparent negligence.

I should like to thank Susan le Roux, Jeremy Lewis, and Michael Poulton of Oxford University Press for their continued help and enthusiasm, and in particular my editor, Judith Chamberlain, for the enormous assistance she gave me over many months.

Finally I must thank Lady Flower, who with great generosity, and without proviso, lent me all her late husband, Sir Fordham Flower's, papers pertaining to the Shakespeare Memorial Theatre and the Royal Shakespeare Company. Uncatalogued, and previously unexamined, they proved to chronicle vividly, and occasionally explosively, some ninety years of the RSC's 102-year past, and I have drawn on them extensively. So, for her help I am above all grateful; without it, this book could not have been written.

Contents

Illustrations

The author and publishers wish to thank the Royal Shakespeare Company and the Shakespeare Centre for their help in supplying most of the photographs from their archives. They also wish to thank Harvard University Press for permission to reproduce the photographs by Angus McBean; the Trustees of the National Portrait Gallery, London, for that of Frank Benson as Richard II; and the individual photographers, when they could be traced, for permission to reproduce those which are credited to them.

Prelude

In 1767 the town council of Stratford-upon-Avon decided to rebuild the town hall. The councillors chose a modest design in Cotswold stone, ornamented with classic arches on the front and north faces, and accepted a tender for the building for £678. There were two problems only. The first was financial: the prudent burghers of Stratford limited the council's contribution to the building to £200, which meant the rest of the sum had to be raised privately by subscription. The second was that over the central arch on the north side of the building was a large and elegant niche, left glaringly empty in the original designs. By the end of the year it was obvious to the council that the project of the new town hall was failing to catch people's imaginations; subscriptions to it had been few and miserly. What was needed was something which would awaken interest in the project, and the council believed it had hit on the perfect solution – one which would also solve the problem of the empty niche. The niche, they declared, must be adorned, and the most suitable adornment would clearly be a bust of Shakespeare, the town's most illustrious native son.

In the past Stratford had, it was true, felt little obligation to honour William Shakespeare's name in any way whatsoever. It had, for instance, allowed the bicentenary of his birth, in 1764, to pass entirely unremarked. But by 1767 even the town council of Stratford had begun to realize that its association with Shakespeare was a potential asset. Pilgrimage to the town of his birth and death was already becoming popular, so much so that Francis Gastrell, the owner of Shakespeare's house, New Place, had even cut down the celebrated mulberry tree in its garden (said to have been planted by the Bard's own hand) in an effort to deter the worshippers and souvenir-seekers who already plagued him. But his action had merely accelerated the birth of a local industry: Thomas Sharp, a local carpenter and carver, had promptly bought the timber and for the past ten years had been carrying on a highly profitable trade in mulberry wood knick-knacks, which proliferated as inexhaustibly as relics of the true cross. With such an example of enterprise before them, the councillors' choice of a bust of Shakespeare seemed astute. The only problem was to find someone else to pay for it.

It was the Steward of the County Records for Stratford who suggested the perfect candidate: David Garrick. Garrick was the leading actor of his day, and the manager and part-owner of the Drury Lane Theatre; much of the increased popularity of Shakespeare's plays that century was due to his performances and productions. He was also rich. In return for his donation the council proposed to honour Garrick with the Freedom of the Borough, the deed to be couched in a box of – inevitably – sacred Shakespearian mulberry wood.[1] Garrick accepted the council's proposals graciously, but his fertile mind soon soared beyond the simplicities of a statue and some deeds in a wooden box. From the council's meanness and the Steward's letter, sprang Garrick's idea for an elaborate celebration in honour of Shakespeare – the Shakespeare Jubilee. And from that Jubilee stretched the long chain of events that culminated in the building of a theatre at Stratford; from that theatre evolved the company now known as the Royal Shakespeare Company, one of the greatest theatre groups in the world.

None of these developments might have happened had it not been for the scale and notoriety of Garrick's Jubilee. It took place in September 1769 and lasted just three days. But from the moment Garrick announced it from the stage of the Drury Lane Theatre, it captured the imagination of the age. Before the Jubilee even occurred it was the subject of innumerable articles, poems, satires, jokes, and discussions. Long after it was over it continued to be written about, argued over, plagiarized, and reproduced in numerous theatrical forms. To attend the Jubilee, in this small Warwickshire town, soon became the ambition of every person with any literary, dramatic, or fashionable pretensions. James Boswell attended, eager for publicity and attired as a Corsican revolutionary. 'My bosom glowed with joy', he wrote, 'when I beheld a numerous and brilliant company of nobility and gentry, the rich, the brave, the witty and the fair, assembled to pay their tribute to Shakespeare.'[2] The celebrations were elaborate and ingenious. They included a firework display, an oratorio, processions, numerous public breakfasts and dinners, and a final grand costume ball held in a specially built wooden Rotunda on the banks of the Avon; they included everything, in fact, except the production of a single Shakespeare play. But despite Garrick's ambitious plans the Jubilee was not, for numerous reasons (not least the appalling weather) the glittering success he had intended. Garrick lost £2,000 on the enterprise, and disillusioned with the proliferation of bad debts in Stratford never set foot there again. But Stratford's attitude to the Jubilee was somewhat different. It gained a leaden bust of Shakespeare for its new town hall, and it gained a new tradition. The Jubilee was remembered as a heady and unmarred success, a model for all future Shakespeare celebrations – of which there would be many.

For the next six years there continued to be sporadic Shakespeare festivals at Stratford, organized on more modest lines. Then the habit died out until the early years of the nineteenth century. By then Bardolatry had taken on the dimensions of a national religion, and Stratford – like many other towns that century – had formed its own Shakespeare Club. The Club arranged a festival in 1827, when the foundation stone of a small theatre was laid in New Place gardens. In 1830 it organized a second, chiefly remarkable for the fact that included in the festivities for the first time was a performance of a play by Shakespeare. It was *Richard III*, with the young Charles Kean in the title-role, and it was given in the new theatre. The Shakespeare Club regarded the performance as very much a footnote to the rest of the proceedings; the success of their feasts and processions inspired them to declare that nothing less than a triennial festival was sufficient to honour Shakespeare in the town of his birth.[3] This admirable resolution was then forgotten for the next thirty years, until the Club was galvanized once more into activity by the imminence of an event impossible to overlook: the tercentenary of Shakespeare's birth.

Stratford, in 1864, was no longer the insignificant country town it had been at the time of Garrick's Jubilee ninety-five years earlier. Gradually the few poor tangible links between the town and Shakespeare were being preserved. The Birthplace had been bought for the nation (and immediately heavily restored) in 1847. The gardens of New Place, including the foundations of Shakespeare's house (which the infamous Francis Gastrell had razed to the ground as a final act of defiance, shortly after his attack on the Bard's mulberry tree) had likewise been bought, and were being laid out. The railway had reached Stratford in 1860. Londoners might still regard the town as outlandishly remote, but with better transport and restored relics, Stratford's appeal to tourists was growing. Pilgrimage there was becoming increasingly popular; the visitors' book at the Birthplace included American names. Stratford was becoming a shrine, and its plans for the Tercentenary were appropriately ambitious. After prolonged preliminary rumblings and many Pickwickian public meetings a large committee was finally formed in 1863 and given the task of organizing a major festival. It promptly created no less than sixteen impressive sub-committees (including Finance, Building, and – less impressively – Déjeuner), and the now traditional Garrick formula was readopted, complete with pageants, breakfasts, and balls. But there was one major innovation; this time there were to be several performances of Shakespeare's plays, and they were to provide the backbone of the festivities. That this not altogether popular resolution succeeded was largely due to the influence of two people: Edward Fordham Flower, founder and owner of the local brewery and the Mayor of Stratford for 1864, and his eldest son, Charles Flower. But even as the committee began to plan it began also to wrangle. It was hoped the festival would raise money, and the question of how to spend that money caused passionate local dissent. Numerous proposals were made, and it was the most controversial one which was finally adopted: that Stratford should erect a memorial statue to Shakespeare. Both Edward and Charles Flower opposed this suggestion fiercely, considering a statue a useless piece of piety, but the idea had great popular support in the town, and was eventually carried by general acclaim.

Although the Stratford Tercentenary gradually attracted the support of a number of distinguished men, among them Tennyson and Ruskin, the actual work of organizing the festival devolved upon Edward Flower. As the months passed, the plans for the festival became increasingly elaborate. It was to last an unprecedented ten days. A special wooden pavilion theatre would be built; five or six productions of Shakespeare plays were being planned in addition to all the other activities, and leading members of the theatrical profession were to be invited to perform in them. It was here that things began to go amiss. Knowing little of the vanities and rivalries of the London stage, the committee saw nothing wrong in approaching several actors more or less simultaneously. They wrote to Benjamin Webster, of the Adelphi; to Samuel Phelps, whose long reign at Sadler's Wells had just ended; to Charles Fechter, the French actor whose recent Hamlet had been a sensation; to Helen Faucit, then technically in retirement, but still very much the doyenne of the London stage.[4] To their delight Webster, Phelps, and Fechter all agreed enthusiastically to co-operate, and even Helen Faucit expressed interest, although somewhat more cautiously. Happily the committee went ahead with its plans: Phelps would play in *Cymbeline;* Fechter would give his Hamlet; Helen Faucit would play Rosalind, and a young French actress, Stella Colas, would play Juliet. All the actors concerned proved perfectly agreeable to this – until they discovered the parts the others would be playing; then there was uproar. Phelps wrote to Edward Flower in tones of injured dignity: 'The Stratford committee have insulted me,' he wrote, 'by asking any man in this country to play Hamlet on such an occasion, without first having offered a choice of characters to . . . Yours faithfully, Samuel Phelps.'⁵ He then published his entire correspondence with the committee in pamphlet form, complete with vituperative commentary, and flatly refused to have anything further to do with the Tercentenary.

After this, others were swift to defect. Fechter, who was being mercilessly lampooned by Phelps, became ill, and thankfully withdrew. Helen Faucit, on discovering that a younger, foreign, actress was to play Juliet informed the hapless committee that 'it was not for the Siddons of the age to come forth in comedy after a French lady had played Juliet'.⁶ Webster left the sinking ship without even the pretence of an excuse, and for a short while it looked as if the Tercentenary would include no Shakespeare productions.

The Stratford committee was saved by the manager of the Princess's Theatre who, risking the ire of his peers, agreed to bring up not just Miss Stella Colas, but also the rest of his company. So the plays were not, after all, the glittering affair they might have been, but they *were* put on: *Twelfth Night, The Comedy of Errors, Romeo and Juliet, As You Like It, Much Ado about Nothing, Othello,* and the trial scene from *The Merchant of Venice* each received one performance. It was a Shakespearian feast unprecedented in the town.

Unfortunately, the plays, the beautiful pavilion theatre, and the attendant junketings, all cost a great deal. Instead of the profits so confidently expected, when the festival was over there remained a deficit of more than £3,000. It was paid off by pulling down the pavilion theatre and selling off its contents, and by personal contributions from Edward Flower, Charles Flower, and other members of the committee, but the fact that there was now no money for the memorial statue to Shakespeare caused great resentment in the town. Criticism of the Tercentenary celebration and its management was not, however, confined to Stratford. The national newspapers took great delight in pointing out its follies, and roundly blamed the local organizers for them. The worst attack came from *The Times* in a long, patronizing and scornful summing-up of what it called 'this recent essay in organised hero-worship'. In the newspaper's view, to seek to commemorate Shakespeare by performances of his plays was ill-judged; to attempt it at Stratford, doubly so:

We testify our gratitude to Shakespeare by calling for edition after edition of his works, by making household words of his language, and by claiming for him the first place among the poets of all time. Yet zealous believers have been known to confess that they did not care to see Shakespeare's plays acted, and of those who go from time to time, out of pure love, to see them acted in London, not one in ten thousand would go out of his way to see them acted at Stratford . . .[7]

This attitude was to bedevil Stratford for many years to come. Rooted in the old Puritan distaste for theatre, it was a view to which numerous critics and commentators had lent weight, Coleridge and Lamb among them. But *The Times*'s arguments were not based solely on the widespread nineteenth-century belief that appreciation of Shakespeare's plays was better achieved in the study than the theatre; it was also based on a mandarin confidence in the innate superiority of the capital. Only there, it was felt, could adequate performances be given; only there was to be found a sufficiently large, and sufficiently responsive audience. The divide between London and the provinces was deep and absolute, and Stratford was the wrong side of the line; that belief was to have a radical effect on the future of theatre there for the next fifty years.

All in all the experiences of 1864 were not encouraging to those who had hoped that out of the Tercentenary might have grown a better memorial to Shakespeare than any statue: a permanent, not a pavilion theatre, for the performance of his plays. The financial problems, the committee imbroglios, the brushes with egotistical actors, the derision of the press – all these weighed against such a project. And yet, as it later became clear, Charles Flower at least had entertained such hopes, and was obstinate enough not to be deterred. It was he who had been mainly responsible for the design and erection of the Tercentenary pavilion theatre, on which, as *The Times* noted when it was pulled down, so much care had been lavished that 'one would have supposed the building was to have been used permanently for a theatre'.[8] Once the Tercentenary was over, and that little wooden theatre gone, Charles Flower appeared to abandon any further theatrical ambitions. He ran the brewery that his father Edward had founded, and prospered. He built himself a large house on the banks of the Avon, and purchased a great estate in Sutherland. He served on the town and county council and on innumerable local committees, and engaged in charitable work. For the next decade he appeared to be a conventional, successful, Victorian businessman, with an interest in Shakespeare's plays which he was content to pursue in private. Then, in 1874, at the age of forty-four, he embarked on a very unconventional project, the planning of a permanent theatre in Stratford, for the performance of Shakespeare's plays. Five years later that theatre opened, and the chorus of derision that greeted it was louder than anything Garrick or the Tercentenary committee had had to endure.

1

Monumental Mockery

In the few existing accounts of the founding of the Shakespeare Memorial Theatre, Charles Flower is tactfully, but summarily, dismissed. He is briefly portrayed as a fine philanthropic Victorian gentleman, a kind of less eccentric Mr Jarndyce, whose benevolence to widows and orphans happened to extend to an artistic enterprise. It is a view of him that is reinforced, unfortunately, by the only surviving portrait of him, painted the year before he died, and now hanging in the foyer of the theatre at Stratford. An unimaginative, pedestrian painting, executed at the behest of the town council at a time when Charles Flower had been very ill, it suggests the same worthy dullness common to most written accounts of the man. Both portraits are misleading.

Charles Flower came from an unusual and unconventional family from whom he inherited a strong tradition of radical politics and religious dissension, as well as a certain daring and romanticism. His great-uncle, Benjamin Flower, was a free thinker and pamphleteer, who wrote many scurrilous attacks on the established Church and the Tory politicians of his day. His grandfather, Richard Flower, was an articulate opponent of William Cobbett and a passionate advocate of emigration, who at the age of fifty-six, and with an impulsiveness and determination that were to mark his descendants, sold up his rich estate in Hertfordshire and embarked for the New World where he founded a pioneer town, Albion, on prairie land in Illinois. Charles's father, Edward, spent part of his youth there, travelling to Albion in a covered wagon, but he returned to settle in Stratford with the young Quaker girl who became his wife. There Edward started a timber business, but his heart was not in it. When his father died in 1830, leaving him the bulk of his money, Edward promptly sold the timber-yard and opened a brewery.

Edward and his wife Celina had three sons, Charles, William, and Edgar, all born within three years. They were poor and the family life was strained by Edward's difficulty in establishing his new business, and his wife's problems (she was a semi-invalid) in coping with a family of three young boys. They lived in a succession of modest houses until Charles was seven, when there was just enough money to build the family a house next door to the brewery. Charles received an interrupted education, at a series of different schools and in 1845, when he was fifteen, he went straight into the family business which was still on a shaky footing. His father, generous, hot-tempered, and impetuous, chafed at life in Warwickshire, and dreamed of emigrating once more: 'We should all have gone to Australia', Charles wrote, 'if my Father could have disposed of the business, and had had £500 to land us with.'[1] Not long afterwards, however, things began to improve and under the triumvirate of Edward and two of his sons, Charles and Edgar, Flower and Sons Brewery gradually became one of the leading companies in the Midlands. By 1857 it had agencies in London, Manchester, and Birmingham, and its sales were twelve times what they had been when Charles first joined the company. Edward and his wife marked their new-found prosperity in the manner of most Victorian manufacturers: they moved into a new house, well away from their premises. The house was called The Hill; it stood in extensive grounds on the Warwick Road, just outside Stratford. It was furnished in the height of fashion with stained-glass windows, hand-painted wallpaper, vast oak chimney-pieces, heavy furniture, tiger-skin rugs, stags' heads, and a proliferation of palms. Successive generations of the Flower family were to live there, and the house (which is still standing) was to play a significant part in the history of the theatre at Stratford.

Of the three sons it was Charles who was closest to, and most like, his father. He resembled him physically, being tall, strongly built, and – in later life – luxuriantly bearded. And he resembled him in character also; he had inherited the Flower business acumen, but also the strain of adventurousness and romanticism that had passed from Richard Flower to his father. He possessed a similar kindness and generosity to Edward's, but a milder temper, and perhaps more perseverance; if he once resolved upon a thing, his wife noted, he never failed to carry it through. He was a perfectionist, whether balancing the books of the brewery to the last penny, or building that temporary pavilion for the Tercentenary. But as a child, he considered, he had been something of a dreamer, a builder of 'castles-in-the-air' – an odd trait for such a practical businessman, and one he felt he never lost. It caused, he noted, much mocking from his family.

Charles had three great passions in life: one was horses; one was travel; and the other was theatre. The love of theatre, which was shared by his brother Edgar, seems to have sprung, full-blown, from nowhere. As a child he had little opportunity to see plays, and his first visit to a London theatre did not come until he was fourteen, when he was taken to the Haymarket Theatre, and saw a Madame Celeste dance the polka. He read Shakespeare omnivorously, and with a taste that was catholic for his day. All his life he remained a champion of the then lesser-known plays, many of which – *Cymbeline*, for instance, *Richard II*, *The Winter's Tale*, the *Henry VI* trilogy – were rarely or never performed. He was a particularly energetic advocate of the *Henry VI* plays, and it was due to his influence that they were first performed at Stratford. When he sat for his portrait, the year before he died, it was a copy of *Henry VI, Part I* that he chose to have next to him. In the last decade of his life he produced an entire edition of Shakespeare's plays – the Memorial Theatre edition – which he intended for use in his theatre. It was remarkable in that it used full unbowdlerized texts, but he bowed to the taste of his time by printing in two typefaces: a large face for the parts of the plays he considered useful in an acting version; a small face for lines he considered obscure or 'immodest'.

He met his wife Sarah at the age of eighteen, and married her four years later. It was a tranquil, long and happy marriage, marred only by their inability to have children. They spent their early years together in a succession of houses. They travelled widely and adventurously; they entertained generously; they became the perfect uncle and aunt to their numerous nieces and nephews. By the late 1860s the brewery had become the town's major employer, and Charles Flower himself, through his work on the council and on local committees, a person of considerable local influence.[2] Shortly after the Tercentenary celebrations he began building a new home, Avonbank, which rivalled The Hill in its splendour and modernity. There he and Sarah were to live for the rest of their lives, in a huge, ugly, Italianate house with gardens bordered on one side by the Avon and on the other by Holy Trinity Church, where Shakespeare is buried. In 1867, shortly after they moved in, they discussed the making of Charles Flower's will. He found himself 'worth about

£30,000' (a great amount at that time) and he was already considering whether Avonbank could not eventually be a useful annexe to 'the Shakespeare Memorial Theatre' at Stratford.[3] So, clearly, plans for such a theatre were present in his mind even then.

Exactly what finally decided him to take action is uncertain. The fact that in 1872 the tiny theatre in New Place gardens was demolished certainly influenced him. Stratford no longer had even the poorest pretensions to a theatre. But the most pressing motive seems to have been a personal one. His wife was forty-six years old, and an invalid; there was clearly no further hope of children. Charles, two years younger than his wife, was at the height of his powers. The care and absorption another man might have devoted to his children found, in him, another outlet: the theatre at Stratford.

In the late summer of 1874 Charles Flower bought two acres of land in the Bancroft meadow, the same site on which Garrick's Rotunda had stood over a century before. At one end lay the gardens of Avonbank; at the other a canal basin at the foot of the fifteenth-century Clopton Bridge – the main entrance to the town. Assuming that he merely intended to extend his own gardens no one took a great deal of notice; the land he bought had once been common pasture; it was marshy, and there were no other bidders for it. Then, in October, he announced that he proposed to donate the land to Stratford town council, provided that part of it 'should be appropriated to a Shakespeare Memorial Theatre, should a fund be raised for that object'. Since Charles Flower intended to launch such a fund himself, and could perfectly well have retained the ownership of the land, this manoeuvre seemed odd and unnecessary. But Flower judged, correctly, that by acting in this way he achieved two objects. Firstly, he ensured the co-operation and interest of the council, who could hardly ignore such a gift from one of the town's leading citizens. And, secondly, the fact that the theatre would be built on land owned by the town, rather than a private individual, gave the project more authority; the proposed theatre assumed the air of a corporate, not a personal, endeavour. The council duly accepted his gift, and sat back to await his next move which was to form a small committee of eight in April 1875, calling itself the Council for the Shakespeare Memorial Association. The lesson of the Tercentenary had been learnt: there were no long lists of distinguished supporters and positively no sub-committees, although six of the eight men on the Council had also been on the Tercentenary committee. The Association was pledged, it announced, 'to build a small theatre in which to have occasional performances of Shakespeare's plays . . . a library, and a gallery to contain pictures and statuary of Shakespearean subjects'.[4] It was a modest pitch, since an appeal was also being launched nationally for subscriptions. Added encouragement was given by the announcement that Charles Flower had donated the first £1,000, and that anyone who gave £100 or more would automatically become a governor of the proposed theatre.

The inducement was apparently insufficient, for donations came in very slowly. Undeterred, in October 1875 the Association advertised for architects to submit designs for the proposed theatre. By January of the following year Sarah Flower noted in her diary that Charles 'was very busy selecting plans for the Memorial Theatre, Library and Picture Gallery'.[5] That he continued to do so, and calmly, in spite of the fact that very little money had been raised, was no doubt due to the fact that from the first he had been absolutely determined that the theatre should be built – even if he had to pay for every last hand-rail himself. Shortly afterwards, on 1 May 1876, it was announced that the winning design came from a firm of London architects, Messrs. Dodgshun and Unsworth of Westminster. Their design reflected the full flowering of the Gothic revival, and resembled a small cathedral rather than a theatre. The building was to have a small horseshoe-shaped auditorium seating 700, with stalls, dress circle, and gallery. It had a small but serviceable stage, with a proscenium arch 26 feet wide and 27½ feet high. There were seven dressing-rooms, 'The West side to be appropriated to the ladies, the East to the gentlemen'.[6] The inside of the theatre also had an oddly ecclesiastical appearance, emphasized by a high pointed roof, and Gothic arches which flanked the gallery.

The outside of the building was frankly fantastical. Clearly a struggle had gone on in the architect's heart between the fashionable style of his day, and the Elizabethan half-timbering he felt evocative of Shakespeare. The result, built of red brick with dressings of stone, was a weird and unsuccessful mixture of architectural styles, incorporating Tudor gabling, Elizabethan chimneys, Gothic turrets, and minarets. The theatre was flanked by a tall observation tower containing a water-tank for use in case of fire. Linked to this by an arched, gabled bridge was the secondary building which would house the library and picture-gallery. The entire structure was to cost £20,000: £11,000 for the theatre; £8,000 for the tower, library, and gallery; and £1,000 for architect's fees and extras. The Shakespeare Memorial Association was immensely proud of the design. Pointing out that whereas most theatres had to be built on narrow town sites, and were little more than a 'mere shed, with a pseudo-classical front', its members announced that *their* theatre would be 'one of the best, if not *the* best, constructed and most handsomely fitted-up theatres in the kingdom'.[7] No expense was to be spared in the construction; the same painstaking care which had been lavished on the Tercentenary pavilion was to be lavished on this more lasting enterprise. It was to be *solidly* built, in an age which placed great value on solidity and permanence. The steps would be of York stone, the hand-rails of solid oak; all internal woodwork the finest Christiania yellow pine. Purbeck marble and Caen stone were to be used for the interior, and the proportions were more those of a medieval castle than a nineteenth-century theatre.

As soon as the plans for the building were announced, questions began to be asked. The very scale and ambition of the project was already beginning to irritate certain sections of the Press. This irritation was to build into a major campaign of criticism and vilification, but it began with sniping. The *Observer* began the attack with the old complaint that London alone was the fit place for such a theatre; to propose to erect a Shakespeare Memorial Theatre in Stratford, it commented, '110 miles from London, and possessing only about 7000 inhabitants . . . verges on the ridiculous'. This carping was echoed in most national newspapers, and even some local ones. There was general agreement (as there had been in 1864) that a statue was by far the most suitable memorial to a poet, but that if it had to be a theatre then obviously the West End, not Warwickshire, was the place for it.

It was clearly necessary for the Memorial Association to come up with something weightier than their initial, modest request for support. They accordingly drafted some further appeals. These had a faint but perceptible note of defensiveness in them, heavily laced with good poetic sentiment. When even these appeals seemed to be failing them – for the subscriptions were still meagre – they turned to the Continent for support for their arguments. They announced that the theatre would, they hoped, also contain a dramatic school for the training of actors, similar to those that already existed in Europe.

They played on what they thought was a trump card: the existence of a theatre in the small town of Bayreuth in Germany. Wagner's opera-house opened (opportunely) in 1876. Bayreuth was equally as small and remote a town as Stratford: if success could be achieved there, why not in Warwickshire? But even this argument misfired. The *Daily News* was quick to counter-attack: 'If Stratford-upon-Avon', it announced loftily, 'could obtain such distinguished – not to say royal – patronage as at Bayreuth, it would be fortunate as long as it were fashionable. . . . Unluckily, Stratford is too distant, and has too little accommodation to become the scene and centre of a great and permanent sort of Shakespearean pilgrimage.'

Amidst all this bickering Charles Flower made an extraordinary speech at the local Mayor's Banquet on 2 November 1876. It went unremarked and unrecorded except by the Stratford Press. Devoid of the flowery language of the public appeals, it remains the clearest, and indeed almost the only, full statement he ever made as to what he hoped for the theatre at Stratford. It shows that Flower had ambitions that were far ahead of his time, which were concerned – not with pieties about the Bard and his birthplace – but with the business of theatre itself, with what kind of company of actors could work at Stratford, and what work they could do. It sprang, as he made clear, from reports which *The Times* had published the previous April, of the revolutionary work of the Duke of Meiningen's company in Germany.

The Meiningen Company, which had been formed some ten years earlier, did not appear in England until 1881. But their work was already celebrated in Europe, and was to influence some of the greatest directors of the European stage, including Antoine in France, and Stanislavsky in Russia. It was an odd occurrence for a man to be discussing what was then little-known and radical theatrical work at a mayor's banquet in a small provincial English town. But Charles Flower's speech reads very much as if, in learning of the methods of the Meiningen Company, his own ideas had suddenly crystallized:

The company is managed by an able director under the control of the Duke himself. The actors are each of them thoroughly instructed, and the utmost attention is given not only to the principal parts, but also to the minor characters . . . the dresses and accessories . . . are as correct as possible, and this not with any extraordinary or lavish outlay. The secret seems to be that the outlay is not dependent on the money realised for admissions, but is guaranteed by the Duke himself. The actors feel therefore that as long as they do their duty, their position is secured and permanent . . . they feel an *esprit de corps*, and work together as members of one body. In every representation the whole of the company is employed, and the actor who takes a leading role one evening may take a minor one the next, or even appear in those parts which, in England, are only filled by supernumeraries. The result is a production as near perfection as possible, and the prestige of the company is great . . . Well, what a Duke has done at Meiningen, the world at large may do at Stratford . . .[8]

What Charles Flower was describing was, essentially, a privately subsidized ensemble company. That he had to spell it out in such detail is a measure of how unfamiliar such a concept was to those used to the practices of the theatre in the 1870s, a theatre still reliant on lavish staging and star performances, which cared hardly a jot for the supporting players; a theatre in which subsidy was unheard of, and where box-office appeal was the ultimate arbiter. The Lyceum in London was its perfect embodiment.

Henry Irving opened that theatre under his management shortly before the Memorial Theatre opened in Stratford, and it became, for the last quarter of the nineteenth century, the nearest thing to a National Theatre this country had. There Irving mounted a series of sumptuous Shakespearian productions, alternating them with equally sumptuous productions of poor plays which provided a starring role for himself. It was a repertoire which Bernard Shaw was later, slightly unfairly, to dismiss as 'obsolete tomfooleries . . . schoolgirl charades . . . blank verse by Wills, Comyns-Carr and Calmour, with intervals of hashed Shakespeare';[9] it made the Lyceum, for nearly twenty years, the most successful theatre of its day. Irving would spend as much as £7,000 to mount a new Shakespearian production (his *Henry VIII* cost £12,000); if it was successful he would keep it in the repertoire for what was then a long run – perhaps one hundred performances or more. If it was unsuccessful he had no alternative but to take it off. Such a theatre afforded actors no security. Irving himself died penniless, and less famous actors had a severe struggle to stay in employment. Most drifted from company to company, with no possibility of controlled development of their work. The system encouraged not only the mounting of inferior plays, but also poor performances – the shortcuts, the paraphrasing, the hogging of the limelight – which was to bedevil the theatre until well into the twentieth century.

Charles Flower seems to have grasped the then revolutionary concept that a permanent company, affording security and free of box-office domination through some form of subsidy, could present work of a totally new standard and authority. And this *was* revolutionary: Irving opposed the idea of state subsidy to the end of his days; in spite of many later energetic advocates, it did not become a reality until the time of the Second World War. Charles Flower spoke, in 1876, of a permanent company, subsidized from some form of endowment:

If they (the actors) could be made to feel that their income and position were dependent upon the efficiency of the whole, and that they might insure a steady income, and perhaps a pension in old age, I am sure a Company might be trained to work here as it has proved to have done in Germany, and that its performance of Shakespeare's plays would be an intellectual treat such as yet has never been experienced in England ... The performances at Stratford would, in fact, be a series of rehearsals resulting in a highly finished representation that would serve as a standard of acting throughout the country. So much for a possible future for the Shakespeare Memorial.[10]

It was to be many decades after his death before any of Charles Flower's ideas were resurrected, and longer still before they became a reality.

Meanwhile, the preparations for the new theatre went on. The foundation stone was laid the following April 1877, on Shakespeare's birthday, with full Masonic ritual. It was hoped that H.R.H. Prince Leopold might be present at the ceremony (in token of the *Daily News's* 'royal patronage', perhaps) but the Prince was indisposed, and the Lord-Lieutenant of the County had to suffice. There was a luncheon afterwards with a great many toasts, and lengthy speeches. No one spoke of the kind of theatre company that might evolve at Stratford, and the work it might do. The keynote was England, Empire, and Shakespeare as the prime exemplar of all that was greatest in the English genius. 'To the Immortal Memory of William Shakespeare!' announced Sir J. Eardley Wilmot, MP.

As long as language has utterance, as long as England's glory lives, coeval with her glory on the battlefield, her glory on the ocean, her far greater glory in endeavouring to promote peace among the nations, coeval with all that is good, great and glorious that England can boast of or even hope for, will be the honours paid to that master mind.[11]

The assembled company, enthused by this rousing portrait of Shakespeare as a kind of literary ancestor to Henry Newbolt, clinked their glasses.

The theatre that was to be the result of all these worthy sentiments gradually reared its turrets above the protective wooden palings surrounding the site. But even as the building progressed, the financing of it was still causing problems. The response to appeals for hard cash rather than speeches remained poor. Six thousand copies of a new appeal were sent out: to the Press; to every member of the House of Lords and the House of Commons; to every alderman and common councillor in the British Isles; to the entire landed gentry of England; to the principal residents in the county of Warwick; and to the owners and managers of every major British theatre. The appeal netted precisely £1,000. The sad fact of the matter was that, when the theatre was completed, in 1879, the site and at least £6,000 of the £11,000 it cost, came from one man – Charles Flower. Of the further £9,000 which then had to be raised to complete the tower, library, and gallery, £6,000 also came from Charles Flower. The remaining £3,000 was raised in subsequent appeals in Britain and America which continued until the whole building was completed in 1882.[12] When the lists of subscribers were eventually published, there were some interesting contributors. They included the American tragedian Edwin Booth; Heinrich Schliemann, the archaeologist and discoverer of Troy; H. M. Stanley, the journalist and explorer; and P. T. Barnum (who had once attempted to buy Shakespeare's Birthplace, and transport it brick by brick to America). Several English theatrical managers donated the requisite £100 to become governors of the new theatre, and there were numerous contributions from amateur dramatic companies, Shakespeare Clubs, and Freemasons. Various members of the Flower family also donated money, and Charles's nephews, Masters Archibald, Richard, and Oswald Flower, each gave five guineas. That the bulk of the money came from one man was modestly obscured by the fact that the lists of subscribers were published at intervals, so that Charles Flower's contribution was never printed in total. Apart from the £12,000 he gave then, the largest donations came from the two leading actors of the day – Henry Irving and Barry Sullivan – who each gave one hundred guineas.

The opening day for the theatre was to be, inevitably, on Shakespeare's birthday, 23 April. As the building neared completion at the end of 1878 the attacks from the Press rose to a climax. Content to snipe while the theatre had remained merely a proposal, the London newspapers were outraged once they realized that the building was there, and what was more, was actually going to open, irritatingly on schedule. It had taken just four years from first announcement to opening. Where had been the customary ponderings, the manoeuvrings of committees, the correspondence in *The Times*, the weighty discussions by celebrated patrons, all the laborious preliminaries considered proper to such undertakings? Almost all of them weighed in to the attack. 'A theatre built on beer,' sneered the *St. James's Magazine*. 'Practically,' wrote the *Athenaeum*, 'the scheme has not much more chance of permanent success than would that of a hospital on Salisbury plain.' The local newspapers bravely attempted a defence of what they liked to term 'a small temple to Thespis'.[13] But the *Stratford Herald*, the *Leamington Spa Gazette*, and the *Evesham Journal* were no match for the outcry from the metropolis.

Virtually the only major support came from America. There Mark Twain, who had recently stayed with Charles Flower at Avonbank, wrote an enthusiastic letter of support to the *New York Times*, and the paper followed it up with a leader endorsing the scheme. But even the support of the *New York Times* counted for little when the most vicious attack of all on the theatre was published during March 1879 in the *Daily Telegraph:*

What likelihood is there that a company, either resident in Stratford, or collected for the nonce, could give anything like a good representation of even his least difficult plays? Then, who will the spectators be? An actor catches something from a good audience, a stimulus without which even his best interpretations will lack fire, an intelligent appreciation of his conscientious care. Who can expect such merits in the inhabitants of a country town, or the gentry of the neighbourhood, not habitually familiar with the highest standards of representation?

Not content with portraying the potential audience at Stratford as a collection of yokels, it added, for good measure, that the governing body was singularly parochial, undistinguished, and unimpressive. It then clinched its arguments by pointing out that – as was common knowledge – Shakespeare himself had got out of Stratford at the first opportunity, and had written all his major work in London, except, it noted, 'for the last six plays, which exhibit a distinct falling-off'.

Even allowing for the previous jibes by other newspapers, it was an unprecedented onslaught. Fortunately for Stratford, it had the effect of an over-kill. The *Telegraph* was not a paper popular among other journalists, and this swingeing attack, coming so shortly before the opening of the theatre, did much to turn opinions in Stratford's favour. As the first night approached, other newspapers began to modify their criticisms, and even to find something favourable to say for the project.

Wisely, the events for the opening festival were kept comparatively simple. The opening play, on Wednesday 23 April 1879, was to be *Much Ado about Nothing* (a play whose title gave further ammunition to some critics). This was to be followed by *Hamlet,* on the Thursday night; a concert of Shakespearian songs on the Friday, and a matinée of *Hamlet* on the Saturday. The following week there would be a recitation of *The Tempest,* repeat performances of *Much Ado* and *Hamlet,* and one performance of *As You Like It.* This modest programme was augmented by only a few other events: the inevitable luncheon on the opening day; a ball at the town hall, and the preaching of a special sermon at Holy Trinity Church. In all the festival would last precisely eight days. With such a short programme, and uncertainty as to what might happen to the theatre once it was over, there was no question (nor was there the money) of hiring a special Stratford company. An existing company had to be found, of good reputation, who could give the opening performances, and acquit themselves well. The company chosen was Barry Sullivan's.

Sullivan had been approached by Charles Flower the previous year, and had entered into the project with enthusiasm and generosity. Not only did he donate his hundred guineas to the theatre, he also undertook to bring down his company at his own expense, and perform free of charge. Sullivan thus gave the theatre not only financial and artistic help, but also the benefit of his reputation, which was still considerable. He was fifty-eight years old in 1879, and had begun his career in the old stock companies and worked his way up, playing opposite all the leading actors of his day, including Charles Kean, Samuel Phelps, and Macready (to whose Othello he played Iago). By the 1860s he had become one of England's most celebrated tragedians, but his reign had been short-lived; he was eclipsed by the rising star of Henry Irving. As Irving's reputation in London grew, so Sullivan found disfavour with audiences in the capital. He retired to tour the provinces, where he could reign more or less supreme. He continued to tour to the end of his life, and died a rich man, leaving over £100,000 in his will – then an unprecedented sum for an actor. He was a short, squarely-built man, with a face scarred by smallpox and a magnificent voice whose rolling crescendos and diminuendos could bring a gallery shouting to its feet. Irving had introduced to the theatre of his day what was then regarded as a more naturalistic school of acting; Sullivan remained resolutely a bravura actor of the old school, unafraid of the magnificent gesture, rejoicing in the richness of his voice, and many critics, among them Bernard Shaw, considered him a superb actor.[14] Others found him old-fashioned and declamatory, and even Shaw considered that Sullivan's best work was done in the 1860s; by 1879 he was a little over the hill.

Sullivan was Irish and had an Irish temper; he was, as his biographer Robert Sillard put it, 'liable to blaze, as the phrase was, very quickly'.[15] He stood on his dignity, and was abnormally sensitive to any slight or insult. Once, when he was booed by the gallery at a provincial performance of his most famous role, Richard III, he stopped speaking, marched off stage, and ordered the stage-manager to ring down the curtain. After a well-timed pause, he re-appeared in front of it and told his audience roundly that this was not the treatment an actor of his eminence was used to, or expected. The gallery was suitably chastened, and the play continued.[16] According to Frank Benson, this grand behaviour continued out of the theatre. 'On the days when he played Hamlet,' Benson wrote, 'if addressed in the street by friends and acquaintances, "Good morning, Mr Sullivan", with a lordly wafture of his hand, he would reply, "Today I am Hamlet", and stalk on in stately silence.'[17]

Anecdotes such as this, and the fact that many critics were happy to dismiss him as an old-fashioned ranter, affected his later reputation. Compared to Irving, Sullivan has been almost forgotten. But his method of working was not that of the slap-dash rhetorician. Like Irving, he was infinitely painstaking in rehearsal with his actors, and something of a martinet. He was interested in experimenting, both with texts and staging, and was a keen student of various editions, and different readings, of Shakespeare's lines. Often he would introduce an unfamiliar emendation, such as Dr Johnson's suggestion that Macbeth's 'My way of life/Is fall'n into the sere', should read 'My May of Life . . . '. These substitutions and changes frequently caused problems with critics, and they were to do so at the opening performances in Stratford.

Sullivan numbered some good actors among his company, most notably the young Edward Compton (the father of Compton Mackenzie and Fay Compton, and an accomplished comedian), but clearly it was felt that such an occasion demanded another celebrated name: Helen Faucit was therefore persuaded to come out of retirement again, to play two performances as Beatrice. Helen Faucit, who had been among those actors to withdraw from the Tercentenary celebrations, was now sixty-two years old – more than a little advanced in years to play Beatrice, even opposite a fifty-eight-year-old Benedick. In her youth she had been one of the most beautiful and renowned actresses of her day, a precursor of Ellen Terry, with the same unfailing ability to charm. She brought with her to Stratford not only the advantage of her reputation, but also a certain social imprimatur, since she counted among her friends Queen Victoria and many leading men of letters and the arts.

The morning of 23 April was rainy. The town was decorated with flags and flowers, and was very crowded for almost every London newspaper and magazine had sent a reporter or critic to cover the events. The tickets for the first performances were sold out, mainly to local people. Fashionable London theatre-goers had other events on their minds, which eclipsed the preparations at Stratford. On 17 April, five days before the opening at the Shakespeare Memorial Theatre, Henry Irving was opening *The Lady of Lyons* at the Lyceum Theatre, Covent Garden, his first new production since he took over the theatre, and the first time he and Ellen Terry would be seen together in new roles. *The Lady of Lyons* was a poor and somewhat dated play by Bulwer Lytton but its production at the Lyceum drew attention away from Stratford and emphasized the fact that both the leading players there were ageing, and no longer regarded as front-rank.[18]

On the morning of 23 April the governors of the new theatre held their first official meeting. There were thirty-two of them, with an executive council of thirteen. Charles Flower was chairman; his wife, his brother Edgar, and his father Edward, were all on the board. Almost all the other governors were either local men, or actors or theatrical managers who had donated their £100 to the theatre, and thereafter played little part in its organization. The meeting was brief and jubilant, and in high spirits the governors then decamped to join 200 guests at a luncheon in the town hall. At six-thirty in the evening, still in the rain, the first carriages began to draw up at the theatre. Backstage, nerves were taut. Barry Sullivan, discovering that Helen Faucit's dressing-room had been decorated with flowers, and that his own was unadorned, immediately felt slighted and showed signs of beginning to blaze. Messengers were hurriedly dispatched to The Hill, and more flowers were sent down from the well-stocked conservatory.[19]

The success of the performance depended on Helen Faucit, Barry Sullivan, and the company, but Charles and Sarah Flower had done everything else in their power to make the occasion go well. Staff from the brewery had been drafted to the theatre to sell tickets and programmes. Sarah Flower had decorated the sides of the stage with banks of palms and ferns. She was still ill, but was well enough to attend the performance, although she had to travel there in a Bath chair. She and Charles Flower sat next to Helen Faucit's husband, Theodore Martin, all three, she wrote, shaking with nervousness. Every effort had been taken to make the production as splendid as possible to the eye. The costumes and sets were new; their cost had been met by Charles Flower.

The anonymous critic of the *Stratford Herald* was enthralled by what he saw: 'Mrs Theodore Martin', he wrote, 'played with consummate skill. She was frequently and heartily applauded, and at the close of the second act, nothing but her appearance before the curtain would satisfy the audience . . . Mr Barry Sullivan also achieved a great success. He was said to have surpassed himself . . .' Exactly who said this is unclear, for none of the London critics went so far. But even their reviews were, on the whole, favourable, and they remained to see how Stratford would cope with the strong meat of tragedy – *Hamlet* – the following night.

Hamlet was one of Sullivan's favourite roles. Although he was most famous for his portrayal of Richard III, he played Hamlet many times, with great success, particularly in America. His performance at Stratford was the 3,061st time he had played the role. He introduced into it some of his textual emendations, and played the Prince of Denmark not as a gentle introspective, a sweet prince, but as a man of suppressed fire, burning with bitter sarcasm. But the part of Hamlet – that 'hoop through which every eminent actor must, sooner or later, jump', as Max Beerbohm put it, had already been annexed for a generation by Henry Irving. London critics had first seen Irving's celebrated and innovatory Hamlet in 1874, when it had run for 200 nights. They had just had the opportunity of seeing it revived at the Lyceum, strengthened by the presence of Ellen Terry, in a splendid new mounting of the play which had cost £4,000. Sullivan's Hamlet in contrast seemed hollow and declamatory; he could achieve neither Irving's naturalistic restraint, nor his sudden demonism. The critic of the *Stratford Herald* was again impressed, and considered Sullivan gave a powerful performance throughout. 'The play scene was a fine histrionic display, rising to positive genius,' he wrote. The London critics were unanimous in their distaste. The reviewer for the *Daily Telegraph* found at last the chance to attack both player and audience, thus fulfilling his own newspaper's prophecies. 'The audience', he wrote, 'was far more appreciative than critical, and solecisms were permitted and passed of so glaring a nature as to make poor Shakespeare turn in his adjacent grave . . . when the dramatic school is founded there will probably be a rule established that will forbid, or promptly suppress, such fanciful readings as "I know a hawk from a heron – pshaw!"'. But the hardest words of all came from the periodical *The Theatre*, which summed up the opening tersely: 'A memorial less adequate to the occasion than that of last month can scarcely be conceived . . .The mountains have been in labour . . . and it is impossible to help being struck by the absurdity of the mouse which has appeared.' The author of this article was anonymous; there was nothing anywhere in the magazine to indicate the fact that it was owned at that time by Henry Irving, who used it to insert puffs for his productions at the Lyceum, and who kept his ownership profoundly secret.[20] There was little love lost between Irving and Sullivan, so perhaps at least some of the antipathy to Stratford was less honest than it seemed.

Once *Hamlet* was over the London journalists, having served their two-day term an uncomfortable 110 miles from the metropolis, departed. They did not stay for the rest of the performances, and they did not assemble again, in such numbers, until 1932 when the new theatre, on the same site, opened. For the next fifty years with a few infrequent exceptions, the editors of the large national newspapers were content to leave the reviewing of productions at Stratford to their provincial counterparts. Judgement had been pronounced; few critics bothered to find out whether it needed, subsequently, to be modified. This early exodus prevented their reviewing the performance of *As You Like It* the following week, which would undoubtedly – and justifiably – have deepened their prejudice. The highlight of this production was the appearance of a stuffed stag, brought from the deer park of the neighbouring Charlecote House, where – tradition has it – Shakespeare once poached a deer from the Lucy family. The stag was the centrepiece of the Forest of Arden, hoisted on poles by keepers from Charlecote, who appeared with their dogs as supernumeraries. One of the keepers was even given a new line, 'Lots of people came from all round the country, and even from *London* to see me and my dogs.' This pleased the Stratford audience mightily.[21] After the performance the stag was carefully preserved, to hang in the theatre's picture-gallery. Its reappearance, progressively moth-eaten, became obligatory in all future productions of *As You Like It* at Stratford. So strong was the local tradition that no director dared to flout it until 1919.

With the final performance on Thursday 31 April the eight days festival ended. The actors were presented with bouquets and laurel wreaths. Charles Flower gave a supper-party for Sullivan and his company in his palm house. In Stratford, the theatre and the plays were pronounced a success. The theatre itself had been widely praised, *The Times* bestowing the ultimate accolade in saying that 'in decoration and appointments it is quite up to the standards of the metropolis'. The governors felt confident enough to announce that although the theatre would remain closed for most of the following year, there would be a second festival the next April, and Mr Sullivan and his company would again be appearing. This announcement was greeted with jubilation when Charles Flower made it from the stage on the final night. Yet as he spoke he must have known that the promise was a measure of the difficulties that faced the theatre. The building had opened, but it had no endowment. The critics of the scheme had been correct when they said that local audiences were too small to do more than keep the theatre open for one or two weeks a year. And that meant that the Stratford theatre would have to rely on touring companies giving special performances – all very well, but a long way from the Meiningen ideal.

Few local people saw this future for the Memorial Theatre as inadequate. Even Sarah Flower, when she congratulated her husband after the first night, told him that it had all been worthwhile, even if the new theatre should open for just one *day* a year – Shakespeare's birthday. But the dream-castle in Purbeck marble and Caen stone had not been built to house one production a year, in ritual tribute to a great playwright. And Charles Flower, significantly, did not answer his wife's congratulations.[22] Perhaps, even to her, he could not admit the gulf which lay between what he had achieved and what he hoped for.

2

A Rash Young Gentleman

Early in 1885, six years after the opening of the Stratford theatre, Charles Flower and his wife were invited to nearby Leamington to see a production of *Macbeth* given by a young actor, Frank Benson, and his company. The object of the visit was to discover whether Benson was suitable to give the performances at Stratford the following year.

Little more could be said of the festivals since 1879 than that they had marked time. The theatre had opened each April, and various visiting companies had appeared. Sullivan had returned, as promised, in 1880, but shortly afterwards had fallen ill, and a substitute had to be found. Edward Compton, who had by then formed his own company, directed the festivals – successfully – in 1881 and 1882. The years 1883-5 were undistinguished, and Charles Flower was looking for new blood. In some respects the young Frank Benson promised well. He was only twenty-six, and had an unconventional background for an actor at that time. He had been educated at Winchester, where Charles Flower's nephew had been his contemporary, and had then gone up to New College, Oxford, where he had distinguished himself as an athlete, and an amateur actor. He had been manager of his own company for only two years, but it included some notable actors, particularly George Weir, a dumpy little man who was a great Shakespearian comic (though rather too fond of drink to be wholly reliable), and Janet Achurch, an actress who later became the greatest interpreter of Ibsen for her generation. In *Macbeth*, Benson was playing the title-role, Janet Achurch was Lady Macbeth, and George Weir was somewhat oddly cast as the First Witch.

The performance was a disaster. Weir was gloriously drunk – a fact that was evident immediately: 'He came down to the footlights in a friendly cheery way', Benson recalled, 'beamed vacuously at the audience, and then, in a confidential whisper informed them that

"The cat has mewed three times".[1] This did not exactly launch the play well, but Benson, who was a man of unflagging optimism, hoped that he and Janet Achurch could galvanize matters by the fire of their performances. The hope was short-lived. The lights failed several times, and, just as Benson was about to embark on 'Is this a dagger which I see before me . . . ' the stage-manager rang down the curtain.

The Flowers departed half-way through the performance. It says much for Charles Flower's perseverance that Benson was still invited to Avonbank for luncheon the following Sunday; and equally much for Benson's eloquence and charm that he was requested, after all, to give the festival of 1886 at Stratford.

He and Charles Flower seem to have liked each other from the first. Benson had none of Flower's practicality, but he shared his passion for Shakespeare's plays, and was – like him – a dreamer. Fixing his eyes somewhere in the middle distance, he was given to launching into long, sentimental, but heartfelt speeches about Shakespeare, England, and 'the Actor's Proud Task'. At twenty-six Benson looked like Galahad as Rossetti might have painted him, or Lancelot as Tennyson described him. There was a purity and zealousness about him which exactly suited the Victorian conception of an Arthurian knight. There was also a great deal of both Micawber – Benson always believed something would turn up – and Don Quixote, but those aspects of his character were less noticeable when he was young. Whatever it was about him – his youth, his charm, his optimistic idealism – Charles Flower decided to give him his backing. Benson was also an avowed believer in the Meiningen Company and its methods, and this may have been an additional factor.

Frank Benson was never shy of making grandiose announcements at the top of his playbills – few Victorian actor-managers were. The first announcement of his company's appearance had been in 1883, when Benson was twenty-four. Then he had trumpeted the fact that Mr F. R. Benson was 'late of the Lyceum Theatre, London'. Benson had indeed appeared at the Lyceum, for precisely one month the previous year, when he had taken over the role of Paris, with marked lack of success, in Irving's production of *Romeo and Juliet*. He had not been invited to remain with the company. About as accurate was the announcement that succeeded it at the top of his playbills, that his company was 'conducted on the Meiningen system'. The

Meiningen Company had become far more celebrated and fashionable by that time than they had been in 1876 when Charles Flower
upheld them as a model for the Stratford theatre. In 1881 the
company had appeared in London, and Benson – straight from
Oxford – had seen their performances at the Drury Lane Theatre,
and been deeply impressed. When he had his own company he
appended the Meiningen name to his bills, and lectured his actors,
with all the eagerness of an extremely inexperienced young man, on
the desirability of their playing walk-ons as well as leading roles. The
influence of the Meiningen seems not to have gone very deep,
however, and the company made up a song about it:

> The Meiningen system is nothing but rot;
> Goodbye, poor actor, goodbye;
> For Benson's parts are the best of the lot;
> Goodbye, fond actor, goodbye.[2]

In this they were perfectly justified, since once he became a manager,
Benson never played a minor role, let alone a walk-on, again. His
first action on taking over the company was to promote himself from
the role of Rosencrantz to that of Hamlet – followed in quick
succession by Romeo, Othello, and Captain Absolute in *The Rivals*.
Benson seems to have been less interested in the other artistic lessons
the Meiningen had to impart – revolutionary set designs and lighting
effects, and careful handling of crowd scenes. The greatest resemb-
lance between the young Benson's company and the Meiningen was
not artistic at all, but lay in the fact that Benson's patient father had
constantly to rescue the company with financial support, thus
providing a form of (paternal) subsidy.

So, on 26 April 1886, the Shakespeare Memorial Theatre opened
once more for its annual festival. Frank Benson, tall, pale, with
waving black hair worn aesthetically long, came downstage in a suit
of black velvet; the first Hamlet at Stratford since Barry Sullivan. At
the end of one week, having also given his *Othello*, and his *Richard
III*, he departed, with promises from the stage to return the following
year. He returned, in fact, for thirty years. From 1886 until 1919
Benson conducted all but five of the Stratford seasons. His fortunes,
and those of the Memorial Theatre, became inextricably entangled.
In some ways he was to hold the theatre back; in others he helped it
greatly. What he did undeniably was establish it, for he brought it
continuity. Had it continued to present short annual seasons

by companies of varying ability, Stratford would certainly have degenerated into little more than a small provincial theatre, fitted in on touring dates, with no aims, no policies, no identity of its own. Benson prevented that; he laid the foundations for what came after.

Benson had left Oxford intoxicated with his own success, resolutely determined to adopt the stage as his profession and convinced that the transformation from amateur actor to professional could be quickly achieved. He launched himself into the theatre with the same *élan*, optimism, and arrogance that would mark many of his later activities. He undertook intense physical preparation, including boxing, wrestling, fencing, and dancing, with elocution and singing lessons for good measure. After some months of this, satisfied he now had all the requirements necessary save experience, he joined Henry Irving's company and was given the role of Paris in the Lyceum's *Romeo and Juliet*. He entered that great theatre stuffed full of theories and self-confidence, and never lost his lifelong ambition to return one day as its manager and star.

Benson's first rehearsal at the Lyceum was not the success he had hoped for, but he had no doubts that all would be well in performance. The first time he appeared he wore no make-up. He had a theory about make-up, as he had about many theatrical matters: it was unnecessary. This was a bold action, particularly in a theatre where Irving painstakingly painted his face before each performance with the old dry colours. Benson survived one scene with a bare face before he was pounced on by the formidable Bram Stoker, Irving's business manager. Stoker informed him that from out front his face looked dirty: 'It's a hot night, Benson, you are nervous, and sweating like a pig in a blue funk . . . get him some greasepaint and show him how to use it.'[3] The final humiliation came when he reached his great moment – the duel scene between himself as Paris, and Irving as Romeo. Benson could fence well, and knew it. He had also paid a special visit to St George's hospital to observe death spasms and he was looking forward to demonstrating his refinement in both in the scene with the great man. Irving took one look at the Oxford graduate, poised perfectly *en garde*, seized his foil with one hand, rapped him over the knuckles with the other, kneed him in the stomach, and muttering 'Die, me boy, die; down, down!' elbowed and kneed him into an ignominious and entirely invisible death at the mouth of Juliet's tomb.

From the exalted atmosphere of the Lyceum Benson departed, chastened, to touring companies in the provinces. Less than a year later, when Paris was still the largest part he had played, he found himself in Scotland with no prospect of a salary at the end of the week's performances. The company's actor-manager had absconded. Benson seized his chance, and with £100 from his father took over the company. Three years later, precariously solvent, he was appearing as Hamlet at Stratford.

His eccentricity was still marked. There was little about him to suggest the actor-manager. Constance Featherstonhaugh, a young actress who was later to marry him and become his leading lady on stage, recalled meeting him for the first time in 1885:

It was a bitterly cold December morning with snow deep on the ground . . . I was shown into a room without a fire, the windows open, the snow drifting in and lying in mounds on the carpet. I saw a handsome boyish figure . . . sipping cold milk. . . . His dress was strange, not to say eccentric; a pair of very baggy ill-fitting trousers of an enormous check, a well-cut Norfolk coat, showing a torn flannel collar, once white, now yellowed by many visits to the laundry; a peacock blue tie, with long ragged ends, and big Jaeger cloth boots with shiny toes. His hair flowed in wavy tresses over his collar. . . He told me he never felt the cold, but his fingers were icy, and his nose decidedly pink.[4]

When she came to know him better, Constance discovered that the curious clothes were not due to carelessness, but to his *theories.* 'He was *full* of theories,' she wrote.

Clothes and food were ruled by theories. It hardened a man, he thought, to be cold, to eat only twice a day. It was healthy to wear digited socks, and sleep in flannel sheets, with his jaws tied up like Lazarus to avoid an open mouth. It was healthy to have the windows open day and night, and have no fires; to drink quarts of milk, and have only apple tart for supper. . . . However, many of these eccentricities he abandoned in later years.[5]

Benson's theories were not confined to matters of clothes, food, and sleep. He believed he had a mission 'to reform the English stage',[6] and he had a number of theories about how he would achieve it. He believed that England and the English theatre became impoverished spiritually if Shakespeare's plays were not constantly performed. He dedicated himself to changing that, and adopted for his company a repertoire which gradually came to depend almost exclusively on

Shakespeare. He also had a lifelong antipathy to long runs, believing that they deadened an actor's performance. Benson's dearest wish was to re-introduce repertoire playing in London, mounting several productions at once, which could be given on successive nights within the same week. It was a splendid ideal, and one which has now become the norm for both the National Theatre and the Royal Shakespeare Company; but although Benson succeeded with repertoire in the provinces, in London he was always to fail.

Benson's other theories for the reform of the English stage were less precise. Taken with the idea of himelf as an evangelical reformer, he tended to assume that all his ideas – no matter how conventional – were tinged with reforming zeal. By the time he first came to Stratford some of his earlier brashness had been eroded by the exigencies of touring. Nevertheless, he entered the theatre there ready to sweep away all its fustian traditions in one sweep. He was impressed by the theatre's equipment and sets,[7] but friends who knew them both predicted that he and Charles Flower were bound to clash. In his *Memoirs* Benson adopted an affectionate but patronizing tone towards Flower, and portrayed himself as a dashing reformer. But it was not an accurate or very honest portrayal. Benson's work was not, in fact, characterized by daring and experiment, but for the most part by the degree to which it conformed entirely to the taste of his time. On many occasions it was not Benson, but Charles Flower, who provided the impetus for the 'daring experiments'; the choice of repertoire was one instance.

Benson made a straightforward business agreement with the governors of the Memorial Theatre. He brought his company to the town each year, and performed plays which were already in his repertoire, and which he toured around the rest of the country. For his performances he received a percentage of the takings, usually 60 per cent to Benson, 40 per cent to the theatre. The theatre made no profits; any money left at the end of the season was used to maintain the building, or to mount future productions. Each year, Benson gave one new production at Stratford, which was given on Shakespeare's birthday and became known as the Birthday play. These productions, often of rarely performed plays, were paid for by the governors or by Charles Flower himself, who financed the making of costumes and sets. Benson was then able to tour the production with his other plays. Since it was Charles Flower's ambition to present the entire canon of Shakespeare's plays at Stratford, and Benson's to perform it, this arrangement suited both parties. Benson was able to put on plays like *Timon of Athens*, *The Winter's Tale*, or *King John* which he could never otherwise have attempted, and to mount more spectacular productions of certain plays – *Antony and Cleopatra*, for instance, first given in 1898 – than he could have afforded himself. Benson sometimes lost money with these productions when he attempted to tour with them, either because they proved unpopular with provincial audiences, or because they were so elaborate that travelling with them was hugely costly. But the fact that he presented such little-known plays added immensely to his reputation as guardian of the Shakespearian sacred flame, a reputation not undeserved, and one which he valued highly.

The system worked to Stratford's advantage as well. Although audiences grew during the thirty years Benson appeared there, and enabled the governors gradually to extend the duration of the festivals, they were composed mainly of local people. To ensure their attendance it was essential to present a large number of plays; there were not enough people to fill the theatre for the same play for several nights in a row. Benson, whose repertoire became so extensive that he could mount rehearsed productions of twenty or more Shakespeare plays, solved the difficulty. It became the custom for Stratford playgoers to visit the theatre every night during the short festivals, and to see a different play on each occasion. This expectation was later to cause the theatre grave problems, but during Benson's years there it could always be fulfilled.

Benson, however, was often reluctant to perform the less familiar plays, sometimes because he knew they would be unprofitable to tour, more often because they did not contain suitable leading roles for himself and his wife. It was Flower's idea, for instance, to present a complete cycle of history plays, a project never before attempted, and one which Benson resisted for years. He was happy to include in his repertoire those history plays which provided him with a superb leading role – *Richard II* for example, which became one of his most famous parts, and *Henry V* and *Richard III*. He was far less enthusiastic about the two *Henry IV* plays, and the *Henry VI* trilogy of which Flower was a passionate advocate. When *Henry VI, Part I* was first produced at Stratford, in 1889, in a version reworked by Charles Flower, Osmond Tearle's company, not Benson's, performed it. Ten years later, in 1899, when Charles Flower was dead, his widow Sarah was still trying to persuade Benson to undertake a

History cycle, but without success. It was a 'daring experiment' of a kind that did not appeal to him. The full cycle was not given by Benson until 1906. It had taken twenty years to get him to do it, and it was Charles's nephew and successor, Archibald Flower, an extremely formidable and determined man, who persuaded him.

Benson did, it is true, embrace some attempts to widen the narrow repertoire of Shakespeare plays popular in his time. The increasing popularity of *Richard II*, for example (of which Benson's production was the first for forty years), was largely due to his influence. He was the first actor to attempt a full-text *Hamlet* (at Stratford first, in 1899). He also did a great deal to rescue *Richard III* from Colley Cibber's adaptation, which had remained popular despite earlier attempts to dislodge it. But the bulk of Benson's repertoire was less daring and innovatory. The three overwhelmingly popular plays were *The Merchant of Venice, The Taming of the Shrew,* and *The Merry Wives of Windsor,* which were given so frequently that the Benson company itself spoke of its repertoire as *The Merry Shrews of Venice*. One of the three was given every year or every other year at Stratford from the 1890s until the end of the First World War. This meant that audiences at Stratford who had first seen Benson play Shylock in 1887, when he was twenty-nine, could see him again in the same part in a virtually identical production at the age of fifty-eight, in 1916. They also had the opportunity of seeing every gradation in his performances in the years between, had they the stamina. The extraordinary thing was that many of them had. Benson's productions became institutions. The fact that they remained the same year after year, with familiar sets and costumes, familiar business and familiar performances, created not boredom, but a cosy and complacent pleasure. Predictability became a virtue. Each time the stuffed stag from Charlecote was trundled out for a performance of *As You Like It*, it was greeted with rapturous applause. When Benson played Caliban in a scaley suit with a dead fish in his mouth in his 1891 Birthday production of *The Tempest*, audiences were delighted. They were still delighted by it in 1916. Change, innovation, experiment – the very qualities Benson had wanted to bring there – were what his audiences least expected or demanded. Benson and Stratford entered into a conspiracy of mutual congratulation. The London critics stayed away and the local critics, conscious that their first duty was to be 'loyal', were unstinting in their annual praise. Both the theatre, and Benson's work, suffered as a result. As he grew older and his London ambitions faded, Stratford became a haven where Benson could rely on unfailing approbation and applause.

Benson's finest work at Stratford was given during the 1890s, when he was in his thirties. But even then his work was not noticeable for innovatory production methods, but for the excellence of the companies he gathered together, and the strength of their acting. At that time he and his wife, Constance, played the leading roles. They were supported by older actors like George Weir, and younger players of the calibre of Oscar Asche, Matheson Lang, Frank Rodney, Arthur Whitby, Lily Brayton, and Harcourt Williams. All these actors went on to become leading players on the London stage, and Harcourt Williams the director who ushered in the great days of the Old Vic, with John Gielgud as his leading man. James Agate said of Rodney, Weir, and Whitby that they were three of the greatest Shakespearian actors he had ever seen: 'Benson's company,' he said 'was the nursery of modern Shakespearian acting.'[8] There was much truth in this; but Benson's company – fine though it then was – was most certainly not the nursery of modern Shakespearian production. In his methods of mounting the plays, Benson remained resolutely Victorian. He adored spectacle, elaborate scenery and costumes, the introduction of pageants, processions, and 'ballets' and dances – which Charles Flower deplored. This was the taste of his time. The fashion for 'upholstering Shakespeare', as *Punch* aptly termed it, had begun in the eighteenth century and had been taken even further by Charles Kean's sumptuous productions in the 1850s. Irving's productions at the Lyceum were all notable for their stunning, and very expensive, *mise en scène*. Benson, with fewer resources, did the best he could afford, although he was outdone by Beerbohm Tree's productions at Her Majesty's, in which the fashion for opulent staging reached its apogee. Benson, although he never went as far as having live rabbits on the stage, as Tree did for his production of *A Midsummer Night's Dream*, loved scenic excess.

In his Stratford production of *Antony and Cleopatra* the sets were lumbering canvas reproductions of Roman and Egyptian architecture; Cleopatra and Antony were surrounded by retinues of supernumeraries, and when Antony bade his Egyptian Queen farewell, 'twenty or thirty girls advanced rhythmically, with a low sweeping movement, and strewed roses before the lovers'. This was

Constance Benson's recollection in her memoirs; she recalled similar effects in numerous other plays. In *The Tempest* Ferdinand entered the stage 'drawn by a silver thread held by two tiny cupids'. In Benson's *A Midsummer Night's Dream* (in the days when there were no restrictions on children working in theatres), there were fifty tiny children as fairies, many of them not more than four or five years old, clothed only in fleshlings, with tiny wings on their heads and backs. The effect was exquisitely fairy-like . . . FRB arranged a fight between a spider and a wasp, which was certainly original and amusing, but a most expensive innovation as the spider's legs came in for such rough treatment that they had to be renewed each night.'[9] These elaborations delighted Benson but the text of the plays had to be cut severely to accommodate them. In *Henry V*, for example, Benson cut the Chorus completely for many years. The forty-two scenes of *Antony and Cleopatra* were reduced to fourteen, playing havoc with the plot, let alone the artistic sense of the play.

The best example of the textual liberties Benson took comes from the working stagebook of his Stratford *A Midsummer Night's Dream*, compiled in 1897 and used for many subsequent productions of the play. Unlike many of Benson's prompt-books, which were hastily put together and often detailed only textual cuts, it gives a complete account of the production, including calls, lighting, cuts, movements on stage, and scenery.[10] It shows that Benson employed not just troops of children, but also 'twelve red soldiers, four slaves, two old men, two priests, two crowd, and six Amazons' – some of whom, presumably, were doubling. Every location – Theseus's palace, the wood near Athens, Quince's house, Titania's bower – had a different set. The last scene of the play (the performance of the play of Pyramus and Thisbe, before Theseus and the lovers) took place in an elaborate Graeco-Roman temple, on either side of which were great urns filled with flaming oil. The scene began with a long procession led by two togaed priests who flung salt on the flames. The text was heavily cut throughout, particularly towards the end of the play. The performance lasted three hours and ten minutes, with four intervals of varying lengths, the shortest being four minutes and the others of between eight and ten minutes. During these breaks the orchestra played Mendelssohn's music to the play. With this method of production – and all Benson's performances had a similar number of intervals – not only was the text despoiled, but the *structure* of the plays was damaged irreparably. The interlocking of scenes, the commentary and ironic juxtaposition of one upon another, became impossible to convey; the intervals and constant scene-changes fragmented their unity.

Benson cut the plays for other reasons besides playing-time, and the wish to include dances and processions. When a play was cut with especial savagery it was always to remove all offending traces of sexual explicitness. This prudery meant that certain plays became almost impossible to stage; Benson never did succeed in performing the whole canon and the two plays that eluded him were *Measure for Measure*, and *Troilus and Cressida*. Other plays were extensively bowdlerized. This was common theatrical practice in the 1890s but Benson continued it well into the twentieth century when such tender precautions were no longer necessary. The production that suffered most was *Othello,* which Benson's companies played frequently. Since not even the word 'whore' could be uttered on the stage of a Benson production, the play created serious difficulties. The crux of *Othello* – the sexual nature of the Moor's jealousy, carefully fanned by Iago – had somehow to be disguised. Iago's description of Cassio in bed, dreaming of Desdemona, was removed, as were the vicious animal imagery ('as prime as goats, as salt as monkeys'), Othello's seizure, the eavesdropping on Iago and Cassio, even Othello's magnificent barbaric 'I will chop her into messes – cuckold me!' Othello's jealousy became unmotivated since Desdemona seemed – at worst – to have done no more than give Cassio her handkerchief. This travesty reached its final heights of absurdity in the scene in which Othello confronts Desdemona with her adultery and calls her 'whore' to her face. Throughout this scene the accusations 'whore', 'strumpet', 'bawd', toll like bells. Benson was forced to find substitutes for them, of which the strongest was 'wanton', and the most usual 'one'. Thus, 'I took you for that cunning whore of Venice' became 'I took you for that cunning one of Venice'. Othello's 'What, not a whore?' became simply 'What, not a . . .' followed by a dramatic pause reverberating with the unsaid and the unsayable.[11] The scene became known in the Benson company as the 'Notta' scene, and younger members of the company had difficulty in watching it with straight faces.

Benson also cut Desdemona's willow-song scene, which he considered unnecessary, and the play ended in good actor-manager tradition, with Benson dying centre-stage, in a shaft of limelight, uttering the words, 'Killing myself, to die upon a kiss'. The two last speeches of the play were thus sacrificed to a strong curtain, but Victorian audiences were used to that.

Benson's greatest strength was as an actor, not a director. His problem was that he was born on the cusp of two irreconcilable theatrical methods. Twenty years younger than Irving and twenty years older than Harley Granville-Barker – the two theatrical revolutionaries whose lives he spanned – he was born a little too late to be a great actor-manager, and too early to be that product of the twentieth century, the director. He seems to have been torn in two directions. His desire to be a reformer warred with a great and nostalgic love for a kind of theatre that was disappearing. He spoke and wrote frequently of the old stock companies, which clearly represented to him an ideal. But the stock companies, which were attached to particular provincial theatres and supported, at short notice, visiting stars from London, had almost ceased to exist by 1880, when they were superseded by touring companies like Benson's own. To Benson, their way of working, which he had never encountered at first hand, was glossed with romance. He admired them, above all, for their resourcefulness – perhaps because that quality was also so vital to his own companies. Benson praised stock company actors for their ability to get by with inadequate rehearsal, for the elegance with which they could extricate themselves from a scene they had inadvertently entered, and for their skill at 'ponging' – the capacity to continue speaking in blank verse when you had forgotten your lines. But then Benson's companies were very good at 'ponging'; Benson himself was notorious for it. Such shortcomings, all of which would be vigorously attacked by Granville-Barker, could be approved by Benson when they were linked in this way with an earlier generation of actors who, whatever their failings, at least were true pros.[12]

Benson's manner of speaking Shakespearian verse was also in the tradition of earlier nineteenth-century actors. It was slow and drawn out, with lengthened vowels; 'war' rhymed with 'star', 'chop' became 'charp', 'my' was invariably 'me'. Irving used a similar kind of pronunciation, and both he and Benson (especially as he grew older) were attacked for it. Irving defended himself, and other actors, against such charges of mannered speaking: 'The accents of pleasure,' he once said, 'are different from the accents of pain, and if a feeling is more accurately expressed as in nature by a variation of

sound not provided by the laws of pronunciation, then such imperfect laws must be disregarded, and nature vindicated!'[13] At its best,
Benson's manner of speaking *was* vindicated; there are many testimonies to the power of his voice in a theatre. At its worst it came
too close to the old manner of 'quavering out their tragic notes', that
Colley Cibber said he had learned from actors of the Restoration
period. Certainly it was slow, and could sometimes debilitate an
entire production. Gordon Crosse recalled that 'Benson and his
colleagues sometimes spoke too deliberately, with many pauses and
much repetition of words and phrases. And in going off the
stage. . .they backed and shunted like a South-Eastern train trying to
get into Cannon Street.'[14] Yet the repetition of phrases – a Benson
trait – often met with critical approval. When C. E. Montague wrote
his famous review of Benson's *Richard II*, he praised Benson
particularly for the repetition of the phrase 'to die', after the lines:

> Mount, mount, my soul! Thy seat is up on high,
> Whilst my gross flesh sinks downwards, here to die.

This, Montague thought, was 'a beautiful little piece of insight', and
'a brilliant thought of Mr Benson's to end on such a note'.[15]
Montague's review passed, via James Agate, into theatrical legend,
and his description of Benson as Richard haunted many future actors
of the part, including John Gielgud. Agate himself, rushing to see the
performance after reading Montague's account of it, considered it
'astonishing . . . the finest piece of Shakespearian acting I have ever
seen'. Yet Granville-Barker, a brilliant critic, saw the performance
within a few months of Montague and Agate, and remembered it
chiefly for Benson's inability to recall his lines.[16] Such conflicting
testimonies make it now virtually impossible to assess Benson as an
actor. Yeats admired him; Ellen Terry considered him best in difficult
parts, Agate continued to defend him to the last. But there were many
critics in London, and later in America, who found Benson careless
and second-rate. Perhaps it was simply that he was very erratic.
Certainly Baliol Holloway, who acted with him for many years,
considered that 'He always gave his best performances on a Tuesday
night, usually in somewhere like Peterborough'.

Although he could give critics the impression of being haphazard
and undisciplined (particularly as he grew older), Benson worked
puritanically hard at being an actor, and strove both to break with
stale traditions, and to perfect his technique. He tried, for instance, to

break with the rigid conventions of stage 'business' which were almost inviolable when he was a young actor. These conventions had grown up gradually, and had become a strait-jacket confining the production of plays, particularly Shakespeare's. Whole sequences of gesture, stance, and by-play had hardened into unbreakable rules, from which an actor departed at his peril. Macready, in the 1820s, was once hissed for *retreating* as Macbeth before the ghost of Banquo; it was traditional to *advance*. Victorian audiences knew the conventions, and were reluctant to accept departures from them. Benson found, when he first went on the stage, that these rules were preserved in prompt-books, and in the memories of older actors. He had such actors in his own companies. George Weir, for instance, was a repository of such traditions and a fierce defender of them. As the grave-digger in *Hamlet* he would always remove numerous waistcoats before he began digging the grave. As Bottom, when he awoke from his dream, he would discover a wisp of hay in the pouch around his waist; in his book all grave-diggers, and all Bottoms, must do the same. But his knowledge extended beyond his own roles and encompassed the play. 'When you had to play a Shakespearian part that was strange to you,' Benson wrote, 'you could and did go to any one of a score of small-part actors in the company, and ask him how it was done. He knew, every actor knew, the traditions that had grown up about the playing of eighty, a hundred, or even more characters. And if you told him that you intended to do something different, he would answer flatly, "You can't do that, it's wrong".'[17]

Benson wanted to break with this paralysing influence and some-times did so, particularly when he was a young man. Arthur Machen, an actor and journalist who worked with Benson for a period, remembered that when Benson rehearsed his company, 'everything was open to discussion, to a reasoned enquiry into the right and wrong way of doing it'.[18] But gradually this changed; moves, interpretations, business which he had introduced into his produc-tions hardened in turn into formal rules. This adoption of the very conventions he had set out to break was, of course, partly due to the way in which Benson was forced to work. Always short of time and money, always travelling, constantly fitting in actors as late replace-ments, Benson and his companies never had the leisure to investigate Shakespeare's plays freshly as a modern company can do. Aware as he was of the deadening effect of long runs, it seems never to have occurred to him that the exigencies of touring could also produce tired, stale work, and short cuts.

Benson drove himself and his actors hard. They worked six days a week, rehearsing during the day and playing at night, and on the seventh day they usually travelled to the next venue. The only activity allowed to interrupt this routine was games-playing. Benson's passion for sport became myth, and his companies became notorious for zeal on the cricket pitch, at football, rugby, and hockey. Benson, a gifted athlete himself, certainly had a weakness for engaging actors who were better at first bat than at speaking Shakespearian verse. So well known was this foible that when he once wired an actor, 'Can you play Rugby tomorrow?', the actor wired back 'Yes', and arrived the next day with his boots, to discover that Benson had meant the part of Rugby in *Merry Wives of Windsor* for which he urgently needed a word-perfect replacement. But the emphasis on sports-playing was not just another Benson eccentricity, as most people assumed. It sprang from his belief that it aided an actor, and improved his performance. Benson deplored lack of practice in physical technique, comparing the actor with a pianist practising scales, or a ballet-dancer doing routine exercises. He wrote at length upon the subject in his book *I Want To Go On the Stage: Do, Don't, How!*, his words oddly foreshadowing those of Peter Brook, in *The Empty Space*, written some forty years later:

To acquire grace and power, [Benson wrote] let him [the actor] supplement the toils of his daily work by a training similar to that practised by all acrobats, gymnasts, trapeze-artists, runners, wrestlers, boxers, athletes. Let him copy the scale-playing of the pianist, violinist, singer. Free calisthenics, drill, games, dancing, fencing; these two latter will give him grace, balance, and rhythmic gesture. Keep up swimming and walking, sword and foil play with either hand, breathing exercises . . .

At the peak of Benson's career he had as many as four companies on the road at the same time, and they were uniformly clannish and schoolboyish. Their attitude to Benson was that of a boy to an admired but feared headmaster. When members left the Benson companies, they became 'Old Bensonians', and were proud of it. 'I would rather be an old Bensonian,' Cedric Hardwicke said, in 1931, 'than an Old Etonian, or an Old Oxonian.'[19] They had annual dinners at which Benson was guest of honour. 'We still feel in the same position to Sir Frank [Benson was knighted in 1916],' Henry Ainley said in 1929, 'as in the old days when we were young actors timidly waiting outside the door, summoning up the courage to go into the presence. To us he is what Jowett was to the undergraduates of Oxford . . . what the Bensonian feels towards Sir Frank is a mixture of love and fear. It is almost a religious feeling, compelled by the blazing spirit of the man.'[20] Benson kept himself remote, and expected to be treated with respect by the company; new members were subject to strict discipline. There was a fondness for schoolboy practical jokes, and an intolerance of women. 'We never took stock of what women were in the company,' Oscar Asche wrote. 'Women did not count with us in those days. We were too fond of athletics . . .'[21] It was a strange company, unimaginable now, but for many years it was permanent and tight-knit, with a strong nucleus of actors. And however hearty its camaraderie, however snobbish its traditions, its loyalty to Benson was absolute.

In 1897, the year of Queen Victoria's Diamond Jubilee, Frank Benson and his company played one of their most successful seasons at Stratford. It lasted two weeks, and Benson put on twelve plays. They included *Othello*, his first production of *Henry V* (without the Chorus), *The Tempest*, and *The Taming of the Shrew* (Katharina was one of his wife's favourite parts). In the space of two weeks Benson played Henry V, Caliban, Dr Caius (in *Merry Wives*), Othello, Orlando, Romeo, Shylock, Petruchio, Benedick, and Richard III. It was a range of parts that no modern actor would think of undertaking, or have in his repertoire at any one time. Benson played them, and then resumed his touring, and other equally exhausting roles. He had a repertoire which extended to about twenty-five Shakespeare plays, and he was at the height of his powers as an actor. He had played Richard II for the first time the previous year, and would create Antony (in *Antony and Cleopatra*) – a part in which Agate considered him unsurpassed – the following year.

It was the first time the season at Stratford had been extended from the traditional one week, and the theatre performances were supplemented by all the junketings that accompanied celebration of the Diamond Jubilee. The festival was a resounding success, and the governors announced that future festivals would continue to be of two weeks' duration. But even at the moment when the early Stratford festivals reached a high point, Benson began to look elsewhere. He was looking for a seal to his reputation, and the opportunity to advance his work as an actor-manager. He looked, inevitably, not to Stratford, but to London. His long-held ambition to return as manager of the Lyceum Theatre had never been forgotten, and by the late 1890s Benson believed his moment had come. He had a growing reputation, a strong company, a wide repertoire of work. In London, the great days of the Lyceum were ending. It was losing money; Irving was ill, and his long partnership with Ellen Terry was drawing to a close. As far as Benson was concerned, the battle was on as to who should be Irving's successor. In London it was assumed that the mantle would fall on the energetic Herbert Beerbohm Tree, who opened the sumptuous Her Majesty's Theatre in 1897. But Benson regarded himself as the natural heir, and began planning a London season, a season which was, as it turned out, to conflict cruelly with his obligations to Stratford.

Benson used the three Stratford festivals 1897-9 to introduce three productions which, together with his earlier *Richard II,* would provide the backbone for his London season. *Henry V,* the Birthday play at Stratford in 1897, was his opening play for London. *Antony and Cleopatra,* the Birthday production for 1898, was also included. And in 1899 he first produced at Stratford his full-text *Hamlet,* a production that would be the third play in his London season. His repertoire thus fortified, he secured Irving's own theatre, the Lyceum, for seven weeks in 1900.

Before Benson even arrived in London, he suffered a disaster. His company was on tour in Newcastle, one of Benson's last provincial dates before the assault on the capital. There was a fire in the theatre, and all Benson's costumes, sets, and props, painstakingly acquired over years of touring, were destroyed. He was not insured. It was a measure of how much the London season meant to him that he refused absolutely to postpone it. Sets and props were lent by other managements, including Irving's, and the Benson company sat up late each night sewing new costumes. The opening date, 15 February 1900, remained firm. The eighth and final production would close on 11 April; it seemed perfectly feasible for Benson to appear at the festival season in Stratford, which opened on 24 April. He was committed to it; the theatre governors and the town were expecting him. There was some concern in Stratford, however, about the plays Benson would be presenting. Sarah Flower wrote to him in November 1899, suggesting the cycle of history plays. Whatever other plays Benson gave, the Birthday play had to be fixed. Benson, always a bad correspondent, and tied up with preparations for the

London season, seems to have left the matter unconfirmed. But this was characteristic; the Flowers were used to receiving a hasty, near-illegible scrawl from Benson, which always arrived at the last minute, confirming the details of the festival. His silence was not, therefore, unexpected.

The London season opened with comparative success. The advance bookings were quite good, and at the first night, *Henry V* was well received by the audience. The Boer War was then at its height and the first night coincided with the relief of Kimberley; the audience was clearly stirred by the parallels between Henry's band of brothers, outnumbered at Agincourt, and the beleaguered British in the Transvaal. 'A great success was the universal verdict on *Henry V*,' Benson wrote in his *Memoirs,* 'and for a moment my hopes of achieving my dearest wishes ran high.' But this was typical Benson overstatement. The reviews were no more than cool and – nine days after the opening – a criticism of the production by Max Beerbohm appeared in the *Saturday Review* which not even Benson could have pretended was favourable. It has often been quoted, and it did Benson lasting and irreparable harm. It was a cruelly funny, shallow piece of writing, almost certainly unfair to the strength of the company:

Alertness, agility, grace, physical strength – all these good attributes are obvious in the mimes who were, last week, playing *Henry the Fifth* at the Lyceum. Every member of the cast seemed in tip-top condition – thoroughly 'fit'. Subordinates and principals worked well together. The fielding was excellent, and so was the batting. Speech after speech was sent spinning across the boundary, and one was constantly inclined to shout 'Well played, sir! Well played *indeed*!'. As a branch of university cricket, the whole performance was, indeed, beyond praise. But as a form of acting, it was less impressive . . .

Of the remaining Benson productions only one – *Richard II* received good notices after this fusillade. The result was inevitable, but Benson refused to acknowledge it. Audiences dwindled; he began losing money. But he had gambled so much on this season that he seemed unable to believe he had failed. Defiantly, he resolved not just to continue the season for the appointed seven weeks, but to extend it – through Lent, a notoriously bad time for theatres – until the end of May. Not only was this foolhardy, it meant that it was now impossible for him to play the festival at Stratford, as expected. But so intoxicated was Benson with the idea of staying in London, and forcing a success, that this seems not to have worried him. He hit on a way of extricating himself that he must have known would be disastrous.

The previous November, when Sarah Flower had written to him about the History cycle, Benson had been considering *Pericles*. Sarah Flower opposed the idea. *Pericles* had a stage history of neglect almost as bad as that of the *Henry VI* plays. But Sarah Flower's objection to it was not due to its unpopularity, but to the fact that the play contained much bawdy, and a scene in a brothel. '*Pericles*,' she wrote firmly to Benson, 'will never do to act here.'[22] Benson, now desperate to extricate himself from the Stratford engagement, ignored her feelings. At some point, possibly as early as November 1899 when he first mentioned the play, possibly later, he had discovered that an old actor of seventy-two, John Coleman, had a version of *Pericles* of his own devising. Coleman's version could not offend the most sensitive taste, since he had excised from it not only the offending brothel scene, but also what he called 'the irrelevant, inept and revolting lubricity of the first and second acts'. Leaving it until the last possible moment, Benson managed to palm off Coleman and his *Pericles* on Stratford. Sarah Flower had, by then, little alternative, and Benson wrote to her on 17 April from the Lyceum – seven days before the play was due to open – to calm her lingering doubts. '*Pericles*', he wrote, 'will, I think, be pretty, and there is *nothing objectionable* in Coleman's version. I should not mind my little girl of 10 coming to see it.'[23]

The production was hastily rehearsed at the Lyceum, and Benson released some of his company to play in it. He had read Coleman's text, and he cannot entirely have avoided the few rehearsals; he must have known, therefore, that what he was sending to Stratford was the worst travesty of a Shakespeare play ever to be presented there. In his *Memoirs* he glossed over his role in the whole affair, merely remarking that 'Being fully occupied at the Lyceum, I had to send another company down to do *Pericles* . . . at the Stratford-on-Avon Festival . . .', and that 'the impression was confirmed that *Pericles* was a play which has rightly been consigned into that region reserved for the "unwept, unhonoured, and unsung"'. This was a little unfair on *Pericles*, since Coleman's version bore little relation to the original. He removed the first act; cut most of the second; cut Gower completely, and eliminated all sexual explicitness, including most of the fourth act. There was not much of the play left after this radical surgery, but Coleman supplied the lack with verses of his own devising. He changed the plot, and several of the characters, and created a play which was almost totally incomprehensible. Coleman elected to play the part of Pericles himself – a difficult feat for an actor of seventy-two, but he was not worried by such niceties.[24]

Most of the reviewers were unsparing, and the critic of *Literature* described the production as 'tragic bungling'. He was in no doubt where the blame lay, and he said so roundly: 'Mr Benson is in some sort responsible. When I remember how much admirable work he has done, and in this Memorial Theatre too, I do not like to blame him . . . But it is a grave discredit to him that this miserable travesty of *Pericles* should have been produced .' Benson never referred to the matter again. With dwindling audiences, harsh reviews, diminishing returns at the box-office, he obstinately set his face against reality and pressed on with the season. At the end of it he was nearly bankrupt. Still he would not acknowledge failure. After a brief return to the provinces, and against all advice, he determined to return to London. This time he was not in Irving's great theatre, but in the little Comedy Theatre in Panton Street, close to Herbert Tree's magnificent Her Majesty's. He did not even have sole tenancy; it was also occupied by a German company. Benson proposed to mount a four-month season of eight plays, from mid-December 1900 until April 1901. He would perform on three evenings and one afternoon each week, when the German company was not appearing. It was a suicidal plan, and inevitably a failure.

In the middle of the season, on 22 January 1901, when Benson was already losing money, Queen Victoria died. The theatre had to close for a short period, and when it reopened it was to rows of empty seats. The company, loyal to Benson to the last, turned itself into a commonwealth and struggled on with reduced salaries. Benson and his wife sold everything they had of any value; the strain on Benson himself finally told, and he became ill with a gastric ulcer. Thin, drawn, and suddenly aged, he made a gallant speech on the last night in April 1901, and the London company was wound up.

The death of Victoria marked the end of an era; the theatre, which so mirrored its time, with its buildings, with its bowdlerized texts, its unquestioning and sentimental homage to Shakespeare, its relish for pretty elaboration and spectacle, would change too. Herbert Tree's productions at the renamed His Majesty's would continue – the last lavish examples of a tradition already dying – until 1914. But after the war it would be the influence of very different men like William Poel and Granville-Barker, which held sway. Into this changing world, Frank Benson – quintessentially a Victorian – moved like a sad ghost. The year 1901 marked a watershed in his own life and work. His ambitions to be Irving's successor, to establish a repertoire theatre in London, were over; he never gave a major season there again. His marriage was severely strained; his finances increasingly precarious. His way of working was too entrenched to adapt. He reformed his company, and recommenced touring, although many of his best actors left him. He drove himself as hard as he had always done, but something of his verve and conviction seem to have left him. G. F. Hannam-Clark, an actor in his company during 1902, recalled tired, bored performances from Benson that year. During the graveyard scene in *Hamlet* he would turn his back on the audience, and, shielded from their view by a long cloak, would draw diagrams of hockey-match tactics on the floor of the stage.[25]

With the total eclipse of his London hopes he turned increasingly to Stratford, forging tighter links with a theatre he had treated so shabbily and cavalierly a year before. Audiences there gave him the same unfailing loyalty and approbation. But change was, year by year, more overdue. It became inevitable after 1903, when Archibald Flower became chairman of the theatre's governors. Even then, such was the affection felt for Benson in the Memorial Theatre and the town, it was slow in coming. For the next eighteen years Charles Flower's ideal for his theatre remained as remote as ever.

3

The New Chairman

Charles Flower first became ill only two years after Benson began to direct the Stratford festivals. From 1888 onwards his health was weak; he retired from the brewery, and it passed into the hands of his brother Edgar, and his son, Archibald. He was no longer able to take as full a part in the running of the Memorial Theatre as he had done before, which was one of the reasons why Benson was invited annually to return, and given virtual *carte blanche* in the organizing of the festivals. Charles lived to see Osmond Tearle's production of *Henry VI, Part I* in 1889, and felt that his belief in the play's stageability and dramatic power was vindicated.[1] But he was by then a very sick man, and had to spend months in France and Algeria trying to regain his health. In 1891 the town council, knowing that he was ill, commissioned his portrait, and the following year, three days after the theatre festival had ended, he died quite suddenly from a heart attack. He had lived to see a few of his ambitions for the Memorial Theatre achieved – it did, at least, still have an annual festival, even if it was in his lifetime only of a week's duration, and its popularity with local audiences was growing. The theatre had not been forced into the ignominious closure so many journalists had predicted. But his visions of a great company like the Meiningen, of a theatre as renowned as the opera house in Bayreuth, and of a drama school, had not materialized.

Charles Flower was given a civic funeral with full pomp. On the Saturday after his death a long procession wound its way through the town to the cemetery in the Evesham Road where, in a last Nonconformist gesture, he had elected to be buried in unconsecrated ground. Not one member of the theatrical profession was present, although Frank Benson sent a wreath and Henry Irving a telegram expressing his 'deepest and true regret'. His illness and death left a vacuum in the affairs of the theatre which took years to fill. His brother Edgar became chairman in his place, and he and Sarah

Flower ensured that the festivals continued, that the theatre opened each spring, and that the annual invitation to Benson was renewed.

Edgar was a very different man from his brother. He had a family of ten children. He owned, and lived in, two houses, The Hill in Stratford, and Middle Hill, a large estate near Broadway which he purchased from Halliwell-Phillipps, the Shakespearian archivist and scholar. He loved painting, country life, and the administration of his estates. He ensured that the Memorial Theatre did not run into debt, and that the festivals continued, but he was, for his eleven years as chairman, little more than a custodian of his brother's venture. It was, in any case, obvious that the Flower family had produced a natural successor to Charles in Edgar's son, Archibald, and that it would be only a matter of time before he took over; when Edgar died in 1903, he did so.

Archie's appointment was not purely nepotistic, as it might have seemed. That he became chairman was due not just to family precedence, but also to the force of his personality and to a passionate dedication to the Memorial Theatre, which matched that of his late uncle Charles. He was to remain chairman for the next forty years, until the end of the Second World War. It was to be a long reign, and it was absolute. During those forty years Archie ruled the Stratford theatre – managed is too gentle a word – totally. Every decision, artistic, financial, bureaucratic, was referred to him. Archie appointed the directors of the festivals, and – when they resigned – their successors. He checked the books; he fixed the production budgets; often he decided which plays should be put on, and who should appear in them. He was involved in casting, contracts, salaries, touring, advertising, the design of the theatre, and any changes to its structure. No set could be made, or costume sewn, until he had previously vetted the cost.

Archie's rule of the Memorial Theatre lasted as long as that of Lilian Baylis at the Old Vic, and covered almost exactly the same period. Yet Archie's work, unlike that of Lilian Baylis, has been almost totally ignored. He was not the eccentric that she was, and the Stratford theatre did not enjoy under his aegis the *réclame* which the Old Vic did under hers. Artistically Archie held the Stratford theatre back, just as, it has been argued, Lilian Baylis sometimes did the Old Vic.[2] But he achieved at Stratford many things that must have seemed impossible in 1903 when he took over as chairman. He brought the theatre its own company, a new building, growing audiences, and financial prosperity. None of the celebrated work at Stratford after the Second World War would have been possible without the theatre buildings Archie fought for and the money he amassed. By the time he retired in 1944 the Stratford theatre was the richest in the country, and potentially one of the finest equipped. Without that legacy the artistic development which came later would have been virtually impossible. His years of charming, despotic rule had many disadvantages, but they were, ultimately, of incalculable value.

In age Archie and Frank Benson were close contemporaries. Archie was born in 1865, seven years after Benson. Like Benson he came from a protected traditionalist background. By the time Archie was born the Flower family business was well established, and he was brought up from his earliest years in an atmosphere of affluence and security, with none of the hardships his father and uncles had experienced as children. His childhood was spent mainly at The Hill, which his father took over from his grandfather. There was a billiard. room, a stable of horses, large gardens with a tennis court. Both his father and his mother were artistic; Edgar was a gifted amateur painter, his wife a talented singer. They entertained constantly, and a stream of distinguished guests from America and England passed through the house. General Grant, the ex-President of the United States, stayed with them, shocking Archie's mother by his addiction to smoking. Ellen Terry, Emerson, and Longfellow also stayed there, so did Professor Huxley, Dean Stanley, Tennyson, Tenniel, and many late-Victorian painters.[3]

Edgar's sons did not receive the same piecemeal education which he and his brothers had suffered. Archie went to Clifton, other brothers to Eton and Wellington. Archie did not distinguish himself academically at school; he went up to Clare College, Cambridge, and came down with an indifferent degree, and a Blue for his rowing. He came home to Stratford to live, and became a director of the brewery, and a governor of the other 'family business', the Memorial Theatre. He had little interest in Shakespeare, and did not begin to read the plays until after he came down from Cambridge. But when he did a curious conversion took place. Archie discovered the plays were enjoyable. More than that, they provided him with a kind of religious and moral vantage-point from which he could survey life and the world around him. From then onwards he treated Shakespeare in a friendly and companionable way, rather as if he were a man he rubbed shoulders with in the course of a day's work.

He was, Archie thought, 'a man of wonderful human understanding',[4] and his plays provided him with all manner of useful rubrics and maxims in everyday life. There was nothing particularly exalted in his view of Shakespeare, and no smack of Bard-worship; Shakespeare was a sound chap, and Archie liked to read bits of the plays at bedtime. He became extremely adept at making speeches on the subject of Shakespeare-the-ordinary-man and Archie's audiences, at Rotarian Clubs, Freemasons' assemblies, town council dinners, took to the view. There was also the advantage that when Archie was appealing for money for the theatre – as he frequently was – these speeches made people reach for their cheque-books with amazing alacrity.

In many ways Archie was a much more conventional man than his forebears. He inherited their energy and determination, but the streak of romanticism and Nonconformity was missing. Like them Archie became a pillar of the local community, serving on some forty different committees and charities and dominating the town council. But his politics differed; he was not a Liberal as his grandfather and uncle Charles had been, but a lifelong supporter of the Conservative party. He was Church of England, and an ardent Rotarian; he was unworldly and not in the least materialistic, but status was important to him – particularly the status of the theatre. Archie was not content for it to be a small provincial house, dedicated to short annual seasons of Shakespeare. References to Bayreuth and Salzburg – of which little had been heard since the flurry of publicity when the theatre was founded – were revived.

His attitude to the Stratford theatre was very much connected with his attitude to his uncle Charles. In many ways he was not the natural man to run the Memorial; he had little understanding of the processes of theatre, and his critical judgement of productions, acting, and design was unreliable. But for the theatre and its development, he was prepared to fight tirelessly and passionately. He regarded it very much as a family inheritance, whose future had been entrusted to him. His love and his admiration for his uncle were very strong; he studied the aims and proposals which Charles – whom he called the 'Founder' – had laid down for the theatre, and he systematically set about achieving them. The old ideas of the 1870s – the resident company at Stratford, the development of the seasons, the possibilities of touring, even of establishing a pension fund for actors – had been in abeyance for over twenty years. During the next forty years, with varying degrees of success, Archie brought each of these aims about. His will was indomitable, and legendary. The phrase Donald Wolfit once used of him – a 'benevolent autocrat'[5]– is echoed by all who knew him, and Wolfit (no mean autocrat himself) was presumably a good judge. Part of his strength was that he was always well-informed. He was a great letter-writer, and letters, cables, memorandums, and postcards flowed in abundance to and from The Hill and the theatre. Even George Bernard Shaw, whom Archie brought on to the board of governors in the early 1920s, treated him with the circumspection of one *force de nature* for another. Shaw corresponded regularly with Archie (whom, after his knighthood, he addressed affectionately as 'Dear Srarchie') and from time to time disagreed with him over theatre policy. But Shaw never allowed the disagreements to flare up into a major fight; he bowed to Archie's views, and contented himself by firing off witty barbs from Ayot St Lawrence.

Archie ruled the board of governors with a rod of iron. He was extremely careful who got on to it, and always made sure that he had a loyal body of support on the executive council – which continued, as it always had, to be packed with family and family friends. The governors existed, for the most part, to give their official imprimatur to decisions Archie had already taken. Oddly for such an autocratic man, Archie was also a great canvasser of other people's views, particularly with respect to the theatre. He could occasionally be influenced in major ways by a chance remark made at a dinner party, or a report by a journalist he had never met. He often encouraged people who had few qualifications to judge to give him their opinions of an actor, a production, or set designs. But he was utterly selective in those he listened to; he could ignore good advice with profligate abandon, but pay credence to ill advice, particularly if it happened to reinforce views which he already partially held. Once he had made up his mind he never changed it, no matter how obviously mistaken he might be, or how public and vociferous the opposition. Opposition served only to make his views more entrenched, and those who understood him practised a more circuitous approach. Both Archie's wife, Florence, and his favourite brother, Spenser, operated in this way, with varying degrees of success, and both also knew that there was one factor always likely to influence Archie when all else failed, and that was economy. For Archie's other most pronounced characteristic was his financial caution, a trait which became more marked as he grew older. This caution was partially inherited but it was intensified by Archie's own experiences in running the family brewery. For the brewery's fortunes fluctuated, and at around the period of Archie's marriage to Florence Keane in 1900 went through a very bad patch, when liquidation seemed a possibility. He rescued the business with the bank's support, but the shock of that near-collapse seems to have haunted him and affected all his financial dealings thereafter. It says much for his devotion to the Memorial Theatre that although there were long periods, especially in the 1920s, when it consistently made a loss on each season, Archie not only continued to champion it, but also helped to cover its losses from his own pocket, a fact never publicly disclosed.

The theatre at Stratford in 1903 came under the joint auspices of two very different men, Archie and Frank Benson. Both were, in different ways, autocratic. But beyond that shared characteristic they could hardly have been less alike. Where Benson was scatter-brained, Archie was methodical. Where Benson was Micawber-like, always optimistically believing that something would turn up, Archie was a careful planner and organizer. Where Benson was financially inept, Archie was clever and obsessively cautious. It was inevitable that their partnership would become strained. That it was some years before that happened was due to the fact that Archie both admired Benson and liked him. Also Archie was conservative by nature, and not usually a man given to sudden and precipitate action. Archie's theatrical tastes had, of course, been forged by Benson's productions.

For his first few years in office Archie made few changes at the theatre, and gave Benson his head. He was newly married, and deeply involved in the affairs of the brewery. From 1903 to 1907 the festivals at Stratford continued much as they had before. The only major difference was that they lasted three weeks each year rather than two, an experiment which had first been tried out successfully in 1902. But there were hints that all was not as settled at Stratford as it appeared to be. In 1903 the governors had considered issuing an invitation to Herbert Tree to conduct at least part of the next year's festival; Tree wrecked their plans by announcing the fact at the 1903 Birthday luncheon, and it had to be hastily denied. In 1905 an invitation was issued to Henry Irving to act in Stratford with the Benson company, but Irving was by then too ill to come. The romantic novelist Marie Corelli, who lived in Stratford and was a constant critic of the Memorial, promptly entered the fray by announcing that she considered Irving was not to be blamed 'for putting a wide distance between himself and the historic building on the banks of the Avon'.[6] Archie was used to attacks from Marie Corelli, and continued a long irritable correspondence with her on the subject of the theatre, but her views seem to have stung him – perhaps because they echoed his own unexpressed opinions. Certainly the invitation to the two surviving pillars of the late-Victorian stage was a bid for status; to have secured the services of either Tree or Irving would have been a considerable coup for Stratford. The bid failed, and Archie was forced to be patient.

The first signs of change came in 1907. That year electric light was installed on the stage and in the orchestra pit of the theatre and, as if to honour this modernity, Archie arranged for the festival season to be a significant break with tradition. As the governors' reports put it, it was planned that 'additional variety should be given to the programme by generous help from many leading artists outside Mr Benson's company'.[7] What this meant was that Benson would give the festival as usual, but that a large number of 'stars' would be imported from London to play with his company for one or two performances in their favoured roles. It was a tacit acknowledgement that 'additional variety' was well overdue, and the roster of splendid names would undoubtedly add to the prestige of the theatre. It was easy enough to persuade the London actors to come; they were usually required to do no more than give one performance, either in a role for which they were famous or in one which they coveted but had not yet secured on the London stage. There was virtually no rehearsal; the stars could be back in London next day.

For the next five years, from 1907 to 1911, many of the leading actors of the English theatre travelled to Stratford, gave their Hamlet, Portia, or Henry V, and duly returned to the West End. Lewis Waller, golden-voiced and the darling of the galleries, came to give Othello, and his famous Henry V. In 1908 Johnston Forbes-Robertson played Hamlet; in 1909 it was Matheson Lang; in 1910 both Martin Harvey and Herbert Tree played the part. Many other actors, including some who had worked with Benson, but who had left his company and were now famous in London, appeared at the Memorial Theatre playing Shakespearian roles they had few chances to attempt in the West End: they included Henry Ainley, Oscar Asche, and Lilian Braithwaite. The leading actors were kind in their comments on the Benson company; they acted with it, Constance Collier said, 'in a spirit of love, not criticism'[8] – a comment which implied, nevertheless, that there were criticisms to make if judgement had not been temporarily suspended. 'Your company,' Lewis Waller told Constance Benson, 'give a better show with half an hour's rehearsal than many do with weeks.'⁹ But such remarks were back-handed compliments, and Benson and his company were forced into an ignominious position by these seasons; to support star actors at short notice – often playing roles for which Benson himself had been famous – was never what he had intended for his company.

This policy continued, however, without tangible opposition from Benson, and reached its pinnacle in two heady seasons in the years 1910 and 1911. In 1910, for the first time, a three-week summer festival was introduced in addition to the established one in the spring.¹⁰ An impressive list of stars came up from London: besides Herbert Tree and Martin Harvey as the Prince of Denmark, there was Ellen Terry – old and unsure of her words, but still possessed of great charm – as Portia; Lewis Waller, Violet Vanbrugh, Henry Ainley, and Marion Terry also appeared. There was the much vaunted performance of a singularly bad play called *The Piper* which had won a competition organized by the governors to discover new playwrights. There was a special 'Old Bensonian Matinée', in which almost every Old Bensonian of note made an appearance. There was an elaborate festival of folk-songs and dance, during which Benson crowned the May Queen of Stratford. It was the year he was granted the Freedom of the Borough, the first man to receive it since David Garrick. Benson was at the height of his popularity in the town. After the ceremony in the town hall, he and his wife were drawn through the streets in a landau by members of his company, and loaded with floral bouquets and wreaths of bay. The 1911 seasons were equally star-studded, and the governors were delighted to discover that the new summer seasons could make money. 'This day, ' said Benson, on the day he was made a Freeman of Stratford, 'you have constituted me your knight, your friend, your serving man.'¹¹ Ironically it was just at this time that the first major strains in the relationship between Archie and Benson were beginning to show. Even as he coined the term, Benson's years as Stratford's knight and serving man were drawing to a close.

The first problems were, almost inevitably, financial. Benson had an inexhaustible capacity for getting himself into debt, and during 1910 and 1911 the debts became an embarrassment to the Memorial Theatre. In 1910 both Archie and the governors lent Benson successive sums of money, totalling £400, of which only £100 was repaid. During the summer festival he became embroiled in another financial muddle. It was then still possible to become a governor of the Memorial Theatre by subscribing the sum of £100; Mrs Pethick Lawrence, a leading figure in the suffragette movement and a supporter of the theatre, wanted to obtain this honour for her husband. Somewhat unwisely, she encountered Frank Benson at the Shakespeare Hotel in Stratford (where he always stayed), and made out the cheque on her husband's behalf to Benson. Benson, vague and short of cash, did not pay it in to the theatre. Archie, some weeks later, then had (as he put it) 'to undertake the delicate task of asking FRB when he was going to pay it in'.[12] Benson handed over the money, and promptly approached Archie for another loan.

He was also further in debt at Stratford. During 1910 he borrowed the sum of £500 from the Justins family, old friends of his, who ran the Shakespeare Hotel. He gave as security 'all my scenery, wardrobe, and stage effects, belonging to my company . . . and a policy to cover the first insurance on the same the premium of which I undertake to keep up'. He also owed the hotel a further £112.14s. for accommodation.[13] He had no way of repaying the debt, and no way of repaying the Justins' loan. 'All these transactions', Archie wrote in a memorandum for the theatre governors, 'gave evidence of the perilous financial position, and I feared a crash would come, which I was most anxious to avoid both for F's sake, and for that of the Memorial Theatre which he was directing.'[14]

Archie's solution was to form a syndicate to take over Frank Benson's company, to be called The Stratford-upon-Avon Players Ltd.; it would employ Benson as 'dramatic and artistic expert', pay him a salary of £20 a week whether he was acting or not (£40 a week when abroad) plus a percentage of the profits, and remove from his incautious hands all the financial problems of running a company. Benson agreed with enthusiasm. 'I think it is all very sound and good,' he wrote to Archie in September 1910. 'Good for Stratford, good for drama and very good for FRB. There are no liabilities of mine that are likely in any way to make the starting of this scheme hard.'[15] He was, as usual, being wildly optimistic. He did not even mention at this point the debt to the Shakespeare Hotel or the fact that the effects of the very company the syndicate was taking over were security on a loan. That was brought to Archie's attention some months later, by the Justins family. Before the syndicate could even begin operating it had to pay off debts of Benson's totalling nearly £2,000.

On 19 February 1911, the new company came into being. Since Archie was the main force on the syndicate which owned Benson's company, the Memorial Theatre almost had – for the first time – its own company; but not quite. Archie at once attempted to make changes, which were long overdue but difficult to make. Chiefly they involved casting. The fact that so many stars had been imported from London for the last five seasons had somewhat obscured the fact that, normally, both Benson and his wife continued to play leading roles for which they were now too old. In 1911 Benson was fifty-three, and Constance forty-eight. Both continued to play parts they had first created when they were in their twenties and early thirties; Benson still played Lysander in *A Midsummer Night's Dream*, Richard II and Henry V. In 1907 he had insisted on playing Berowne in *Love's Labour's Lost*, with a Longaville and Dumain half his age. His wife continued to play Rosalind, Katharina, Titania (usually with a much younger Oberon), and in 1910 had really stretched credibility by appearing as Julia in *Two Gentlemen of Verona*. About the only roles they had conceded were Romeo and Juliet. Furthermore Constance Benson was a less accomplished actor than her husband, with a somewhat raucous and strident technique. She had a sharp tongue, and did not get on with Archie.

Archie boldly suggested that the syndicate should employ a younger actress for the younger leading parts. Constance Benson was angry, and resisted the suggestion. Benson fought loyally on her behalf, but Archie was adamant. The result was that Constance Benson played the first season at Stratford under the syndicate, in spring 1911; that summer she departed. She did not act at Stratford again until spring 1913, and then only in three parts. This was a major concession, so it was not surprising that the syndicate should be asked to make a concession also. The 1911 season continued the now-established practice of importing London stars to Stratford, but there had been murmurings about this for some time, chiefly from Benson's general manager, Bill Savery. Savery was dogged and practical, and Archie admired him; some years later Archie brought him back to Stratford as manager of the Memorial Theatre, a position he held for over twenty years. Archie agreed, therefore, that the 1912 season should be given by Benson's company alone, and that no famous names should be invited. It was something of a test, after five years of a different system which had brought the theatre prestige and good audiences. Benson rose to the challenge; he decided to put on a spectacular production of *Antony and Cleopatra* (the first he had given for fourteen years) with himself as Antony, and Dorothy Green, a promising young actress who later became one of the leading Shakespearian actresses of her generation, as Cleopatra.

The resulting season must have confirmed Archie's doubts about Benson's capabilities. It relied heavily on old Benson productions, brought out, dusted down, partly recast, but not rethought. There was *A Midsummer Night's Dream* (a fourteen-year-old production); *The Merchant of Venice* (fifteen years old); and Benson played roles including Henry V, Richard III, Coriolanus, and Hamlet (the complete text), which were now a severe strain on his energy. *Antony and Cleopatra*, the 'new' production and the Birthday play, was given in the same version of fourteen years standing, still very heavily cut and compressed. It was under-rehearsed. By the time of the dress rehearsal Benson had still not rehearsed any of the scenes between himself as Antony, and Dorothy Green as Cleopatra. When Dorothy Green protested, Benson agreed to run through the scenes with her at six o'clock on the morning of the first night. He then travelled up to London, spoke at Shakespeare celebrations on the South Bank, returned to Stratford, and went on.[16]

The productions satisfied the Stratford critics; Archie gave no overt indication that they did not satisfy him. But it happened that the year 1912 was something of a watershed in the history of the English theatre and Archie, conservative though he was, could not have ignored the contrast between the work Benson was doing at Stratford and the work which was given, the same year, in London. That autumn Harley Granville-Barker directed two Shakespearian productions in London. *The Winter's Tale* opened on 21 September, some three weeks after the end of the summer season at Stratford; *Twelfth Night* opened on 15 November; both were given at the Savoy Theatre. They were productions which changed the course of English theatrical history, and haunted the memories of a generation of actors, directors, and critics. The casts, which were led by Granville-Barker's first wife Lillah McCarthy, also included several ex-Bensonians – Henry Ainley was Leontes, Arthur Whitby Autolycus, and Nigel Playfair also had a small part in *Winter's Tale*. But the productions could hardly have differed more from Benson's. *The Winter's Tale* was staged with a projecting apron platform; the footlights were abolished, and the stage was lit with the aid of electric arc spotlights positioned at the front of the dress circle – a method of lighting so unconventional and unfamiliar that *The Times* spoke of 'search-lamps converging on the stage'. Only six lines of the text were cut, and the play was given fast, with only one interval, which amazed the critics who were used to slower delivery and time-consuming business.

Granville-Barker was greatly influenced by the ideas of William Poel, for whom he had played Richard II shortly before seeing Benson's performance in the part. Both Poel and Granville-Barker believed in simplicity of staging, and had no patience with the elaborate productions which were still the fashion in Beerbohm Tree's theatre, and – when there was the money – at Stratford. When it came to the question of scenery for *The Winter's Tale*, Barker announced that he would have none of it.[17] He left the design to Albert Rutherston (costumes), and the brilliant Norman Wilkinson (sets). The result was not, perhaps, as austere as he had intended, but still highly original. *Winter's Tale* was given on a neo-classical set of white and silver, with tall pilasters; *Twelfth Night* in a brightly coloured garden, with cut-out trees that resembled a child's painting. The costumes for *Winter's Tale*, in particular, were heavily influenced by the Russian Ballet (whose first appearance in London, in 1910, had caused a sensation). The colours were vivid, the style eclectic; Hermione made one of her entrances under the shade of a great, gold, fringed umbrella – like an Indian potentate's. To an age used to stage naturalism, to the painstaking evocation of period, where electric light had only recently replaced the softness and chiaroscuro of gaslight, the brilliant stage, the formalized sets, the swift speech, were revolutionary.

There is no record of whether Archie Flower saw either of these productions, but certainly by 1912 he was moving in theatrical circles in London which included Granville-Barker and the *avant-garde* of writers, actors, and directors. He and his wife were present, for instance, at a dinner given in honour of William Poel, at the Trocadero restaurant in London on 21 December 1912, two weeks after the opening of Barker's production of *Twelfth Night*.[18] This dinner, the most formal public tribute Poel ever received, was attended by many of the leading actors of an earlier generation, including Ellen Terry, and by all the young lions of the contemporary theatre. Granville-Barker was in the chair, and the guests included

Sybil Thorndike and Lewis Casson, Bernard Shaw, Edith Evans (then still a milliner, but flirting with a stage career), Lillah McCarthy, Nigel Playfair, and Ben Iden Payne, a young director/actor who had founded the first English repertory theatre in Manchester, and who would many years later become the artistic director at Stratford. Poel's praises were warmly sung by the assembled company; he was, Shaw asserted, 'one of the greatest and finest influences on the English theatre'.

Next year Poel was invited by the governors to bring his latest production to Stratford, for the Spring Festival of 1913. Poel had had brief contact with Stratford before – he had brought an earlier production of *Measure for Measure* there in 1908. His new production was of *Troilus and Cressida*, a play Benson never performed and which had then been seen only once in England since its original production in 1603. Poel produced it first for the English Stage Society, a group he had founded in 1894, which was dedicated to performing the plays 'in an Elizabethan manner', swiftly and simply on a bare stage. The ESS paid actors the sum of two guineas for rehearsing and performing, and used a number of amateur as well as professional actors. The productions were given in a variety of church and parish halls, and were often sparsely attended; Shaw recalled going to see Poel's production of *Romeo and Juliet* with Granville-Barker, with only about six other people in the house.[19] Yet Poel exerted a great and lasting influence both on productions at Stratford and on many of the leading actors and directors of his day, including Harcourt Williams, John Gielgud, and Tyrone Guthrie. Of the future directors at Stratford no less than four – William Bridges-Adams, Iden Payne, Robert Atkins, and Barry Jackson – were deeply influenced by his work.

Poel's production of *Troilus and Cressida* was by far the most interesting event in the otherwise unoriginal 1913 seasons, though it was not recognized as such at Stratford. The rest of the programme consisted mainly of old Benson productions, and *Troilus* was given only two performances. It was not the Birthday play, in spite of its rarity; Archie might be flirting with the *avant-garde*, but he was clearly not prepared to risk this play, with its reputation for bawdiness, as the highlight of the festival. Nor was Poel given a great deal of financial help. He wrote to Esmé Percy, the actor who played Troilus in London, trying to persuade him to play again in Stratford, and his letter says much about the conditions at the theatre: 'It is now definitely confirmed,' he wrote, 'we give two shows of *Troilus and Cressida* on Whit Monday, May 12th . . . There is not much money to be got out of the Stratford authorities, as the theatre only holds £50 when full, and I have promised to keep the expenses down to £100. Will you come and do it for a £5 note?'[20] The five-pound note seems to have been an insufficient temptation; Percy refused, and the part of Troilus was taken by the young Ion Swinley. Poel himself played Pandarus, Edith Evans played Cressida, and Hermione Gingold, aged sixteen, played Cassandra. Poel's productions were marked by his own considerable eccentricities, and one of his oddest foibles was a penchant for casting women in men's parts, something he continued to do throughout his life as a director, no matter how unsuitable the role, or the actress. William Bridges-Adams encountered this trait when he worked for him as an assistant stage manager on a production of *Two Gentlemen of Verona*. He came down to the rehearsal room one morning to find

Poel, wrapped in a grey muffler, nibbling a biscuit and sipping a glass of milk. In front of him a lady, shimmering with sequins, and no longer in her first youth, was in an attitude of visible distress. Poel's voice was raised in querulous criticism; 'I am disappointed,' he said, 'very disappointed. Of all Shakespeare's heroes, Valentine is one of the most romantic, one of the most virile. I have chosen you out of all London for this part, but so far you have shown me no virility whatsoever.'[21]

In his production of *Troilus* the parts of Aeneas, Paris, and Thersites were all played by women. No man could play Thersites, Poel considered – 'he would be sure to over-act'. The costumes for the production were as unconventional as the casting. The Greeks and the Trojans wore a somewhat shabby array of Elizabethan knicker-bockers and wrinkled hose. Cassandra wore a Greek tunic. As Cressida, Edith Evans, looking like a large but youthful Lady Bracknell, wore an Elizabethan frock and a feathered cavalier hat.[22] But then Poel did not believe in any kind of uniformity of costume, and still less in the relentless faithfulness to period dress which was the fashion of his day. When he directed *Coriolanus* with Robert Speaight, Coriolanus wore a leopard skin, Volumnia a Gainsborough dress with a plumed hat, Virgilia a Pre-Raphaelite smock, and the citizens an attire similar to that of French railway porters.[23] Costume, he considered, was there to express character – nothing else. At Stratford, Poel was unable to have an apron-stage built, but he managed to produce *Troilus* in an approximation of what he considered to be the Elizabethan manner, on a bare stage, with a curtained inner recess. The play was given with one interval and comparatively few cuts. Poel, an advocate of full texts, was still capable of making alterations which would appal a modern director, though they were minimal compared to the kind of tinkerings that went on in Benson productions. Occasionally even Poel found Shakespeare's bawdy unacceptable. In his production of *Measure for Measure* Lucio's 'He has got a wench with child', was unaccountably amended to 'He will shortly become a father'. Surprisingly, most of Thersites' vicious sexual imagery survived intact in Poel's production, but Ulysses' long and intricate speech about Time was, for no clear reason, heavily cut.[24]

The two performances of *Troilus and Cressida* at Stratford did not receive a great deal of attention. The production was seen by two later Stratford directors, Bridges-Adams and Barry Jackson, both of whom admired it, and it brought lasting benefit to the English theatre in that it convinced Edith Evans to give up millinery and become an actress. But *The Times* (reviewing the London production) considered the three-hundred years neglect of the play to be thoroughly deserved; it was, wrote its critic, degenerate, decadent, and unstageable. At Stratford, where change was long overdue, Poel's approach to the production of Shakespeare's plays could have been encouraged and utilized. The freshness of his approach, the insistence on simplicity of staging, fairly full texts, and Poel's marked ability to spot outstanding actors when they were young and inexperienced, were all qualities needed at Stratford. But he was not invited to work there again and might anyway have refused if he had been; he had a deep mistrust of the commercial theatre, even a non-profit-making enterprise such as the Memorial. Archie was still reluctant to make radical changes at Stratford, and was not the man to appreciate Poel's innovations. Poel might enjoy the esteem of his peers, but most of his work was given in shabby halls, with poor audiences, and he was unlikely to bring Stratford the fame and prestige that Archie hungered for. So *Troilus and Cressida* came and went, unremarked in the tide of old Benson productions. Archie had other plans for Stratford, and those plans were still dependent on Frank Benson.

In 1913 Archie had decided, and the governors and syndicate had agreed, that the Stratford-upon-Avon Players Ltd. should go on tour. Two companies were to be formed; one, under Benson, would go to

Canada and the United States, and the other would go to South Africa. It was an extremely ambitious project, and one dear to Archie's heart. His own family ties with America were close; American tourists already visited Stratford and the Memorial Theatre in quite large numbers. Archie foresaw, with great accuracy, that support for the Memorial Theatre in America could pay dividends in the future. A successful American tour would bring the Memorial Theatre precisely the kind of notice Archie desired: an international reputation. It was also possible that it would bring in a great deal of money. As Archie was well aware, touring in America could be highly profitable. Even in the 1880s and 1890s, for instance, Henry Irving had been able to make such large profits from his four American tours that they subsidized costly productions at the Lyceum. Benson, obviously, would not be going to America with the advantage of a reputation as great as Irving's, nor with such celebrated productions. But he went as a representative of Stratford, for which Archie believed Americans had a more sentimental regard than many Englishmen. The tour meant that the Stratford-upon-Avon Players would be kept together, in Stratford's employ, for a full year, from the summer season of 1913 through to that of 1914. The governors provided the money necessary for the tour, and announced in their annual report that they hoped that their 'substantial aid' might be 'the means of establishing a repertory company on a permanent footing'.[25] The plan therefore gave Archie the hopes not only of making Stratford famous, but also of fulfilling Charles Flower's original ideal of a resident company. The tour of America, and the smaller-scale one to South Africa, obsessed him throughout 1913.

The American tour was to last eight months. It involved long and arduous journeys between thirty-seven different cities, with a large repertoire of plays. Benson would be playing all his old leading roles; Constance Benson, who could not reach agreement with Archie as to the parts she would play, was not going. Benson had Dorothy Green as his leading lady, and a good supporting cast, including the handsome young Murray Carrington, Basil Rathbone, and a fine older actor, Randle Ayrton, who had once been his stage manager. Benson, as well as playing a large number of taxing roles, was also to act as a kind of ambassador for the company, giving numerous speeches and press conferences *en route*. He viewed the whole project as a kind of happy crusade. On the last night of the summer season of 1913 he received even more bouquets and bay-wreaths than usual from the Memorial stage. 'We go', he told the audience, 'as ambassadors of Shakespeare and Stratford. We go sailing under the stars, with many sounds ringing in our ears, and singing as we go the rhythms of Shakespeare.'[26] It was a characteristically halcyon vision, and the reality was sadly different.

The tour began well. In Canada the reviews were good, the audiences large; the performances made a substantial profit. Archie, who had accompanied the actors for the Canadian part of the tour, returned home well pleased. The company moved on to Chicago, opened with *Much Ado about Nothing*, and faced a concerted critical attack – much of it directed towards Benson's own performance as Benedick. The *Chicago Tribune* described him as 'a skittish old beldame, peaked, capricious and jerky'. The *Examiner* said his performance was devoid of distinction. The *Record Herald* noted Benson's old failings – his constant paraphrasing, and the heavily cut text. The reviews for his Hamlet, and even for his Richard II ('spoken in one long howl . . . hard, wooden and graceless') were equally bad. Audiences fell off; the company began to lose money.They pressed on with the punishing schedule, but the reviews remained poor, and the receipts disappointing. Benson gallantly continued with his programme of speeches and conferences, but his style of speechmaking – waffly, sentimental, full of grossly purple prose – sounded oddly to American ears: 'Verbal confetti', commented the *San Francisco Chronicle* after a Benson speech in that city.

The reviews and the reports of Benson's speeches were assiduously collected by press-cutting services; they all wended their way back to The Hill, where Archie kept a careful watch on the progress of the tour, and on Benson himself. Archie even went to the lengths of writing to at least one American journalist for a fuller report than the one she had already written for her newspaper. She wrote back to him at length in April 1914, and her comments on Benson were not encouraging.[27] Her letter was carefully kept, annotated and marked, in Archie's files. It was precisely the kind of evidence that always weighed most with him, and her account, echoing earlier ones in newspapers, was clear enough: Benson was failing in his mission in America, and not just as an actor, but as an ambassador also. Within a month of Archie's receiving that letter, as the long tour drew to a close, it was announced that there would be a second American tour, for the autumn of 1914. But Benson was not invited to lead it, or even to go on it. It would be led by the young Murray Carrington who had received uniformly good notices throughout America.

Benson returned to England tired, publicly demoted, to face the news that when all the receipts were in and the expenses paid, the tour had not even made a small profit; it had lost £1,000. But he was still contracted to rehearse, and play, the summer festival at Stratford, which opened on 1 August. War was declared on 4 August. The same month both the syndicate and the Stratford-upon-Avon Players Ltd. were wound up. Almost certainly the moment had come when Archie would have made the break with Benson. As it was, the second tour of America had to be cancelled, and the war won Benson a short reprieve.

Benson's first reaction to war was to mount as many productions of *Henry V* as he could muster. His second was to attempt to join up himself. Recruiting officers dubiously surveyed the thin, somewhat haggard man before them (Benson was fifty-six, and looked older). When asked his age, he would reply crisply, 'Thirty-five'. 'Surely you are older than that?' one questioned. 'Are you here to get soldiers,' Benson replied with spirit, 'or to ask silly questions?'[28] Unable to enlist, Benson continued to act. For 1915 and 1916 (the year of the tercentenary of Shakespeare's death) the festivals continued at Stratford, and Benson continued to run them. In 1916, during the special Tercentenary Matinée in London at the Drury Lane Theatre, Benson was knighted for his services to the theatre by George V. He returned in triumph to Stratford, where a star-studded matinée had also been organized to celebrate the tercentenary. There were speeches, celebrations, bouquets, tributes; it was, ironically, the last festival that Benson would ever organize there. Later the same year he and his wife found work running a canteen for the Red Cross in France. In September, his only son, Eric, was killed in action, a loss from which he never recovered.

The theatre at Stratford closed for the remainder of the war. It did not reopen until the spring of 1919, when a short, token festival was hastily arranged. On paper it looked an *ad hoc* affair, which promised little. Benson, only just back from France, was unable to gather a complete company; too many men still had not been demobbed, and many others would never return. But he agreed to appear at Stratford in a few scenes from *Coriolanus* and *The Merry Wives of Windsor*. The remainder of the week was to be padded out by visits from two other companies, both led by actors who had once worked with Benson, J.B. Fagan, from the Court Theatre, and Nigel Playfair. In fact, this short season marked a turning-point for Stratford, and for Benson; it marked the change between the reign of the old guard and the new. Benson sat in the audience a tired man, newly returned from the ugliness of the front, trying to pick up the threads of his career. He watched Nigel Playfair's production of *As You Like It*, full of sunshine and gaiety, and saw a new generation at work.

Nigel Playfair, who had acted in the Benson companies on several occasions, was then forty-three. His own career provided a link between the old traditions and the *avant-garde*. He had acted for Benson, but he had also acted for Granville-Barker, and it was Barker who had most influenced him. In 1918, with financial help from Arnold Bennett and a covey of press barons, he had taken over the Lyric Theatre, then nearly derelict, in a shabby and unfashionable area of London. Playfair was to transform it into one of the most successful theatres in the country, and to present there some great productions. In 1919 he was just beginning his career as an impresario/director. When he was invited to present *As You Like It* at Stratford he was given five weeks' notice. He invited the brilliant Claude Lovat Fraser to design sets and costumes, and embarked hastily on rehearsals. There was no money. Lovat Fraser's wife made sixty costumes in the five weeks available, for £150.[29]

Stratford had seen Benson's production of *As You Like It* on numerous occasions. It was one of the standard plays in his repertoire, indeed from 1910 onwards it had been given almost every year without fail. Benson's sets consisted of heavy canvas flats festooned with painted ivy, which would quiver and shake when Benson, as Orlando, attempted to nail his verses to them. To convey the Forest of Arden with verisimilitude Benson used to cover the stage ankle-deep with leaves, through which his actors, clad in autumnal russets and greens, tripped and scuffed. Lovat Fraser set the action on the edge of the wood, with deliberately formalized trees framing a delicate artificial landscape. The costumes, which he took from fourteenth-century missals, looked curiously modern. They were vividly coloured blues, whites, scarlets, and yellows, the result of dyeing unbleached linen in the Lovat Fraser bath-tub. They were startlingly beautiful, clearly the work of a designer, and not the hotch-potch of velvet, paste, jewels, slashed taffeta, and wrinkled hose that Stratford had always accepted as the *sine qua non* of a Shakespearian production.[30]

The play was to be given uncut, with only one interval. 'I was determined', Playfair wrote some years later, 'not to cut a single sentence . . . "If they want the Bard," I said to myself, "they shall have him – whole and unadulterated".'[31] But when he arrived at the Memorial Theatre Playfair discovered that Stratford had numerous ideas about how a production of *As You Like It* should be put on, and they had nothing to do with respect for the Bard's text. Chief of these was the obligatory appearance of the stuffed Charlecote stag. Playfair looked at the moth-eaten animal and categorically refused to use it. He was met with stupefied disbelief. 'Such a piece of iconoclasm', he wrote, 'had apparently never been heard of in Stratford before . . . '[32] Resolutely stag-less, the production opened. Sir Frank and Lady Benson were in the first-night audience to give gentle encouragement to their protégé. They saw a play transformed, with young actors playing young parts, with scenes flowing into scenes, lines spoken which they had always cut, a Rosalind (Athene Seyler) who was not the gracious womanly figure they were used to, but giggling and girlish. Their reaction was a common one among Stratford audiences and critics in the years to come. *This* was not the play they knew. 'It was produced', Constance Benson wrote, 'in an entirely novel way, with Futurist scenery and dresses, and was most interesting, but – to my mind – not the *As You Like It* of Shakespeare's fancy . . . I overheard Nigel Playfair say "The Bensons are hating my show"; but they weren't hating it, only they could not see the sylvan play in the very new and original setting.'[33]

Archie Flower was nonplussed by the production, and said as much. Among Stratford theatre-goers the reaction was one of outrage. 'Outside the theatre', Playfair wrote, 'the storm raged, and it attained a ferocity I would hardly have thought possible. When I came into my hotel . . . people turned their backs and got up and walked from the room . . . The rest of the cast fared little better; they were cut and cold-shouldered everywhere. When Lovat Fraser was walking in the street, a woman came up to him and shook her fist in his face. "Young man," she said impressively, "how dare you meddle with our Shakespeare?"'[34]

The production attracted a great deal of attention from the critics, most of it unfavourable. Only the reviewer of the *Manchester Guardian* praised it unreservedly. The others scented innovation, and did not like it. 'It is the voice of Shakespeare,' wrote H.C. Bailey in the *Daily Telegraph*, 'but the hands were those of the twentieth century, those much experienced restless hands which must still be contriving something new . . . '[35] Shakespeare – 'our Shakespeare' – had for so long been annexed as a late-Victorian writer, noble and Tennysonian, that the discovery of the protean nature of the plays was bound to be controversial. In Stratford, where tradition had stiffened into complacency, it was particularly hard. What was surprising was that Archie Flower, who was bewildered by Playfair's production, whose own taste was for more traditional methods, recognized that change was now inevitable. With that short spring season of one week, Frank Benson's years of work for Stratford came to an end. When the summer festival opened the Memorial Theatre had a new company. Its director, William Bridges-Adams, was thirty years old.

4

The First Director

From 1919 onwards the Memorial Theatre was always to have its own resident company in one form or another, and would never have to depend again on the services of an outside touring company such as Benson's. That a resident company at last became a reality was due to two unlikely and incongruous factors: the existence of a small wooden YMCA hut in Bloomsbury, and the collective guilt, after years of inertia, of a body in London rejoicing in the cumbersome title of the Shakespeare Memorial National Theatre Committee.

The affairs of the SMNT Committee and the Stratford theatre were to be entangled for the next forty years, marked occasionally by hostility, and always by rivalry. Even after their relationship entered a new phase when the National Theatre was, at long last, founded in 1962, it remained circumspect, and for some years stormy. In view of that subsequent history, it is ironic that had it not been for the SMNT Committee, and for its confusion about its aims and its role, the Memorial Theatre might never have formed a company, and might have continued to employ touring companies as it had done in the past.

The SMNT Committee was formed in 1908, and was the result of the sudden and unpredictable alliance of two utterly different factions. One faction was committed to the erection in London of a suitable memorial to William Shakespeare, which was to take the form of a statue. The other faction, led by William Archer, the critic and translator of Ibsen, by Granville-Barker and Bernard Shaw, was committed to the founding and building of a British National Theatre. The two factions cordially detested each other, and for years the National Theatre advocates had enjoyed themselves by heaping scorn on the worthies who favoured a memorial statue. William Archer had even contributed a short poem (parodying Milton) to the debate:

What needs my Shakespeare? Nothing. What need we?
A playhouse worthy his supremacy.
Oh bathos! – to the Voice of all our race
We raise dumb carven stones in Portland Place.[1]

In 1908 the faction dedicated to a 'dumb carven stone', undeterred by shafts of wit from Archer and his supporters, announced a world-wide architectural competition to design a suitable monument. There was therefore considerable amazement when, only two weeks later, after energetic lobbying by Herbert Beerbohm Tree and others, the two factions suddenly forgot their differences and came together in fractious alliance, to found the Shakespeare Memorial National Theatre Committee, a group whose very title betrayed the confusion and duality of its aims. The National Theatre was, at its inception, conceived as a memorial to Shakespeare, and it was therefore inevitable that sooner or later its affairs would become embroiled with that other memorial to Shakespeare, the theatre at Stratford.

The Committee's initially tenuous existence was given greater credibility the following year by Edith Lyttelton, who was from the first a driving force, and who persuaded a businessman, Carl Meyer, to donate £70,000 to the project. Meyer was duly rewarded the following year with a baronetcy, and with this new substantial backing the National Theatre began its long slow progress towards birth. In 1913, with Meyer's money, the SMNT Committee bought a theatre site – the first of many – in Bloomsbury, and plans were drawn up for the future building. It was to be a long, low structure, resembling a conglomeration of Stratford tea-shops, and fortunately it was never built. Shortly afterwards war was declared, and for its duration the SMNT Committee was dissolved. Nothing was done except to lease the Bloomsbury site to the YMCA, who built on it a small wooden hut in which to entertain British troops. It was called the Shakespeare Hut.

As the war drew to a close the SMNT Committee decided that, as they now had an embarrassingly large sum of money (by then nearly £100,000) and little else to show for the ten years of its existence other than an unsuitable site in Gower Street, it might release some of its funds to give practical support to a company which would present plays and tour them around the country. This idea was the brain-child of William Archer and the young director William Bridges-Adams. Bridges-Adams had, in 1912, proposed to Lilian Baylis that she should mount Shakespeare seasons at the Old Vic, but nothing had come of his suggestion. During 1918 he had a number of discussions with Archer about the 'establishment of a Shakespearian touring company of a high standard in connection with the National Theatre', and in November 1918 he drew up an outline of the scheme for Archer.[2] His argument – that they should found a company first, and worry about bricks and mortar second – was to haunt the SMNT Committee for many years. To found a National Theatre they would need more funds, and no one on the Committee had any illusions as to how difficult it would be to raise them. Bridges-Adams's argument that fund-raising would be facilitated if a company was in existence, appealed to Archer, and to a number of other people on the Committee. But there were those, among them Shaw, who had considerable reservations about the idea. 'There is not the least doubt in my mind', Shaw wrote to Bridges-Adams in May 1919, 'that the endowment of an ordinary Shakespear tour through the provinces is a gross malversation of the [SMNT] funds . . . Consequently, if you go Bensonizing and Bengreeting, however artistically, I shall have to resign my place on the Committee . . . ' Shaw was, however, prepared to countenance a very similar proposition, what he called a 'Grand Pilgrimage through England with special performances of Shakespear's plays, absolutely uncut (bar impossible indecencies) . . . At these performances the literature of the SMNT and its appeals to the public could be distributed . . .' The distinction between the two proposals was a fine one, which did not prevent Shaw from rhapsodizing it into a major one:

There is nothing more ignominious than the position of a touring manager playing Shakespear without stars: he is the *dernier des derniers*, sans plays, sans stars, sans prestige, sans everything. . . . He is Wopsle in his last ditch. . . . But there is a new stunt available. As the leader of a Pilgrimage, the protagonist of the S.M.N.T., the man . . . compelling Mayors and principals of Colleges to receive him with awe, you could in one single tour get a position that would make you a favorably marked man for life. You would be the successor of Barker instead of the broker who bought up Benson . . . . If the S.M.N.T. ever materialized you would be in the running as its manager. You would be a sort of bishop instead of a stroller.[3]

Shaw's letter was already out of date by the time he wrote it, a fact which illustrates the poor communications within the SMNT Committee. By April of 1919, a month before he wrote, negotiations were already advanced for Bridges-Adams to preside over a company which was to embark neither on a tour, nor even a 'Pilgrimage', but which would be based instead at the Memorial Theatre in Stratford. But Shaw's letter, and the other correspondence relating to the founding of Bridges-Adams's company, is important, for it shows quite clearly that not only Bridges-Adams himself, but also a number of influential people on the SMNT Committee conceived of the new company as the forerunner of a National Theatre company. The fact that a man like Shaw could even dangle before Bridges-Adams the possibility of his becoming the future 'manager' of the National Theatre explains much that happened later. In going to the Memorial Bridges-Adams was not just launching a new company in what was still regarded as a relatively unimportant provincial theatre, he was being groomed for a far more illustrious purpose.

Securing Bridges-Adams and his company and, even more important, a small subsidy to back them, was a considerable coup for Archie Flower and the Memorial, pulled off in the teeth of competition from both the Old Vic and Herbert Beerbohm Tree who, according to Shaw, had 'exhausted every effort to collar the SMNT's funds for His Majesty's'.[4] A joint committee was set up to administer the New Shakespeare Company, as it was called. It was composed evenly of Stratford governors, led by Archie Flower, and the leading members of the SMNT Committee including William Archer, Edith Lyttelton, and Sir Israel Gollancz. The SMNT voted the new company a small subsidy of £3,000 per annum for three years. The sum of money was significant: it was £2,000 less than the cost Bridges-Adams had estimated was needed, and it was precisely the amount that the SMNT Committee received each year in rent for the Shakespeare Hut. The SMNT Committee might be prepared to back Bridges-Adams's scheme to a degree, but it had no intention of touching its capital.

So in August 1919 a resident company opened at the Memorial Theatre, Stratford. It was a company born hurriedly of indecision and compromise, and its future was a precarious one. It depended entirely on the subsidy from the SMNT Committee for its existence, and that subsidy was small and for a limited duration. The company's function was unclear. Bridges-Adams could, and did, conceive of it as a forerunner to a National Theatre. But others on the SMNT

Committee thought differently. They believed a building must come first, not a company; and they believed that, if a company did exist, the last place it should operate was Stratford-upon-Avon.

Bridges-Adams was that child of the new age, the producer, or director. In spite of the fact that the New Shakespeare Company was, in modified form, his brain-child, the job of directing it would never have been his had he been part of what he called 'the demoded royalty of the stage' – an actor-manager in the Benson mould. It was firmly laid down in his contract that he could not act with his company under any circumstances, so perforce he *had* to be a director. The role suited him; like Granville-Barker he had begun his career as an actor, but swiftly concentrated on directing.

The town he came to work in with his New Shakespeare Company was also beginning to change, slowly but irrevocably. In 1919 Stratford was still a small market-town, with a spring and summer festival that lasted a modest five or six weeks a year. Reporters who visited it then, and for some years to come, still delighted their readers with accounts of how quaintly *unspoiled* it all was. Although they rarely reviewed productions, they did quite frequently cover the events which had become traditional adjuncts to the festivals, such as the procession carrying flowers to Shakespeare's grave on the birthday, the unfurling of national flags, and the annual luncheons at which a succession of distinguished guests continued to propose toasts to the Immortal Memory. With one voice they conjured up a Warwickshire idyll. 'Only by the rows of flagstaffs,' W.A. Darlington wrote, in 1921, 'and by the astounding number of small cottages and shops which advertise their desire to store your bicycle and regale you with ham and eggs and still lemonade, could you tell you were in a showplace.'[5] But this atmosphere of pastoral simplicity was not to last many years longer. The days of bicycle expeditions were numbered, and with the advent of the motor car Stratford would change forever. Bridges-Adams realized this from the first: 'The Petrol Age was taking charge of Stratford,' he wrote later, and the implications of that were not lost on him.[6]

After the First World War, as cars and motor-coaches gradually became more widely available, tourism developed at Stratford with amazing speed. There is a reliable index to this development in the records of the visitors to Shakespeare's Birthplace, and in the years after the war these reveal the explosion of interest that took place. In 1920 31,000 people signed the visitors' book at the Birthplace. By

1924 this had more than doubled, to 72,000. By 1926 it was 87,000, of whom over 18,000 were American. The conversion of market-town to tourist mecca had begun. This, inevitably, was to have great influence on the fortunes of the Memorial Theatre. A high percentage of the tourists could be relied upon to attend the theatre, and this meant that the Memorial had, on tap, a large potential audience during the summer months of the year, a time then notoriously bad for London theatres. And the audience was no longer the local one which had complacently cheered Benson, it was drawn from all over Britain, from Europe and America. It was, in fact, the nucleus of an international audience, drawn to Stratford by the allure of a writer in precisely the way Victorian newspapers had predicted was impossible. In view of this, the old references to Bayreuth and Salzburg no longer sounded quite as hyperbolic as they had once done. Hating the other by-products of tourism, Bridges-Adams believed that the theatre could become Stratford's 'one unimpeachable credential',[7] and this realization of the Memorial Theatre's potential gradually changed his attitude to working there. As the wavering about the National's future continued, his loyalties changed; increasingly he concentrated his energies on the Memorial itself, a theatre which might not be ideal, but which actually existed, a theatre where he could realize his ideal – a fine, permanent company.

This pragmatic idealism was shared by Archie Flower. Archie served many years on the SMNT Committee, but he was never closely involved in its affairs, and it was always the theatre his uncle had founded which absorbed his energies, and dominated his life. He too wanted the Memorial to have what Charles Flower had envisaged – a permanent, and resident, company. So, although Archie had not selected Bridges-Adams as director of the New Shakespeare Company (he was William Archer's appointee), the fact that the two men shared similar aims, and a similar belief in the Stratford theatre's potential, ought to have augured well for the future. But although in theory their aims were alike, as individuals they could hardly have differed more strongly, and it was upon their relationship that the future of the Memorial depended.

In background, outlook, and temperament Bridges-Adams represented many of the things of which Archie was most suspicious. His parents were early and ardent Socialists, quite rich, and living at Blackheath, a way of life which did not prevent their despising the 'frivolous' Fabians, with 'their London-made and dividend-bought tweeds'.[8] Their son was educated at the newly-opened Bedales, an acceptable public school in that it was 'progressive', and at Oxford. He was an agnostic, and an intellectual, fluent in both French and German, and with a passion for Shakespeare, Wagner, and Dickens (all nurtured by his father). He shared none of Archie's comfortable attitudes to Shakespeare, and indeed was the first person to work at Stratford whose attitudes were totally untainted by Bard-worship. Whereas Archie would speak of Shakespeare in folksy tones ('Look upon him not as a highbrow poet . . . but as a personal friend . . . a great sportsman . . . as the very best of company once you admit him into the family circle'),[9] Bridges-Adams was concerned with the texts of the plays, and with divining their meaning as fully as possible on a stage. 'His actors sensed that he knew this author backwards,' the actress Fabia Drake wrote of him, 'there was very little that he found either obscure or unreachable. We relied upon him to keep us true to Shakespeare, and no company could ask for more.'[10] At Oxford, Bridges-Adams acted for the Oxford University Dramatic Society (OUDS) and he went into the theatre professionally as soon as he graduated, continuing for a while both to act and direct. By the time he went to Stratford in 1919 his experience was wide: he had worked briefly with Poel, with Laurence Irving and Patrick Kirwan, and he had directed at Bristol, in the West End, and at Liverpool Repertory Theatre (which he rechristened the Playhouse).

When he went to work at the Memorial Theatre he looked deceptively frail, and much younger than thirty. He was tall, with short fair hair, wide-spaced intense blue eyes, and ears that stuck out obstinately and noticeably. It was a curiously old-fashioned and gentle face, which betrayed his sensitivity and vulnerability – but not his wit, determination, or ambition. He was not strong physically. He walked with a stick, and he had a highly-strung nervous temperament which could charge his work, but which always threatened to tip over into breakdown when he was exhausted. This nervousness and weak health could on occasion make his battles with Archie unequal contests, for Archie, although much older, had an iron constitution; he could win because he could wear other people down. But Bridges-Adams had, nonetheless, immense energy, and could work exhausting hours under stress for long periods (a qualification essential in all directors who came after him, many of whom also suffered nervous breakdowns; it has now become almost a badge of office). He was a fighter, never an accommodator, another factor that strained his relationship with Archie, who found it something of a shock to have a director with a mind of his own and an extremely sharp tongue.

In manner Bridges-Adams was restrained, somewhat aloof, and shy, except with close friends. He was reserved with women (his first, unhappy marriage was annulled). He never swore, and – as far as those who worked with him remember – never set foot in a pub. With those he knew really well he liked to eat good food, drink good wine, and talk late into the night. When absent from his friends he was an obsessive and brilliant letter-writer, sharply funny and always perceptive. His judgements of people, of plays, and productions, were acute and unsentimental.

Bridges-Adams was younger by eleven years than Granville-Barker, and it was as a disciple of Barker that critics greeted him when he went to Stratford. Certainly his charter for the New Shakespeare Company smacked of Barker and it was, at that time, revolutionary. He wanted, he said, to create an ensemble company, 'not one star and twenty sticks'. He told journalists he wanted to present the plays 'as plays, irrespective of mutilations made to suit the whim of a star or the exigencies of stage carpentry'. He wanted 'continuity of action, scene following scene, without unnecessary waits'. But although his aims were clearly influenced by William Poel and Granville-Barker, his own sensibilities differed from theirs. 'No one,' he wrote many years later in *The Irresistible Theatre*, 'should produce a play unless he has the instincts of a show-man; least of all should he attempt to produce a play by Shakespeare.'[11] There was much of the showman in Bridges-Adams, and his subsequent work at Stratford was marked by a concern with sets, costume, and lighting, which horrified the purist in Poel. He had little patience with Poel's insistence on what he categorized as 'the bare, the chastely, indescribably bare stage of the Elizabethans', and found Poel's work tainted by a dry austerity, and (with some justification) inadequate knowledge of Elizabethan staging methods.

In Granville-Barker's work Bridges-Adams found something cerebral and anaemic which he never liked. His attitude to Barker and his work was a complex one and reveals a great deal about his own methods of production at Stratford. He admired Barker's Savoy productions, but found them over-clinical and cold; he particularly disliked Barker's use of brilliant white light in both *The Winter's Tale* and *Twelfth Night*, which he described as 'germ-free'. He himself attempted to achieve with electric lights the soft chiaroscuro effects of the gas-lit theatre, the kind of effects Irving had made famous at the Lyceum in productions Bridges-Adams was too young ever to have seen. He considered that Irving's death had opened up a void in English theatrical tradition: 'Irving's death', he wrote, 'left a gap which Tree could not quite fill – soapstone after granite.'[12] Barker, he believed, did not fill it either.

By the time Bridges-Adams went to work at Stratford, Barker had remarried and had abandoned directing for writing, a course actively encouraged by his formidable new wife. Bridges-Adams was one of the few theatre colleagues who continued to see Barker at this time, and he made several attempts to persuade him to direct at Stratford, all of which were amiably refused. But although he admired Barker, he retained strong reservations about his approach to directing, and found discussing theatre with him, after his retirement, a depressing experience. It was, he wrote, 'rather like talking to cheerful Anglicans about the transports of the early fathers'.[13] What Bridges-Adams was searching for was a theatre that could marry the past traditions of actor-manager theatre with the new development of a more conceptual director's theatre which Barker had pioneered. Like Benson, he too was possessed with fierce nostalgia for the 'old' theatre – in his case, the theatre of actor-managers like Irving. His letters constantly reiterated his admiration for the energy and panache of Victorian/ Edwardian actors, 'with their strange lovely vocal athleticism'. He admired the way in which actor-managers like Irving and Tree had been able to people a stage with groupings that recalled paintings 'from Tintoretto to Meissonier'. And he always retained an odd fondness for acting that was larger than life, for 'good unashamed Hams . . . hams in the best sense; every one of them able for his combat, his step-dance, knowing how to take stage, give stage, put his feet right and keep his arms between waist and shoulders'.[14]

Throughout his years at Stratford he depended heavily on actors who had learned their profession in the robust school of Victorian/Edwardian touring companies, men like Baliol Holloway and Randle Ayrton; women like Dorothy Green. Such actors were, in any case, almost indispensable to a hard-pressed company with inadequate rehearsal time, but that was not the only reason for their constant presence in the Memorial Theatre companies. For Bridges-Adams they provided a direct link with a theatrical tradition that was being threatened by the naturalistic acting and throw-away technique of Gerald du Maurier and his successors. For him they sent blood coursing through the veins of productions that might otherwise have been too 'anaemic', too cerebral.

For his first season at Stratford Bridges-Adams lived up to his promises. His New Shakespeare Company was devoid of star names, the plays were performed without cuts, and Stratford audiences had the novel experience of seeing them performed with only one brief interval. For this season Bridges-Adams evolved a technique he continued to use throughout his years at Stratford, which was essentially a compromise between the bareness of Poel's staging and the scenic excess of Benson's. He subdivided the stage with traverse curtains, interspersing scenes which used the full stage with scenes in front of the curtains, so that sets could be changed quickly behind them while the action proceeded in front. This enabled him still to use numerous sets, and to indicate location with a literalness that rivalled Benson's, while maintaining speed of presentation, scene flowing into scene, with none of the old waits and intervals. He directed six plays, opening with that proven crowd-puller, *The Merry Wives of Windsor*, and continuing with *Julius Caesar* and four other plays that were among his favourites, *The Winter's Tale, A Midsummer Night's Dream, The Tempest,* and *Romeo and Juliet.* He had precisely four weeks to rehearse all six, and he worked the company hard, until ten each night. In addition to directing all six plays he also designed the sets for them, and the lighting.

Because the company was new, its early work was reviewed nationally. The first season was well received by the critics, and so was the spring season the following year. The *Observer* praised him for being innovative, but not 'freakish, futurist or rebellious'. 'Mr Bridges-Adams', wrote the critic of the *Daily Telegraph,* 'has learnt nearly all there is to know of the art which conceals art . . . In the New Shakespeare Company we have the nucleus of a very promising national repertory company.' The *Daily Mail* was all breathless praise: 'Last August,' it announced, in 1920, 'the young producer Mr Bridges-Adams was called "the coming man". Now he has arrived.' But from his peers Bridges-Adams received more qualified praise. Both Poel and Granville-Barker had reservations about his first season, and said so – Poel in public, Granville-Barker in a private letter. Their reactions were more interesting than the critics', because both men immediately identified problems that were to bedevil Bridges-Adams's work for many years to come.

Poel, writing in *The Nation,* criticized Bridges-Adams for his methods of staging which, he considered, were still too elaborate. 'The tragedy [*Romeo and Juliet*]', he commented, 'that Shakespeare wrote to be acted in one scene, Mr Bridges-Adams presents in twenty-three scenes, the performance lasting about three and a half hours. It can hardly be said that his production solves the problem of Shakespearian representation . . .' Granville-Barker's criticism was different. He came to see the production of *A Midsummer Night's Dream,* and wrote an impassioned letter about it to Bridges-Adams from his hotel in Leamington. Until almost the end of the production, he wrote, he had liked everything about it – 'I blessed you and felt cheered'. Then, to his horror, in the final moments Bridges-Adams had allowed his actors to introduce all sorts of tired comic business, especially in the scenes of the play before Theseus' court.

What is to be done to a Lysander who spoils his last most beautiful line . . . by splitting it in two with a comic yawn? Would shoot him out of hand. And finally the old obscene clowning of the play. Here would shoot you. . . . I write you this diatribe because I really care that you should do something for Stratford that has not yet been done. If you will I'll fight for you. But if you are not to clean out this rubbish heap then you must be fought against for your own sake and Stratford's sake – and Shakespeare's sake. But that must not be when you have 75 per cent of the thing as right as right.[15]

Granville-Barker, writing about one of Bridges-Adams's very first productions, put his finger on the single problem which, more than any other, was to mar Bridges-Adams's work. Because he was never to have adequate rehearsal time he had to rely on actors experienced at playing Shakespeare; but in using such actors, with only a few days to work on each play, it was virtually impossible for him to rid his productions of the same tired inheritance of 'business' that had worried the young Benson. He knew as well as Granville-Barker that these stale short-cuts, this 'rubbish-heap' of accumulated traditions, had to be cleared away if the plays were to be rethought freshly: but how was it possible with a maximum of five days rehearsal?

In the three years the New Shakespeare Company was subsidized by the SMNT Committee in London, Bridges-Adams did manage to achieve a good deal, even if he was conscious that it was not enough. By 1921 he had strengthened his companies, had lengthened the duration of the festivals, and had introduced short tours between them which kept the company together and helped the work to be played in. But what he could achieve was severely limited by the conditions under which he had to work, and by the fact that the company was desperately insecure financially. The grant from the SMNT, which Bridges-Adams considered was inadequate, was in any case due to expire after the end of the spring season of 1922. Unless this subsidy was continued, it left the New Shakespeare Company without financial support and – if it disbanded – the Memorial Theatre without a company. The governors of the Memorial, seeing this prospect ahead of them, and unable to get any firm assurances of support from the SMNT Committee, sought various ways of making their resident company self-supporting. There was a short-lived, and much ridiculed attempt to convert the Memorial Theatre into a cinema during the winter months, in the hope that profits from that venture could be used to back the company. It was an expensive failure. For the unsubsidized summer season of 1922 Archie Flower organized a guarantee fund through the Stratford Chamber of Commerce, which would have made good any small losses made by the company. In the event it was not called upon, for luckily that season proved to be the most successful on record. Over 30,000 tickets were sold, and the guarantee fund was untouched.

But, as both Bridges-Adams and Archie were well aware, this happy state of affairs could not be relied upon, and was only achieved because most of the plays given during the summer months were already in the repertoire, played by a company already in existence, so costs were lower. At the end of that 1922 season, Bridges-Adams redoubled his attempts to persuade the SMNT Committee in London to provide the company with a larger grant, of £5,000 a year, and to guarantee it for at least three years. He believed that if the company could be kept in year-round existence, by means of a touring season, and a London season when not playing at Stratford, it could become self-supporting. Gradually a company would be built up for which subsidy was unnecessary, and which could be of such a standard that it would bring the realization of the SMNT's aims for a National Theatre that much nearer.

He drew up a scheme on these lines for the SMNT Committee, and sent it to William Archer:

For four years you have had at your disposal an organisation capable of infinite development, and you have made no use of it. At heavy expense you have maintained it in half-life, because by some process of reasoning which I have never been able to fathom, it was held to be more consonant with the terms of your trust to dribble your interest away on a manifestly unsound proposition than to encroach on your capital, even to a less amount, for a sound one . . . all the money in the world would not build up the Meiningen Company in a year. But a very little could lay the foundations, and the rest is mainly a matter of work and time . . .[16]

But at the very moment that Bridges-Adams was arguing his case, backed by detailed figures, the SMNT Committee was already turning its back on his proposals. In 1922 the Bloomsbury site had been sold, and the SMNT Committee's funds invested elsewhere. Since the Committee's money was no longer tied up in land, it seemed to Bridges-Adams, and to Edith Lyttelton who supported him, that there was an even stronger case for increasing the grant to the New Shakespeare Company. But there were two factions on the Committee who felt differently. There was a lobby supporting the Old Vic, who felt that if SMNT money was to go to any theatre company it should go to Lilian Baylis's in London rather than one in Stratford. And there was another faction, led by Sir Israel Gollancz, who felt that the money had been raised to build a National Theatre, and that it was (to use Shaw's term) a 'malversation' to dribble those funds away in the support of a company like the New Shakespeare, or the Old Vic. Unfortunately for Stratford and Bridges-Adams, William Archer, their first champion, increasingly inclined to this view.

Archer acknowledged that there was a 'legal loop-hole' which would have allowed the SMNT Committee to divert capital funds to the New Shakespeare Company, but he felt that was immoral, and in any case was doubtful whether doing so would be 'furthering our great object – the erection and organisation of a National Theatre'.

You know that I have always appreciated your work . . . I think we owe you a great debt for the originality you have shown in developing a system of mounting which was at once agreeable, inexpensive, and susceptible of almost instantaneous changes. If we could open a National Theatre tomorrow, I think you would have a better claim than anyone else to the position of Director – at any rate . . . on the Shakespearean side. But even with a subsidy of £5,000 a year you can't work miracles . . . The company will be praised by some, declared by others to be manifestly inferior to the Old Vic . . . and, as a matter of fact, won't approach the level of finish and accomplishment which you could attain if you had, in the National Theatre, a perfect instrument to work with.[17]

Bridges-Adams fought back, and continued to argue his case, but without Archer as his champion, his efforts were doomed to failure. For the seasons of 1923 the SMNT Committee allocated him a subsidy of only £1,000, and with even-handed justice handed another £1,000 to the Old Vic. Not only was this sum of money significantly less than Bridges-Adams had asked for, it was – as the Committee was well aware – inadequate to subsidize the Stratford company's 1923 work. It meant that, for the first time since the Memorial Theatre had opened, it now had to finance its company itself, or go to the wall.

It was saved by a further guarantee from the Stratford Chamber of Commerce, organized by Archie, and by the fact that the 1923 seasons were particularly successful. Again, the guarantee fund was untouched, and a small surplus was made of £761. Almost imperceptibly, and with few flourishes, the Memorial Theatre made a giant step forward: with the summer season of 1923 it became self-supporting. From then on the New Shakespeare Company became the Memorial's resident company, to be administered not by a cumbersome joint-committee, but by the Stratford governors. That meant in effect administration by Archie.

During the next two years Archie attempted, by various means, to put the theatre on a sounder financial footing, although without much success. At the end of 1922 it had been decided to apply for a Royal Charter of Incorporation for the theatre. (Previously, although it had been categorized as a non-profit making organization, the Memorial had been registered under the Companies Act of 1862.) The Royal Charter, which was finally granted late in 1925, merely reiterated the aims of the Memorial Theatre as laid down by Charles Flower, and confirmed its methods of administration; but it gave the theatre a certain status, and Archie may have felt that this would encourage fund-raising efforts. In 1923 the theatre launched an ambitious endowment appeal for £100,000 which raised precisely £2,000. In July 1923 Archie even made tentative motions towards the granting of a state subsidy, and the theatre appealed in the House of Lords for a government subvention. This, as Archie and the governors must have known, was certain to fail and it did. The idea of state subsidy for the arts was, in 1923, an untenable proposition.

Since, in spite of all these efforts, money was not coming in, there was only one solution: to stop it going out. Archie watched over the theatre's accounts like a hawk; spending was kept to a minimum, and sets were even painted on both sides of the canvas to save money. Even so, the theatre's finances were precarious, and the least attempt to expand its activities dangerous. In 1924 Bridges-Adams persuaded Archie and the governors to increase the length of the company's provincial tour, and the surplus of the previous year was swiftly converted into a £470 loss. This might seem a small sum, but to the Memorial Theatre it was a large one; there were no cash reserves to fall back on. The only reserves the theatre had were the properties it owned in Stratford, most of which had been left to the theatre by Charles Flower and his wife, and some of which, like the Arden Hotel opposite the theatre, had been bought by Archie and the governors with bank loans. These properties brought in modest rents, and some money was raised each year by charging tourists admission to see over the theatre buildings, but the financial security they gave the theatre was minimal. Nevertheless Archie insisted the theatre should hang on to what properties and investments it owned, even when hard pressed for money. It was typical of Archie that when the governors finally acknowledged that the cinema experiment had been a failure (in 1924) the expensive equipment they had bought was not sold for cash to cover the loss the theatre made that year, but was sold to the Stratford-upon-Avon Picture House Company Ltd., in return for a major shareholding. This seemed a strange move to many people, including Bridges-Adams, but – like many of Archie's financial schemes – it was to pay unexpectedly large dividends, in a way no one could have foreseen.

By the end of 1925 this policy of caution was beginning to pay off. The theatre's debts were cleared, and the 1925 seasons again made a surplus, of £850. Archie was jubilant, and declared his policy of penny-pinching vindicated. Bridges-Adams was delighted, and felt his prophecies that the Stratford company (now called the Stratford-upon-Avon Festival Company) could be self-supporting had been proved right. 'The object now in view', he told reporters, 'is a continuous season, from April to September.'

Once the SMNT Committee grant had ended, and Bridges-Adams's initial honeymoon period with the Press had expired, little further interest had been shown in the Memorial by the national newspapers. Its productions were again rarely reviewed except by the local papers, but this had had little effect on the box-office, and the number of American tourists among the audiences had encouraged both Archie and Bridges-Adams to think of attempting an American tour – perhaps in 1926. Bridges-Adams favoured the idea because it would provide him with the means of keeping his company together for an entire year; it was both frustrating and expensive to gather a new company together each spring. It made continuity of work difficult, and it meant that the initial rehearsal period in London, when company salaries had to be paid but there were no box-office returns, had to be kept to a minimum, for they were a severe drain on the theatre's inadequate resources.

The spring season at Stratford now lasted four weeks, and the summer season eight weeks. The attempt at touring before the spring festival had been dropped after the losses in 1924, but between the two seasons the company still went on a short provincial tour to towns like Birmingham, Cheltenham, Malvern, and Oxford – all within a tight radius of Stratford. Eight productions were mounted each spring, and two further new productions each summer. Archie remained convinced that this large repertoire must be maintained, so that audiences could continue to see a different play each night of the week, just as they had done during the Benson era. But whereas Benson had had an established repertoire of work, with complete sets and costumes, and a company who knew their parts and the productions backwards, Bridges-Adams was starting each season from scratch, which made the work-load intense. He was allowed only seven weeks rehearsal for the eight spring plays, and no matter how much he protested that this was inadequate he could not get it extended. Prior to opening in Stratford there was a week of dress rehearsals (one play dress-rehearsed each night, plus one matinée dress rehearsal) followed by a week of first nights (one play opening each night, plus one opening at a matinée). The immense strain this caused was further exacerbated by the fact that he continued not only to direct, but also to design and light all the plays. In addition to this he was also responsible for the day-to-day running of the Memorial itself during the festivals.

Theatre staff was kept to a minimum. Apart from Bridges-Adams there were only two other full-time employees, Bill Savery who had remained at Stratford after Benson left, and Alice Crowhurst, who ran the box-office. Alice Crowhurst was the daughter of the theatre's one-time sole employee, its original caretaker, and her devotion to the theatre was absolute. In Stratford it was rumoured that she slept in the box-office; certainly it was her domain. There were no theatre workshops for the building of sets, and there was no properly organized wardrobe; all other theatre labour was casual. Every decision taken by this odd triumvirate, however minor, had to be channelled through Archie Flower.

Salaries, both for theatre staff, and for the companies, were low. Bridges-Adams himself received a salary that varied slightly from year to year, but which was then generally in the region of £750. The amount he could pay his actors was severely limited by Archie, who could never understand the necessity for a rise. During the 1920s salaries at Stratford were slightly higher than those paid at the Old Vic, with a ceiling that gradually crept up over the years from £20 to £25. (At the Old Vic, a theatre equally as hard-up as the Memorial, where Lilian Baylis was even more parsimonious than Archie, salaries were rarely higher than £17 during this period.) But this was for leading actors only, and it never increased, no matter how many parts they played or how many years they returned to work with the company. Supporting players and beginners received far less, and many had to struggle along on £3 or £4 a week, which compared very unfavourably with what they could receive, even playing small parts, in the West End. Because Stratford productions were rarely reviewed nationally during the 1920s, an actor could make far greater impact by appearing in an Old Vic production than he ever could in a Stratford one, making it comparatively easy for the Vic to poach Stratford actors, and extremely difficult for Bridges-Adams to keep his companies together; he could tempt them neither with money (as West End managers could do) nor with prestige (as Lilian Baylis was increasingly able to do).

Bridges-Adams was well aware of these problems, and aware that there was only one solution to them – money. But he was working for a chairman and board of governors who grew extremely nervous at the first hint of losses, and the first appeal for increased spending. At the end of the 1924 season, when the company had sustained a loss, both Archie and his executive council immediately wanted to introduce cuts in spending. Bridges-Adams drew up a lengthy report, pleading against any cuts. The report remains the clearest account of the problems he faced at Stratford in the 1920s and makes it clear that what he was aiming at was properly rehearsed, individually designed productions, given by a strong ensemble company. What he was often producing, as he was bitterly aware, were hasty revivals, using shabby stock costumes and improvised sets:

Frank Rodney as Bolingbroke in Frank Benson's production of *Richard II*, first played at Stratford in 1896 and in London in 1900.

Left, above, the Forest of Arden in Barry Sullivan's *As You Like It* at the Memorial Theatre, 1879. The stuffed stag makes its first appearance. *Below,* the set for the lists scene from *Richard II,* 1896.

Right, above, Frank Benson as Richard II, 1896 and (*below*) aged 54, as Henry V in 1912.

Randle Ayrton as Macbeth and Dorothy Massingham as Lady Macbeth in Bridges-Adams's 1931 production.

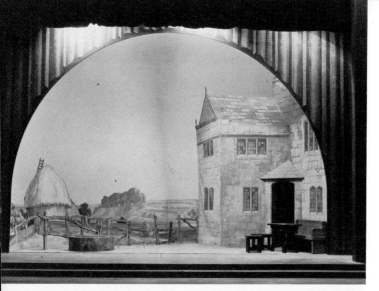

Three examples of set design from the first seasons in the new theatre, 1932: *top*, Shallow's house in *Henry IV, Part II*; *centre*, Theodore Komisarjevsky's brilliant design for the opening scenes of *The Merchant of Venice*; *bottom*, Theseus's palace from Norman Wilkinson's designs for Bridges-Adams's *A Midsummer Night's Dream*.

Three of the actors most acclaimed for their work at Stratford in the inter-war period: *top left*, Baliol Holloway as Malvolio in Bridges-Adams's *Twelfth Night*, 1934; *top right*, Donald Wolfit as Hamlet in Iden Payne's 1936 production; *bottom left*, Randle Ayrton as Shylock in Iden Payne's 1935 *Merchant of Venice* and (*bottom right*) as Quince in *A Midsummer Night's Dream* directed by E. Martin Browne in 1937, the year Ayrton retired.

Two of the finest
productions in the new
theatre during the
1930s: *left*, Bridges-
Adams's production of
Love's Labour's Lost for
his last season, 1934,
with designs by Aubrey
Hammond; *below*,
Komisarjevsky's
celebrated and
iconoclastic production
of *The Comedy of
Errors*, 1938.

Right, Alec Clunes
(right) as Coriolanus and
James Dale as Tullus
Aufidius in Iden Payne's
1939 production of
Coriolanus. *Below*, the
breach scene at Harfleur,
with Clement McCallin
as Henry V in Iden
Payne's 1937
production.

The term *Festival* should imply a certain splendour, the very negation of half-heartedness, shabbiness, or cheese-paring. Although we are bound to proceed with due regard to economy ... it would be a thousand pities if the public got the idea into its head that we had allowed ourselves to fall short of the best in us for a matter of two or three hundred pounds profit or loss. And yet ... this is precisely what we have to do again and again ... Circumstanced as we are, my procedure is invariably the same. I form my conception of the play as I should produce it under ordinary conditions and with reasonable backing. I then obliterate every item in that conception which is likely to entail the expenditure of cash.

But the worst problem of all was clearly the lack of rehearsal time, a problem that could have been solved by reducing the repertoire, or staggering the openings of the plays, which would have involved no expense; here there was no mistaking Bridges-Adams's bitterness and anger:

We rehearse six or seven plays in five weeks. Some companies do it in a fortnight, and no doubt wonder why we should need longer ... Why indeed? One may as well be hung for a sheep as a lamb. If we have reached the point of putting up THE SCHOOL FOR SCANDAL in six rehearsals, and OTHELLO in three, why keep up the farce of striving for perfection? Why not shove them both up in two? ... The truth is (and it had better be told) that it is not possible to produce two plays simultaneously, much less six; that it is not possible to do real justice to one play in the time that we are able to give to any play; that to put OTHELLO on stage in three rehearsals for a festival performance is an insult to the memory of Shakespeare, to any actor worthy of the part, and to the people who pay to see it.[18]

His long and impassioned report achieved something. The governors were persuaded not to make the further threatened cuts in expenditure. Beyond that, as Bridges-Adams had probably foreseen, it had little effect. The money needed for reform simply was not there, and Archie would not deviate from the fixed policy of a large repertoire and immediate openings. It says much for Bridges-Adams's tenacity that he did not give up there and then, but continued to fight. He did so because he still believed that the Memorial Theatre could become more prosperous, and because, in spite of what he wrote, he knew that he was making progress; in view of the obstacles, remarkable progress.

By 1925 he had gradually assembled the nucleus of a strong company, many of whom continued to work for him for years. A number of the middle-range and character actors, such as Eric Maxon, C. Rivers Gadsby, Kenneth Wicksteed, Stanley Lathbury and others, had had years of playing Shakespeare – some of them rarely acted in anything else – and they had an influence on new recruits to the company which was not always for the good. But for his leading parts, Bridges-Adams could call on a number of fine actors. He brought in Roy Byford, an enormously fat man who was a gifted character actor, and excelled as the Falstaff of *Merry Wives*. He used actors who were also frequently at the Old Vic during this period, such as George Hayes and Wilfred Walter. He developed some strong younger actors such as Ernest Hare and John Laurie (to whom he gave a major break by casting him as Hamlet, in 1927). And as the mainstay of his companies, he had his three major actors, Dorothy Green, Baliol Holloway, and Randle Ayrton, all of whom made many appearances at Stratford in the 1920s. Holloway and Ayrton in particular became the twin pillars of the company, acting in successive seasons.

They were very different both as individuals and as actors, but they were alike in one respect. The work which they did at Stratford for Bridges-Adams in the Twenties was consistently ignored at the time, and invariably dismissed later. 'Whenever I look back at Stratford,' a friend once told W. A. Darlington, 'the stage seems to be occupied by Baliol Holloway making a speech, and somehow, whatever the play, the same speech.'[19] In Darlington's view Holloway's reputation was chiefly bound up with Stratford, and 'it was to Stratford that it was sacrificed'. This was perhaps true of Holloway in the 1930s, when he worked almost exclusively at Stratford, and under a less accomplished director than Bridges-Adams, but it was not true of the previous decade. Holloway then played four Stratford seasons, 1921–4, giving performances his fellow actors admired and playing Richard III and Othello, parts in which he was later acclaimed in London. His work was then sufficiently regarded for him to be chosen as leading man opposite Edith Evans for her first Old Vic season of 1925, and he remained at the Vic playing leads the following year.

Holloway was tall and bony, with a strong, saturnine face, and a powerful voice. He had an odd way of speaking verse, which many critics disliked: 'He persists in cutting up every speech into granulated nodules,' James Agate once wrote of him in exasperation. Bridges-Adams admired him greatly, and considered him the finest

Falstaff (in the *Henry IV* plays) and Benedick he had ever seen: 'Stroke after stroke,' he wrote, 'the planned execution of a conception: the painter's mind at work behind the picture. I believe he knows as much about the inner minds of these two parts as any man living.'[20] Holloway had the versatility and the stamina of the Edwardian actor, and both at Stratford and the Vic would undertake in one season a range of roles no modern actor would ever risk. In 1924 at Stratford, for instance, he played Bottom, Othello, Bolingbroke, Claudius, Kent, Antony (in *Antony and Cleopatra*), Petruchio, Falstaff (in *Merry Wives*), Gratiano, and Sir Peter Teazle. Many of the roles were already in his repertoire, in the Benson manner; he played them with the usual minimal rehearsal, and faced eight openings in the first week of the season. Such a way of working inevitably affected his development as an actor, and no doubt accounts for the fact that people who saw him later in his career found him predictable, stale, and operatic. But Agate remembered being 'lifted out of his seat' by the closing moments of Holloway's London Richard III, and considered his Othello ('a magnificent savage')to be one of the finest he had ever seen, succeeding, he wrote later, 'where Irving, Forbes-Robertson, Sofaer, Richardson and Wolfit failed'. But theatrical memories are short, and Holloway's early work when he was still young and vigorous was forgotten. He used to tell the story of how, during the 1960s, when he had not appeared on stage for some years, he was approached by a young radio director to appear in *Othello*. The young man was offering him the part of a senator, and clearly did not know that Holloway had ever played the leading role himself. 'Do you think I'm up to it?' Holloway asked wryly. 'Well, I think so,' replied the young man, immediate doubt and consternation writ large on his face.[21]

The eclipse in Randle Ayrton's reputation was equally dramatic. His name is now unfamiliar except to older actors, to those who worked with him, and those who saw – and never forgot – his performances. He received scant recognition during his lifetime, less after his death, but, without exception to those who remember him, he was a great and original actor. He took up acting comparatively late in life, beginning his career with Benson. When he returned to Stratford for Bridges-Adams in 1925, he was fifty-six, and approaching his greatest years as an actor. He rarely performed in London, which he detested, and eventually moved his home to Stratford where he could live an intensely private and withdrawn existence

which revolved exclusively around his work and his family. Fellow
actor Sebastian Shaw considered him one of the greatest performers
he ever saw or worked with. He remembered him as a 'short squat
man, with grey hair, a broad expansive face, a large nose. He was
ugly . . . but you were never conscious of that, just of his tremendous
power. He had a curious, almost ugly voice too, slightly nasal in
quality, but with the most extraordinary range: it could move in a
moment from lightness and delicacy to rawness and passion.'[22]

Ayrton had a reputation for being 'difficult'. Those who worked
with him all agree that he did not suffer fools gladly. With those he
did not like, or did not respect, he could be waspish, impatient,
crotchety, even cruel. Yet at home, away from the theatre, Ayrton's
demeanour was totally different. His daughter Luise, who also acted
at Stratford during the 1920s, never heard him swear, and rarely saw
him lose his temper. With younger actors who seemed to him
promising he could be warm, patient, helpful.

He seems to have been at his best in the harsher roles: as Ford,
which he played, 'as a blackly funny study of obsessive jealousy,
clutching a riding-crop in his hand throughout';[23] as Shylock, in
which he played 'as a blackly funny study of obsessive jealousy,
role for sympathy; as Leontes; as an embittered Henry IV; and as
Lear – a part he played three times at Stratford. When he made his
rare appearances in London he was highly praised. James Agate saw
him as Ford in a production of *Merry Wives* with Edith Evans and
Dorothy Green, and remembered it, years later, as one of the finest
portrayals he had ever seen. When Ayrton acted at the new Memorial
Theatre in the 1930s, and all the productions were at last regularly
reviewed by national critics, his performances received high acclaim.
But the recognition of his powers came late, only a few years before
he retired.

Later it became the fashion to sneer retrospectively at the acting at
the Memorial, and to assert that the companies there had always
been poor, and inferior to those at the Vic – a view canvassed with
particular energy by W.A. Darlington. But much of this retrospective
criticism was unfair, occasioned partly by Bridges-Adams's refusal to
employ stars, and insistence on trying to build up a company, a
policy that ran directly counter to the theatrical taste of the day. With
a few exceptions, company strength, as opposed to star performances, was not to become of major concern to British theatre until the
late 1950s. The Vic did import stars like Edith Evans for occasional

seasons, but the cross-fertilization between Stratford and the Vic, which continued throughout the 1920s with both companies constantly using the same actors, suggests that the acting standards of the Vic and the Memorial must have been far more on a par than critics chose later to suggest. But whatever the comparative standards of the companies at that time, Stratford had one definite advantage over the Vic in the 1920s: in Bridges-Adams the Memorial had a director who was generally agreed to be an accomplished designer and an imaginative and innovative lighting technician, gifts less noticeable in his Old Vic counterpart, Robert Atkins.

It is now very difficult to assess Bridges-Adams's skill as a set-designer. He was, after all, working on a severely limited stage, with a tiny budget. Most of his designs were sketched on the backs of envelopes, and those that remain were mostly recreated later from memory. The few photographs of his Twenties productions are also a poor witness to his work. They were taken when the stage was bare of actors and lit only with working lights, which emphasize cruelly the 'fake' element in them which he himself criticized. Throughout the decade he continued to rely heavily on the use of traverse curtains and very simple sets – an archway, a flight of steps, a door, a line of pillars – almost always of architectural elements, with few of the attempts to reproduce woods and gardens with the laborious verisimilitude favoured by Benson.

He lit his sets atmospherically, often illuminating only parts of the stage, which irritated some Bensonians in the company who liked a good shaft of light in which to stand and deliver, and which many critics also disliked, dubbing the technique 'murky'. Yet many who saw his productions remember them, above all, for the grace and power of their staging, for Bridges-Adams's gift for grouping actors within a scene (no mean task at a time when as many as twenty or thirty 'supers' were still commonplace), and for the way in which his lighting techniques could shift and transform the moods within the plays, catching and reflecting the nuance of the moment. He seems to have had a particular gift for the elegiac, the dying fall – the clown Feste silhouetted against a slow fading light, at the close of *Twelfth Night,* singing softly of the wind and the rain; Lady Mortimer and Lady Percy alone on the stage at the end of the Glendower scene in *Henry IV, Part I,* the light falling on them through green glass windows, Lady Mortimer humming her song, as the stage slowly faded to darkness.[24] And he had a gift also for orchestrating battle and crowd scenes, despite lack of rehearsal, which gave an epic excitement and flourish to his productions of the history or the Roman plays.

Of his sureness of taste in design there can be little question. When he came to direct the new theatre at Stratford, which provided him at long last with the resources of a modern stage, he was quick to bring some of the finest designers and directors in the country to work there. He had the gift to perceive excellence in others and would certainly have developed his own work more (his later work promised much) had he not been forced to work so long in conditions inimical in every way to excellence. Meanwhile, his attitude towards producing Shakespeare changed in one important way: his respect for the text underwent a gradual and subtle change.

Bridges-Adams had gone to the Memorial with the declared policy of full texts and no cuts, still a revolutionary approach in the theatre of 1919. After his first season of uncut texts, Ben Greet hailed him as 'Una-bridges-Adams'. But by 1922 he was already saying that this policy was an experimental one which needed review, and from about 1923 onwards he began to cut texts much more freely, occasionally savaging them in a manner reminiscent of Benson and Victorian actor-managers at their worst. This seems to have been a tendency in his work quite early, temporarily suppressed by the influence of men like Archer and Shaw on the SMNT Committee. Certainly Shaw, writing to him in 1919 before he even began work at Stratford, had felt a need to reprimand him on this score. 'It is really almost impossible', Shaw wrote to him, 'to do Shakespear at full length without being forced into the right way of playing him. You can imagine my feelings when you calmly remarked that you thought the last part of *Twelfth Night* might very well be cut. Why not the first part, and the middle as well, if Shakespear was a fool who did not know what was good for himself?'[25] Bridges-Adams and many directors who came after him, including Peter Brook, were to disagree with Shaw's argument that the texts of the plays were totally sacrosanct. But his reasons for cutting were often dubious. There was an over-tender sensitivity, a delicate squeamishness in his temperament which could make him rebel against the uncompromising harshness of certain Shakespeare plays, or certain scenes. When that happened he was prepared to cut, and cut badly. In *Othello*, for instance, he shied away just as Benson had done, from the rankness of Iago's sexual innuendo, and preferred to cut the key scene in which Othello eavesdrops on Cassio and Bianca: 'I am never at ease with it,' he once wrote. 'Othello and Iago once well posed, you *don't* want Othello reduced to the ignominy of pushing his black face round the edge of a curtain.'[26] He seemed to have an intense, Bradleian need to keep his Shakespearian heroes on pedestals of unsullied nobility, and if cutting the text helped him do that, he would. He was also quite prepared to hack at a play if, by doing so, he could achieve greater spectacle and so satisfy the 'instincts of the showman' within him.

The play he cut most, removing whole sections and transposing others with a wilful abandon, was *Coriolanus,* a play he directed twice at Stratford and staged spectacularly in the Reinhardt manner, with highly vocal 'supers' teeming on to the stage from the orchestra pit. His changes altered the import of the play significantly but enabled him to stage it (particularly the Corioles scenes) in such a way that its epic excitement was still vividly remembered by some critics over forty years later.[27]

However, although there might be weaknesses in his work, it was still obvious by 1925 that Bridges-Adams had achieved a very great deal at Stratford. It was also becoming obvious that there was, apart from overwork, one major factor which was holding him back, and that was the Memorial Theatre itself. The old Memorial had one great advantage – intimacy; so close were the seats at the side of the circle that it was possible for the audience there to join hands with the actors on stage when they sang the traditional 'Auld Lang Syne' at the end of the last performance of the season. But the theatre had endless disadvantages: it was too small; conditions backstage were cramped; dressing-rooms and storage space were inadequate; the stage itself was tiny, and its technical equipment so old-fashioned that the least attempt at ambitious lighting effects was likely to blow every fuse in the house. Shaw, who had become a governor in 1922, took it upon himself to become one of Bridges-Adams's most loyal champions, and the theatre building's most outspoken critic. In 1925 Shaw was invited to propose the toast to the Immortal Memory of William Shakespeare at the annual Birthday luncheon. He had been invited to do this before, but had always refused, for the excellent reason (he said) that, 'as he never celebrated his own birthday, he could hardly celebrate that of a lesser dramatist'. However, the chance to attack the architecture of the Memorial, in a speech he knew would be widely reported, overcame such scruples and this year he consented:

When you propose a man's health on his 359th birthday, you may be sure that his health requires constant attention . . . What his health requires, like that of many elderly gentlemen, is country air. London is entirely hopeless . . . in London, mastery has been gained by people who regard the theatre as a fashion, and the play as a necessary evil. No one could say that of the Stratford theatre . . . But Stratford wants a new theatre. The Memorial is an admirable building, adapted for every conceivable purpose – except that of a theatre.

Shaw's speech was, predictably, quoted by every major newspaper in the country. By an odd quirk of fate, the theatre he attacked had, within twelve months, been burned to the ground.

5

After the Fire

The Memorial Theatre was closed on the day fire broke out; its cause was never discovered. The smoke was first seen at 2.45 on the afternoon of 6 March 1926. Every available fire-engine from Stratford and the surrounding towns was called in, including an old horse-drawn steamer from Warwick. But their efforts to douse the flames met with little success. Costumes and sets stored under the stage fed the fire, and the mass of half-timbering which had been so proudly chosen to ornament the building provided good dry tinder. The tall observation tower, with its water-tank for use in the event of fire, became a hundred-foot chimney, funnelling the flames. At four o'clock in the afternoon the roof fell in, and by the following morning the building was a blackened shell. Only the library and picture-gallery remained intact; the curved walls of the old auditorium framed a mass of smouldering timber and twisted metal, and where the stage, the dressing-rooms, the seating had been, nothing remained.

It was some time before the full implications of the destruction sank in. Given the many disadvantages of the old building the fire was regarded privately as so fortuitous that both Archie and Bridges-Adams jokingly emphasized that they had cast-iron alibis. Archie had been on the golf-course, and had arrived at the scene of the fire resplendent in plus-fours; Bridges-Adams had been at the Garrick Club in London. Bernard Shaw, aware that some people considered he had inflicted some Celtic curse on the Memorial with his Birthday luncheon speech, sent Archie an unrepentant telegram. 'Congratulations,' it read. 'It will be a tremendous advantage to have a proper modern building. There are a number of other theatres I should like to see burned down . . . '[1]

The theatre was destroyed on a Saturday, just as rehearsals were about to begin for the longest season at Stratford yet attempted – five weeks in the spring, and ten weeks in the summer. On the following day, Archie held a conference at The Hill; it made two decisions. The seasons would continue, and would not even be postponed; and an appeal would be launched immediately to build a new theatre. Thanks to Archie's continual financial caution, the theatre governors were the majority shareholders in Stratford's solitary cinema. It was therefore not difficult to persuade the owners that the cinema should be adapted as a theatre for the duration of the festivals, and the performances given there.

Archie, Bridges-Adams, and a local architect went down on the Sunday to survey the building. There were no dressing-rooms, naturally, and the stage was small, but there was an encouragingly large auditorium. Bridges-Adams drew rough plans in the mud with his umbrella point, indicating the changes he would need made. The main wall at the back of the cinema had to be pulled down, and the stage enlarged; temporary dressing-rooms had to be built. The architect, displaying a confidence no modern counterpart would risk, announced it could all be done in the six weeks available before the start of the next season. The work began the next day and by the following Tuesday most of the money necessary for the conversion had been raised, in fifteen minutes, at a meeting led by Archie in the town hall. Six weeks later the festival opened in the converted cinema on the day appointed.

The major problem, however, was the rebuilding of the theatre, and finding the money to pay for it. Shaw might choose to assume blithely that of course there *would* be a new building, but there was no money to pay for it. The insurance on the old theatre was inadequate to restore it, let alone erect a new one. It was the kind of situation Archie was best at; it involved money, and persuading other people to part with it – at which he was accomplished by nature and hardened by experience. To his credit, there was no talk of patching up the old building, or rebuilding on a similar scale. Both Archie and Bridges-Adams realized that the chance had come to build a great modern theatre.

Archie's first move was to ensure the support of the Press. Viscount Burnham, the proprietor of the *Daily Telegraph,* was approached and he agreed that his newspaper should launch an appeal; ironically, the paper that had published the most vitriolic attacks on the original theatre was now the one that came to its aid. (Burnham's continuing interest and support were cannily ensured by the creation of a new post – President of the Board of Governors – which he filled.) On 26 March, three weeks after the fire, the *Telegraph* launched a major appeal on behalf of the theatre. It asked for the gigantic sum of £250,000, of which £150,000 was needed to build the theatre and £100,000 to endow it. The appeal had the support of Thomas Hardy; of the Prime Minister, Stanley Baldwin; and of the leaders of the Labour and Liberal parties, Ramsay MacDonald and Asquith. An appeal on this scale for a theatre had never been undertaken in Britain before. Since the war the SMNT Committee had made no further appeals for money for a National Theatre. Lilian Baylis had launched an appeal, the previous year, for the rebuilding work necessary on the Sadler's Wells Theatre, the new extension to her empire. That appeal, which also had the support of Baldwin and Asquith and other glittering names from the arts and politics, had been for the comparatively modest sum of £40,000. Lilian Baylis had already discovered how difficult it was even to raise such a small sum.

To begin with, however, all went well. The *Telegraph's* appeal was publicized by almost every provincial newspaper in the country, and a second, Midlands appeal was launched by the *Birmingham Post*. Subscriptions began to come in fast. The *Telegraph* donated the first £1,000; Archie, another £1,000. Within a week cheques had arrived from numerous leading actors, directors, and writers, including Gerald du Maurier, Henry Ainley, Barry Jackson, Sybil Thorndike, Fay Compton, Ivor Novello, Arthur Conan Doyle, Pinero, and Shaw. Over £5,000 was subscribed on the first day alone. King George V agreed to become the patron of the theatre, and even London society took up the project; it was announced that a special Drury Lane matinée, organized by the Marchioness Curzon of Kedleston, and given in the presence of the King, would be held that May. Further publicity was provided by the announcement, on 14 April, that there would be an open competition to appoint the architect of the new theatre, and applications were invited from architects in Britain, Canada, and the United States. An energetic correspondence ensued in the columns of *The Times* and other newspapers, in which all the arguments of fifty years earlier about a Stratford theatre were enthusiastically rehashed. The governors were showered with advice, including the helpful suggestion that the new theatre should be sited in London. Poel and his supporters – the 'Elizabethan Methodists', as Bridges-Adams called them – had a field day. The theatre should

have an apron-stage, and no proscenium arch; it should be constructed in the Elizabethan manner; it should be called, one writer
suggested, as a brilliant compromise, 'The Globe Theatre, Bankside,
Stratford-upon-Avon'.

The publicity given to the appeal not unnaturally stung the SMNT
Committee in London, who had been quietly doing nothing very
much since 1918. Sir Whitworth Wallis, curator of the Birmingham
Art Gallery, and a Stratford governor, suggested, in a letter to *The
Times,* that 'since the National Theatre's Committee's attempt to
provide a National Theatre in London seems as far off success as
ever',[2] it might do better to donate its accumulating funds to
Stratford, thereby achieving its aims at a stroke. Sir Israel Gollancz
replied on the Committee's behalf, haughtily (and, as it proved,
inaccurately): 'We have managed to survive the vicissitudes of twenty
years,' he said, 'without relinquishing our aim, or swerving from our
fixed purpose of . . . seeing a National Theatre in London. I think I
may confidently predict that we shall continue to stand firm for the
little while longer that is necessary . . .'[3] The SMNT Committee
naturally delegated none of its funds to the Stratford appeal, and this
little exchange was to create a residue of ill-will that later caused
Stratford some difficulties.

The high point was reached in November 1926, when the Drury
Lane matinée was finally held, some seven months late. Lady Curzon
gave an at-home, and thanks to her efforts and those of her
committee was able to announce that nearly all the seats had been
sold, including the boxes which cost 100 guineas and more. On the
great day, the King and the assembled audience saw an arrangement
of scenes from Shakespeare, delivered by stars of the West End stage,
including Fay Compton, John Martin-Harvey, Godfrey Tearle, and
Edith Evans. Few actors who had actually worked at the Memorial
were included in the programme. It was a glittering occasion,
attended by precisely the kind of fashionable audience who never
went near Stratford, and it raised £1,863.

Archie Flower was not present at the performance. He went to
Lady Curzon's at-home, and next day sailed on the *Franconia* for
America. Perhaps he enjoyed the fuss attendant on a society matinée,
but he had no illusions as to where he would raise a quarter of a
million pounds.

Archie's visit to America was timely. By the end of 1926 it was obvious to him, and to anyone else keeping a close watch on the growth of the Memorial appeal (which was regularly charted by the *Telegraph*), that there was no way in which the sum of £250,000 was going to be raised in Britain within a reasonable period of time. The timing was unfortunate. Only weeks after its launch the miners' strike began, followed shortly afterwards by the General Strike. It was hardly a propitious moment to raise a quarter of a million pounds to build a theatre and in the meantime the temporary theatre at Stratford was losing money fast – nearly £3,000 during 1926 alone.

Archie travelled to America with his wife Florence, and remained there for five months.[4] During that time both he and his wife embarked on an exhausting, and often dispiriting round of meetings, dinners, assemblies, and parties designed to interest Americans in the appeal and to raise funds. They showed slides; they made speeches; they lobbied, cajoled, and persuaded. But after four months they were making little tangible progress. They had attracted their fair share of cranks and charlatans; they had succeeded in interesting various educational groups, and Shakespearean societies, but there was little chance, and Archie knew it, that such groups would be capable of raising the large sum of money needed. They were armed with a list of influential, and rich Americans, yet their efforts met with little success. Towards the end of their stay Archie was losing hope and becoming uncharacteristically despondent. One of the most influential of the men on their select list was the millionaire Clarence H. Mackay, then the President of the Postal and Commercial Cable Company, a client of Duveen's, and a well-known patron of the arts. Mackay, they had been told, was precisely the man they needed to open doors for them, but Mackay was elusive, and resolutely unavailable. Archie was near to giving up, but Florence insisted on one more approach. She was a beautiful woman, and possessed of an intransigent Irish charm. She wrote to Mackay, pointing out that they had been trying to see him for weeks and had so far got no further than the railings around his residence. Mackay was intrigued, and agreed to help them. From that moment on the Memorial Theatre appeal was assured of success. It did not, however, look that way to English commentators, when Archie returned to England just before the spring festival of 1927 opened. The British fund had, in a year, netted only £29,000 and subscriptions to it were slowing down noticeably. Clarence H. Mackay's name meant nothing in Britain, and when Archie announced that there was in existence, on the other side of the Atlantic, a body calling itself the American Shakespeare Foundation, pledged to raise money in the States, the news was greeted with disappointment. 'When will the people of Stratford learn the plain truth?' commented the *Birmingham Mail*. 'The Memorial Theatre will never be built except by English money, and this begging from the United States (however it is disguised) is not only degrading, but futile.'[5]

On the eve of Shakespeare's birthday, 22 April 1927, the American Shakespeare Foundation held its inaugural dinner at the Hotel Ambassador, New York. The dinner had been arranged with the help of the *Telegraph's* New York correspondent, and numerous people who had been canvassed by the Flowers on their tour. Present were a covey of extremely rich and powerful financiers and politicians, collected together by the intervention of Clarence H. Mackay. The Chairman of the Foundation was Elihu Root, a former Secretary of State; the Honorary Treasurer was Otto Kahn, of the bankers Kahn, Loeb and Co.; and the Chairman of the Advisory Committee, and the man who was to become the Foundation's most influential member, was Thomas W. Lamont, a partner in Messrs. Pierpont Morgan, one of the largest and most powerful financial empires in America. Also present at the dinner were a number of other American multi-millionaires including Solomon Guggenheim, J.P. Morgan Jnr., and Edward Harkness. With this kind of financial muscle behind them, Archie believed the appeal *must* succeed, and he was proved right even more quickly than he expected. On 17 June 1927 Archie received at The Hill a letter from Thomas Lamont.[6] It informed him that the new theatre at Stratford was secured. John D. Rockefeller had agreed to donate £50,000 direct to the British fund, and a further £50,000 to the American. There were further large donations promised: $100,000 from Harkness; $25,000 from Guggenheim; $25,000 each from Archer Huntington and J.P. Morgan; and $25,000 from Lamont himself. This meant that, with £160,000 promised from America together with the £41,000 by then raised in Britain, and investments and property held by the theatre and valued at £29,000, there was £230,000 – only £20,000 short of the original sum named, with a full-scale American appeal still to come.

The American donations were kept secret until 2 November 1927. Then they were triumphantly announced, first at a dinner at the Park Lane Hotel, New York, hosted by Clarence Mackay, and then in the

Daily Telegraph. The announcement was greeted with jubilation in Stratford, and with some sourness by the SMNT Committee in London (who were aware they were being remorselessly up-staged). Archie returned to America to embark on a further fund-raising tour, and to present the Americans with a spring of mulberry (from the True Bush) to be planted in Central Park. In the midst of all this euphoria it occurred to no one that the American contribution might cause difficulties. Archie was to discover, however, that dealing with American financiers of Lamont's ilk was not without problems. From the moment the American donations were announced he had, in effect, a new master: a group of businessmen on the other side of the Atlantic who knew nothing of operating a theatre, little about the organization of the Memorial, and who had every inclination to interfere.

The American donations at first appeared to have been given unconditionally. Lamont mentioned no provisos whatever in his letter of 17 June, nor in any subsequent letters that year. It was recognized that a potential problem might exist in that there were now two funds for the building of the theatre: one, in England, administered by Reginald McKenna, Chairman of the Midland Bank, and an ex-Chancellor of the Exchequer; and one in America, administered by Otto Kahn and Thomas Lamont. The English fund was accruing interest at 4 per cent, the American at 12 per cent. Although the English fund would be swelled by Rockefeller's direct donation to it of £50,000, the American fund was larger to begin with, and accumulating interest more rapidly. Before any of the money held in America could be released to Stratford, the agreement of Kahn, Lamont, and other members of the American Shakespeare Foundation had to be given. In 1927, amidst general jubilation, it was assumed that this was merely a matter of form. But later, as the actual building of the new theatre progressed, Archie and the governors were to discover that this was far from the case.

Meanwhile, in January 1928, two months after the American gifts were made public, an architect for the new theatre was appointed. The winner of the open competition was a woman, Elizabeth Scott, aged twenty-nine, a junior architect in a small London practice. Her designs for the new Memorial Theatre were beautiful, and of a quite different standard to any of the others submitted. The other five designs which were short-listed reveal how unfamiliar a problem it was to design a theatre in the late 1920s. Very few new theatres were built in Britain between the wars; the wave of new civic and repertory theatre building did not begin until after the Second World War. So the architects had few recent precedents to learn from, and had in addition a particularly difficult location to deal with. The theatre had to sit on an island site, bounded on one side by a road and on the other by a river notorious for flooding. It was visible from all sides, whereas most British theatres were built on small town sites, with only their façades visible. At Stratford, a town composed of old, low-built houses, the theatre's fly-tower (for the raising, or flying of scenery) could not be hidden, and most of the architects produced drawings of monstrous edifices, with the fly-tower disguised by various decorative tricks. In contrast to these, Elizabeth Scott's design had a plain beauty and simplicity. The building's function was immediately apparent, with no attempt at fussy disguise. A great fan-shaped auditorium bellied out along the river-bank; the building of her imagination looked like a great liner, uncompromisingly of the machine age, tethered on the banks of the Avon.

Since the new architect was female, Elizabeth Scott's appointment resulted in an avalanche of publicity; she was the first woman ever to win a major architectural competition, and the first to design a British theatre. The newspapers made much of her Eton crop, of her unmarried status, and of the fact that she came from a family of distinguished architects, her great-uncle being Sir George Gilbert Scott, architect of St Pancras Station, Girton College, and the Albert Memorial; and her cousin, Sir Giles Gilbert Scott, architect of Liverpool's Anglican cathedral. They forebore to point out that, though she might have architecture in her blood, she was relatively inexperienced. She had graduated only four years previously from the Architectural Association, and had worked since then in a fairly minor capacity in the offices of a London architect, Maurice Chesterton. Her design might be clever and accomplished, but she was young and untried to be supervising the building of a huge and complex new theatre. Moreover, she had no special knowledge of theatre or stage design, and her plans had been drawn up without the benefit of help from experts in the field. She acknowledged her own inexperience and the size of the task before her by taking into partnership for the project her employer, Maurice Chesterton, and another experienced architect, John Shepherd.

It was agreed from the first that modifications would be necessary to her original designs. The building was, for instance, not built in stone, as Scott had wanted, but in red brick. But the major changes involved the core of the building – the auditorium, and the stage. Bridges-Adams was insistent, and Archie was persuaded, that the designs could not be finalized until the architects had had every opportunity to study the latest advances in theatre architecture in Europe, and seek the advice of professionals – directors and design-ers – who were familiar with the needs and problems of a repertoire theatre.[7] Bridges-Adams clearly feared that either money would be wasted on what he called 'riotous architecture', or that, when it came to planning stage and auditorium, the old penny-pinching Stratford attitudes would prevail. He drew up what he called a 'case for orthodoxy in design' (by which he meant the orthodoxy of the great German theatres), and he presented it, significantly, not to Archie but to Archie's brother Spenser, pleading with him to intercede quickly before final decisions were taken.[8] Bridges-Adams argued for a large stage, with a high grid, and wide wing space to store scenery. He wanted the very latest stage, sound, and lighting equipment; he wanted workshops, rehearsal rooms, and proper store-rooms and paint-shops under the same roof.

For once, it seemed, his arguments prevailed. Spenser Flower proved to be an ally, and to have considerable insight into his brother's character. With his advice as how best to approach Archie regarding the stage construction (which involved stressing the pres-tige an advanced stage would bring Stratford, and repeated reassur-ance that all economy would be observed), Bridges-Adams won Archie over to his point of view. It was announced that building would not commence at Stratford for at least a year, and that in the interim the architects, Archie, and Bridges-Adams, would all embark on a lengthy tour of the best European theatres in order to study their methods of stage construction, and the most up-to-date stage and lighting equipment. The Memorial, Archie announced, would be nothing less than 'the most modern and best equipped theatre in the world'.

In the meantime there were those who, as Bridges-Adams had anticipated, began to wonder what Stratford was up to, and among them was Thomas Lamont. During 1928 he began to take an increasingly active interest in the Memorial Theatre. At first he confined himself to questions about the administration of the Mem-orial, which he found difficult to comprehend. If the theatre had a

Royal Charter, and King George as its Patron, why did the King not play a more active part in the running of it? This having been explained to him, he then began to question whether Archie was really the right man to be the chairman of the governors, a question he put, unblushingly, to Archie himself. Archie answered with remarkable patience and calm – giving, in the process, an interesting definition of his role as chairman:

It is quite natural that you should feel that this position [the chairmanship] should be filled by a more important individual. Believe me, I am not only ready, but anxious, to give way to another, but the difficulty is to find someone ready to sacrifice the necessary money and time . . . My function is to exercise common sense in general administration and to see that money is not wasted . . . In addition to the experience gained in watching the steady development of the festivals, I have had about 35 years experience as a member of Warwickshire County Council and as Chairman of many other committees which have to settle plans and contracts for very large amounts . . . It is all very interesting, trying to steer between the 'Scylla' of the artistic temperament, and the 'Charybdis' of stern finance. When funds permit and the Governors so desire, it may be possible to find a man to do all this, but if he is a paid official it will mean a stiff salary . . .'

Given the years of work, and the money donated to the Memorial Theatre both by Archie and other members of his family, it was the gentlest of rebukes, but it seems to have worked. Lamont ceased cavilling about the composition of the board of governors, but it was not long before he found something else to displease him.

He was most certainly *not* pleased by the year's delay in starting to build, and the visits to European theatres. He clearly suspected that a great deal too much attention was being paid to 'artists and experts', and he also expressed a churlish disappointment that the funds raised in Britain were not larger. Archie struggled to keep him informed, and to allay these worries, but Lamont, a testy man given to writing abrupt and seigneurial letters, was not to be appeased. All might have been well however, had it not been for the appearance on the scene, in April 1929, two months before the laying of the foundation stone of the new theatre, of Harley Granville-Barker.

Granville-Barker was then still living his reclusive life with his second wife Helen Huntington, and remained cut off from most of his former friends and colleagues in the theatre. He had briefly, at

Bridges-Adams's suggestion, been connected with the plans for the new Memorial Theatre, serving on the advisory committee set up immediately after the fire, which had assessed the possible costs of building the new theatre, and the size of endowment necessary for it. Once the figure of £250,000 had been announced, Barker's involvement had ended. His interest, though desultory, had not. He was still among the most passionate campaigners for a National Theatre in London, and in the following year, 1930, was to publish a new book on the subject, which revised the ideas of his earlier *A National Theatre: Scheme and Estimates*, written with William Archer. From his retreat in Devon, Granville-Barker wrote a singularly silly and ill-informed letter to *The Times*, criticizing the new theatre at Stratford. He alleged that there was no information current as to how the governors proposed to spend the 'very considerable sum' of money they had in hand; that the sum of money was quite needlessly large, and that it would have an adverse effect on other theatre appeals, notably those for Sadler's Wells and the National Theatre. His clinching argument was that if Stratford's needs were assessed at £250,000 critics of the National Theatre project would assume that that theatre required 'a million or so (which is absurd, but it will be hard to dispute)'.[10]

Archie had little difficulty in answering Granville-Barker's criticisms. All donors to the theatre were receiving periodic reports on intentions and progress; an endowment of £100,000 could hardly be said to be extravagant, and it was, as Archie pointed out, a little hard that Stratford should be expected to curtail its operations for fear of damaging the prospects of either Sadler's Wells or a putative future National Theatre. Unfortunately the matter did not rest there. Thomas Lamont, on holiday in Paris, saw the Granville-Barker letter. He wrote loftily to Archie, saying that it had been called to the attention of 'the American community' and that, moreover, Granville-Barker had 'expressed the belief on more than one occasion, to American donors, that any sum above £150,000 is bound to be wasted on quite useless expenditure. Mr Granville-Barker is known in America as a competent producer, and his opinion carries weight . . .'[11] The *Times* letter, and this backstairs lobbying by Barker, did great harm to the relationship between the Memorial Theatre and the American Shakespeare Foundation. Lamont now began to believe that the Stratford appeal funds were in dire peril of being mismanaged. For the first time he began to use threats, stating that 'an awkward situation with regard to the transmittal of the American gifts' might arise, unless he received detailed reassurances about how the money was to be spent. He bombarded Archie with enquiries about the size and design of the theatre, about its management structure, about the plans for the endowment funds. He discovered the theatre was to have a cyclorama, and was thrown into another flurry of doubt: why? was it necessary? how much would it cost? Archie's answers, no matter how detailed or courteous, failed to satisfy him. During 1930 Theresa Helburn of the Guild Theatre, New York, was dispatched to England at Lamont's behest, to obtain more information. She spent a great deal of time discovering such facts as the future cubic footage of the theatre, and the cost to the exact penny of a cyclorama, none of which proved very informative to the financier in New York, but which caused endless nuisance to the architects in England. Meanwhile, although the building at Stratford was now progressing fast, and the workmen had to be paid, and materials bought, no money from the American fund was released, and all costs had to be met from the British fund. Not even the sum of £50,000, which Rockefeller had donated directly to the British fund, was transferred.

By March 1931, a year before the new theatre was due to open, Lamont had been sufficiently mollified to release that Rockefeller contribution, which he could hardly continue to hold without provoking an ugly row. But there was still an enormous sum of money under his control in New York: the American fund stood at $612,000. Then on 9 March 1931 Lamont wrote to Archie and proposed that, of this sum, only $250,000 should be released. The balance of $362,000 should continue to be held in America as 'The American Shakespeare Memorial Fund'. The investment income on this sum should then, he proposed, be forwarded to the Stratford governors annually. Even then, there were ties. A group of six people, he suggested, three Americans and three Britons, should be appointed to act as trustees and 'to decide jointly on questions of policy as to how . . . the income should be spent'.[12] This was an arrangement which had never previously been mentioned, and it was a great blow to the theatre. It had been announced that the costs of building should be divided equally between the British and American funds, and that the balance of both should be invested in Britain and the income used to endow the theatre – an arrangement Lamont knew of, which had been extensively publicized. Lamont's proposal meant that the governors would be short of the American money needed just to complete the building.

Lamont was in a powerful position and he knew it. Until his demands were met he would not release a cent. Archie prevaricated; Lamont was adamant. Telegrams and anxious letters winged their way to and fro across the Atlantic. For perhaps the first time in his life Archie was out-manoeuvred, and in the end he had to give in. There was one last element of farce. The governors of the theatre met, and duly passed a resolution agreeing to all of Lamont's demands. They then requested the money now urgently needed for the building work. Lamont refused: first, he said, he must receive a 'certified copy of the Governors' resolution with the seal of the Stratford theatre attached'. 'He has *now* asked for a certified copy,' Archie wrote, in exasperation, to Reginald McKenna, 'whatever *that* may mean . . .'[13] Finally a typed copy of the minutes of the governors' meeting and their resolution was sent to Lamont. The Stratford seal was attached, and it was headed, in bold letters, 'Certified Copy'. Lamont pronounced himself satisfied, and the full sum needed to complete the theatre building and pay its workforce was finally remitted from New York on 19 November 1931, just five months before the theatre was due to open. It had taken a full seven months to get it, and the balance of the American fund, some £52,000, half the theatre's proposed endowment fund, remained tied up.

While Archie struggled with the finances of the new theatre, the work-load on Bridges-Adams relentlessly increased. The seasons in the cramped and unsuitable cinema premises continued, still with a large repertoire and inadequate rehearsal time. It was, of course, even more difficult to persuade good actors to work there than it had been in the old theatre, and the quality of production which could be given in such a theatre, and on such a stage, was obviously limited. Still, Bridges-Adams achieved memorable things, particularly in 1928 and 1929 when he had George Hayes, a fine actor, in his company, who gave some highly praised performances. But the strain was intense, and made worse by the fact that budgets were tighter than ever before. Whereas the governors had held the freehold of the old theatre, they now had to pay rent, and this was enough to tip the precarious finances into deficit. With Archie's careful book-keeping no season under Bridges-Adams's direction in the old theatre had made a loss larger than £500. At the cinema the festivals made a loss each year: the lowest was £1,274 (in 1927), and the highest £5,000 (in 1926).

Working under these conditions had already adversely affected Bridges-Adams's health; he had had a severe nervous breakdown in 1926, and had stayed at The Hill to recover, where he was nursed back to health by Florence Flower. Since then events had compounded the considerable strain under which he normally worked. At the same time as directing the festivals he was deeply involved in plans for the new theatre, and in particular with the design of the stage to which considerable changes and adjustments were being made. He was embroiled in arguments on all sides: with the architects, with the builders, with the technical advisers, with Archie, and with Theresa Helburn. In addition to this, he took his companies on three arduous tours to America and Canada in 1928, 1929, and 1931-2, on the very eve of the opening of the new theatre. These tours were arranged from the best of motives: to show the many Americans who had contributed money to the theatre appeal the actual work of the company they were supporting. They were not, as many people believed, embarked upon in order to raise more funds for the appeal in America; the American fund closed at the time of the first tour, in autumn 1928. Even Thomas Lamont, and other members of the American Shakespeare Foundation, advised against the third and final tour in the autumn of 1931. They argued that America was in the grips of the Depression; that the tour was likely to lose money; that it was dangerously scheduled, finishing only a few weeks before the opening of the new Memorial. But Archie remained undaunted, convinced that the tour would add to the theatre's prestige, and Bridges-Adams, appalled at the thought of opening the new building with a new company, a new repertoire, and the usual inadequate rehearsal time, agreed. The final American tour enabled him to keep the 1931 company together and build up a repertoire of work for the April 1932 opening. He agreed, even though he knew it would mean he would have to leave England for a period when the Stratford building was being finalized; the tour went ahead.

At this time he was also involved in long and protracted negotiations with the governors about his own contract which were far from amicable, and reveal much about the decline in his relationship with Archie. Previously his contracts had been on a yearly basis and had been informally agreed by exchange of letters between himself and Archie. In 1925, when his contract was renewed for the following year, he had, for instance, expressly declined to use a solicitor, on the grounds that a formal contract would be cumbersome and 'would have to set forth many points which are perfectly well understood between us'.[14] By 1930 his attitude had radically changed. When his contract came up for renewal that year he asked that it should be for three years' duration, not one, and he put the matter in the hands of a solicitor. It was, in the circumstances, a perfectly reasonable request. For over ten years he had worked at Stratford under adverse circumstances; with the new theatre in the offing, which would at last give him the opportunity to do all the things at Stratford he had wanted to do for so long, he obviously wished to be sure that he would be given sufficient time to work in it, and to develop his ideas. Perhaps he already had doubts about this; if so they were certainly confirmed by the undignified wrangling that ensued.

The negotiations began on 7 October 1930, and the contract was not finally signed and sealed until 12 March 1931. In the intervening five months no less than forty-eight letters were exchanged and numerous acrimonious meetings convened concerning the contract. Many people were brought into the controversy – Spenser Flower, Bernard Shaw, Barry Jackson, as well as Archie and Bridges-Adams's solicitor. Every conceivable point that could be argued over was disputed: money, expenses, dates, notice.[15] The bestowal of a knighthood on Archie, in the 1930 New Year's Honours List, did not improve the situation. Bridges-Adams had, for an idealistic and high-principled man, an odd and uncharacteristic regard for public honours. He was far too generous to begrudge Archie his title, but he certainly felt his own exclusion from any form of public recognition keenly.[16] A residue of bitterness in his dealings with Archie and the Memorial remained for the rest of his time there.

If his work at this time had been acclaimed, it might have done much to heal these wounds and restore his confidence, but it was not. Having ignored Stratford productions since Bridges-Adams's opening seasons, the national critics became interested once more as the opening of the much-touted new theatre neared. The cinema seasons of 1930 and 1931 received significantly more attention from national reviewers than any Stratford seasons for years. Naturally they attended first nights, when work was woefully under-rehearsed. They usually confined their attendance to one or two plays a season and, in the case of critics for daily newspapers, they left performances before the end to file their notices. But however unfortunate the circumstances under which they attended, the fact remained that almost without exception they found both productions and acting inadequate. Bridges-Adams was attacked for his old-fashioned staging, for his concern with design at the expense of actors, and for their poor verse-speaking. Even Stratford spawned a critic with teeth, the right-wing A.K. Chesterton (later founder of the League of Empire Loyalists), who launched a series of attacks on Bridges-Adams's work, and considered that 'Those things which he orders with superlative skill are all bound up with artifice: he turns his back upon life itself, and positively runs away from emotion . . . he exploits all his materials save his actor [*sic*], and would be quite content, I am sure, that his productions should be judged as so many magnificent charades . . .'[17] Unfortunately Chesterton and Archie were friends, and these attacks happened to reinforce all Archie's theatrical prejudices. He had always underestimated the importance of sets, staging, and lighting, and when a critic like Chesterton attacked Bridges-Adams for over-emphasizing their importance, or criticized his companies for mangled pronunciation and unrhythmic verse-speaking, he spoke with Archie's own voice. Instead of seeing that both staging *and* acting were vital elements in a production, Archie began to believe that they were somehow in opposition to each other, and that only by forgetting about what he dismissed as 'lavish scenery effects' could there be a return to the theatrical values he endorsed: good honest productions with no fuss, and every actor clearly audible at the back of the gallery.

As the highly publicized opening of the new theatre approached, the gulf between the two men's hopes for it was already wide, and widening. Bridges-Adams now wanted a great international theatre, employing outside directors and designers, producing properly rehearsed productions that used to the full the resources of his new modern stage. Archie wanted the 'customary . . . modest scale of production . . . a sober sincere and intelligent tradition of acting of Shakespeare.'[18] Bridges-Adams wanted to spend money on achieving his aims; Archie remained wedded to financial caution. The two visions met in only one ephemeral area: both men wanted the theatre to win prestige, that most evanescent of commodities. But even here they differed. Bridges-Adams saw that as a long-term, hard-fought-for prize. Archie, who was increasingly tied up with the complex arrangements for the opening of the theatre, wanted it at once, in the very first season, when the eyes of the world were to be directed to the new theatre on the banks of the Avon. The 1932 opening was to be a kind of revenge for the opening of 1879, the moment when his uncle's vision was vindicated, and his own years of work finally crowned with approbation.

6

Openings

On 15 February 1932, two months before the new Memorial Theatre was to open, Archie Flower received an unexpected telephone call from Sir Edward Elgar asking if he might be shown over the building. Elgar was then an old man of seventy-five, living not far from Stratford in Worcester. He had had tenuous connections with the Stratford theatre in the past, and it was virtually agreed that he would be its new musical director.

Archie met him outside the new theatre on the river terrace, and found him furiously angry. The building was, he announced, 'so unspeakably ugly and wrong' that he would have nothing further to do with it. He flatly refused to go inside. Archie, exercising all his charm, finally persuaded him to look at the auditorium and the stage, and then brought him out through the main entrance, a foyer of chaste yet aggressive modernity, fearing all the while that the sight of so much stainless steel, of rigorously plain walls and art deco doors, would cause Elgar to faint. But Elgar did not faint; instead he informed Archie that he would very probably be unable to eat for a month, and that not only would he not work in the building under any circumstances, he would never set foot in it again. He also announced that he really felt he ought to write to *The Times* about it.[1] Archie already had good knowledge of what damage unfavourable publicity in the correspondence columns of *The Times* could do, and this threat, from so celebrated a man, reduced him to a state of anguish. It took the combined efforts of Bridges-Adams and Archie, and several letters, to persuade Elgar to keep his opinion to himself.

Bridges-Adams wrote to Archie from London once Elgar had been successfully headed off:

If you take as a personal worry what every elderly buffer says about a public building, you will end by going mental. I couldn't do my job for a week if I put what others say before what I know. What *you* know is that a theatre in which you are keenly interested carries the official approval of the RIBA, and is none the less 'much discussed', a word which, in the theatre, signifies life. What we both know is that we don't personally like a whole lot of it. What I know is that if the Council had given me . . . a free hand with the whole building, as I had with the stage, we should have had a better and cheaper theatre. But that is spilt milk – though not as many gallons, perhaps, as we think.[2]

Neither Bridges-Adams nor Archie then voiced publicly their doubts about the new building. Privately, they were well aware that the theatre, beautiful though it was, had numerous drawbacks. It had finally cost a total of £192,000, and could seat 1,000 people (520 in the stalls, 260 in the circle, and 220 in the balcony). On the fabric of the building no expense had been spared. Certainly, there were none of the traditional accoutrements of a theatre: there was no red plush, and not a gilded cherub or caryatid in sight. Elizabeth Scott was an avowed 'modernist'; the building accordingly appeared functional, simple in line, and almost puritanically plain. But on closer examination it was also rich in detail, resplendent with the arts of a machine age. The entrance foyer was a great empty hall, the floor of Hornton stone with sections of Ashburton marble and Derbyshire fossil; the walls were lined with fawn-coloured brick. Great ebony doors with exquisitely worked finger-plates in aluminium, representing the twin masks of Comedy and Tragedy, and surrounded by pilasters of stainless steel and green Swedish marble, led into the theatre itself. The only ornament and distraction was a little stainless steel and bronze folly in the middle of the hall, which served as a booking-office. (This is still there; the doors have long disappeared.) At one end of this hall was a long couch of ebonized wood, upholstered in green horsehair. That was all; the bookstall, the posters and production photographs which now humanize the foyer and give it an atmosphere of activity were not there. All was icily elegant.

To reach the circle the audience passed by a shallow fountain in Verdi de Prata marble, mounted stairs flanked with more green Swedish marble, and passed through the circle bar. This large room, overlooking the theatre forecourt and the river, was of so chaste a design that even the *Architectural Review* (in a paean of praise for the building) remarked that the architect appeared to have been worried 'lest the colours of the whiskies would not blend with the general colours of the room'.[3] In the circle bar, and throughout the theatre, panelling of rare wood vied with marble as the only ornament. The woods had been selected in an attempt to include at least one from each of the British dominions, and they made an impressive, if abstruse, role-call – stained sycamore, East Indian rosewood, Honduras mahogany, English burr-elm, gurjun and ebony, Indian laurel, and Andaman padank . . .

The *Architectural Review*, a magazine in the forefront of modernist design, pronounced the building a triumph. 'It is uncompromisingly a theatre,' its critic wrote, 'with no attempt at disguise'. The foyer was 'amusing'; the staircase 'beautiful'; even the café (now the restaurant) where the architects had designed everything from light fittings to knives and forks, met with unqualified praise. 'The chairs and tables, chinaware, curtains, handrails like forked lightning, are all worthy of Stockholm Town Hall,' he commented.[4] The critic of the *Architectural Review* could be forgiven for evangelizing perhaps; he was well aware that the consensus of opinion on the new theatre was hostile. Beachcomber dubbed the building 'the new Soviet barracks at Stratford', and conservative critics delightedly followed his lead.

On one point the two camps were united: it was, everyone agreed, a superb *theatre*. Mesmerized by an auditorium uncluttered by pillars, by a stage enormously deep with vast scene docks on either side, and by the revolutionary lighting equipment and the rolling stages which could glide whole scenes out of the docks and on to the stage in seconds, they were almost unanimous in their praise. Ironically, this was precisely where the drawbacks were most apparent. It was backstage, onstage, and in the auditorium, where it mattered most, that the mistakes had been made.

The stage and auditorium had been designed after the exhaustive tour of European theatres, and after taking what had seemed to be the best available advice. Two other eminent men of the theatre, Sir Barry Jackson, and the designer Norman Wilkinson, as well as Bridges-Adams himself, had acted as advisors. In the face of all the energetic lobbying from the 'Elizabethan Methodists', Bridges-Adams had been insistent from the first that the stage should not conform to any one single idea about the staging of Shakespeare, but should be adaptable: 'The need is for absolute flexibility,' he told the *Observer* in 1928, 'a box of tricks out of which the child-like mind of the producer may create whatever shape it pleases. It should be able to offer Mr Poel an Elizabethan stage after his heart's desire. It should be no less adequate to the requirements of Professor Reinhardt.'[5] Bridges-Adams always maintained that the stage, as far as the proscenium arch only, was his design. But this was something of a simplification. In 1926, with Granville-Barker's help, he had drawn up detailed specifications regarding stage *and* auditorium, asking for a two-tiered horseshoe house, good sight-lines, and a removable forestage, among other things. The adjudicators of the competition for an architect felt that these specifications were over-precise and would damp the ardour and imagination of competitors. As a result, the specifications reached competitors only in a very attenuated form. So, when Bridges-Adams came to work on the design of the stage with Elizabeth Scott, he was forced from the first into adapting his ideas to fit in with her plans. And from that point onwards there was constant interference, discussion, and argument. 'What we eventually got,' Bridges-Adams wrote many years later, breaking a long and discreet silence on the subject, 'when the architects, pressure-groups, quacks and empirics had finished with us, was the theatre, of all theatres in England, in which it is hardest to make an audience laugh or cry.'[6]

Everyone concerned with the new Memorial was working at a time when few new theatres were being built, but many cinemas; the result was a theatre that would have made a perfect Odeon. The stage had a proscenium arch which was narrow (30 feet) and too low (21 feet). It was structurally immovable. It was decorated with wood-panelling that distracted the eye, and flanked by what looked like two odd art deco cupboards, lower than the top of the proscenium, which were assemblies, or side entrances, to the fore-stage. The fore-stage itself was too shallow – little more than a shelf perched above the orchestra pit. Beyond the pit lay the fan-shaped curve of the stalls, modelled on the opera house at Bayreuth. The circle ran in a shallow curve across the middle of the auditorium. There were no side balconies or boxes (as there are now), so that the circle was cut off from the stage by an expanse of cold, cream-painted wall, ornamented by more fussy wood-panelling. The effect was to isolate the audience from the stage, and to create a tunnel effect, looking through a narrow opening at a great stage some 40 feet deep. The actors were imprisoned somewhere in the tunnel. 'On a clear day,' commented Baliol Holloway in 1934, when he had just endured the stage for the first time, 'you can just about see the boiled shirts in the first row. It is like acting to Calais from the cliffs of Dover.'

Extraordinary errors had been made, even in the design of the much-vaunted mechanics of the stage. Sections of the stage had been provided with lifts, so that, theoretically, they could be lowered, set with scenery, and raised again. To accomplish this they needed to sink to a depth of about twenty feet; they only went down eight. The whole of the back section of the stage was constructed to rise above normal level, providing a platform; after it had risen only three feet, however, the heads of actors standing on it were cut off from the view of the gallery. The scene docks on either side of the stage had been made exceptionally wide to accommodate the famous rolling stages; but they were not built wide enough, so that the rolling stages could not be fully withdrawn. To compensate for this, the stages were made flexible, so they could slide up the side walls of the scene dock. This meant that it was impossible to build a complete set on them, which had been the main reason for their installation. Changes and modifications to their design were still continuing as late as January 1932. After installation they caused constant problems by sticking obstinately when only half extended, and they were subsequently very rarely used.

Backstage there were other, now inconceivable errors, of an elementary nature. In spite of what Bridges-Adams had said on the subject, there was no rehearsal room, no workshops, no green-room. There were too few dressing-rooms, and they were positioned on the road side of the theatre, with their windows opening directly over the heads of people standing in the gallery queue, so actors were constantly distracted by noise as they prepared to go on.

Although Archie and Bridges-Adams had reservations about the theatre's design, they do not appear to have been aware of the true scale of the mistakes. It was lucky for their peace of mind, for there was little they could have done about it. Small changes and alterations went on until the very last minute, but the completion of the theatre was rushed. The opening, on Shakespeare's birthday, 23 April 1932, had been fixed and was to be conducted with the maximum ceremony and publicity.

It had been announced that the new Memorial Theatre would be opened by the Prince of Wales, a *coup* pulled off after months of negotiations with the Palace, of which Archie was inordinately proud.

If anything, the Royal Family had shown even less inclination to visit Stratford and its theatre than the London critics had done. No member of the Royal Family had ever set foot in the place, despite its Royal Charter. Charles Flower had failed in his attempt to persuade Prince Leopold to lay the foundation stone of the original theatre. It had been hoped at one point that the Duke of Connaught would lay the foundation stone of the new theatre, but that had come to nothing. Archie was told that he might have done so had it not been for the adverse publicity created by Granville-Barker's letter to *The Times* only two months before the ceremony.[7] This neglect was felt keenly by Archie and the governors, the more so because the Old Vic had been favoured with several royal visitations. The Prince of Wales's presence was, therefore, the high point of the planned ceremonial, which involved wreath-laying at Shakespeare's grave, a luncheon for 600 distinguished guests, and unfurling the nations' flags before the Prince would advance upon the bronze and steel doors of the entrance foyer, to be presented with a gold key by Elizabeth Scott, and enter the theatre. He and the rest of the audience would watch a matinée performance of *Henry IV, Part I. Part II* would be given that evening. Over half the seats for the matinée were allocated in advance to ambassadors, governors of the theatre, members of the American Shakespeare Foundation, and to the critics who were assembling from all parts of the globe. The opening ceremony was to be broadcast by the BBC, and – the first time this had ever been attempted – relayed live to America.

All these plans generated an immense amount of publicity; newspapers hurriedly researched Stratford's past and began printing erudite stories about Garrick's Jubilee, and a plethora of interviews with Bensonians. The whole affair was planned, scheduled, and rehearsed with precision. The spectacle outside the theatre took on such dimensions that the spectacle planned for inside – the actual performances – was quite eclipsed.

Bridges-Adams had not found it easy to draw up the schedule of plays for the opening week, nor to decide finally upon his company. He was not helped by the advice (which was really disguised criticism) which began appearing in newspapers and magazines by the end of 1931 to the effect that now Stratford must, at last, employ some star actors. The *Sphere* took it upon itself to suggest names: John Gielgud, Basil Gill, Cedric Hardwicke, Fay Compton, Gwen Ffrangcon-Davies, and Sybil Thorndike – none of whom had ever appeared there. Bridges-Adams ignored these suggestions. He was determined to remain loyal to his concept of an ensemble company, and to the actors who had worked hard in the old theatre and in the cinema.Throughout the January and February before the opening Archie bombarded him with casting advice, although it was by then late in the day. Bridges-Adams answered him with asperity:

Additional engagements for leading parts can only be made from people who have done well for the company in the past, or who will fit in without destroying the balance . . . Supposing I announced the engagement of Alan Aynesworth, Seymour Hicks, Gertrude Lawrence and Leslie Henson? You would no doubt find another £400 a week with pleasure, but would you be so pleased when you saw the plays?[8]

Bridges-Adams had, in fact, the nucleus of a strong company. It was led by Randle Ayrton and by Fabia Drake, who excelled as the heroines of the comedies, making a great success as Rosalind and Viola. They were backed up by several good supporting and charac-ter actors, including men of considerable experience such as Eric Maxon, Ernest Hare, and Roy Byford. Wilfred Walter, a leading actor who had played often at Stratford and at the Old Vic during the 1920s, was brought in after the American tour, to give added strength to the company. Both Bridges-Adams and Archie knew they did not have a good young leading man; they had to content themselves with Gyles Isham, a romantically good-looking young actor who had made a great success with his Hamlet for the OUDS, who had acted at Stratford before, and who had played leading roles at the Old Vic (including Bolingbroke to Gielgud's Richard II in 1929). Although Bridges-Adams was determined, as far as possible, to open the theatre with a repertoire already familiar to this company, the final planning of his first season in the new theatre was left dangerously late. By the beginning of March the plans were still not finalized; Bridges-Adams was still hoping to persuade Archie to reduce the number of plays they would put on. But Archie remained unconvinced, and seven plays for the opening week were announced: the two parts of *Henry IV, Julius Caesar, A Midsummer Night's Dream, As You Like It, Twelfth Night,* and *King Lear.* It was a repertoire chosen as far as possible to disguise the lack of a strong young leading actor, and to exploit the talents of Fabia Drake (Rosalind, Viola, Lady Percy), Randle Ayrton (Henry IV, Lear, Malvolio), and Norman Wilkinson, who wanted to design a new production of the *Dream,* the first he had worked on since Granville-

Barker's celebrated production at the Savoy in 1914. It also had another advantage: all the plays except *Henry IV, Part II* had been in the recent repertoire (in 1930 and 1931) and were known to the company – five of them had been included on the American tour. As far as was humanly possible, Bridges-Adams would open the theatre with productions which were played-in, not under-rehearsed. This was an essential consideration. Because of the duration of the American tour, Bridges-Adams had even less rehearsal time available to him than usual. The company arrived back in England on 24 March; after a short break they began rehearsals at Stratford on 4 April, with just three weeks to the opening performance. Bridges-Adams travelled to Canada for nine days work with the company early in March; after that he had only the three-week period in Stratford.

The Stratford rehearsals came at the end of a punishing seven-month tour during which a number of the company, including Randle Ayrton, had been ill. The theatre at Stratford should theoretically have been finished by the end of February; in fact a considerable amount of last-minute work was still being done to the stage as late as April, and only a limited number of rehearsals could be held on the actual stage. Most rehearsals on stage, and all dress rehearsals, had to be held at night (leaving the theatre free to workmen during the day). They continued late, often until three o'clock in the morning, and tempers were frayed.[9] The company had perilously little time to accustom themselves to the stage, and there was even less time adequately to test all the elaborate stage machinery. 'I take no risks,' Bridges-Adams wrote to Archie, that January. 'If the contraptions are uncertain in the working I shall not use them.'[10] Then he believed there was time to test them, but last-minute hitches and snags proved him wrong. Because the schedule of the opening plays was finalized so late, insufficient time had been left to design new sets and costumes, which Bridges-Adams insisted upon. They were made in London at short notice, and were accordingly expensive. The sets by outside designers, such as Wilkinson (*Midsummer Night's Dream*), Aubrey Hammond (*Julius Caesar*), and George Sheringham (*Twelfth Night*) were beautiful; those designed by Bridges-Adams (including the two *Henry IV* plays chosen for the opening performances) reflected the rush in which they were created.

The decision to open the theatre with the *Henry IV* plays was also a tardy one. Late in February 1932 Bridges-Adams had written to Archie about the question and had ruled them out. The alternatives, he suggested, were the *Dream* or *Julius Caesar*. The idea of opening with *Caesar* was eventually dropped because there was insufficient time to rehearse the crowd scenes, with many supers, on stage. Bridges-Adams finally decided against the *Dream* because the play had been given the previous year, and because he was having considerable problems with Norman Wilkinson over the designs for it. Wilkinson's fondness for alcohol could incapacitate him for days at a time. The *Henry IV* plays were selected *faute de mieux*, and it was an unlucky decision. Gyles Isham, as Hal, had a demanding role beyond his talents and Roy Byford, who was too genial and lightweight a Falstaff for those plays, nevertheless had to take the part because there was no one else capable of it in the company (Ayrton, the only other possibility, was playing the King). Fabia Drake had only the tiny part of Lady Percy.

The two plays were dress-rehearsed the day before the opening. The actors finished work at 3 a.m., a few hours before the whole carnival swung into action.

Over 100,000 people came to Stratford that 23 April to watch the opening ceremony and join in the general festivities. Prince Edward arrived in some style, piloting his own Red Puss monoplane, and was driven into Stratford in a Rolls Royce, accompanied by Archie's son, Fordham Flower. Archie, who had been made Mayor of Stratford in 1932, as his uncle had been in 1879, greeted them. Newly-installed electrical equipment ensured that seventy-four flags of the nations fluttered to the head of their masts without one eminent man having to touch a guy rope. Archie made a speech which was a variation upon all his Shakespeare speeches, and the Prince of Wales, who had never been noted for his interest in the theatre, replied with an elegant address, in similar vein. 'Shakespeare,' he said, 'was above all an Englishman'; he delighted in 'all swift true things', such as the galloping of horses, the skill and backbone of men-at-arms, and the quiet courage so often found in the simplest human heart. The key to the theatre was then presented to him by Elizabeth Scott, and the audience slowly followed Prince Edward into the building, to watch a play in which an earlier Prince of Wales found temporary solace in a tavern, among companions notable for many things, but not exactly the quiet courage of their simple hearts.

Since there was no Royal Box, the Prince and the rest of his party were seated in a specially screened-off section right at the very back of the dress circle – some of the worst seats in the house. The stalls were filled with the specially invited audience, the ambassadors, diplomats, governors, and critics, together with their elegantly dressed wives. John Masefield, the Poet Laureate, had written a special ode for the occasion, and was among the audience to see it performed. Lady Keeble (formerly the actress Lillah McCarthy, Granville-Barker's first wife) had the unhappy task of speaking this ode, composed of twenty-eight lines of dispiritingly lumpen verse. Then the curtain rose on the Palace of Westminster, a disappointing affair. Inside Elizabeth Scott's obtrusive proscenium arch hung a canvas flat, painted with a Norman arch. The sides and back of the stage were enclosed with drab curtains, giving an acting area only twenty feet deep. Randle Ayrton, as King Henry IV, was seated upon a throne which resembled an up-ended box with a canopy. His voice obviously affected by nerves, he began: 'So shaken as we are, so wan with care . . .' There could hardly have been a more appropriate beginning to a play.

Apart from the fact that there was only one interval, it was as if the Memorial Theatre had stood still since the days of Frank Benson. Each location of the play had a different, relentlessly literal set, made up of canvas flats and curtains. The Boar's Head Inn had flats with painted timbering and windows, and a fireplace surmounted by a boar's head. Other rooms in the Palace of Westminster were suggested by ill-painted stained-glass windows, and pillars like up-ended bolsters. The lighting, presumably because Bridges-Adams had had insufficient time to work on it, was murky. It was a dull, bad, depressing performance of a difficult play that was, in any case, an unwise choice for such an occasion, and such an audience. Things were made worse by the fact that the actors were only half audible. After all the advance publicity about a 'world theatre', with an audience well aware that this was the most costly new theatre ever built in Britain, waiting to see evidence of what they had been told was a stage with revolutionary possibilities, it appeared all the worse.

The performance began at 3 p.m; the interval came at 4.20 p.m. During the interval, the Prince and the royal party left to fly back to Windsor. This was not a reaction to the production; his departure at 4.45 p.m. had been scheduled from the first. But it had assiduously not been publicized, and it contributed to the general atmosphere of deflation and anti-climax.

The rest of the audience returned, and the second half of the play dragged to a close. Archie Flower left the theatre in a state of cold anger; at some point, either then, or the next day (there is dissension on this point) he passed Bridges-Adams, and cut him.

Most of the critics departed immediately, only a few remaining to see the second part of the play that evening and fewer still to see all the plays in the opening week. Their reviews of the matinée spoke with one voice: the production had been a disastrous failure. Some were disposed to make allowances. Both *The Times* and the *Guardian* were prepared to be merciful. They could not pronounce the production a success, but they emphasized the mitigating factors, the 'refrigerative' effect of a modern theatre, the formality of the occasion. W.A. Darlington, in the *Daily Telegraph,* thought the production had failed because the actors were tired, which was partly the case. *Henry IV, Part I* was, he wrote, 'a dull and spiritless affair . . . The fact was that the players. . .were tired out. They had not got the feel of the theatre with an audience in it. Accordingly, the effort to "put over" a difficult play was more than they could manage.'

Other critics, however, were not disposed to be as charitable as these three, or to lay the blame on exhaustion, and the formality of the occasion. They were not prepared to excuse the tired imagination revealed in the staging, and the acting, as C.B. Purdom, writing in *Everyman,* described:

The play was staged in a series of picture sets, well designed and paint- ed – in the nineteenth-century tradition. The changes were quickly made on the rolling stage, but the play had to stop a dozen. . . times for that to be done, though only for a minute or so. The continuity of action was nonetheless broken. And the forestage was never used. . . the lighting system, the best that any theatre has today, was hardly used at all, even the cyclorama not being properly lit . . . Falstaff had to sit away from us, sometimes in semi-darkness, speaking his golden words to the painted scene, not to us to whom they were written.[11]

It was left to A.E. Baughan, in *Era,* to pin down the problem that was – apart from the theatre building itself – at the root of the trouble:

The company *must* be given longer for rehearsals and I doubt if this can be done under the present arrangements. The season is to last five weeks, and during that time no fewer than seven of Shakespeare's plays have to be . . . produced . . . Most of these are in the recent repertory, which means that nothing very new will be done in producing them. I can truthfully declare that there is hardly a single play in the repertory which does not require a new production.[12]

The most successful production of that first season in the new theatre was, in fact, a new one, and one on which a considerable amount of money had been spent. It was *A Midsummer Night's Dream,* directed by Bridges-Adams and designed by Norman Wilkinson. Although the cast for this production remained virtually the same as that for the 1931 production, the play had been rethought and recharged by a great designer.

Norman Wilkinson had been a governor of the Memorial Theatre since 1919, the first member of the theatrical *avant-garde* to gain a place on the board. He was a considerable force on the executive council, and very often an ally to Bridges-Adams in his arguments with Archie; the *Dream* was, however, the first production he designed at Stratford. It was clearly the work of the man who had designed Granville-Barker's greatest Shakespearian production, the 1914 *Dream,* with the celebrated fairies with gilded faces. Traces of that production remained in his designs for Stratford: Puck, for instance, was again a strange, wizened, crouching creature, clad in a scarlet hunting-jacket. The wood was hung with soft drifting gauzes in blue and silver, lit with an evanescent light. The fairies, wearing costumes of the same colours, disappeared when they stood in certain positions against the gauzes. Theseus and his court wore Elizabethan dress, and Titania and Oberon wore costumes heavily influenced by Bakst, with formalized silver wigs; Titania's transparent hooped skirt, and Oberon's stiff transparent gauze cloak had a circus quality far removed from traditional prettiness. The play began in a great Palladian palace, and Bridges-Adams conceived it as a 'joyous epithalamion'; those who saw it remember it vividly to this day.

Unfortunately, the production opened on the fourth night of the festival, by which time most of the critics had departed; the *Dream* was, that year, reviewed only locally, and the opening season, so heralded, so publicized, so worked for, was regarded as a failure.

No modern director would have agreed to open a theatre under the conditions that Bridges-Adams faced in opening the new Memorial. And they would almost certainly have been more cautious about preliminary fanfares of publicity and highly elaborate opening ceremonies. When the National Theatre opened, productions played to audiences and Press *before* a Royal Gala 'opening'. Most modern directors would also endorse the phrase originally coined by George Devine and often used by Peter Hall: 'the right to fail' is a concept now widely accepted in the subsidized theatre. In 1932 Bridges-Adams would not have dared to use such an expression, even though he saw clearly it would take years to achieve the work and the company he wanted. It was a concept Archie would have found almost incomprehensible; to him failure – and particularly public failure – was anathema. He had worked ceaselessly and passionately to raise money, to get the new theatre built; for six years it had absorbed him. The year the theatre opened he was sixty-seven, and he was impatient for achievement. Bridges-Adams had worked equally as hard, and equally as passionately, but in Archie's view he had had his chance, and he had failed to deliver the goods. Their relationship, upon which the development and welfare of the theatre depended, had been strained before the opening; after that first matinée, it never recovered.

The first season ended in May 1932. By the beginning of June, when planning for the summer season began, Bridges-Adams was exhausted, ill, and close to another nervous breakdown. Archie, meanwhile, was besieged with letters from governors, old friends, even acquaintances, echoing the earlier criticisms of A.K. Chesterton. They all agreed that what was wrong at Stratford was that the acting (by which most of them meant the speaking) was not good enough. The reason, they suggested, was not the over-ambitious repertoire, the lack of rehearsal time, or defects in the theatre building; it was that Bridges-Adams was more concerned with sets and lighting than he was with directing actors.

On 1 June 1932 Dame Edith Lyttelton wrote to Archie about the opening season from London. Dame Edith had remained a friend and champion to Bridges-Adams ever since his first season in 1919, and she had on numerous occasions interceded with Archie on his behalf. But she was also a friend of Archie and his family, and she was a woman to whose views he gave weight. Her letter was carefully preserved by Archie, annotated, and underlined:

It all boils down to this, the castes [*sic*] are not good enough. If all were up to the level of Ayrton, and Byford, and Walter, no more need be said. But there is a curious lack of spirit and vitality in the productions . . . BA's productions used to be so full of gaiety and spirit and life; why has it vanished? . . . Could not someone be engaged to work under BA's general direction to infuse unity and vigour of conception, and rehearse and rehearse? I hate feeling like this because, as you know, I am a tremendous admirer of BA in all ways.[13]

The letter was more generous to Bridges-Adams than many that Archie received, and the answer as to what had happened to Bridges-Adams's gaiety and spirit was obvious enough. Archie, however, latched on to only part of the letter, the suggestion that the company should employ someone under Bridges-Adams who could act as a kind of kapellmeister, rehearsing the company after first nights, and coaching them in verse-speaking. From this it was only a short jump to the idea that Bridges-Adams would have to be replaced. That opinion, which strengthened over the next two years, was exacerbated by Bridges-Adams's behaviour.

Bridges-Adams had waited thirteen years to work in a modern theatre, and thirteen years to have the money and freedom to achieve his ideal of an ensemble company. 'I confess I chafe somewhat', he had written to Archie earlier that year, 'to think what fine shows, and what fine casts, I could have put on in London, with half the frittering away of nervous energy that Stratford involves. Mr Micawber has waited a *very* long time for something to turn up – but I don't intend to desert him as long as I am given a free hand – ye gods, a free financial hand, to do things now as I think they should be done.'[14] Once the theatre was open, he began to fight, and fight hard, for that privilege. A crisis came almost immediately, in June 1932. Bridges-Adams proposed that long-term spending on productions should be increased, the repertoire reduced, the seasons extended, and that guest directors as well as designers be brought in, thus gaining the benefit of fresh talent and reducing the impossible workload upon himself. He suggested Komisarjevsky and Max Reinhardt, who was coming to England to direct the OUDS the next year. Archie agreed with none of this, and the tone of the letters between the two men became increasingly formal and irritable; the customary 'Dear Archie' gave way to 'Dear Flower', and even occasionally to 'Dear Chairman'. On 5 June a meeting of the governors' executive council was held to discuss plans for the forthcoming summer season, and the longer-term policies of the theatre. Bridges-Adams was invited to be 'in attendance'. That the meeting was also partly to discuss Bridges-Adams's capabilities and future as a director was made clear in a letter that Norman Wilkinson sent Archie the day before the meeting: 'The job before us', he wrote, 'is like mending an old bridge, or building a new one while the traffic is still kept going. (This is not intentionally a pun!)'[15]

The result of the meeting incensed Bridges-Adams. It was decided to add two productions to the spring repertoire – *The Winter's Tale* and *The Merchant of Venice*. Opening dates, rehearsal time, and the extensive repertoire would continue unchanged. Nothing was agreed about guest directors, and no funds were allocated for the new productions. The decision to include *Winter's Tale* had been made against Bridges-Adams's express wishes; he felt the production which was in the repertoire (and which had toured America) was poor. He had agreed to include it only if the governors would vote a total of £3,000 (to include director/designer fees) to be spent on the two new productions, with Wilkinson designing *Winter's Tale*. Adding insult to injury, the governors requested that, as Edith Lyttelton had suggested, Bridges-Adams employ someone to coach the company in verse-speaking and rehearse productions after they had opened.

So angry was Bridges-Adams that the next day in spite of the meeting he went ahead and asked Komisarjevsky to direct at Stratford. He then wrote to Archie:

I have today seen Komisarjevsky with a view to his producing *The Merchant of Venice*. As he is a first-rate man, he naturally wishes to undertake the production as a whole. On the other hand he is of the opinion that on simple lines it can be done for about £800, including his own fee as designer and director.

As matters stand, the allocation for the plays is precisely nil. Where the *Merchant* is concerned, I earnestly hope that yesterday's vote may be modified . . . As for *Winter's Tale;* if the Council are really satisfied with the old production of a play that calls for more exquisite treatment than any I know, then I can only recommend to them that they drop it out of the bill . . . I hoped to start rehearsals this week, but can do very little until this matter is settled. At the moment, in the absence of any allocation, we are at a standstill.[16]

Archie's reply was frosty.

The Council felt strongly that any further call on our meagre surplus should be spent on trying to strengthen the company . . . costly scenic productions, made for our Stratford stage . . . are available for at most 18 or 20 performances here, so that there is little hope of getting back much of the cost ... I agree with you that we got a lot of publicity from Norman's dresses and setting, [for the *Dream*] but I feel, taking the long view, that this has been more than counter-balanced by the severe things which have been said and written about the acting and inaudibility of many members of the company.[17]

Meanwhile, Archie took the negotiations with Komisarjevsky out of Bridges-Adams's hands, and put them into Bill Savery's, knowing quite well that Savery, now ageing, was even more conservative with money than he was. Savery was in ignorance of the company's financial position, and was used to thinking in terms of pence rather than pounds. He was appalled at the suggestion of spending £800 on the *Merchant*. 'With the costs Bridges has in mind,' he wrote to Archie, 'we could not possibly take the money in Stratford to pay our way. This being so, the loss has to be provided out of the endowment fund. Can the endowment fund stand it?'[18] As it happened the endowment fund could, but Archie did not inform Savery of this, and Savery embarked on protracted hagglings which lasted the best part of a month. They were concluded only because Bridges-Adams was ill, angry, and threatening resignation, and because Komisarjevsky agreed to reduce the figure of £800, and to use existing Stratford costumes. Because of the delay Komisarjevsky did not arrive in Stratford until 7 July. He had ten days rehearsal. The irony of all this was that Komisarjevsky's production of *The Merchant of Venice*, with Randle Ayrton and Fabia Drake, marked a turning-point for the Stratford theatre. It provided them with a much-praised production that, far from making a loss, was a box-office hit, and brought the theatre a lot of money.

Theodore Komisarjevsky was then one of the most talented and sought-after directors in England. He came from an aristocratic Russian family, and was the brother of the celebrated actress Vera Komisarjevskaya – who was regarded by many as an equal to Duse and Bernhardt in the theatre of the early 1900s, and considered by Chekhov to be one of the greatest interpreters of his plays he had ever seen. Komisarjevskaya owned her own theatre for some years in St Petersburg, and her young and talented brother began his career there, working as an assistant to her *régisseur*, Meyerhold. He later became the director of Moscow's two greatest theatres, the Imperial and the State, and he continued to work in Russia after the Revolution. He then left Russia for England, and first made his name with his famous productions of Chekhov at the tiny Barnes Theatre in Hammersmith, in the mid-1920s. He was respected by many English actors; John Gielgud, for instance, considered him one of the most contradictory and fascinating characters he had ever met in the theatre: 'bitter and cynical about the English stage and the English public, destructive, pessimistic, and at the same time a real artist, a wise and brilliant teacher, and often an inspired producer.'[19]

Komisarjevsky was small and balding, with a crackerjack ebullience and a mordant wit. He was totally without sober reverence for Shakespeare's plays – of which, prior to 1932, he had directed only one: *King Lear,* for the OUDS, in 1927. He brought to the plays a fine intelligence, an insistence on truth and the discarding of all tired second-hand conventions, and a frank and startling love of sheer theatricality which amazed English audiences. He designed all his own sets, which were thirty years ahead of their time and much misunderstood, and he lit his productions himself, using formalized, sometimes almost expressionistic techniques. He seemed to move with aplomb and aptitude from comedy to tragedy, and perhaps his one major weakness was that he could, occasionally, be flash and superficial. His association with Stratford, instigated by Bridges-Adams, was to continue for the next eight years, until 1939, and to provide the theatre with some of its greatest and most revolutionary productions.

The Merchant of Venice proved Bridges-Adams right. Komisarjevsky was working with precisely the same company that had been greeted as uneven and inadequate that spring; he had only ten days rehearsal, and a small budget.[20] But a fresh mind (and a superb director) was able to inject verve into the performances. Even the stage, with all its manifest disadvantages, seemed transformed. Gone were the tired pseudo-realistic sets, and in their place were gaily painted, frankly artificial scenes of Venice. At the end of the first scene, as the play moved from Venice to Belmont, the set split down the middle, the curvaceous lion of St Mark's departed stage left, and the drunkenly lopsided Rialto stage right, while Belmont and Portia's garden – with the caskets painted in a Rex Whistlerish manner on a curtain – rose casually from the depths of the stage to the music of Johann Sebastian Bach. Komisarjevsky had a box of tricks at his disposal, and he used it with insouciance. He saw the play as a comedy, having no patience with the more sentimental ideas which had gradually adhered to it since the nineteenth century. The action was preceded by a *commedia dell'arte* harlequinade (with Launcelot Gobbo as Harlequin), and the whole play, which had become stale with years of repetition at Stratford, was transformed into a sharp romantic comedy with, at its centre, a dark point – Randle Ayrton's harsh and unsympathetic portrait of Shylock.

Some critics, faced with a Portia in wig and owlish spectacles in the trial scene, with a Prince of Morocco as a farcical blackamoor under a red umbrella, hated the irreverence of the production. *The Times*'s critic found it 'striking, but reckless and affected'. Other critics recognized the vivacity of the performance, and saw that the challenge it threw down to traditional attitudes was a necessary and belated one. The actors in the company loved it, and Bridges-Adams was delighted. He had that rare capacity, the ability to be as pleased by the success of other directors in his theatre as he was by his own. His instinct in asking Komisarjevsky to work at the Memorial had paid off; Stratford had a production that sent people out of the theatre arguing, not dulled into complacency. Feeling that his policies had been vindicated, and that Archie would be convinced, if not by the production itself, at least by the phenomenal box-office returns, Bridges-Adams left for a holiday in Salzburg. He was full of plans for the next season, including another invitation to Komisarjevsky, a *Hamlet* directed by Max Reinhardt, and productions by Granville-Barker (now in Olympian retirement in Paris) and William Poel. While he was away, the governors discussed replacing him when his contract with the theatre (the hard-fought-for three-year one) expired in 1934.

Archie did not act immediately; he had a lingering personal regard for Bridges-Adams. Besides, he could not dismiss him, and to have provoked his resignation only months after the opening of the new building would have caused overwhelmingly unfavourable publicity. Instead, for the year 1933 Bridges-Adams was given his head. Because he was threatening to resign many of the ideas he had advocated for years were adopted, though with considerable misgivings on Archie's part.[21] The first continuous season was announced, lasting twenty-one weeks, from April to September. Ten plays were to be in repertoire, but their openings were to be staggered: six opened in the first fortnight, the rest at intervals throughout the season. Reinhardt and Poel were unable to come to Stratford, and Granville-Barker would not; but there were two guest directors, Komisarjevsky again, and Tyrone Guthrie, then thirty-two, who had just been appointed to succeed Harcourt Williams at the Old Vic. The three most successful plays from the 1932 seasons were to be revived, with cast changes: they were *As You Like It,* the *Dream,* and Komisarjevsky's *The Merchant of Venice.* All this meant that the work-load on Bridges-Adams was substantially reduced, and he had only two first-nights in the opening weeks to contend with. The company was slightly larger, and there were two leading men, George Hayes and Anew McMaster, which helped to spread the work-load on the actors. John Wyse, who had joined the company the previous summer, was the young leading man and Fabia Drake remained as leading lady, with Rachel Kempson, straight from RADA, playing Juliet, Ophelia, Hero, and other parts. Most of the supporting players remained from the previous seasons, so continuity was not broken. It was a capable company, not as star-studded as the casts Guthrie assembled the same year for his Old Vic season (which included Charles Laughton, Flora Robson, Leon Quartermaine, and Athene Seyler) but imaginative, and well-balanced.

Bridges-Adams asked for a budget of £6,000 for seven new productions, including guest director and designer fees, and was given £5,000 reluctantly. Archie was dubious about the expenditure, and the length of the season, and at the beginning of the year Bridges-Adams wrote to him to try and allay his doubts:

Don't think I don't see Stratford's point of view – I do. But what we have to think of is the world's point of view . . . Even if you fail in an honest attempt to 'go big', you can draw in your horns at any time . . . but I don't feel you can do that until you have at least tried the other . . . I believe your first duty to subscribers is to shew them that you are giving them as first-rate a thing as they subscribed for, and that a (relatively small) sum lost at this end would be readily forgiven you.[22]

From this letter it would seem that Archie was still worried about the attitudes of the American Shakespeare Foundation, which continued to hold a sum of over £52,000 in New York. In fact, his worries were unfounded and proceeded more from a lifetime's habit of financial caution than from any real difficulty. As the Governors' Report for 1933 made clear, the Memorial Theatre was, in fact, rich: compared to any other theatre in the country, very rich. The new theatre was rent-free; the 'Corporation' of the SMT, as the president and governors were designated by the Royal Charter, also owned a library, a picture-gallery, and numerous properties in Stratford which brought in annual rents. Quite substantial profits were now being made from catering, and from charging admission to see over the new buildings. The interest on the capital being held in New York was being transmitted to Stratford with few of the problems Archie had anticipated; no Anglo-American committee of trustees had ever been formed, and Thomas Lamont had subsided into tranquillity once the new theatre had opened. There was also a considerable amount of money left standing in the British fund, far more than anyone had envisaged. It had been swelled by insurance from the old theatre, and by judicious investment. In 1933 the fund stood at £75,000 (this sum was designated the 'Endowment Fund') and there was a further £25,000 accumulated interest in a 'Reserve Fund'. The theatre therefore had liquid assets of £100,000 in England alone – a very large sum in 1933.[23] And there was already every indication that, just as Bridges-Adams had predicted, the annual seasons could make money: in 1932 they made a surplus of £2,787 and, in 1933, of £3,117.[24] Obviously the theatre could not afford to throw money around too cavalierly; on the other hand the days of haggling over a £2 rise for an actor, or the cost of new sets, should have been over.

Archie *was* prepared to spend money on projects which seemed to him of tangible benefit. During 1933, for instance, he authorized the conversion of the shell of the old theatre into a modern, well-equipped conference hall, at a cost of £10,000. Even then, so conservative was he in financial matters, this capital expenditure was charged against revenue for the current year.[25] The conference hall was precisely the kind of bricks-and-mortar investment that Archie understood; it could be hired out, and would produce further revenue for the theatre. But he could not understand that to spend money on productions was also a form of investment, and the primary business of the theatre. Nor was he prepared to spend money on salaries. Bridges-Adams's salary had been raised by the three-year contract to a reasonable £1,550 per annum, but only after a great deal of haggling. Bill Savery, who was paid £850 a year, asked for a rise in 1933 and was refused. Actors' salaries remained pegged at pre-war levels. Randle Ayrton, in 1932, received £20 a week – the same salary the syndicate had paid Frank Benson in 1913. Only Roy Byford and Fabia Drake were ever paid more, and their salary – £25 a week – was the ceiling.[26] These wages were still slightly higher than those at the Old Vic, where that year Charles Laughton was being paid an exceptional £20 a week by a reluctant Lilian Baylis.[27] But the Old Vic was genuinely a poor theatre; Stratford no longer was.

The year 1933 proved to be the most successful the company had ever had. It was successful artistically, and successful at the box-office. A record 140,000 people saw the plays during the season, and there was no falling-off in audiences during the months of June and early July, when the theatre had always been closed, as some governors had feared there would be. Rail fares to Stratford were cheap: an excursion ticket from London cost five shillings and sixpence return. The most expensive seat in the theatre cost nine shillings, and a good seat in the stalls could be obtained for as little as three shillings and sixpence. In spite of the world-wide depression there were still large numbers of tourists in Stratford, and the theatre enjoyed the novel experience of being frequently sold out. It was, in fact, already becoming apparent that it was too small. People who had laughed when Bridges-Adams had said, years earlier, that the Memorial was 'a cast-iron financial proposition' began to think again. Provided tourists continued to troop to the Shakespearian shrines, the theatre was virtually assured of an audience for the plays, even if productions were poor – a dangerous state of affairs. But their numbers were undoubtedly swollen, in 1933, not only by the novelty of the theatre and the continuing controversy over its design, but by the fact that the level of production was high, and critical reaction vigorous and on the whole favourable.

   The most controversial production of the season was once again Komisarjevsky's. His *Macbeth,* a production far ahead of its time, was disliked by almost every major critic, but the subject of so much argument that it sold out. As had been clear from his production of *The Merchant,* Komisarjevsky had no patience with the literal and realistic sets which were still the prevailing fashion in the theatre, a hangover from the Edwardian era which paid no heed to the advances made in stage design by such pioneers as Granville-Barker and Norman Wilkinson in England, and Copeau, Gordon Craig, and Adolphe Appia in Europe. Komisarjevsky's attitude to design was expressionistic; he believed that

the ideal stage environment should be three dimensional and material, made of wood, glass, metal, genuine tissues – not faked with papier mâché, glued and painted canvas [it should] move the imagination of the spectators so as to enable them to imagine not only the events which happened before them, but those happening off-stage ... The sounds, lighting coming from all directions around the actors, and forming a kind of counter-point to the acting [should] reveal the unseen to the imaginations of the public, and stimulate their emotions.[28]

The set he designed for *Macbeth* (with Lesley Blanch – now famous as a writer – working on the costumes) was made of aluminium. The stage had a permanent setting which left it virtually bare except for a staircase and, in later scenes, a platform. Sheets of twisted aluminium hung at the back of the stage. The lighting was atmospheric, relying mainly on the use of spotlights which illuminated only parts of the stage, and colour which washed over the cyclorama. The costumes appeared equally unconventional. It was comparatively few years since Frank Benson had been accustomed to double the costumes for *Macbeth* and for his production of *Rob Roy*. Macbeth and his thanes in kilts had been the tradition. That had been superseded by what might be called modified Scottish/Nordic, in which the characters looked wild and uncivilized, and the men wore furs and horny Norse helmets. This kind of costume had frequently been used, for instance, at the Old Vic and by Bridges-Adams at Stratford. Komisarjevsky abandoned all this. The men's costumes were of no period or any period, although they conformed most closely to uniforms of the First World War. The witches, wrote *The Times,* 'are no longer the weird sisters, secret, black, and midnight hags, on a blasted heath, but horrible old crones, plundering not only corpses but skeletons on the battlefield, under the shadow of modern guns, while steel-helmeted soldiers carrying rifles pass on into battle'.

Grey costumes, the silvery-grey aluminium set, and shadowy lighting, created a phantasmagoric world where the edges of reality were blurred: Banquo's ghost was Macbeth's own shadow, cast huge on the aluminium walls behind him. Komisarjevsky created, the *Telegraph* wrote, 'a baleful atmosphere, in which murders and horrors seem to have their natural habitation . . . the men and women in the play seem to dwindle to shadows blown hither and thither by the wind of evil forces . . .' George Hayes and Fabia Drake, as Macbeth and Lady Macbeth, were encouraged to speak the text swiftly and sharply, which the critics disliked: 'A series of spasmodic rushes', commented the *Morning Post,* 'which destroys the music and rhythm of the verse . . .' The fashion then was still for melodious periods and graceful cadences, rather than the more rugged manner of speaking verse to which modern audiences have grown accustomed; for the approach of a Gielgud, say, rather than an Olivier. But it was not just the verse-speaking they disliked, it was practically everything about the production. 'Producer's Shakespeare', sniffed *The Times*. Ivor Brown disliked the aluminium sets because he thought no 'temple-haunting martlet' would nest in them. They did not like the costumes: *Hamlet* in plus-fours, or *Macbeth* in evening-dress (experiments conducted by Sir Barry Jackson in the 1920s), that they could accept, even if they did not like it. But this – a director seeking to find a visual statement of what he felt to be the poetic heart of the play – they could not accept. They dubbed it 'futurist', a word which had succeeded 'modernist' as a general term of abuse for innovatory productions.

The actors were also unhappy. George Hayes was too gentle an actor to succeed as Macbeth, and Fabia Drake felt her Lady Macbeth was a failure. Komisarjevsky asked her to wear salad-oil on her arms so that she would gleam against the aluminium walls, and her costume, which incorporated a considerable amount of iron-mongery, was much ridiculed. Her crown in the banquet scene was made of saucepan scourers; two old ladies were heard in the interval discussing in shocked tones the fact that her breasts were covered by what appeared to be saucepan lids. Fabia Drake thought the costume effective, but she disliked the set, particularly the staircase which was steep and curved with no rails, and down which she had to walk, staring ahead and apparently sightless, in the sleep-walking scene.[29]

None of the other productions that season was as revolutionary, or as controversial as the *Macbeth,* but they had a pace, a style and grace that was new to Stratford. Guthrie directed a strong, hieratic production of *Richard II,* and Bridges-Adams an acclaimed *Romeo and Juliet,* with superb designs by Wilkinson. His production of *Coriolanus,* with Anew McMaster in full voice in the title-role, provided him with the chance for considerable spectacle, achieved, as it had been in his earlier production of the play, at great cost to the text. But although the production of *Coriolanus* gave him the chance to demonstrate his considerable skill with crowd scenes, it was not the kind of Shakespearian play he was happiest with, either as a director or a man. He was drawn always to the gentler plays (or those he considered gentler) in which he could, with 'exquisite treatment' as he called it, summon up a world of gaiety and magic in a wood near Athens, an enchanted island, or the forest of Arden. Plays inescapably shot through with a harsher vision did not attract him (*Troilus and Cressida,* for instance, which he never directed, or

Measure for Measure, or even *Macbeth*). The productions he directed in the 1933 season, however, demonstrated in the main his gifts as a director rather than his weaknesses – his sensitivity, his technical finesse, his ability to orchestrate a play, his capacity, so often denied, to coax a performance from an actor. Rachel Kempson, a novice actress thrown in at the deep end with Juliet, found him 'infinitely painstaking and patient'; she experienced none of the reticence and aloofness that Archie believed made Bridges-Adams a poor director of actors.[30] But above all the season demonstrated his other great gift – his ability as an administrator/impresario of a theatre. In his choice of designers and directors he showed his discernment; in his encouragement of them, his generosity. This was a gift which could have been an enormous asset to Stratford. But it was not to be used. Two days before the 1934 season was due to open, on 15 April, he resigned.

The reasons for Bridges-Adams's resignation were many. Some were personal; he had recently remarried, and had a new-born son – an event of great importance to him, which came late in his life. His wife, Peggy, to whom he was devoted, was a rich woman, so that Bridges-Adams was no longer tied financially to the Memorial Theatre. But the main reasons were professional, and could be summed up in one word – Archie. To achieve what he had achieved in 1933 required constant fighting and arguing and manoeuvring in the face of Archie's opposition. And when it came to planning the 1934 season, almost all that had been achieved the previous year was thrown away. The production budget was cut back to £4,000 and a new sub-committee of governors was formed to supervise spending. Out of a repertoire of eight productions, five were revivals in order to save money that did not need saving. There was only one guest director, Robert Atkins. There was to be no increase in rehearsal time, no increases in salaries. The executive council, and Archie, turned a deaf ear to Bridges-Adams's latest proposals (hatched with Tyrone Guthrie) that Stratford and the Old Vic should have closer links – proposals Bridges-Adams favoured because he saw in them a way of securing a London appearance for his company. It must finally have been clear to him that the theatre's new financial prosperity was never going to influence its artistic policies while Archie was still chairman. Far from utilizing the money now available to improve production standards, Archie used affluence as an argument for retrenchment; if low-budget, hastily rehearsed productions could still attract an audience then why was it necessary to spend money? Archie and Bridges-Adams had reached impasse. Then, in February 1934, while he was working on the designs for Bridges-Adams's new production of *The Tempest*, Norman Wilkinson suddenly died. In him Bridges-Adams lost the chief member of the executive council who was sympathetic to his ideas; he must have known that, without Wilkinson's alliance, his negotiations with Archie and the council were likely to be even less fruitful. Finally, he was almost certainly aware that Archie had decided not to renew his contract when it expired that autumn. The matter had been discussed among the governors' executive council and Archie had already met, and was wooing, Bridges-Adams's successor, though Bridges-Adams did not then know who he was.[31] But Bridges-Adams was a proud man; resignation was preferable to dismissal.

He wrote a letter of resignation to Archie Flower, and then did not send it for some days. On 14 April he had supper with Victor Cookman, the second-string critic of *The Times* and an old friend. When Cookman left him at the Shakespeare Hotel in the early hours of the morning, he took with him the letter of resignation and dropped it off at The Hill. The next day, as Bridges-Adams knew, there was an executive council meeting called to announce the appointment of C.B. Cochran to the seat on the council left vacant by the death of Norman Wilkinson. At this meeting Bridges-Adams's resignation was announced and, to Archie's extreme annoyance, it completely eclipsed the news of Cochran's appointment. There was much speculation, particularly in Midlands newspapers, as to the reasons for the resignation, and a great deal of rumour about 'friction' between director and governors. Bridges-Adams wrote a second letter, explaining his reasons for resigning in more detail. It was diplomatically expressed, but the drift of it was clear. Archie, at a second meeting of the governors on 23 April, made no reference to it, merely remarking with uncharacteristic lack of generosity, that 'while we all admire the flair of Mr Bridges-Adams for a beautiful picture, I have personally expressed the opinion sometimes, that more attention should be given to the actor, the speech and the acting'. This slur, which was widely reported, angered Bridges-Adams, the more so because he knew Archie was trying to pretend that his reasons for resigning were exhaustion and ill health. He leaked the text of his second letter to the Press:

I have resigned for the sole reason that the Stratford theatre, like any other vital institution, needs from time to time the infusion of new blood. It is my hope that, by resigning myself I may encourage the local administration to face this fact, and all that the facing of it implies.

Bridges-Adams was then forty-five, Archie sixty-nine, and he had been chairman since 1903; the implication was obvious.

A public row ensued, in spite of all Archie's efforts to hush things up. For the first time newspapers began publicly criticizing the way in which the Memorial Theatre was governed. As they pointed out, although the list of Stratford governors then numbered over one hundred, including some celebrated names, very few of them attended meetings or took any part in the running of the theatre. The governing force was the executive council and that was still packed with Archie Flower's family and close friends. Its sixteen members, in 1934, included Archie, his wife, his brother Spenser and his wife, his son Fordham, Frank Benson, and Reginald McKenna who rarely attended, and at least four other people who had been friends of Archie's for over thirty years and who could be relied upon to agree with anything he proposed. Of the remaining five, who included Shaw (then seventy-eight) and Sir Barry Jackson, none seemed inclined to voice strong independent views.

Archie, upset by this publicity, attempted to heal matters, and made one further mistake: he invited Bridges-Adams to become a governor. Bridges-Adams told him succinctly to Go to Hell. This news finally filtered through to Shaw, who then made an odd and clumsy attempt to patch matters up. He admitted that he did not know the circumstances of the quarrel:

Such correspondence as I have read leaves me perplexed as to whether you and Archie are the dearest friends on earth or utter incompatibles. However, it doesnt matter now, since it is fixed up that you retire . . . But it is important that you should retire with all the honors. Your name should be connected with Stratford as the George Washington of the revolution against Bensonism . . . If you were to vanish now without any recognition of this historic position – without a peerage, so to speak – your retirement would be open to all sorts of misconstruction. The proper and only possible recognition is the offer to you of an honorary governorship, making you a privileged person in Stratford for all time . . . If I were you I should not only accept the governorship but insist on a bust or portrait in the Gallery. I assure you this is the correct *Public* aspect of the case.[32]

But Bridges-Adams, then on holiday in the Outer Hebrides, did not care a jot for the public aspect of the case. 'I really had no choice but "Go to Hell"', he answered.

I resigned, not in a momentary fit of impatience, but after at least three years consideration of the matter. My stated reason for resigning . . . as gently worded as might be, did none the less imply strong criticism of Chairman and Council. To accept a Governorship would have amounted to saying that my criticism really was not seriously meant . . . it is my considered opinion that no further progress is likely without drastic reforms, even perhaps some amendments of your Constitution. Holding views as strong as that, I can't come into the fold.[33]

What Bridges-Adams did was to put on two productions for the 1934 season that were a last throwing-down of the gauntlet. He directed *The Tempest,* using Norman Wilkinson's beautiful designs, with unapologetic spectacle. The masque scenes had elaborate and exquisite costumes by Rex Whistler; the play opened with a storm scene that used to the full the resources of his stage. A huge galleon, illuminated only by swaying lanterns and flashes of lightning, surged, heaved, and staggered on waves projected on to the cyclorama from a camera, and finally sank below the water which seemed to flood the stage. 'It is all stage trickery, of course,' commented W.A. Darlington, 'but it is stage trickery of a quality that would have driven even the designers of the old Drury Lane spectacles to impotent envy.' And then, as if to demonstrate once and for all his versatility, he directed a production of *Love's Labour's Lost* (with designs by Aubrey Hammond) of the utmost simplicity and calm, with a permanent setting of a single great oak-tree, whose branches roofed the stage and marked the progress of the play towards autumn. As soon as his highly-praised productions were on, he left Stratford and returned only for the usual ceremonies on the final night of the season. Then, both he and Archie made generously polite speeches, which disguised the very real bitterness both felt. 'If I and Sir Archie put our hands upon our hearts,' Bridges-Adams said, 'we would have to admit that there has often been friction between us. But without friction, there is no progress . . . Although we have often disagreed as to the means, we have always been at one concerning the end.' The following day he left, and for twelve years after his departure the Memorial Theatre languished and declined. There can be no question but that his resignation was a tragic mistake which should not and would not have happened had it not been for Archie's obduracy, tight-fistedness, and unwavering conviction that he knew best.

Bridges-Adams took up work for the Drama Department of the British Council and eventually retired to a house in a remote part of the west coast of Ireland to concentrate on his writing. He began a history of the English theatre, remarkable for its erudition and wit, which he never completed. He never directed in the theatre again. Over twenty years later Fordham Flower, Archie's son, who had always admired him, began to make overtures to him to visit Stratford, where the Memorial was at last enjoying a renaissance. 'No, sir,' Bridges-Adams wrote to a friend,

I'm not going back to Stratford, even if they do ask me, which they know too much, and are too proud to do. I stared at the theatre for two whole hours one wet August night, standing in the rain in the Bancroft gardens, remembering and meditating, in 1934; then went to Scotland; fished; slew a stag; came back in time for my good-bye speech at the end of the Festival, and *knew*, when I let in the clutch next morning, I should never set eyes on the place again. Too rich a memory to monkey with; it must stand, as it has done, to this day . . .[34]

7

Veering to Charybdis

The choice of Bridges-Adams's successor was made abruptly by Archie some months before Bridges-Adams tendered his formal resignation. He selected Ben Iden Payne, who had for the last twenty-one years been living and working in America. Archie's first overtures came so suddenly, and after so brief a meeting, that they surprised even Iden Payne himself, as he recorded many years later in his memoirs.

During the late summer of 1933, when the Memorial Theatre was enjoying its most successful season ever, and when Bridges-Adams's policies were at last being allowed trial, Iden Payne came to England on holiday for the purpose of visiting William Poel. Poel was by then an old man of eighty-two, and Iden Payne regarded him as his mentor; Iden Payne brought with him numerous photographs of productions he had directed in America using a method of Elizabethan staging similar to that which Poel had advocated for Shakespeare for so long. Towards the end of his holiday he visited Stratford where, Iden Payne wrote, 'I was introduced to Sir Archibald Flower . . . I happened to tell him of my recent visit to Poel, and he asked me to show him my photographs. Soon after my return to America I was surprised to receive a letter from Sir Archibald inviting me to return to Stratford, all expenses paid, to consider an offer to become Director of the Festival company. I accepted . . . '[1] This meeting, which Iden Payne does not date precisely, in fact took place on 14 October 1933, which means that Archie had decided not to renew Bridges-Adams's contract, and was making overtures to his successor, at least four or five months before Bridges-Adams resigned.[2] Iden Payne's second visit to Stratford came in May 1934, after Bridges-Adams's resignation, and his appointment was announced on 18 July. Archie, who had been so loyal and so dilatory in his dealings with Frank Benson, was somewhat less so in his dealings with Bridges-Adams. The new appointment was an example of Archie's iron whim; of his tendency to take decisions suddenly, without consultation and discussion, and of his resolute refusal, once they were taken, to deviate from them. The reason for Archie's choice was transparently clear: he believed Iden Payne to be the antithesis of Bridges-Adams. Iden Payne resembled an ageing cherub, and had a gentle, rather schoolmasterly manner, which was deceptive. It concealed a certain narrow-mindedness and some obstinacy – particularly where his theories of Elizabethan staging were concerned – but it seems to have convinced Archie that he was appointing someone who would toe the line a great deal more than Bridges-Adams had done. Members of Archie's family still consider that he made the appointment because he judged Iden Payne to be a 'yes-man', and he was not altogether wrong.

Although Archie had never seen a single production by Iden Payne, his methods provided welcome corroboration for all Archie's theatrical prejudices – particularly his belief in good clear speaking and his distaste for 'lavish' scenery or spectacle. Iden Payne was used to working in small theatres, on restricted budgets, which Archie considered another point in his favour. But his strongest recommendation was unconnected with theatre: it was the fact that Iden Payne had been working for many years in America. Archie, like many members of his family, was strongly drawn to the United States. He had his family connections there, and he had had positive evidence of the importance of American support for the Memorial. Possibly he believed that the appointment of a man who had worked so long in America would further sweeten his relationship with the American Shakespeare Foundation. If so, he was proved correct, for it was shortly after Iden Payne's first season that the Foundation finally consented to remit the £52,000 which they still held, although even then there were provisos.[3]

If Archie had been less swayed by such considerations he might have seen that there were numerous reasons why Iden Payne might not be the ideal director of the Stratford festivals. The Memorial Theatre, at considerable expense, and with Archie's full approval, was equipped with a proscenium-arch stage which did not adapt easily to the methods of staging favoured by Iden Payne. At the time of its design when the 'Elizabethan Methodists' had campaigned energetically for the erection of a platform stage and an auditorium based on Twenties reconstructions of the Globe, their arguments had been publicly rejected, both by Bridges-Adams and the governors.

Yet, in Iden Payne, Archie appointed a man who was opposed to the design of the very theatre he was to direct, and who said so from the beginning. His first, and only, public comment when he was appointed was that he was 'against the picture view of Shakespeare', and 'was rather sorry that the Memorial Theatre proscenium was thrown back from the audience'. For all the expensive equipment which had been installed in the Memorial Theatre only two years previously, and for the possibilities which that equipment afforded a director, Iden Payne had no use. He was concerned with continuing his experiments in what he called 'modified Elizabethan staging', experiments which it would have been easier to pursue in a simple church hall than in the Memorial.

There were other reasons why the appointment was ill-judged. When he became Director, Iden Payne was fifty-three. He had not administered a professional theatre for over twenty years; he was out of touch with British and European theatre, had no acquaintance with the work of contemporary British actors and found their company a strain, preferring to work with amateurs rather than professionals. Finally, according to Bridges-Adams, he had the worst handicap of all: he needed the job badly, badly enough to make him prepared to compromise from the beginning. Bridges-Adams enlightened him one day over lunch:

Told him the Facts of Life; showed him my contract (he having at that time not signed his), and locked him up for a couple of hours with all my Stratford files. I am afraid that at that time he needed the job so much that he read everything thinking to himself that this was what he must not do if he wanted to get the job. Can you imagine a worse start for the Director of the Stratford Festivals in ten-thousand a year Warwickshire?[4]

Iden Payne accepted a salary of £1,500 a year, the same amount Bridges-Adams had been receiving under his three-year contract, though his own contract was initially for a year only. But the weakness of his position was not, as Bridges-Adams somewhat bitterly suggested, solely the weakness of a salary-dependent employee versus the independently rich chairman. The position of *any* Stratford director was weak, because of the authoritarian way in which Archie ran the Memorial Theatre, and it needed a man of great will-power, with the deviousness of a machiavel and the suavity and charm of a diplomat, to circumvent it. Iden Payne was none of those things. It was virtually inevitable that the balance of power between

Archie and his artistic director, which Bridges-Adams had fought to keep even, would swing decisively in Archie's favour.

Iden Payne's early career in England had been promising. After some years as an actor, he worked for Yeats as stage-director at the Abbey Theatre, Dublin, and then for three years as director of England's first repertory theatre, the Gaiety, Manchester, where he presented strong companies (that included Lewis Casson and Sybil Thorndike) in some innovative and acclaimed work. In 1913 he left to work in America, taking a job with Charles Frohman Inc., the biggest production company on the East Coast, and his career took a turn for the worse. He stayed six years, hating it and demoralized by it, but condemned to the work by financial need. He accepted the job, he later wrote, 'with a bitter sense of shame. It meant identifying myself with the "star system" which I had always condemned.'[5] Iden Payne endured the work, the stars' temperaments, and the succession of generally mediocre boulevard plays, until 1922. Then he suddenly found himself a haven. He took up an appointment with the Carnegie Institute of Technology (now the Carnegie-Mellon University) and found in the academic world an atmosphere in which he was happy, and work which he did not despise. In 1926 he was made Visiting Professor of Drama, and there he remained until he came to Stratford in 1935. At Carnegie, and at various small American theatres, he was able to pursue his experiments in 'modified Elizabethan staging', and also to work frequently with student actors, which he liked. It was interesting, tranquil, unpressured work, free of outside interference, and generally unencumbered by box-office considerations. It was no preparation at all for the circumstances he found when he came to Stratford.

When Iden Payne arrived to begin work at the Memorial he discovered the same conditions that had driven Bridges-Adams to nervous breakdown on several occasions. The theatre was still run by a minimal number of staff: Bill Savery remained as General Manager, and Alice Crowhurst continued to be responsible for the box-office. In addition there was now Henry Tossell, an amiable man with a weakness for Stratford bars, and little theatrical experience, who was secretary to the governors and general intermediary between Archie (who had recruited him) and the rest of the staff. All three were intensely loyal and prepared to work for low salaries, but Savery was the only one with any degree of solid experience or theatrical judgement. Savery and Bridges-Adams had been close to each other and, although they had done battle on occasion, had achieved together a good working relationship. Savery continued to write to Bridges-Adams after his departure, and his letters (allowing for a certain bias) give a good indication of what happened to the company when Iden Payne took over. His first letter was written in September 1934, when Iden Payne had just arrived and was beginning preparations for his first season:

I.P. seems very keen and interested, but I hope he will . . . not overdo the scholastic touch. At the moment I feel he thinks he can teach actors to speak Shakespeare. If he or anyone else had the available time it might be possible, but there is no time. For repertory the old Shakespearian actors have to be brought in, and I doubt if their way can be altered . . . the young members of the profession will not be taught . . . they look out for L.S.D. and know that besides ourselves and The Old Vic there is no scope for them.[6]

Savery was merely restating a problem which Bridges-Adams had identified at Stratford as early as 1924, but it was a problem that Iden Payne, fresh from teaching American students to speak Shakespearian verse, and as yet unaware of the pressure of work at Stratford, was not to understand until later.

He began his plans rather as if he were launching a drama school than administering a theatre. He weeded out those members of the company who did not meet his standards. Large numbers of very young and inexperienced actors were auditioned, and Iden Payne spent hours coaching both those he hired, and those he turned down, in verse-speaking and deportment. There were long sessions in the director's office, with young actors parading back and forth with oranges on their heads to improve posture.[7] In the end, as Savery wrote to Bridges-Adams, Iden Payne assembled a company which was composed mainly of the same old-Bensonians whom Bridges-Adams had retained for so many years. By February 1935 he had realized that in order to meet the Stratford schedules and get productions on with so little rehearsal time, it was impossible to bring in many new actors. 'I have had a devil of a job,' Savery wrote, 'as I.P. would not make up his mind, so that at the last moment we had to call up all the old reinforcements . . . it goes a bit hard when time is wasted on youngsters and people that you know will never be needed . . . you can see from the company names how many *new* people came from hundreds of callers and auditions galore . . . Archie of course at the moment is full of the teaching idea; he will wake up directly.'[8]

Over two-thirds of Iden Payne's 1935 company, as Savery indicated, were inherited from Bridges-Adams, and many of them were to remain in his companies throughout the eight years he worked at Stratford. Actors like Stanley Howlett, who had worked with Benson as early as 1906, and Gerald Kay Souper, who had been in a Benson company at Stratford in 1897, had both been used, intermittently, by Bridges-Adams, and under Iden Payne took up permanent residence, along with other ageing actors like Kenneth Wicksteed and Eric Maxon, first introduced by Bridges-Adams in the early 1920s. These men, and others, formed a nucleus to the company which became over the years progressively more cliquish and more hostile to innovation, whether from directors or other actors. A director like Komisarjevsky, who combined genius with authority, could force them to work as he wanted, and could disguise their limitations by the *élan* and artistry with which he used sets, costumes, lighting, and music. But Bridges-Adams had found them problematical, and Iden Payne with his didactic manner found it impossible to change them.

Only two new actors joined the company to play major roles for Iden Payne's first season: Catherine Lacey, appearing in Shakespeare for the first time, and her future husband, Roy Emerton. Lacey was playing, among other parts, Cleopatra, and Roy Emerton was cast as Antony, a decision which horrified the traditionalist Bill Savery, who wrote apprehensively to Bridges-Adams that Emerton a) had a glass eye, b) was a film actor, and c) was 'a very rough and ready diamond *indeed*'.[9] Eight productions were to be mounted: three were revivals from the Bridges-Adams period, Komisarjevsky was to direct *The Merry Wives of Windsor,* and the other four were new productions directed by Iden Payne himself. The invitation to Komisarjevsky had now become a recurring one, and he continued to direct productions at Stratford through Iden Payne's years as Director. He became, as *The Times* put it, 'the theatre's chartered revolutionary', and his work at the Memorial was to stand head and shoulders above the other work done there during that decade. But his continuing presence at Stratford was due to the fact that Archie, and not Iden Payne, championed him. Archie appreciated the fact that Komisarjevsky productions attracted publicity and sold tickets. Iden Payne tolerated his presence but did not admire his work; its stylized brilliance was the antithesis of the simple approach he himself favoured. He made little attempt, as Bridges-Adams had done, to use other guest directors of equal calibre. Occasionally he would invite an actor in the company to undertake a production (usually a revival) but otherwise in 1935 and thereafter he chose to direct most of the plays himself, with the result that he became as exhausted and overworked as Bridges-Adams had been in the Twenties. In such circumstances the training of actors he had envisaged, which was in any case of a dubious and untheatrical kind, became an impossibility.

In 1935 Komisarjevsky produced a gay, fast-paced production of *Merry Wives* with brightly painted sets, Viennese costumes, and the general atmosphere of an Offenbach opera; indeed, some of the speeches were spoken as recitative to music. Of the four new productions directed by Iden Payne, three were produced on his 'modified Elizabethan stage' and only one, *Antony and Cleopatra*, had the services of a designer. Iden Payne begged Aubrey Hammond to produce 'austere' sets, a request that Hammond, a highly talented designer, largely ignored. When Iden Payne saw the pillars, the flights of steps, the rich costumes, the torch-bearers, he was horrified. These 'charming pictures' he considered (unconsciously echoing one of Archie's favourite phrases) interfered with the play, and 'diverted attention from the language and action to themselves'.[10] Hammond departed and never returned. For the other three plays Iden Payne directed he was safe from such excrescences; instead Stratford audiences saw for the first time Iden Payne's version of an Elizabethan stage, a device of which they were to grow thoroughly tired over the next eight years.

When William Poel had first advocated Elizabethan methods of staging Shakespeare at the end of the nineteenth century, his arguments, and his experiments, had been new and radical. To a theatre which still relied upon opulent sets and which hacked the plays to accommodate the lengthy set-changes they necessitated, Poel's work had brought a new vision and a new orientation. But by the mid-1930s other directors, like Guthrie and Komisarjevsky, were discovering ways of staging Shakespeare which involved full use of the resources of the modern stage, especially of lighting. The old arguments Poel had used, and which Iden Payne reiterated in defence of his methods – that such staging brought swifter playing, greater continuity, permitted fuller texts etc. – were no longer so relevant.

All those things could be achieved by directors like Guthrie without recourse to reproductions of a sixteenth-century stage. Iden Payne, however, was committed to it; in him Poel's vision of forty years earlier had become fossilized. He embarked upon his directorship at Stratford with an apostolic zeal, determined to prove, in lectures, talks, pamphlets, and productions, that this method of presenting Shakespeare was the one true way. Accordingly he constructed on the Memorial Theatre stage an elaborate reproduction of an Elizabethan stage, based closely on the celebrated De Witt sketch of the Swan Theatre. The resulting structure was an uneasy and inelegant compromise, drastically limiting the possibilities of the stage, and dulling the eye. Just inside the Memorial's proscenium arch an elaborate penthouse roof was erected, supported by two tall Corinthian columns of wood. Under the jutting roof there was a two-tiered inner stage; the upper part of this acted as a balcony, and the lower as an inner room, or cave, or tomb – whatever was required by the text. Both inner rooms were curtained, and Iden Payne used 'curtain boys' (two actresses dressed as page-boys) to open and draw these when necessary. Occasionally, in an unhappy admixture of Elizabethan and more modern traditions, he incorporated painted scenery into this edifice: the lower curtains, drawn back, might reveal a garden vista on a canvas drop, or the interior of a room. The upper balcony was frequently used to group supers, who would hang over its rails in the full Tudor fig Iden Payne favoured, and watch the events going on below. The whole edifice was rendered the more ineffectual because there was no extension to the forestage, so that the acting area (on a stage over forty feet deep) became shallow and confined. Nor was it easy to light, because of the overhanging penthouse roof.[11]

In 1935 Iden Payne used this staging for *All's Well that Ends Well*, (a play rarely performed at Stratford), and for two of the hardiest perennials in the Stratford repertoire, *The Merchant of Venice* (with Ayrton as Shylock), and *The Taming of the Shrew*. Neither these productions nor the hastily reassembled revivals were greeted warmly by the critics; Komisarjevsky's *opéra bouffe* version of *Merry Wives* caused predictable outrage, and *Antony and Cleopatra* received mixed reviews. This had no effect on the box-office whatsoever. The theatre itself still had curiosity value; the tourists continued to visit the Shakespearian shrines in ever-increasing numbers, and the attendance figures for the season climbed again, to reach a new peak of 150,000. Helped by the fact that in 1935 the

Memorial was, for the first time, exempted from paying entertainment tax on the festivals, an increased surplus was made of £9,720.[12] It was becoming clear, as Bridges-Adams had predicted, that whatever the standard of productions at the Memorial they were virtually assured of an audience – a state of affairs bound to engender complacency. But complacency was the last risk that the governors, particularly Archie, feared. After so many years of precarious existence it was difficult for them to realize that a larger theatre, longer seasons, increasing tourism, had changed the Memorial forever. The ghosts of old financial troubles still haunted them, and it was not surprising that the new phenomena of full houses and increasing surpluses should become their criteria for success. Within a year of Bridges-Adams's departure it was obvious that what progress he had been able to make was already being eroded. The idea of inviting guest directors and designers of international stature was dropped; his plans to enlarge the company, to tour, to take productions to London, were dropped. Iden Payne saw as clearly as his predecessor the need for much longer rehearsals, for staggered openings, higher salaries, and production budgets, but he never risked the kind of aggressive confrontation on these points that Bridges-Adams had done. He complained periodically, but he was no match for Archie, and under his aegis there was actually a regression. The rehearsal period shrank once more; it was down to five weeks for seven opening productions in 1936.

Given these conditions of work, lack of prestige, and low salaries, it was hardly surprising that Iden Payne failed to attract new actors to Stratford. He found a number who promised well, but because the companies were still under strength, these young actors were constantly required to play parts beyond their range. Peter Glenville, for instance, joined the company in 1936 at the age of twenty-two, two years out of Oxford where he had scored notable successes with the OUDS. At Stratford he was called upon to play Romeo, Petruchio, Mark Antony, Feste, Hector, and other roles, all in the same season. Not surprisingly, he suffered under the strain, received progressively poor reviews, and gave up playing Petruchio after a few weeks. He did not return to Stratford again and neither did the Cressida and Juliet of that season, Pamela Brown, one of Iden Payne's most notable finds. Several other talented young actors joined the company during the years 1939-42, including Joyce Bland, Trevor Howard, Alec Clunes, Geoffrey Keen, Clement McCallin, and the slightly older Donald Wolfit. None of them remained more than two seasons. From the peace of exile, Bridges-Adams saw clearly that there would be a decline: 'My own view,' he wrote to Bill Savery, 'is that as Stratford has elected to go local rather than national, it must stew in its own juice until so big a storm is raised that Stratford will have to revise its policy altogether.'[13]

By the mid-Thirties that storm was already well overdue. It came finally in 1938, but for the two years before that Stratford won a stay of execution thanks to the work of three men: Komisarjevsky, Randle Ayrton, and Donald Wolfit. Their contribution in those two years was such that it eclipsed the general failings of the company and drew attention away from the retrogressive policies instigated by Archie. Komisarjevsky and Ayrton were assets Iden Payne inherited from Bridges-Adams; Donald Wolfit he discovered himself. All three came together to work on the production which was the great success of the 1936-7 seasons, and one of the greatest productions at Stratford that decade – the Ayrton/Komisarjevsky *King Lear*.

Apart from his production of *Macbeth*, *Lear* was the only Shakespearian tragedy Komisarjevsky directed at Stratford. It was equally as radical and unconventional a production as the *Macbeth* had been, but it was received with almost unqualified praise, helped by the fact that it had at its centre (as *Macbeth* had not) a monumental single performance, Randle Ayrton as Lear, giving what was in effect his farewell to the stage. As many traditions had adhered to *King Lear* as they had done to *Macbeth*. In particular, it had become the convention to set the play in a vaguely early-English setting, with Lear and his entourage in Druidic robes. Gielgud, for instance, in Harcourt Williams's 1931 Old Vic production, wore flowing white robes emblazoned with a scarlet Celtic pattern. Bridges-Adams followed this convention closely in all three of his productions of *Lear* at Stratford, in each case using a set like Stonehenge, with a rough circle of huge stones and costumes suggestive of some shaggy Nordic/Celtic culture. Komisarjevsky came to the play wishing to abandon such conventions, and also to rid himself of the reputation he had for deliberately impudent staging. 'I am producing it', he told the *Observer* in March 1936, 'for the sake of the acting, and not for the *mise-en-scène*. I have no sets (except the simplest) and no *décors*. I am not giving it a "barbaric" atmosphere or surroundings or costumes, because to my mind there is nothing barbaric about the

play. It is inspired by the ideas of the Renaissance period . . . ' Like
many of Komisarjevsky's remarks this was somewhat misleading.
True, he removed from the production all suggestion of a Celtic state,
and the set *was* simple – a permanent staging consisting of angled
flights of steps which almost filled the stage. Both steps and the
cyclorama behind them were lit with coloured light, which changed
with the mood of the play. It was, in its simplicity, flamboyantly
theatrical and occasionally extremely obtrusive. To Ivor Brown of
the *Observer* it 'unhappily suggested the site for a big production
number in a revue'. Most other critics did not agree with him, but the
actors disliked it also. The steps were constructed so narrowly that it
was almost impossible to walk straight up or down them except on
tiptoe, and most elected to negotiate them sideways, in a crablike
fashion.[14] Komisarjevsky, concerned with visual impact, did not
consider such matters. Apart from the flights of steps the stage was
totally bare for the whole production, and Komisarjevsky relied
solely on the use of light to convey not only mood, but also to define
location. The play began with Lear seated on a golden throne at the
very top of the steps, flanked by his courtiers, the staircase lined on
either side by rows of attendants holding aloft long slender golden
trumpets which they slowly raised as the curtain went up, 'A
spectacle which,' wrote the *Birmingham Mail,* 'when its full glory
burst upon the senses, drew applause from the crowded house'. Once
Lear had divided his kingdom, the action and the light moved
symbolically downwards, to the foot of the steps, while the throne, in
shadow, descended into the depths of the stage. Such was the
spectacle that not one critic complained that Komisarjevsky had cut
the preliminary opening scene of the play.

Most reviewers found that the bareness, and Komisarjevsky's use
of light, emphasized rather than weakened the sense of elemental
forces at work both in nature itself and within the characters. 'The
storm scenes', wrote Darlington in the *Telegraph,* 'are carried
through without any scenery at all. The only effect is given by
scudding green and black clouds in an angry sky; yet never before
had I so clearly the feeling that I was out in that tempest.' This
dramatic use of light, which marked all Komisarjevsky productions,
was an innovation in Britain. Komisarjevsky was using techniques
that others, like Gordon Craig, had experimented with, but which
were not to be widely used in the English theatre for at least another
thirty years. Now, perhaps, his use of coloured light might seem

crude or overstated, but in 1936 it was a bold attempt at freeing the plays from laboriously literal sets, bringing possibilities of a new poetic intensity to the action. *Lear* was a production filled with ideas which might fruitfully have been explored and the fact that it was to have artistically no influence at Stratford at all was perhaps the worst indictment that could be made of the Memorial Theatre, its director, and its policies.

Randle Ayrton had played Lear at Stratford twice before, but the acclaim which greeted this performance was in part due to a production which did everything to emphasize the power of his acting. Those who saw it, and those who acted with him, agree that Ayrton was one of the greatest Lears of this century. There was, perhaps, something of Lear in Ayrton's own strange temperament; difficult, crotchety, remote, suspicious, capable of conveying such passion on stage that it could galvanize an audience, Ayrton knew that this production would mark his last performance as Lear. He was sixty-seven and did not have long to live, although there were then no signs of the heart disease which was to cause his death four years later. He could bring to the role an old man's understanding, and the same harsh unsentimentality which had marked his Shylock, his Henry IV, his acclaimed Enobarbus.

At the outset he is already trembling on the edge of senile decay; a gnarled, snarling, vehement figure of unreasoning impulse, easily amused, easily deluded by words, as easily blinded to the eternal verities. His progress to disillusionment is pitifully rapid and direct, his struggle against complete madness pitifully futile. It is a performance in which majesty and helplessness, dominion and pathetic submission to stronger wills are perfectly blent. Mr. Ayrton does not now command oratorical power with the ease of former years, but he can still give – and does give – a Lear such as the younger acting generation cannot even conceive.[15]

Ayrton had received high praise, such as this in the *Birmingham Mail*, from local critics before. This time it was echoed to the full by the national critics. 'Here is a *Lear*', wrote *The Times*, 'worth a long journey to see.'

The production was revived the following year in 1937, and then Randle Ayrton retired to his house on the outskirts of Stratford to run a theatre school. Had his performances in the great Shakespearian roles been given in London (say at the Old Vic) rather than at Stratford, there can be little doubt that his achievements would have been remembered, and discussed, for years to come. As it was, they have been largely forgotten except by those who actually saw him, or worked with him. His influence on Donald Wolfit, who was in the 1936 and 1937 companies and played Kent to his Lear, was particularly strong. Wolfit acknowledged it, and also its immediate influence on his own conception of Lear, which he played to great acclaim some years later.

Wolfit came to Stratford at a crucial point in his career, even (he considered) at a crisis point. He was thirty-four years old, and had been acting since he was eighteen, gaining none of the recognition he felt was his due, and which he saw being given to John Gielgud, his direct contemporary. His bitterness and dissatisfaction had been intensified by his season at the Old Vic (with Gielgud playing the leading roles) in 1929-30, at the end of which his contract had not been renewed. He passionately wanted to act in Shakespeare, but had had, he felt, too few opportunities. When Iden Payne invited him to come to Stratford he accepted with alacrity. Arriving there, he was very much an unknown quantity. The *Stratford Herald,* called upon to introduce this young man to its readers, could think of nothing better to say than that here was an actor 'with a wide range of dialect parts'. He was given the roles of Orsino, Ulysses, Cassius, Gratiano, Kent, and Don Pedro. It was a good range of parts and was improved later when Peter Glenville fell ill, and the part of Petruchio fell into his lap. Then, halfway through the season, Iden Payne decided to direct *Hamlet,* and cast Wolfit in the title-role. This was an astute move of Iden Payne's for Wolfit had received ecstatic praise for every part he had played, and the announcement that he was to play Hamlet attracted a good deal of publicity.

Wolfit was happy at Stratford. He liked Warwickshire, and had a romantic attachment rivalling Frank Benson's to playing in the town where Shakespeare had been born and lay buried. He had earned, as he put it, 'golden opinions' for his performances, and he admired, and was learning from, Randle Ayrton, whose Lear he called magnificent, and whose Shylock was, he wrote, 'the finest study of the part I ever saw'.[16] Hamlet was still regarded, as Wolfit was well aware, as that 'hoop, through which every eminent actor must, sooner or later, leap'. He approached the hoop with his customary combination of pugilism and self-confidence.

On the first night Ayrton came into his dressing-room two minutes before his call was due. 'I saw the face of the old warrior reflected in the mirror', Wolfit wrote. 'He touched me lightly on the shoulder:

"Give them a bit of the old," he said, and vanished . . . '[17] 'A bit of the old' was exactly what Ayrton, and Wolfit, were able to bring to Shakespeare. In both men's acting there was a roughness (sometimes amounting to crudity), a histrionic daring, and a ruggedness that were far from fashionable in the theatre of the 1930s. Critics, struggling to define this quality in Wolfit's performances, would compare him to what they thought an earlier generation of actors must have been like – actors such as Burbage. Naturally they had little idea of what Burbage *had* been like, but they recognized a vigour, a masculine attack, which was remote from the more delicate approach favoured at that time. Not for nothing was Gielgud already acknowledged as the Hamlet of his generation by the kind of critics who took pleasure in such labels. Gielgud's classical approach to the part, developing a tradition handed down from Forbes-Robertson, had established Hamlet as a prince of finely-shaded sensibility, his appearance both beautiful and romantic, his words delivered in exquisitely modulated cadences. This fashion did not augur well for Wolfit's Hamlet. For a start, according to popular conception, he did not *look* right. His strong-planed features and large athletic frame did not suit a character conceived of as princely, elegant, and possessed of a matinée-idol's profile. James Agate was later to write of Wolfit as Hamlet that his reluctance to put paid to his step-father's account was 'almost as inexplicable as it would be in the case of a heavy-weight boxer, or a Woolwich Arsenal centre-forward . . . there is no aloofness, and little suggestion of the princely; this is a bourgeois Hamlet'. At Stratford Wolfit did his best to conform physically to the taste of the time, and photographs of him in the part show him achieving surprising success. Dark, slightly wavy hair fell across his forehead; pale make-up, and carefully painted eyes, brows, and mouth, softened and romanticized the strength of his own features. His costume was totally traditional: a white shirt open at the throat; a suit of black velvet; a medallion around his neck showing a portrait of his father. But in his acting Wolfit seems to have made no attempt to conform to the taste of the time; his Hamlet was 'rough-hewn, passionate, dangerous and in danger'. It is a measure of its power that it was highly praised, although it was so against the contemporary grain. It elevated him, his biographer Ronald Harwood considered, to 'the ranks of the leading players',[18] even though it had the added disadvantage of being given not in London but in Stratford.

Wolfit played both Hamlet and Kent again in the revivals in 1937. He was also a fine, wolfish Iachimo in an interesting masque production of *Cymbeline* by Iden Payne, the Chorus in *Henry V*, Touchstone, Autolycus, and Ford (one of Ayrton's favourite parts when younger). Then, at the end of the season, he decided, as he put it, to 'don the mantle of the actor-manager', and form his own touring company. The fact that he was prepared to do this, with only his own savings of between five and six hundred pounds as backing, was a further illustration of the unadventurousness of the Memorial Theatre and its governors. The Stratford company was supposed to tour; it had been one of the theatre's articles of intent that the plays should be taken out (as the governors' reports had somewhat hyperbolically put it) 'to audiences far and wide in the great cities of the world'.[19] Since Bridges-Adams had left, no Stratford company had ventured as far as Birmingham, let alone further afield. Yet, far from being pleased at Wolfit's enterprise Archie Flower was put out to learn that one of his leading actors was preparing a nine-week tour at the end of the festival, and was taking with him a large section of the 1937 company. Wolfit received a summons to The Hill. 'He told me severely,' Wolfit wrote, 'that such a scheme as I had in mind was most inopportune, and frankly quite impossible . . . he assured me that I should lose every penny I could find to back me, that others had gone out and come limping home without a rag to their backs . . . '[20] The confrontation between Archie and Wolfit, each such formidable autocrats, must have been worth witnessing. Wolfit refused to be browbeaten, and Archie – in a gesture of magnanimous parsimony – finally agreed to lend him some old and unused costumes from the Stratford wardrobe. At the end of the season Wolfit duly set off, ignoring Archie's doom-laden prophecies. He completed the tour with some success, and did not lose a penny on it. It is extraordinary, in retrospect, that Archie did not seize upon this opportunity and give Wolfit his backing. Here was one of the most gifted actors in the Stratford company, eager to take a company on tour; had he helped Wolfit, he might have retained him for further Stratford seasons and also built up once more a touring company, as the theatre was committed to do. But he did not. Both men were, in any case, probably too temperamental ever to have worked in harness together, but the fact remained that Wolfit, with virtually no money, pulled off a tour and proved Archie wrong. The Memorial Theatre continued to pretend that actors could not be persuaded to tour (it made the engagement too long) and that reliable dates could not be obtained.

Wolfit left Stratford with a parting gift from Randle Ayrton: the whip he had used as Petruchio. He never returned. The same year Ayrton retired and, at a stroke, the theatre lost the services of two of the best actors ever to work there. With their departure the flood-gates of angry criticism opened, just as Bridges-Adams had predicted they would. From 1937 onwards both Archie and Iden Payne were in a siege position, assaulted on all sides by hostile attacks on their work, on the system that produced it, on the policies of the governors. Their response, in both cases, was to nip smartly back inside the castle and pull up the drawbridge against the 'crabbers', as Archie was pleased to call them. The criticisms rained down: Iden Payne suffered them; Archie rejected them; and the governors, drilled into obedience for years, bowed their heads to the inevitable.

The battle was begun by W.A. Darlington in the *Daily Telegraph*, at the end of the 1937 season. Darlington attended more productions at Stratford than any other national critic and had been one of the theatre's most persistent attackers since 1920 – sometimes unfairly so. His often-quoted assessment of Stratford as compared to the Old Vic, 'For team-work and acting the Old Vic has it nine times out of ten', was made in 1921, when Bridges-Adams's work had scarcely begun and when Darlington himself had attended only two brief seasons at Stratford. Some of Darlington's criticisms seem to have been influenced by his dislike of Archie, clearly apparent in much he wrote; others stemmed from intimacy with members of the company and directors, who conveyed to him in private the appalling conditions under which they had to work. In what he wrote about the Memorial in 1937, however, Darlington was unbiased and accurate. His criticisms were contained in a long article, which came to one major conclusion:

Every criticism I have made can be met fully and completely by the expenditure of cash . . . one thing is wrong and one only. The new theatre is being run, so far as productions are concerned, on the same scale as the old one. The authorities who carried on so heroically in the old days, running short seasons of plays, often at a heavy loss, have not adjusted themselves to the new conditions in which a season lasts six months, and plays to a steady profit.

Archie's reply contained all the old fusty hallowed arguments: that it was still the governors' cardinal belief that a different play must be mounted each night; that star actors would not come to Stratford because it interfered with their lucrative film-work, and that in any case the theatre could not afford star salaries of £50 a week; that rehearsals could not be 'extended indefinitely'. Most of this was rubbish.

Although the theatre had been enlarged by a further 150 seats during 1936, it was still turning away patrons from its more successful productions (Komisarjevsky's for instance) because the repertoire was so large, the seasons only six months, and too few performances of each play were given. The audience was no longer a local one, expecting different plays every night. It would have been perfectly possible to open a season with two or three productions and to introduce others later in the season. It would have been possible to tour, so that these productions had a longer life, and could recoup their expenses. Salaries could have been raised, and rehearsal periods lengthened; larger companies were well within the theatre's means. All these changes, which Darlington had advocated, would have helped to raise standards, and it was above all the generally mediocre standards – the belief that the theatre was no more than a parochial rep – which kept leading actors away from the Memorial. The Old Vic paid equally poorly, and had, admittedly, the advantage of being situated in London, but the Old Vic could draw major actors for Shakespeare because of its prestige and the growing quality of its work under Guthrie. It was in any case becoming increasingly risible for Archie to continue to plead poverty. Parts of the governors' annual reports, including the figures for the previous year's operations, were published each year, and there was no arguing with the figures: Stratford was rich.

From the year the new theatre opened, as Darlington had said, each festival produced a surplus. To begin with they were comparatively small, though adequate. Under Iden Payne's direction, when spending was, at Archie's behest, kept to a minimum, they grew annually to alarming proportions. Rounding off to the nearest figure, the season of 1935 made a £10,000 surplus, and in the next three years it never fell below £13,000. The exact surplus for 1937, the year Darlington launched his attack, was £13,486, of which £6,000 came from productions and the rest from miscellaneous sources such as rents from properties, catering, cloakrooms, and so on. None of this surplus was invested in the productions for 1938. £2,000 went to the theatre's fund for needy actors. £1,250 was spent on enclosing a riverside loggia to improve the facilities of the conference hall; £2,160 was spent on a new scenery store, and the rest was diverted to the theatre's swelling reserve fund. [21]

In spite of the blandness of his letter to the *Daily Telegraph* Archie was stung by Darlington's criticisms. He drafted two long private letters to him in reply, neither of which he sent. Both repeated the excuses made in the *Telegraph* letter, and both contained the following sentence: 'I always see all the plays through at first and generally feel rather unhappy about it – then I go away to Scotland to fish and when I get back often find it hard to believe it is the same company. I wish you had seen them again before you wrote, for then I could have attached more weight to what you felt . . . '[22] It was characteristic of Archie that he could see nothing funny in this bizarre statement. Since he went to Scotland to fish each year for three months, from the beginning of May until the end of July, he was admitting that as far as he knew the first three months of the six-month season were below standard – a quite extraordinary admission from the chairman of the theatre's governors.

Instead of sending these letters, Archie sought Darlington out at the Garrick Club in London, presumably hoping to lend the weight of his personality to his arguments. He then returned to Stratford secure in the belief that he had headed Darlington off. He was wrong.[23] By the end of 1938 the attack had swollen to a climax, fuelled by the fact that that year's season was one of Stratford's poorest on record. With the exception of Komisarjevsky's witty *Comedy of Errors*, the remaining seven plays were directed by Iden Payne. The company, affected by the departure of Ayrton and Wolfit, was weak.

Mr. Iden Payne appears to ask little more of his actors save that they should speak their lines clearly and intelligibly. By this curious compromise [the modified Elizabethan staging] he misses both the simplicity of the bare Elizabethan stage, and the persuasiveness of the picture stage . . . Most of the acting, responsive to the producer's almost morbid fear of theatricality, gives an impression of flatness . . .

So wrote Charles Morgan in *The Times*, and in the *Observer* St John Ervine commented that the company was 'the worst I have ever seen at Stratford. I do not know why the company . . . is so poor. I only know that it is, and I venture to prophesy that unless a very great improvement in the acting *and* in the production takes place promptly, the Memorial Theatre will find itself without an audience.' Other critics besides Darlington noted the anomaly that a theatre making a large annual surplus was prepared to spend money improving facilities such as the conference hall and restaurant, but not on improving the standard of its work.

For yet another year large profits have been made, both in the supply of Shakespeare and of cakes, coffee and ale. Once more the year's surplus . . . enables extensions and improvements, really capital charges, to be paid out of ready money. So much for cash. What of cachet? Somehow or other the well-endowed and highly prosperous Stratford theatre will have to find new outlets for its profits. It cannot build tea-rooms for ever.

But in spite of widespread comments such as this from Ivor Brown in the *Manchester Guardian*, Archie and his fellow governors seemed impervious both to criticism and to irony.

The governors' report on the 1938 season was couched in a particularly ridiculous way, guaranteed further to inflame criticism. The poorly received productions were dismissed in one sentence, and the governors then went on to congratulate themselves at length on the number of dinners and teas that had been served, and the increased profits derived from them. 'Theatre funds have benefited to the extent of £2,575,' they announced triumphantly. To congratulate themselves on such sums from such sources was ridiculous enough, in view of the standard of work the theatre was producing. But it was even more ridiculous in view of the reserve funds which, by that time, the theatre had at its disposal, figures which were *not* published and therefore could not be used as ammunition by critics. By the end of 1939 the Memorial's assets, swollen by careful investment and penny-pinching, had grown to the sum of £366,414.[24] It was a measure of Archie's financial caution that with this kind of reserve he was still proud to make a catering profit of some £2,000, and was still adamant that salaries and production budgets could be increased only minimally.

Unfortunately for Archie and Iden Payne, the contrast between Stratford's affluence and the poverty of its work was emphasized by the flowering of the work at the Vic, still genuinely a poor theatre. In 1937 Tyrone Guthrie had assembled one of the greatest companies ever to work there, including Edith Evans, Michael Redgrave, Alec Guinness, and Laurence Olivier (playing a full-text Hamlet, Henry V, Sir Toby Belch, and Macbeth). Olivier returned to the Vic for part of the 1938 season, playing Coriolanus, and Iago to Ralph Richard-son's Othello. These were productions that could only highlight the shabbiness and second-rate quality of the majority of Stratford productions, and they were achieved on equally small budgets. They made the Vic the lodestar for any would-be classical actor. Anthony Quayle, for instance, who began acting in 1931 (and after the war became Director at the Memorial) shared the ambition of many young actors: to join the company at the Old Vic. Stratford he never considered at all.

In November 1937 Lilian Baylis died, and in April 1938 Guthrie again revived his appeal for some kind of alliance between the Memorial Theatre and the Old Vic.[25] The idea was immediately taken up by several influential critics, including Ivor Brown and St John Ervine, and was used as a further bludgeon to attack the Memorial. Clearly, they argued, an alliance between the Memorial, with a lot of money and no prestige, and the Old Vic with much prestige and no money, made sense. Guthrie persisted in his overtures throughout 1939. He was acting largely for pragmatic reasons, and he was quite open about this, as he made clear in a letter to Iden Payne that October:

I think I should say frankly that one is aware that in making overtures to Stratford the Vic is in the undignified and suspect position of a poor relation making overtures to a rich one. It would be foolish to pretend that the Vic would not be the financial gainer, and Stratford the financial loser in an alliance. But, seeing that the object of neither body is to earn private profit, I still feel hopeful that your governors may take a generous view of the matter; the more so since they recognise that the Vic has certain assets that can usefully be pooled in such a partnership . . . [26]

This was tactfully put. The Old Vic's assets (as Guthrie was well aware) included not only a London theatre, but some of the finest actors in the country and, above all, himself, a quixotic but brilliantly original director.

His suggestion was not a new one, and it was to be made again in various forms over the next twenty years. In 1939, given the state of Stratford's productions, it had many things to recommend it, particularly since Guthrie was not envisaging immediate and total amalgamation (difficult in view of the two theatres' different charters) but rather increased co-operation between the two companies, beginning with a joint tour. Had Guthrie been dealing with Bridges-Adams he would almost certainly have met encouragement. He had championed such an arrangement as early as 1922, and he would have seen the advantages for Stratford. But Guthrie was dealing with Iden Payne, who was cautious and ready to bow to Archie's wishes in the matter. 'I have been entirely non-committal,' he told Archie, sending him Guthrie's letter.[27] Archie, naturally, was against the idea. He would never countenance any suggestion which threatened Stratford's autonomy, and therefore his own. And, since he considered that the standard of work at Stratford was adequate, Guthrie and the Vic held no attraction for him.

The degree to which Archie had, by this time, turned his face to all suggestion of change or reform was marked in his private correspondence. He received many personal letters of criticism about the Memorial almost all of which echoed exactly what the critics had been saying for the last two years. His defence was the one which has been used by commercial managements on Broadway or in the West End from time immemorial: the box-office cannot lie. His adoption of it in old age (he was then seventy-four) showed how far the idealism inherited from his uncle had been conquered by his own obsession with the balance sheet. The sad and paradoxical fact was that Archie, who had devoted a major part of his life to the Stratford theatre, and without whom the new building would not have existed, was, from the moment that building opened in 1932, the very force holding it back. None of the many reforms advocated by the Memorial's critics was possible while he remained chairman, and while his appointees ran the theatre. By the end of the 1930s it was clear that Bridges-Adams had been right: if the Memorial was ever to achieve the stature that Archie had wanted for it, it was Archie who had to go.

The last season at Stratford before the declaration of war with Germany was also the Diamond Jubilee of the theatre. In celebration of that fact (and not in response to criticism) more money was spent. Several guest directors were brought in; Irene Hentschel (the wife of Ivor Brown), Robert Atkins, Komisarjevsky, and Baliol Holloway all undertook productions, leaving only three in the hands of Iden Payne. The company was strengthened by the presence of four leading men – Holloway, James Dale, the young Alec Clunes, and John Laurie, returning to Stratford for the first time for twelve years. Both Clunes, playing among other parts, Benedick, Petruchio, Iago, and Coriolanus, and Laurie playing Othello, Malvolio, Jaques, and

Richard III, received high praise for their work. But Laurie was not happy under Iden Payne's direction. He found him 'dull, finicky and anaemic, with no understanding of actors – he treated them like school-children'.[28] Great time and trouble had been expended on the production of *Richard III*, which had elaborate neo-Gothic sets and faultlessly correct period costumes by Herbert Norris, but Laurie found the sets old-fashioned and over-elaborate, constantly impeding the action of the play; he categorized them as 'tuppence-coloured'. The most innovatory production from the design point of view was Irene Hentschel's *Twelfth Night*. She was the first woman to direct at Stratford, and she brought in a team of designers, Motley, who had worked frequently with Gielgud and with Michel Saint-Denis and George Devine at the London Theatre Studio. They were to work constantly at Stratford in the 1950s. They set the play in an austere and frankly artificial garden. The women's costumes were early Victorian, and Olivia and her household wore heavy mourning. The production was praised for its originality and verve, and for the delicacy of its staging – in such marked contrast to the heavy-handed pictorial approach generally favoured at Stratford. But the production caused controversy mainly because of the playing of Olivia as a spoilt young heiress rather than the conventionally mature and sympathetic heroine. This innovation, which could be well justified by the text, startled and displeased the critics. It was one example among many of how easily attitudes to Shakespeare's plays could become entrenched, and of how necessary it was to challenge them.

This function of theatre, to reinterpret and rediscover the classic plays by returning to the text and examining it without preconception or prejudice, was particularly vital at Stratford, where directors and companies were working almost exclusively on the plays of one dramatist.[29] It was a function that Stratford generally failed to undertake. One of the most remarkable things about the Diamond Jubilee season and the Memorial's productions generally after sixty years of existence was the predictability of its directorial vision, which hampered even the most talented of its actors. It could be seen most clearly in the staging of the plays, in the use of debased Edwardian-style sets, in the fustian and conventional costuming, in the waxwork groupings of supers. But it was not just the staging which had fossilized; the playing of certain scenes, the conceptions of many characters, even decisions about the texts, once taken, remained sacrosanct. Iden Payne, like Bridges-Adams before him, worked from old prompt-books when redirecting the same play, so that again and again cuts, transpositions and business used the first time he directed a play remained the same in all succeeding productions. *A Midsummer Night's Dream* provided the worst example of this process. It was given five times (directed by different people) during the years 1937 to 1944. Yet on no occasion was it given a completely fresh production. Instead progressively debased elements from Norman Wilkinson's superb 1932 designs were reused. First both his sets and costumes were preserved; then parts of the sets with the original costumes (now delapidated); finally new sets were introduced, made up of a hotch-potch of standard drops from the stores, together with a bizarre array of costumes containing some original dresses unhappily married with other oddments totally unsuited to them.

There was, finally, no recognition that Shakespeare's plays had any relevance to a modern audience. During the decade of the Thirties, the decade of depression, of widespread unemployment and political unrest, of the Spanish Civil War, and the rise of European Fascism – all events that left their mark on the work of a generation of British artists – the work at Stratford continued serenely unaffected by the turmoil of the outside world. It was as if the Memorial Theatre existed in a world of its own, hermetically sealed against events outside. Shakespeare was treated, not as a writer who transcended his era, but as an Elizabethan dramatist, his plays museum pieces as remote from the experiences of modern audiences as those of John Lyly.

An example of the way in which this insularity and misplaced reverence affected the work at Stratford was the last production in the 1939 season. This was *Coriolanus,* directed by Iden Payne, and it opened on 9 May, just three and a half months before Hitler ordered the invasion of Poland. By May conscription in Britain had already been introduced and war with Germany seemed inevitable. Of all the plays in the canon *Coriolanus,* with its complex and impassioned political argument, its subtly balanced dialectic, its investigation of democracy and authoritarianism, was a play that had obvious and immediate relevance to the events which were at that very moment dividing Europe. Yet Iden Payne's production appeared totally unrelated to and unaware of those events, and was cocooned in theatrical traditions from the past. It was played in a Palladian set, with the Romans in Elizabethan costume, and the Volscians resembling refugees from a Turkish harem. Most of the political argument of the play was cut; the production relied heavily on the crowd spectacle traditional at Stratford since Bridges-Adams's first production of the play in 1926. Iden Payne's chief concern was to defend his use of Elizabethan costume, rather than togas. It seems to have occurred to no one, certainly not the critics, that the play was as much about the Europe of 1939 as it was about primitive Italian warring states. The *Birmingham Mail* described the plot as centring on a by-election. *The Times* brought out the well-worn opinion that 'the play smelled of the oil-lamp and was clearly born of the literary process'; Darlington, in the *Daily Telegraph,* stated (with equal lack of originality) that the play had 'little of the subtle humanity of Shakespeare's best work'. Both these assertions could be traced back at least as far as 1912 and A. C. Bradley's commentary on the play.[30]

When war was declared the Memorial Theatre closed, reopening just over a month later on 9 October. It was announced that the seasons would continue, although the theatre was beset with problems. Few younger actors were available because of enlistment; the plays had to be severely cut to finish before black-out; at the beginning of the war (before servicemen swelled their numbers) audiences dwindled. Yet the seasons did continue, and for the next three years Iden Payne continued to direct them, relying heavily on the services of Baliol Holloway both as an actor and as a director (not his forte). The war threw Archie into a panic about finance, and the entire staff and company were at first put on reduced salaries. In the first year of the war the theatre did make a small loss of £404. Archie immediately claimed that his much-criticized financial caution was vindicated. But his claims were premature. From 1941 onwards the theatre made a substantial surplus on each of the wartime seasons, which never fell below £8,000, and reached a peak of £23,000 in 1944.[31] But although the Memorial Theatre was able to continue its charmed life despite the exigencies of war, it was at last recognized that change in its artistic policies was inevitable. A new voice began to make itself heard on the theatre's executive council, that of Lord Iliffe, who had succeeded Lord Burnham as President in 1935. On several occasions during the war Iliffe acknowledged that there must be change, that more money must be spent. He expressed himself cautiously, but the acknowledgement was made.

Like Burnham, Iliffe was a press baron. Unlike him, he was to have some considerable influence at Stratford, and to make the title of President into something more than a purely honorary one. Unfortunately Iliffe's financial astuteness and his finesse in committee, qualities which were later to be of influence in the Memorial's affairs, were not harnessed by Archie during the Thirties. The two men seem to have had a wary respect for each other, and Archie kept him at arm's length. When Iliffe began to speak out about the Memorial and allude to future change, his words always carried the proviso 'after the war', and the phrase carried with it a secondary meaning. For Archie was ill, although the fact was never publicized, and it was only his illness that enabled Iliffe to comment at all; 'after the war' meant after Archie's retirement.

One evening in 1941 Archie suffered a severe stroke. He recovered completely, with no paralysis, but the attack effected a sudden and extraordinary change in his personality. From that moment onwards he lost all interest in the activities which had been the mainspring of his life. The town council, the forty committees he had sat on, the Birthplace Trust, even the Memorial Theatre, all the affairs and institutions which had been his consuming interest for over half a century suddenly became of no concern to him. He took up an invalid's life, spending much of the day wrapped in rugs on a sofa at The Hill, looked after by a nurse, and simply closed his mind to all the projects he had fought for for so long. His daughter-in-law, Hersey, Lady Flower, recalled the suddenness of this transformation. 'It was', she said, 'as if the committees, the theatre, had never existed. All he cared about was one thing, that Fordham [her husband, Archie's eldest son] should come back from the war and carry on where he had left off. I think if he had not been determined on that, and determined to see Fordham again, he would simply have turned his face to the wall.'[32] This sudden affliction in the man who had – for good and ill – been the driving force at the Memorial since the turn of the century, left a vacuum in the theatre's affairs. Everyone – the governors, the director, Bill Savery, Henry Tossell, the entire staff – had been used to taking his cue from Archie for over forty years. The habit of obedience to his wishes was so ingrained that, even after his illness, they continued to consult him. In the absence of new directives they muddled on, frightened to make changes, terrified to take a decision of which Archie might have disapproved.

Many people of Archie's generation who had been associated with the Memorial for years died during the war. It marked a further watershed in the theatre's history, a break between the rule of those associated with it since Edwardian days, and the new generation who came after. Sir Frank Benson died in a bed-sitting room in Holland

Road, Kensington, frail and alone, looked after in his last years by his landlady. Randle Ayrton died in 1940, only three years after opening his theatre school. Spenser Flower, the brother closest to Archie, died at the beginning of the war. Many of the older governors died, including the actress Mary Anderson, whom Archie had often consulted, and Canon Melville, who had been involved, years before, in the Benson syndicate. Those older members of the governing board and staff who, like Archie, lived on, clung tenaciously to the past as their numbers dwindled. They knew Archie's state of health, but that intensified their loyalty to him, and their resistance to change. Mrs Melville, Canon Melville's widow, became the theatre's deputy chairman. Like her husband she had been associated closely with the theatre for over forty years, and she remembered the 'dark times', as she called them, when they had 'not known where to turn for money, and so had turned to themselves'. 'I have always consulted Sir Archie,' she said, 'and I always shall. Whatever he says should be done, will be.'[33] But Archie had withdrawn behind the shield of his invalidism, and was issuing no directives. All that was known was that he wanted his son to succeed him as chairman, so everyone patiently awaited the end of the war and the return of Fordham Flower from active service. Until then no one, not even Lord Iliffe, was prepared to risk reform.

In the meantime the theatre had three changes of director. At the end of the Stratford season of 1942, Iden Payne resigned. There was no publicity; he simply departed as quietly and suddenly as he had arrived. The immediate reason was that he had been offered a lecture tour of America; the real reason that he had found a chance to escape from work which had become increasingly frustrating. Like Bridges-Adams he had been worn down by the job of director, and his health had suffered. It was not surprising that when he had a chance to return to America, he took it. He later became Visiting Professor of Drama at the University of Austin, Texas, a position he held until the age of eighty-eight. He was able to pursue his experiments with Elizabethan staging and work with student actors; he died in 1976 aged ninety-five. In his lengthy memoirs, *A Life in a Wooden O,* he dismissed his eight years' work at Stratford in a few brief paragraphs.

He was succeeded by Milton Rosmer, who had had a long career as an actor-manager, who stayed at Stratford for only one disastrous season, and whose departure was anything but quiet. Rosmer made public his reasons for resigning in a series of letters and interviews. It was, he said, 'in the nature of a personal protest . . . against the inadequacy of the festivals'.

Rosmer was followed by Robert Atkins, who imparted some of his customary panache to the festivals and gave them a temporary injection of life. Atkins, a man who had done battle in his time with Lilian Baylis, was not one to be easily thwarted, and the publicity surrounding Rosmer's departure gave him a certain leverage for reform. He was able to make some changes at the Memorial. He built on a forestage, and greatly improved the standard of design. He reintroduced touring to the provinces prior to Stratford openings, and he secured for himself a notably higher salary. His second season at Stratford, in 1945, was well-received and attracted a great deal of publicity nationally, largely due to the fact that Atkins had in his company the young and extremely beautiful Claire Luce, playing Cleopatra, Beatrice, and Viola. The blonde Miss Luce's voluptuous charms dazzled the critics to such a degree that they devoted columns to her artistry. Periodicals such as *Picture Post* gave considerable space to photographs of her as Cleopatra, scantily clad, heavily made-up in the Hollywood manner, a serpent of Old Nile whose salad days were clearly far from over. The young Anthony Quayle picked up one of those magazines in an officers' mess overseas, and remembered it afterwards; it was the first time it had occurred to him that the Stratford theatre might offer possibilities to an astute director.[34] Certainly the publicity surrounding Miss Luce helped to attract a record audience of 250,000 people to the festival, producing the record surplus of £23,000. For the first time the Memorial Theatre had been given a hint of what could happen when a 'star', even a film star, appeared there.

While Atkins was still director, on 23 April 1944, the long-awaited transference of power from Archie to Fordham Flower took place. Fordham was granted special leave from his regiment and went to Stratford to attend the executive council meeting. He was stationed in an ante-room while his father, making a rare expedition from The Hill, chaired his last meeting behind closed doors. Archie informed the governors that his son was waiting outside, and that he wished to be succeeded by him. No voice was raised in dissent; there was no discussion of the matter. Fordham was finally ushered in, and formally invited to occupy the chair. He accepted. Next day he was back with his regiment.[35] He remained on active service until August 1945, and then returned to Stratford. As soon as he returned, all his father's roles descended upon him. The Birthplace, the town council, the theatre, the brewery, the countless committees, all the organizations his father had worked for now looked to him. Within days there was a deputation from the town asking him to be mayor.

The main and immediate problem at the theatre was who should be its post-war artistic director. Atkins seems not to have been seriously in the running, and forestalled any embarrassment by resigning that August. In October his successor, who was to play a key role in the future evolution of the Stratford theatre, was announced. It was Sir Barry Jackson, the founder and director of the Birmingham Repertory Theatre, who had been a governor at Stratford since 1929.

Jackson and Fordham Flower together took over the running of a theatre whose assets, by the end of the war, totalled a remarkable £446,581, but whose prestige was nil. Both made it clear from the beginning that they knew radical changes had to be made, and that they were prepared to make them. 'May it never be said again of the Governors of the Stratford-upon-Avon Theatre,' Fordham Flower said in his first public speech as chairman, 'that the tinkle of silver and the rustle of notes deafened their ears to the criticism and comments of their many well-wishers.' It was a brave remark, the braver since it was against his own father that that allegation had chiefly been made.

8

Decay and Change

Sir Barry Jackson was a man of habit. He lived in Malvern, but it was his custom when working at his theatre, the Birmingham Rep, to stay at the modest Station Hotel and to eat all his meals at a corner table in the hotel's dining-room. He was in Birmingham, and at that hotel, when the offer to become artistic director at Stratford was first made, and one of the first people to whom he confided the news was the young Peter Brook, then aged twenty and just down from Oxford. Jackson had just given Brook his first major break by giving him a production to direct at Birmingham; he had also taken him under his wing, protecting him from the Rep's stage management (who were very suspicious of this schoolboy director who turned up for rehearsals in a tomato-coloured suit), obtaining for him a room at the Station Hotel and issuing constant grave invitations to luncheon or to dinner. It was over luncheon at the corner table, when Brook commented on Jackson's unusual air of elation, that the news was broken. Jackson announced that he was going down to Stratford to look over the Memorial the next day, and asked if Brook would like to accompany him. Flattered and excited, Brook agreed. The visit was, however, something of a shock. The two men found a building in which the ravages of wear and war had gone unchecked. Elizabeth Scott's modernist palace had weathered the last thirteen years badly. It had become a theatrical Satis House, a place where time had stood still, and where decay had been allowed to take its course. With mounting depression Brook tramped round an auditorium with torn carpets, sagging seats; a stage hung with filthy tabs, much of its machinery damaged and unrepaired. Backstage they found a now badly out-dated switchboard, no Tannoy, a litter of unclassified scenery, and everywhere hampers of musty smelling costumes. The theatre that had been hailed as one of the most advanced in Europe had fallen on hard times.

The urbane Sir Barry, to Brook's amazement, surveyed it all with equanimity. He gave the younger director a sharp glance, smiled, and lit a cigarette in his long holder. 'Oh yes,' he said finally, 'I think we could turn this into another Salzburg, don't you?'[1]

Jackson was not a young man when he took on the task of renovating and revitalizing the Stratford theatre. In 1945 he was sixty-six, precisely the same age as the theatre of which he became director. He came to the Memorial with an almost unmatched record for fine, brave, innovatory work that went back to 1913, and a high reputation as an administrator, director, and as a discoverer of some of the finest actors to emerge during the first half of this century. His connections with the Memorial, direct and indirect, went back to the year of its opening.

He was born in Birmingham on 6 September 1879, a few months after that first one-week season at the new Stratford theatre. He was given the Christian name 'Barry' in honour of one of his father's favourite actors, Barry Sullivan, who that year had given his Benedick and ill-fated Hamlet at the Memorial. His father had founded the Maypole Dairy chain of grocery shops, and had made for himself a considerable fortune. Barry Jackson was his second son, and the youngest child in the family by ten years. He was brought up in a succession of large houses on the fringes of Birmingham, in an atmosphere not dissimilar to the upbringing of Charles Flower's family of nephews and nieces. His father was a liberal Victorian businessman interested in the arts, and with a passion for theatre. The Jackson home boasted a good library; the walls were hung with the paintings of contemporary Victorian artists, and there was a family tradition of amateur theatricals in which Barry, a late child, was too young to participate. He was frequently taken to the theatre as a little boy, and his first introduction to Shakespeare was the plush opulence of the old Theatre Royal, Birmingham, and the swaggering braggadocio of Frank Benson as Petruchio. Isolated from the rest of his family by the ten-year gap, he was further isolated from his contemporaries by his father's decision to have him educated by a tutor rather than sending him to school, and by eighteen months in Geneva studying French rather than a period at an English university. As a boy he read with an only child's voracity, plundering the books in his father's library; his first colouring book was the pictures in Staunton's edition of Shakespeare. He grew up marked by that childhood – erudite, widely cultured, speaking several languages, but somewhat wary of friendship, and close to only a few chosen people. He was also homosexual.

His father's death, in 1906, left him, at twenty-seven, a very rich man. Nancy Burman, who knew him for many years and was his production manager at Stratford, considered that his wealth cut him off from other people: 'It didn't exactly make him suspicious, but it made him cautious, because, of course, only too often people were trying to get something out of him.'[2] But not everyone who knew Jackson would agree with this; Peter Brook, for instance, found him 'an essentially simple, direct man. An English gentleman of a kind that is now virtually extinct. He was kind, formal, impeccably courteous certainly, but I never thought of him as aloof.'[3] Jackson's inheritance changed the course of his life. It meant that he was free to pursue whatever line of interest he liked, and that meant, not architecture, for which he had trained, but theatre. In 1907, the year after his father's death, Jackson, together with his friend John Drinkwater, gathered a group of amateur actor friends together to form the Pilgrim Players. They performed in places like the St Jude's Mission Hall and the Edgbaston Assembly Rooms, and between 1907 and 1912 produced twenty-eight plays including works by Shakespeare, Ibsen, Yeats, and Shaw. The theatre Jackson founded, paid for, directed, and nursed for the best part of his life, grew up from these amateur theatricals in a way which would not be possible today, when distinctions between theatre amateurs and professionals are sharp, and the gulf between the two difficult to traverse. But these amateur origins left their mark on both Jackson himself and the Birmingham Rep, in a willingness to experiment and take risks, in a simple dedication to work, in enthusiasm, and in a distrust of the glitter of show business.

Jackson first approached an architect friend about building his theatre in April 1912. It opened, less than a year later, in February 1913. It was the fourth repertory theatre to open in Britain, and of those four precarious enterprises only Birmingham and Liverpool survived long beyond the First World War.[4] The reputation that the Birmingham Rep earned itself in the post-1918 period was due very largely to Jackson's gifts as an administrator, to his refusal to compromise over repertoire, and to his uncanny ability to perceive talent in the untried and inexperienced. The survival of the Rep was due to his determination, and to the fact that he was prepared to subsidize it himself. It has been estimated that between 1913 and

1934 (when the theatre was taken over by a local trust) Jackson lost over £100,000 of his own money on the enterprise.[5] Because of this personal subsidy the Rep was able from the first to put on a programme of work that was consistently bold and far-sighted, and that made little concession to its frequent unpopularity with local audiences. Much of the work, inevitably, for the Rep put on a large number of new plays, was ephemeral and quickly dated, written by authors now long forgotten. But mixed with this new work was an amazingly catholic pot-pourri of plays that reflected Jackson's own scholarship and the breadth of his interests. He introduced audiences to many of the rarely performed Shakespeare plays, and was the first man to mount modern-dress Shakespeare productions. There was a constant diet of plays by Jackson's close friend, Shaw, including the first performance of his marathon *Back to Methuselah*. Even in the early 1920s, when their work was still little known in England, there were productions of Chekhov, Ibsen, and Strindberg. There were plays by contemporary authors such as Maugham, Eden Philpotts, Bridie, Barrie, Coward, Lonsdale, St John Ervine, Pinero, and Synge. There were revivals of virtually forgotten Elizabethan and Jacobean plays; restoration plays; nineteenth-century actor-manager vehicles like *The Corsican Brothers*, mixed together with verse plays from Auden and Isherwood and the work of then little-known European playwrights such as Capek, Schnitzler, Giraudoux, Molnar, Kaiser, and Andreyev.

During the years Jackson ran it the Birmingham Rep became famous not only for the daring of its repertoire, but also for its ability to attract many young actors who went on to become major figures in British theatre: it was a training ground for Laurence Olivier, Ralph Richardson, Gwen Ffrangcon-Davies, Cedric Hardwicke, Margaret Leighton, Paul Scofield, and many others. Jackson never lost his capacity to take a risk on young talent; it was typical of him that he was prepared to risk employing the extremely inexperienced Peter Brook as a director in 1945, and to entrust him in his first season with *Man and Superman, King John*, and *The Lady from the Sea*, thus beginning a theatrical partnership (for Paul Scofield appeared in all three productions) which was to bear fruit over the next twenty years. But Jackson's theatrical activities were not confined to Birmingham. He had spectacular successes, and spectacular failures, on the West End stage, the successes – such as *The Apple Cart* and *The Barretts of Wimpole Street* – helping to subsidize the work at Birmingham. His companies toured abroad and in the provinces. He was also the founder of the Malvern Festival, which he directed from 1929 to 1937, and it was perhaps significant that, while the Memorial found it so difficult to tempt London critics to Stratford, Jackson had no difficulty in persuading them to troop off annually to the Malvern Hills.

Jackson made the move from Birmingham to Stratford at a key moment in the Memorial Theatre's history. The war was over, and for those who survived it there was a deep-felt need to start building something new, a wish which carried a Labour government to massive victory at the polls in 1945. What Anthony Quayle called 'this surge of post-war energy and idealism' was felt particularly at the Memorial, not just because of the war years, but because of the stasis which had affected the theatre for years before that. Reforms had been promised; the funds were there to pay for them; the theatre had both a new chairman and a new director to effect them. Jackson might not be a young man, but everything about his past record suggested that he was just the man to bring the changes that were needed.

Certainly the Press thought so. Jackson's appointment was widely welcomed, not just by the Midlands newspapers where he had many friends, but by national critics like Darlington of the *Telegraph*, and Victor Cookman of *The Times*. He entered the Memorial on a tide of approbation and applause: 'We never realised,' wrote the *Birmingham Mail*, 'how much bigger than the Rep he is . . . He is emphatically the man for Stratford if the Governors desire to make it at once the world force and the National Theatre which it could, and should, be . . . ' Any residual doubts which journalists might have had about Stratford's intentions were removed by the way in which the new chairman and Lord Iliffe greeted his arrival.

On 21 January 1946 Iliffe gave a luncheon for the governors and the Press, to introduce Jackson as director and announce the details of his first Stratford season. The luncheon was an extraordinary occasion for a number of reasons, not least because it was held at the Savoy Hotel in London – the last venue on earth to which any journalist used to the old ways of the Memorial would expect to be invited. The engraved invitations had the desired effect. The reception was a glittering affair attended by numerous celebrated actors, producers, and critics, including James Agate, Beverley Baxter, and Sidney Carroll – all of whom had been conspicuous for their indifference to Stratford in the past. Even scouts from the William Hickey column turned up. Fordham Flower had prepared a remarkable speech, a public *mea culpa* on behalf of the governing body, and its tone was unequivocal:

The Governors have imposed upon themselves a little frank self-examination. There was a time when we were too prone to measure our achievements by the intake at the box-office, or the shape of the balance-sheet. Today, however, the Governors are determined that quality in acting and production should take precedence over profits, and to prove that the charge of local complacency is no longer valid . . . The Director *must* be the key man of the theatre, responsible only to the Governors, and he must be given more latitude and power than has been the practice at Stratford in the past.[6]

There could have been no more accurate an assessment of the theatre's history, no more frank an acknowledgement of it, and no clearer a statement of intent. Barry Jackson's way appeared to be clear.

In spite of this speech, Fordham Flower remained very much an unknown quantity. He was, after all, his father's eldest son, and there were many who feared that, for all his protestations, it might be a case of 'Amurath an Amurath succeeds'. Fordham seems to have been assessed completely differently, according to how well people knew him. To those who had brief, or marginal, acquaintance with him, there was Lieut.-Col. Flower, Wykehamist, Sandhurst trained, professional army officer, a conventional product of his upbringing, whom such people were inclined to underestimate. To those who knew him well, there was 'Fordy', a man of great warmth, of mercurial flights of enthusiasm, a superb organizer, a brilliant committee-man, someone who could recognize, and who respected, creativity in others: in short, the perfect person for the job. Those who did not know him well might underestimate him, but they respected him; those close to him speak of him now with an unmistakable and unqualified regard. He was, without question, a much-loved man, a fact to which his three living artistic directors, Anthony Quayle, Glen Byam Shaw, and Peter Hall, all pay eloquent testimony. And that, as anyone familiar with the relationships frequent between theatre directors and the heads of their governing bodies will know, is an extremely rare phenomenon.

From his earliest childhood Fordham was immersed in the affairs of the Memorial Theatre. When he was six years old he walked on in the production of *The Merchant of Venice* in which Ellen Terry was playing Portia. In his teens he ran a 'Festival Club' during the Benson seasons, where members could take tea and join in discussions about productions. During the Twenties he became a close friend of Bridges-Adams and it seems to have been his admiration for Bridges-Adams that first caused him seriously to question his father's policies for the Memorial. After Winchester, he followed a family tradition of entering the army. He went to the Royal Military College, Sandhurst, was commissioned in 1924, and from 1924 to 1932 served with the 9th Queens Royal Lancers in Palestine, Egypt, and India.[7] In 1932, when he decided to leave the army, he returned to Stratford and took up the work expected of him as heir apparent, entering the brewery as junior director, following his father on to the town council, the Birthplace Trust, and numerous local organizations. In 1934 he married Hersey Balfour, a niece of Dame Edith Lyttelton.

Fordham was immensely loyal to Archie, but not blind to his failings, and having the example of Archie's autocracy always before him seems to have been crucial in making him the very different man he was from his father. His wife considered that, unlike Archie, Fordham had a very clear knowledge of his own limitations. The prospect of taking on the chairmanship of the Memorial worried him greatly; he knew that reforms had to be made but he felt that as far as theatre was concerned he was an amateur, and that what the Memorial needed urgently was to be run by a professional. 'What am I going to do?' he asked her, when he was appointed; '*I* don't know how to run a theatre.'[8] What he did, initially, was to downgrade the role of chairman, and insist, as he had done in his Savoy Hotel speech, that the director of the theatre must have greater power. But Fordham had been a career soldier, and he did expect other qualities from his theatre's director besides professional expertise; in particular he expected what he termed 'leadership' – his concept of leadership being defined in a somewhat military way.

His new director was not a man who easily fitted this concept. Jackson was reserved; he continued to live at Malvern, and disliked the social activities connected with the Memorial that provided a chance to promote its new policies. He could be tactless: backstage he knew everyone, from the master carpenter to the cleaners, and he was quite likely to stop a cleaner in the foyer and ask her how her asthma was, and then fail to recognize a governor immediately behind her – a tendency that did not endear him to some governors. Even with his companies he was somewhat retiring. His gift was for finding good people to work for him; then he would not interfere, but let them proceed with absolute freedom – and this was sometimes interpreted as unconcern by those who did not know him well. He was much older than Fordham – too old to have served in the war, so they lacked that common experience – and his manner, erudite, urbane, slightly mandarin, was not one to appeal to Fordham, who was always drawn to those of powerfully expressed enthusiasms. But more important than any of this, their relationship began on a bad footing.

Jackson insisted from the first that if he was to administer the Memorial properly, he had to have the right staff. Bill Savery, Alice Crowhurst, and Henry Tossell were still running the theatre. To Fordham they were a little like old family retainers; he had known Alice Crowhurst and Savery since he was a boy and he knew that they had given most of their lives to the Memorial. All three were elderly. Alice Crowhurst had worked for the theatre for fifty years; Savery, as manager, for over thirty; Tossell for twenty. Someone had to sack them, or persuade them to resign, or send them into honourable retirement. However it was done, or phrased, it was painful, and neither Fordham nor Barry Jackson wanted to do it. Savery retired, with a pension, before Jackson's first season – Fordham having broken the news to him. By the end of that season it was obvious that Alice Crowhurst and Henry Tossell would have to go too. Fordham tried to persuade Barry Jackson that this time they must tell them jointly. According to Lady Flower and others, Jackson could not face it, and retreated to Malvern. Fordham never forgot, nor wholly forgave his cowardice. When he told Tossell he would have to retire, Tossell burst into tears: thus Fordham severed the last links with his father's regime. If the theatre was to be administered professionally it was obvious these three elderly people could not do it, and a colder man might have retired them without a qualm. But to Fordham, a man of intense loyalties, it was traumatic; Barry Jackson's refusal to be involved was, in his eyes, a failure of responsibility, and of leadership, and on that note their working relationship began.

Jackson's first season of 1946 was a complete break with the past. He brought in a completely new company consisting mainly of young actors, and resolutely refused to employ anyone who had ever appeared at Stratford in the old days – a decision that caused lasting bitterness to actors like Baliol Holloway. Eight plays were in the repertoire, each one directed by a guest director; Jackson chose not to direct himself. Each play was given a full month's rehearsal, and only three plays were in repertoire each week. Their openings were staggered throughout the season. These reforms aroused intense opposition in Stratford. Many of the hotels had been closed, or requisitioned, during the war, and the local hoteliers were looking forward to starting up their businesses again, secure in the knowledge that many Stratford visitors would stay several days, even a week, in order to see a large number of plays. If that were no longer possible, what would happen to their revenue? Angry letters began appearing in the *Stratford Herald*; the governors were lobbied; Jackson turned a blind eye.

The directors for that first season were an extremely odd and heterogeneous bunch. They included Brook, still virtually unknown, directing *Love's Labour's Lost,* with Paul Scofield as Armado. There was Eric Crozier, a young director who had made his name in opera and who was, like Brook, considered adventurous, and who was responsible for the opening production of *The Tempest*. There was Nugent Monck, a Poel disciple who was nearly seventy and who had for years run the amateur Maddermarket Theatre, directing *Cymbeline*. Dorothy Green, Benson's old leading lady, directed Scofield as Henry V, and Michael MacOwan, previously a West End director, and Frank McMullan, an academic who had just succeeded Jackson's friend Allardyce Nicoll as Professor of Drama at Yale, were also invited. This was, indeed, casting the net wide; no matter how hard Jackson had tried he could hardly have collected together a more dissimilar group of directors, all working in totally different styles, and with a company largely unknown to any of them. He wanted to create a permanent company of younger actors who could be developed. He had little wish to employ stars, and in any case the Memorial's reputation was so low few would have gone there. The term 'second eleven' is rather unfairly associated with his choice, and Jackson did better than the description implies. His leading players were Robert Harris and Valerie Taylor. Harris, if not a star in the Gielgud league, was a good, experienced, sensitive actor, and a great improvement on many of the leads Stratford had seen in the recent past. Valerie Taylor was then a film and West End actress of some repute, whom Brook considered 'fine, fragile and sensitive, and something of a catch'. Apart from this, the new company had some promising young actors, Donald Sinden among them, and one trump card – the virtually unknown Paul Scofield.

The beginning of the season was chaotic. The old guard, in the shape of Alice Crowhurst, Henry Tossell, and Barbara Curtis, a stage-manager who had ruled the backstage and the costume departments for a considerable number of years, were still *in situ*. Meanwhile, the new guard, Nancy Burman from Birmingham as productions manager, Jackson himself, his assistant and Press officer Tom English, the new company and the assortment of new directors, were endeavouring to take over in a theatre hopelessly ill-equipped to deal with the scale of work being done. Supervising it all was Bill Savery's replacement, the new general manager Leonard Crainford, who Jackson considered had metropolitan experience but who lasted only two years in the position. Crainford hired a number of new stagehands and they settled down extremely ill with the old survivors of the Barbara Curtis regime. Hostilities developed on all sides, and neither the old hands nor the new were ready to deal with the demands being made upon them by the new crew of directors. The confusion was exacerbated by the numerous vital repairs to the theatre's stage equipment which had not yet been made.

The opening production was Eric Crozier's *Tempest*, which had a highly elaborate operatic set by Paul Shelving. It had been giving problems, and Jackson was worried about it. But after the dress rehearsal the old stage carpenter assured everyone that it would be all right. In fact, nothing went right. The second production was the dull, and extremely heavily cut production of *Cymbeline* by Nugent Monck. The season could not be said to have got off to a good start. The third production was Brook's *Love's Labour's Lost*, and Brook, having witnessed the confusion surrounding *The Tempest*, was nervous about it. In fact it went without a hitch, the production became the hit of the season, and Brook, at twenty-one the youngest director ever to have worked at Stratford, was launched. His reputation quickly grew from local to national; it modulated from boy wonder to *enfant terrible*. One newspaper, perhaps having heard Jackson's description of him as 'the youngest earthquake I know', compounded it with his plumply beneficent appearance, and described him as 'a teddy-bear filled with dynamite'. Brook has been scathing about the Stratford he found when he came to work on this production. 'Every conceivable value', he wrote, 'was buried in deadly sentimentality and complacent worthiness – a traditionalism largely approved by town, scholar and Press.'⁹ His judgement, if harsh, was accurate – certainly of the attitudes that had prevailed at Stratford in the twelve years since Bridges-Adams's departure. And yet the work he did in that first season was not without precedents at Stratford; to an extraordinary degree it chimed with the earlier work of Komisarjevsky, a man whose productions he had never seen, and whom he never met.

The production of *Love's Labour's* is usually remembered now as 'Watteau-esque', and Brook did base many of his ideas for it on Watteau's *L'Embarquement pour l'Île de Cythère,* an influence detectable in the grace of the groupings and the pretty artifice of the costumes, which Brook felt were 'the ideal visual correlative of the play's essential sweet-sad mood'. But if Watteau was an interesting correlative for the aristocratic young lovers, journeying from illusion and artifice to greater maturity, it was difficult to see how that vision fitted some of Shakespeare's other creations in the play – Armado, for instance, or Costard. Brook made no attempt to make them fit; the production teemed with ideas that owed nothing to Watteau. The Princess was accompanied by a chalk-faced *commedia dell'arte* clown, who never spoke; Constable Dull was a Punch-and-Judy policeman with a truncheon and a string of sausages; Armado was a sixteenth-century grandee whom Velázquez might have painted. The play began with insolent aplomb by confronting the audience with a gigantic drop on which was painted a great barred gate and the words of the King of Navarre's proclamation banning women, writ large like a song-scroll in a pantomime. The production was far more heretic, rag-bag, and anarchic than the adjective 'Watteau-esque' conveys.¹⁰ It was played fast, except for the famous long silence that greeted that messenger of death, Mercade; it had a delight in artifice as great as that of any of the characters, and it was *funny*, belying the play's reputation for difficult-to-comprehend jokes. The whole affair, wrote *The Times*, 'had a puff-ball lightness'. The audacity of some of the sets, the rejection of consistency, the carefree mixing of visual styles and the resulting unpredictable homogeneity, all these things Komisarjevsky would have delighted in. Brook's *Love's Labour's* of 1946 was the spiritual heir of Komisarjevsky's 1932 *Merchant,* poetic justice at last, when Komisarjevsky's great contribution to the production of Shakespeare had been ignored at Stratford for so long.

It was fortunate for Jackson that the production was the runaway success it was, and it was fortunate that he had Paul Scofield in his company, whose gifts were immediately recognized. Together they saved a season that was otherwise not notably interesting. But Jackson had opened doors, taken risks, let air into a building that had been stifling with conformity for years, with the result that the season played to packed houses, in spite of petrol rationing, in spite of there being no great West End stars in the company, and in spite of the fact that the repertoire contained no less than four 'unpopular' plays: *Cymbeline, Love's Labour's Lost, Measure for Measure,* and Marlowe's *Dr Faustus.* It did not, however, make a surplus, as the *News Chronicle* reported in January 1947:

This week I saw and heard something I would not have believed possible: a theatre director announcing, with a broad smile, and a note of pride in his voice, that under his direction a theatre had shown a financial deficit . . . It is immensely refreshing to find a man who is obviously more interested in theatrical standards than in a whopping surplus year after year . . .

Barry Jackson announced a deficit of £13,385, the largest loss a season at the Memorial had ever sustained. When revenue from other sources was balanced against this, the deficit shrank to £5,993 – still more than the theatre had ever lost in a year before.[11]

Jackson, who had had twenty-one years of fairly consistent deficits at Birmingham, was not likely to be upset by such figures, particularly in a first season that had involved changes backstage, and in a theatre with assets as large as those of the Memorial. The governors were still, however, deeply imbued with the habits of financial caution. Their nerve was being tested, perhaps not yet too severely, considering the theatre had liquid assets in the form of investments that, in 1946, totalled over £190,000.[12] A surplus of £23,000 had been made in the previous year alone, and it had been foreseen that costs would go up. But far from cushioning the blow, the scale of the reversal from 1945 to 1946 was such that trouble was brewing after only a year of the new reforms. 'This theatre is heading for bankruptcy!' trumpeted one of the governors, Captain Cunningham-Reid, at the next governors' meeting. It took the combined efforts of Fordham Flower and Lord Iliffe, aided by that gentleman's silky finesse in committee, to squash him.

Cunningham-Reid became the spokesman for those governors who were for many different reasons becoming disgruntled with the new

way in which the Memorial was being run. He was Fordham
Flower's cousin, and had been a governor of the Memorial for some
years, another of the numerous Flower wives, aunts, cousins, uncles,
and sisters brought in by Archie. It turned out in his case to be an unfortunate act of nepotism that caused endless problems. Cunningham-
Reid was a politician, author, and something of a playboy. After his
marriage to, reputedly, 'the richest girl in England', his activities had
made him a favourite subject for the gossip columnists of the day,
with the result that when he decided to 'speak out' about the way in
which the Memorial was governed, directed, and generally administered, his remarks were given vastly inflated publicity, and widely
reported in every newspaper from *The Times* to the *Daily Mirror*.
His speciality at this time was the disruption of governors' meetings
by provoking argument about matters either already decided or
entirely irrelevant. Quite what moved him to speak out once his
cousin became chairman is uncertain; he had preserved, as far as the
records show, a marked disinclination to speak at the meetings he
had attended before that. But once Fordham was in the chair he
launched his attack. He had begun, in fact, as early as April 1946,
selecting with perfect timing the moment when Jackson's first season
was just beginning. Then it had been the role of the governors and
the autocracy of the previous chairman which had been his target.
'We have been treated like shop-window dummies,' he announced.
'It is quite wrong that we have been called together only once a year,
and that our only function has been a subservient chanting of Yes,
Yes, Yes . . . ' All this was quite true, though it might have been more
impressive had it been addressed at the time to the chief culprit,
Archie. But it was now less relevant. Fordham had already
announced that full governors' meetings would now be held every
quarter, and he had acknowledged quite frankly the embarrassment
of the number of Flowers on the executive council. At the very
moment Cunningham-Reid made his highly publicized criticisms the
conditions for governorship were in the process of being changed, as
he certainly knew. The old prerequisite, the donating of £100 to the
theatre, which went back to 1875, was being abolished so that more
people with genuine expertise and interest in the theatre could be
invited to become governors. But, as Cunningham-Reid also knew,
this could not be done overnight because it involved changes to the
theatre's Royal Charter.

Cunningham-Reid made a number of other embarrassing remarks

during 1946, in particular about the level of salaries being paid to actors. On learning that the top salary had been raised to £50 a week, he announced that this was too low: the theatre should be paying £100 to £300 a week, like the West End. The poor salaries, he considered, explained the 'lack of front rank talent' in that year's festival company. This was hardly the most tactful thing for a theatre governor to say, especially at the beginning of a new season. The company was understandably furious; Valerie Taylor demanded a public apology, and rumours of writs fluttered back and forth. At the end of Jackson's first season, however, Cunningham-Reid switched his attack to the profligacy of the Jackson regime, apparently seeing no inconsistency between demanding £300-a-week salaries one moment, and presaging bankruptcy for the theatre the next. He was here on much stronger ground, and although he was not formulating any clear or useful policy for the theatre, he became a rallying-figure for other governors and the spokesman for all kinds of generalized dissent. Some governors supported him because they too feared overspending; some because they believed the general governing board rather than the executive council should have more say in the day-to-day decision-making of the theatre. Others simply could not stomach Barry Jackson's policies.

This opposition reached a climax at the end of 1946, when it was known Jackson's first season had made a substantial deficit, and when Jackson's term of office, and power, was increased. His contract was extended from the initial two-year period to three years, so that it expired at the end of 1948; and he was made Director of the Theatre, rather than just Director of the Festivals, as all his predecessors had been. This meant that Jackson was responsible not only for the festivals but also for the hire of the theatre during the winter (previously the province of Henry Tossell). Both were necessary moves; if Jackson was to effect change at the Memorial he needed time, and two years was too brief. And it was clearly ridiculous that the director of the theatre should have no influence over the quality of the winter seasons, which had in the past been unambitious, relying heavily on performances by local amateur opera and dramatic societies, or productions hastily got up by Memorial actors like Baliol Holloway. Jackson wanted to change this, making Stratford into an important touring date for the best pre-West End shows and for companies like the Royal Ballet, thereby making the winter seasons an important source of revenue. These two decisions, coupled with the fact that the previous season had lost money, caused a discernible split in the governing body. A feud developed between, as one governor put it, 'Local' and 'London', and Fordham found himself with something of a palace revolution on his hands. The local contingent objected to practically everything Jackson had done: to the increased seat prices (up in 1947, with a modest top price of ten shillings and sixpence); to the reduction in the number of plays in repertoire each week, and its effect on the livelihood of local hoteliers; to the curtailment of the town's use of the conference hall, which was no longer to be so frequently available for local functions; to the new winter-season policy, and Jackson's distaste for the amateur performances which had always played such a cosy part in Stratford Decembers; and – above all – to the fact that the theatre was losing money. The London contingent, so categorized because its ambitions for Stratford were national rather than parochial, was led by Fordham and was committed to expansion, to turning the Memorial at last into a major, prestigious British theatre. This contingent was understood to support Jackson.

The feud extended beyond the confines of the governors themselves, and began to affect, for the first time, the whole relationship between the town of Stratford and the theatre. It marked the point at which a certain hostility between the two bodies began, a kind of town/gown division still extremely palpable in Stratford today. The theatre's refusal to placate local interests caused great resentment and had numerous repercussions. It made it extremely difficult, for instance, for the Memorial to obtain a liquor licence for its restaurant – the application being seen as another attempt to take bread from the mouths of local hostelries. And it meant that Fordham Flower's later attempts to get the theatre's rates reduced (arguing that the theatre brought tourists to the town and that since Stratford contributed nothing to the upkeep of the theatre this was a comparatively painless way of helping it) were doomed from the first to failure. Jackson, meanwhile, in the face of this vociferous hostility among the governors, and dislike within the town, was trying to get the theatre machine in working order again. The scale of the problems he faced is perhaps one of the reasons why he left his general manager and directors to get on with the production side of the theatre. During 1947 he wrote a long report for the governors about the state of the theatre as he found it, and what he was doing to amend it. It made blackly entertaining reading.[13]

King John, 1948; one of the productions which marked the beginning of the post-war renaissance in the work at Stratford. Robert Helpmann (centre) in the title-role. Directed by Michael Benthall, designs by Audrey Cruddas.

Peter Brook's second and highly controversial production at Stratford, *Romeo and Juliet*, 1947, with revolutionary designs by Rolf Gérard. Laurence Payne (facing camera) as Romeo and John Harrison as Benvolio in the opening scenes of the play.

Michael Benthall's 1951 staging of *The Tempest*, III. iii, Alonso and the spirits. Michael Redgrave (bottom right) as Prospero. Designs by Loudon Sainthill.

Right, Paul Scofield as Hamlet and Claire Bloom as Ophelia in the play scene from Michael Benthall's 1948 production. Sets and costumes by James Bailey. *Below left*, John Gielgud as Lear and Alan Badel as the Fool in Anthony Quayle and John Gielgud's production of *King Lear*, 1950, with designs by Leslie Hurry. *Below right*, *Henry V*, the final production in Anthony Quayle and Michael Redgrave's 1951 Histories season, with Richard Burton in the title-role and Hazel Penwarden as Princess Katharine.

Peter Hall's first production at Stratford, *Love's Labour's Lost*, 1956, with designs by James Bailey. Geraldine McEwan (seated centre) played the Princess of France.

Glen Byam Shaw's much acclaimed 1953 production of *Antony and Cleopatra*, with Michael Redgrave and Peggy Ashcroft in the title-roles.

Peter Hall's 1959 production of *Coriolanus*, with Laurence Olivier (right) as Coriolanus and Anthony Nicholls as Tullus Aufidius.

Anthony Quayle as Aaron in Peter Brook's celebrated 1955 production of *Titus Andronicus*. Laurence Olivier played Titus, Vivien Leigh, Lavinia.

Glen Byam Shaw's final Stratford production: *King Lear*, 1959, with (left to right) Albert Finney as Edgar, Anthony Nicholls as Kent, Charles Laughton as Lear, and Ian Holm as the Fool.

From guttering to sewers, the Memorial was in a mess. The exterior and interior of the building needed extensive repairs and redecoration. The auditorium was shabby, and needed recarpeting and new seating. Stage machinery and lighting equipment, never serviced or repaired, was broken, dangerous, and frequently non-functional. Dressing-room and office accommodation, ill-planned from the first, was inadequate; there were not enough telephones for the offices to function properly, and the existing switchboard needed replacing; in order to pass from the front of house to the offices, staff had the choice of going outside the building or walking through the auditorium. Costumes and scenery were in an appalling state, unclassified, and unstored. Nancy Burman found hundreds of baskets dumped all over the theatre, full of priceless costumes made of brocades, silks, and velvets – all unobtainable materials just after the war – and all eaten by moth, threadbare, and musty. There were no workshops for the building or painting of sets. Plinths, pillars, ramps, steps, frames, canvases, all in short supply and expensive, had been left all over the theatre, including a cellar under the conference hall which was periodically flooded by sewage from an out-of-date drainage system.

The picture-gallery was a gloomy depository for unique theatrical memorabilia and some fine paintings, cheek-by-jowl with rubbish. The theatre library had never been properly catalogued, and was also a *mélange* of irreplaceable books and junk-shop rejects. The theatre's numerous rented properties in the town were all in need of urgent repairs. Avoncliffe, Randle Ayrton's old home, had been taken on by the theatre with the aim of founding its own drama school, but because of the war nothing had come of it, and it was being used as an actors' hostel.

All these tasks Jackson began to deal with. Nancy Burman reorganized the wardrobe, saving what costumes could be salvaged, classifying it, and dividing it properly between production and maintenance. New workshops were opened and set in motion, so that all sets and props could be made in Stratford without recourse to expensive London firms. Backstage, Tannoy was installed, dressing-rooms and offices improved; stage machinery repaired and replaced. The picture-gallery was closed and completely reorganized; the library was put in the hands of a qualified librarian, Levi Fox, for complete recataloguing. Jackson, as his successor Anthony Quayle acknowledged, created an efficient theatre machine for the directors who came after him. But, immersed in these problems, Jackson maintained more than ever a certain aloofness from the production side of the theatre. For the season of 1947 he hired five, rather than eight directors: four from the previous season returned, including Peter Brook, and there was one new director, the young and gifted Michael Benthall. He then left them to get on with it. The company was led by Robert Harris and Beatrix Lehmann, with Paul Scofield and some of the younger actors returning. With multitudinous problems of administration, burgeoning rebellion among the governors, and the worry over the previous season's deficit all in the background, this company launched Barry Jackson's second season at the Memorial.

It was chiefly notable for three things: Paul Scofield's performances, Brook's production of *Romeo and Juliet* (playing in tandem with a revival of the previous year's *Love's Labour's Lost*), and the arrival of Michael Benthall directing *The Merchant of Venice*. On the strength of his previous year's *succès fou*, it was decided that Brook's *Romeo and Juliet* should open the season.

The advance publicity for the production was stupendous. It was fed by Brook's growing reputation, which had been strengthened meanwhile by two London productions starring Alec Guinness, *The Brothers Karamazov* and Sartre's *Huis clos*. It was then whipped into a fervour by the highly publicized search for the right actors for the leading roles, who, Brook was insisting, had to be young, and preferably unknown. Brook's view of directing at that time was somewhat dictatorial, and still highly conceptualized. Thirty years later he would maintain that that was unavoidable, because many of the companies he was working with did not contain enough strong actors:

In every production of that period, productions by Guthrie, Benthall, myself, for instance, the director *had* to find a way of injecting animation into actors. One had to play a sort of game: you'd take a small part actor who had been bored all season, and say, 'Why don't you play this part as a hunchback with one eye?' – that sort of thing, you *had* to make a stage picture, and bring as much vitality out of the actors as you could. To bring out ensemble strength was impossible.[14]

Although when working on *Love's Labour's* he had come to the first rehearsal with every move of the blocking worked out in advance, and had then abandoned it, his way of working was still far more schematized than it is now. He sought for a keynote to each play – Watteau for *Love's Labour's,* one particular line from *Romeo and Juliet* ('In these hot days is the mad blood stirring'). When he found that, he said in 1947, then he felt he had 'caught on' to the style of the play, and from that moment he knew 'how the actors must sit or stand, how they must speak, whether they must behave naturally or artificially'.[15] Brook's ideas for *Romeo* foreshadowed those of Zeffirelli in his celebrated Old Vic production of the play some thirteen years later. He tried to fill the production with a sense of heat, youth, fire, impetuosity, to restore an Italian vigour to a play that had for years languished in an atmosphere of Pre-Raphaelite romance. As designer he used Rolf Gérard who had worked with him on *Huis clos,* and who produced some superb sets far ahead of their time which were heartily disliked by most critics. The stage was bare, except for a miniature crenellated wall defining its outer limits; it was backed by a great empty indigo sky.[16] Brook took fencing lessons before beginning work on the play, and he placed great emphasis on the fights, which were long, spectacularly choreographed, and which suddenly blazed forth without warning from the atmosphere of heat and torpor conveyed by the street scenes of Verona.

For his leads, after numerous auditions, Brook chose two young and inexperienced actors: Daphne Slater, aged nineteen, and Laurence Payne. According to some of his cast, he concentrated his energies during rehearsals on them, and on the crowd scenes, neglecting the smaller parts. He was, John Harrison (playing Chorus and Benvolio) considered 'somewhat dictatorial in his methods . . . He was very high-handed with us all in the ball and fight scenes, masterminding through a megaphone, and only Nancy Burman, pouring oil on troubled waters, prevented downright mutiny'.[17] According to Harrison it was only at the dress rehearsal that Brook decided on one of his controversial cuts (the reconciliation at the end of the play between the Montagues and Capulets), a decision which, together with the cutting of the Friar Laurence/Juliet potion scene, caused scandal when the production opened. Other changes were made at this stage, including the elimination of scenery worth several thousand pounds, an action that caused outrage backstage and offended even Barry Jackson, although, according to Brook, he uttered not one word of reproach.[18]

Jackson was perhaps anticipating another great success, but when the production opened it was to a concerted attack. Too many puffs preliminary, Brook's own burgeoning reputation, his previous success, all this seemed to determine some of the critics to find fault, and find fault they did. 'Sacrifices poetry, acting, even the story itself to pictorial splendour', wrote *The Times*. The *Guardian* commented that Shakespeare 'seemed to be fighting a losing battle with his determined producer'; the *Mail*, echoing this, that the production was 'a contest of ballet versus the Bard, with the Bard an easy loser'. Only two people defended the production – Peter Ustinov, who pointed out that there was hardly a dull moment all evening, and Philip Hope-Wallace, who wrote that if this production 'were to be given in Prague or Moscow we should never hear the end of it'. Certainly some of the adverse criticism could be attributed to the reviewers' desire to put this infant prodigy in his place, and also to the fact that the stripping away of romance and prettiness, what Brook called 'poetry and gauzes', was in 1947 predictably unpopular. There was little acknowledgement of the imaginative force behind the production, of the innovative vision of sets and staging; instead every critic focused on the unfortunate cuts, and the comparative pallor of the acting. In Brook's view there was some justification for this; he later acknowledged that his leading actors had been somewhat under-strength, but in his view it was then particularly difficult to find good *young* actors. English actors (with the notable exception of Scofield) were, he felt, 'only any good if they were over thirty-five to forty. It was impossible to cast parts like Ferdinand, or Orlando; the young actors were all in the RADA image, stiff, conventional, and boring, either genuinely upper class, or stilted working class. My Romeo, for instance, was born with a Cockney accent. *Now* he would have kept it; *then* he had to learn to talk like a gentleman, and so he could not speak from his heart'. It was a difficulty that made Brook doubt Jackson's central policy; in his view 'Barry Jackson did not have a hope of making a permanent company out of young unknowns'.[19]

The other productions that season were of a more even standard than they had been the previous year, with a notable performance as Richard II from Robert Harris, and a very beautiful, but undercast, production of *The Merchant of Venice* by Michael Benthall, with sets and costumes by Sophie Fedorovich, the ballet designer. In the autumn, three of the productions, *Richard II*, Brook's *Romeo* (with some of the cuts restored), and *Twelfth Night*, went to London for a season at His Majesty's Theatre; it was the first time a Stratford company had appeared in the West End since Bridges-Adams had taken his production of *Henry V* to the Strand Theatre in 1920 for a few special performances.

The notices were respectable, short, and lukewarm. The season did not attract a smart metropolitan audience, unlike the productions at the Old Vic, which was still basking in the glories of the Olivier/Richardson seasons from 1944–6 at the New. 'Though the smarties who would willingly be crushed to death to see the Old Vic may absent themselves,' Philip Hope-Wallace commented, 'London people who want to see Shakespeare should not miss this visit from Stratford-upon-Avon.' At the end of that engagement the company disbanded. Few returned the following year, except Paul Scofield. All the directors except Michael Benthall departed also, including Peter Brook. When the plans for the next season were announced, late in 1947, there were substantial and dramatic changes. There were only two guest directors, Michael Benthall and Anthony Quayle; the company was significantly older, more experienced, and included a number of stars – Godfrey Tearle, Robert Helpmann, Diana Wynyard. Clearly some effort was being made both to strengthen the company, remove the 'second-eleven' taint, and perhaps attract the 'smarties' who so far had shown their preference for the Old Vic.

The impact of this announcement was somewhat diminished by the fact that, before the season even began, on 7 January 1948, Barry Jackson's retirement was announced.

Jackson's resignation, which was to come into effect at the end of the season, was the cue for an outcry from the Press, and not just from his Midlands supporters but nationally as well. The prevailing view, from which there was not one dissenter, was that this was a disaster for the Memorial Theatre. 'A bad business,' commented the *Birmingham Mail*. 'The Memorial Theatre cannot afford to lose its most distinguished director after only three years in the saddle . . . No one imagined Sir Barry could work a miracle overnight. It can only be done by steady consistent policies.' The *Sunday Times* pointed out that Jackson was the fourth director to depart in six years, and that his resignation was not discussed – or indeed even known about – by many members of the theatre's executive council.

On 9 January Jackson gave an interview to his old friend T. C.

Kemp of the *Birmingham Post,* in which he made it clear that he was prepared to retract his resignation:

The *Birmingham Post* understands that his statement was based . . . more on a desire to counteract rumours which have been spreading about his position, and less an absolute decision to retire. The facts are that no offer has yet been made to Sir Barry of a renewal of his contract, and in the circumstances he had no alternative but to say he would be retiring . . . if an offer of renewal were made, he would seriously consider it . . .

Jackson was therefore opening the door to the governors, and most particularly to Fordham Flower, to invite him to remain. No invitation was forthcoming; the following day the *Post* reported that the announcement of Jackson's retirement had been made 'with the full approval of Lieut.-Col. Fordham Flower'. The door had been firmly banged shut.

Then and since numerous people have constructed scenarios to explain this odd resignation, which came at such a crucial point in the theatre's history. Jackson's friends and supporters believe to this day that Jackson was ousted by the Machiavellian manoeuvres of Michael Benthall and Anthony Quayle, who – according to their version – infiltrated themselves into the Memorial under Jackson's generous aegis, and then set about stabbing him in the back, each, meanwhile, keeping a close eye on the other's prospects of promotion. But this scenario, though it has a certain Jacobean appeal, ignores the timing of Jackson's resignation, which took effect in the winter. Benthall had then been in Stratford only briefly, to direct the previous season's *Merchant of Venice,* and it was Jackson who invited him to return the next year; Benthall then invited Quayle. Neither Benthall nor Quayle was in a position to do extensive lobbying that winter to influence Jackson's position one way or the other. Certainly, according to Anthony Quayle some thirty years later, Michael Benthall had seen the possibilities of Stratford, and was less than impressed by Jackson's direction of the theatre. But this was predictable. Benthall was young (then only twenty-eight), extremely gifted and, like Quayle, in a hurry. He came from a distinguished family, was educated at Eton and Oxford, and his career in the theatre had only just begun when war was declared and he joined the Royal Artillery. After the war the progress of his reputation was meteoric: he co-directed *Hamlet* at the Old Vic in 1944 with Tyrone Guthrie, and it was he who was largely responsible for persuading his close friend Robert Helpmann to pursue an acting career in tandem with his work in ballet. In 1947 Benthall and Helpmann had taken over the Duchess Theatre for a period, presenting a superbly designed production of *The White Devil*. Quayle had met Benthall shortly after the war, through Guthrie, and was for a short time involved in a plan to take over the Duchess for a longer period (together with Peter Ustinov) and mount highly finished, star productions rather in the manner of the Gielgud seasons at the New. But Ustinov dropped out from the triumvirate, and the plans fell through. At about that time, Barry Jackson invited Benthall to return to Stratford for the 1948 season and direct a number of plays there. Benthall then approached Quayle and suggested they both went to Stratford, where 'with one big heave' he believed they could 'make the Memorial the centre of classical theatre in Britain'.[20] Jackson gave them *carte blanche* and the company for the 1948 season was chosen entirely by the two young directors.

During the winter, before Jackson's resignation and while these plans were going on, there was a certain amount of contact between Benthall, Quayle, and Fordham Flower. It was, for instance, Quayle who persuaded Godfrey Tearle to come to Stratford to play Othello, and there was some correspondence between him and Fordham Flower about that arrangement, and about how the next season should best be presented to the board of governors.[21] During this period Quayle, who was responsible for hiring most of the 1948 company through his Tennent's contacts, gradually assumed the more senior role in the Benthall/Quayle partnership.[22] But his contacts with Fordham were few and concerned mainly with casting. They were sufficient, however, to start rumours, and it was the rumours that pushed Barry Jackson into hasty resignation. But the most basic reason why that resignation was accepted with alacrity was that Fordham Flower *was* unhappy with Jackson's term as director.

The two men had an uneasy working relationship. It was difficult, in any case, for a new young chairman, intent upon revolutionizing his theatre, and insecure about his ability to do so, to work with a man twenty-five years his senior. But this, according to those who were close to Fordham, was exacerbated by the difference in their personalities. Fordham was one of the people who found Jackson mandarin, unable to convey enthusiasm. He could not understand

Jackson's refusal to involve himself more in the day-to-day running of the theatre, and interpreted it as an Olympian detachment. Above all, he felt that Jackson could not make decisions. The seeds of this feeling had been sown at the time of the retiring of Savery, Tossell, and Alice Crowhurst, and had grown since. Whenever a problem came up, Fordham found, Jackson would duck for cover. He would disappear to Malvern or Cornwall, where he frequently stayed, and no one would be able to reach him, even by telephone. And there were other problems. Fordham wanted the Memorial to break with all the old amateur traditions of the past, and make the leap to a prestigious world theatre which had been postponed so long. Jackson, with his insistence on a young company, on the impossibility and undesirability of bringing stars to Stratford, seemed to him to be endangering this policy. He was also worried by Jackson's contacts with academics like Allardyce Nicoll, and Jackson's vision of promoting those contacts to make Stratford into what he called 'a Shakespeare university'. He did not feel the influence of academics was a help — but then he had seen what the dead hand of academicism could do to a theatre during the Iden Payne years. There was also the fact that by the end of 1947 it was known that Jackson's second season had made another deficit, of some £8,000, which was bound to give ammunition to the rebellious among the theatre governors. But this did not influence Fordham greatly. His main reason for wanting Jackson to go was that — to him — he lacked one vital quality, leadership.

During May 1948 he made this clear in a letter to Lord Iliffe. Iliffe was asking him to reconsider Jackson's departure, mainly because he had been in contact with newspaper critics like T. C. Kemp, W. A. Darlington, Ivor Brown, and Victor Cookman, all of whom had been canvassing him forcefully on Jackson's behalf. He realized Jackson was 'a bad business-man', he wrote, but would it be possible to retain him as artistic director, in partnership with a strong business manager? Fordham replied:

Personally, I think that B.J.'s shortcomings on the purely business and commercial side don't really matter a damn if you take the broad view. Artists are apt to be like that. The real and important thing that has been lacking is *Leadership*. You already know my views about the vital necessity of the leadership of the S.M.T. passing from an individual member of the Flower family to the Director, who should be the key man of the theatre, i.e. the Leader. Under this present regime there has been no real leadership. In particular, the company must have leadership. Any Director who fails to provide this, vis à vis the company, is bound to fall down on his job. If Tom Kemp really believes that B.J. has achieved the respect of this company, I think he must be a little out of touch with the acting profession.[23]

By this time, although Iliffe did not know it, Fordham had already decided who he wanted to succeed Barry Jackson, and had un-officially offered him the job. He did not tell Iliffe this, nor did he tell him about the small squib of an affair, late in 1947, which seems to have convinced him finally that Jackson did lack 'leadership'. Then, as now, there were frequent leaks about plans for forthcoming seasons, and before the full programme for 1948 was officially announced it was already known in the local press that the season was to include some star names, among them Robert Helpmann. One of the productions, it was also known, was to be *The Taming of the Shrew*, directed by Michael Benthall. Someone leaked the fact that it had been considered a 'rather amusing' idea to cast a man – Helpmann – as Katharina. This, in 1947, caused predictable scandal, the more so because Benthall was well known to be homosexual. Barry Jackson, always drawn to daring schemes, did not oppose the suggestion with the resolute firmness the governors expected of him. He thought, in fact, that it was an interesting proposal. His slowness to crush the nascent idea was seen as the ultimate instance of a director failing to rule, and it was felt that his own homosexuality had clouded his judgement. The rumour was hastily squashed, but it did final damage to Fordham Flower's confidence in his director, and it was also to influence the choice of Jackson's successor.

Ironically, 1948 was a brilliant season, and a testimony to Jackson's policy of opening doors to young directors, to the generous freedom he gave them, and to the energy and talent of the two directors involved. It brought to the stage of the Memorial productions less quirky and uneven than those of Jackson's two previous years, for it brought to the theatre for the first time the style, the standards, and the bravura of the West End. It established the style that was to dominate Stratford for the next decade, the Tennent formula: the best star actors, exquisite and sumptuous costumes, highly elaborate, superbly designed sets, tightly controlled, sure-footed productions. Its essence was captured in the photographs of Angus McBean, the photographer for that season and for Stratford productions through-out the late 1940s and 50s. More than any other he conveyed the strengths of that work, the force of the great actors playing the leading roles, their features dramatized by the heavy make-up of the period, and the sheer visual splendour of the staging. It was a style of theatre that was later to become unfashionable; 'very Tennent's' became a term of abuse to many of the new generation of actors, directors, and designers who began to emerge in the mid-Fifties. But this later reaction unfairly belittled the very considerable achievements of the Tennent production company during three decades, a period when Tennent was responsible for many of the finest classical revivals in the West End, and was, indeed, one of the few London managements consistently prepared to risk money on classical work. To a radical director like Brook, who worked frequently for them, H. M. Tennent was 'the great bastion of quality, the nearest thing we then had to a National Theatre'. 'When Tennent had one of their top West End casts,' Brook considered, 'with actors like Gielgud, Ashcroft and Evans, they could play as well as the Moscow Arts, and on one month's rehearsal.'[24]

Quayle's and Benthall's policy was, from the first, to bring this best of the West End to Stratford. The Memorial Theatre held, as they saw it, a trump card: it could offer leading actors a range of roles they might wait years to play in London, and the chance of working with one company over a period of some months. The money was available to rival Tennent's in the style of staging, if not in salaries; all that was lacking, in spite of Jackson's two seasons, was prestige. Both men felt that Stratford needed to produce good work, the kind of work that would make the Memorial fashionable – fashionable in the sense, as Quayle put it, that metropolitan magazines like *Vogue* would write about it. 'It was no good the same old local critics writing about the place,' Quayle considered, 'it had to be smarter than that.'[25] It was. The whole atmosphere of the Memorial changed radically with the productions of the 1948 season in both small and large ways. Suddenly telegrams and flowers began appearing in actors' dressing-rooms where, in the past, there had been a simple handwritten note from Jackson, and perhaps a single rose. 'Suddenly,' Brook remembered, 'the directors were West End, the actors were West End. I think it terrified Barry Jackson – he was always proud of being a provincial, and he had a deep distrust of the London theatre.'[26]

The 'West End' company that Quayle and Benthall drew together was a fine one. It was led by Helpmann and Diana Wynyard, an actress of great beauty who had previously appeared mainly in modern plays, and by Paul Scofield, who returned to play Hamlet (alternating in the role with Helpmann), Troilus, Bassanio, and the Clown in *Winter's Tale*. Godfrey Tearle came in at the end of the season for the *Othello*, and the company included a number of actors from the 1946 Tennent production of *Antony and Cleopatra,* which had had Tearle and Edith Evans in the title-roles, and Anthony Quayle as Enobarbus. At Stratford, Quayle was acting as well as directing, and there was a supporting company of extremely talented character and younger actors, including Claire Bloom, aged seventeen, Paul Hardwick, William Squire, Robert Urquhart, Michael Gwynn, Michael Bates, Heather Stannard, and John Justin. Edmund Purdom, son of the critic C. B. Purdom, that castigator of Stratford in the past, played minor roles and was shortly to set a precedent by being snapped up for films. Clifford Williams, now an RSC associate director, played walk-ons. Right across the board it was one of the strongest companies ever to have worked at Stratford.

Quayle and Benthall also brought in a covey of talented designers, including Audrey Cruddas who, together with Benthall, devised a brilliant set of screens and tattered banners for *King John,* and Motley, returning for the first time since 1939 to design *Troilus and Cressida*, and an elaborate *Winter's Tale* with sets and costumes reminiscent of Russian icon scenes. Working with Rosemary Vercoe, Benthall directed a *Shrew* in which Sly and Bartholomew, ensconced in a large bed, watched a group of actors perform a play within a play, rustling their costumes out of a basket crammed with clothes of different styles and periods, so that Petruchio resembled a cowboy, Katharina sometimes a Wild West heroine and sometimes Lily Langtry, and the rest of the characters seemed to have picked out the coats and periwigs of eighteenth-century comedy. It received bad notices; Peter Brook remembered it years afterwards as marvellously funny, daring, and inventive. But the most spectacular designs of the season were for the most publicized, and most popular production – *Hamlet,* with Scofield and Helpmann alternating in the leading role.

The designer was James Bailey, a young man in his early twenties who had previously worked on opera and ballet at Covent Garden. He set the play in a palace that resembled a great Gothic cathedral, its arches receding, heavily shadowed, and lit by dim backlighting. The costumes were early Victorian, the men in frock-coats, the women in crinolines. Ophelia and Gertrude wore low-cut dresses revealing bare shoulders that gleamed whitely against their jewels and the shadowy backgrounds, Claudius had mutton-chop whiskers and wore full dress uniform with sashes, ribbons, and stars emblazoned across his chest; the whole staging conveyed both opulence and threat. It was magnificently operatic, superbly designed and executed, particularly in view of the fact that materials then were rationed, and the costume department had an allocation of only 2,000 coupons per production and made many of the clothes by unpicking and restoring what old costumes they could from the decaying theatre wardrobe.

Hamlet was the Birthday production, and opened the season, Scofield giving the first performance in the title-role, and Helpmann the second. This doubling, by an actor already acclaimed as a great discovery and an older actor famed as a dancer and choreographer, but with a growing reputation as an actor, attracted a huge amount of interest. The theatre was besieged with applications for tickets: 10,000 applications arrived for *Hamlet* on the first day of booking. It was clear that Benthall's and Quayle's policies were going to pay off. Benthall and Bailey had found, in their conception of *Hamlet*, an ingenious correlative for a play to which romantic attitudes had attached themselves. By setting it at the tail-end of a period obsessed with the romance of ruins, Gothic architecture, ghosts, madness, and the eroticism of decay, romantic attitudes to the play were harnessed to the production of it, and Elsinore moved with surprising ease to the world of Horace Walpole. The production was just sufficiently on the edge of two eras to use to the full the aura of repressed Victorian sexuality.

Both Hamlets – clearly very different – received acclaim and detraction, the consensus being that Scofield was the more moving, though immature in technique, and Helpmann the more technically accomplished ('exquisitely mimed and spoken', *Punch* commented) but affecting the head rather than the heart. But some critics dissented from this balanced view. Scofield's Hamlet, wrote Siriol Hugh-Jones in *Vogue*,

is of a profound tenderness ... [he] downplays ... the savagely bitter comedy latent in the role ... he is a romantic, fore-doomed figure in the vast echoing Gothic castle which James Bailey has designed so magnificently ... [it is] a rare performance, and not one to be described as an excellent attempt which will be improved with maturity – much of Hamlet *is* immature, and the performance is young and touching . . . it releases the imagination and touches the heart with an immediate urgency.

Vogue carried a long article about the season, with McBean photographs. One of the directors' ambitions was swiftly realized: work of this kind *could* attract the attention of chic metropolitan publications.

There were, however, some voices raised against this new opulence of conception and design. Ted Willis, writing in *New Theatre,* criticized what he saw as the growing dominance of directors and designers:

By and large the actor is reduced to the level of a tailor's dummy. He is required to wear clothes well, and stand in certain beautiful positions. His acting ability, of which there is no lack this season, is a secondary factor. Costume, décor, lighting, grouping, these reign supreme in Mr. Benthall's productions, and the prime elements of theatre, script and actor, are forced into second place.

But in spite of such strictures as these, the season was a resounding success, crowned by the final production with Godfrey Tearle as Othello, a production more in the old actor-manager tradition than those which had preceded it, but greeted with uniform praise.

In the midst of this satisfactory state of affairs, with the box-office breaking all records yet again, one question remained: who was to succeed Barry Jackson? The immediately obvious answer was Benthall. Although younger than Quayle, and less experienced, he was the more senior of the two in the sense that it was he who had brought Quayle to Stratford in the first place. He was original, a brilliantly promising young director; he had had brief experience of running a theatre in his season at the Duchess. Quayle was primarily an actor, though he had had some success as a West End director since the war; but the Memorial had fought shy of employing an actor-director since 1919. The decision was in fact made early in January 1948, within a week of Barry Jackson's resignation, although it was not announced until the following June. It was taken solely by Fordham, with a swiftness reminiscent of his father. Shortly after the row about Jackson's resignation erupted he had to travel to London, and made a tentative arrangement to meet Quayle in order to discuss the forthcoming season; the same day Quayle was meeting emissaries from MGM who wanted him to work in films. According to Quayle, he and Fordham, who did not know each other well, walked round and round St James's Park until, quite suddenly, Fordham offered him the directorship of the theatre. Quayle hesitated; he was worried about Benthall's reaction. Finally he agreed to think it over, and consulted Guthrie. Guthrie advised him to accept: 'What a thing to be able to influence,' he told him. 'You will regret it if you don't.' So Quayle returned to Stratford and told Benthall, and Benthall appeared 'not to mind in the least'.[27]

All this had happened by 18 January 1948, when Quayle wrote to Fordham informally accepting the informal offer of the directorship.[28] So there was no question of Quayle's wooing Fordham during the 1948 season, as his enemies believed. But although his overtures to Fordham were minimal, Quayle did hold one advantage over Benthall in the contest for the Stratford directorship. He was, very much, an ex-soldier. Both he and Fordham had been staff officers, and had been deeply affected by the experience of war; Quayle was ambitious, forceful, and in Fordham's view, a natural leader. His rival was also an ex-soldier, and might possess similar qualities, but Benthall was homosexual. The little fracas over *The Taming of the Shrew* had not been forgotten.

Fordham's decision was finally ratified by the governors, and in the mid-summer of 1948, when Quayle was thirty-five, his appointment was announced. It was the signal for an outcry from the Press, particularly from Midlands newspapers. The *Birmingham Evening Dispatch* took a typical line: 'Sir Barry Jackson . . . a man of vision, energy and purpose,' it commented, 'is allowed to depart at the moment when his policies are beginning to bear fruit, and is succeeded by – well, we can only say, is succeeded by Anthony Quayle . . .' Within the Memorial itself there was further hostility. There was resentment of Quayle from Benthall's supporters (if not from Benthall himself). There was hatred from staff brought in by Jackson who were totally loyal to him. There was gathering hostility among the governors, many of whom opposed Quayle's appointment. And there was very real anger from Quayle himself, who considered that Jackson was 'fostering the fire' behind his back. According to Quayle the two men had only one brief discussion about the handover: Jackson advised him 'not to ignore the academic side', and to encourage the theatre's relationship with Shakespearian scholars. Quayle replied that as far as he was concerned the academics were the ivy on the tree, and it was the tree that needed to flourish. Neither made any further attempt at *rapprochement.*[29] Jackson refused point-blank to attend the traditional ceremonies and speech-making on the last night of the season, and it was left to Lord Iliffe to arrange a graceful leave-taking. A formal luncheon at Claridge's was organized, and Sir Barry was presented with a portrait of Paul Scofield by Dame Laura Knight as a parting gift.[30] The customary tributes were made, and Jackson made an ironic speech of farewell: 'It has been', he said, 'a labour of love. I may have been a rather expensive luxury, but there has been a great deal of spring cleaning to be done. If I have left some tidiness to my successor, I am satisfied.' Jackson then left, and returned to the Birmingham Rep. At Stratford Quayle began work on his first season.

Jackson was the sixth director to leave the Memorial in an atmosphere clouded by dissent and hostility, and it was sad that he did so, for in many ways he laid the foundations for what came after. 'He opened doors,' Peter Brook considered, 'and because of that he, personally, lost control of the theatre. But in a sense his job was done, historically, with those first few weeks of that first season, with his belief in what that theatre could be. He changed the theatre's destiny. And after him it became, I suppose, a success story.'[31]

9

The Triumvirate

Quayle was thirty-five when he became artistic director at Stratford, and he was of the generation whose lives had been interrupted and reshaped by war. He was tall and burly, built like a rugby-forward, and the characteristic everyone commented upon was his energy, which allowed him to work sixteen-hour days for weeks in succession without faltering. He cultivated a bluff frankness (which he also used professionally to great effect in two of his finest performances, as Henry VIII and Iago) which charmed many, and annoyed others. Fordham Flower admired him greatly, and described him as 'robust and Elizabethan'. Older actors like Gielgud respected his drive and forceful persuasiveness, while younger actors who had not shared his war experiences sometimes found his manner so military that they ridiculed it.

Quayle came from a middle-class family with no theatrical background, and was educated at Rugby. He left school early, trained at RADA and began his career as an actor at the age of eighteen. He continued as such until the outbreak of war, playing mainly younger supporting parts but with the finest companies, including Gielgud's at the New and the Vic's, and this training was to leave its mark on his theatrical tastes and judgement. It was only after the war that he began to develop his other talents: as a novelist (he wrote two novels towards the end of the war), as a director, and then – at Stratford – as an administrator. This diversity of talents was regarded with some suspicion by his contemporaries, for it ran counter to the current theatrical fashion where the distinction between actors and directors was hardening. Quayle, characteristically, had no time for such distinctions, and dismissed them impatiently, but the triple role he assumed at Stratford was a particularly difficult one, and it caused him much private heart-searching. His apparently ebullient self-confidence disguised this, but in private the resolution of the three roles worried him; just when he was succeeding best in one area, he would begin to fret about his progress in the others.

Those who worked with him at Stratford share a remarkably uniform view of him. Everyone, actors, directors, and management, agree that he was a superb administrator, stimulating, generous, and adept at getting what he wanted. Peter Brook likened him to Peter Hall, both men possessed of great charm and apparent simplicity, but with an element of the machiavellian guile needed by any major theatre impresario who wants to succeed.[1] As a director he was straightforward, unintellectual, suspicious of theory, dubious about experimental techniques. He was not an innovator like Benthall, but he was forceful, capable, and discerning, and – perhaps because he was an actor himself – good at coaxing performances from other actors. In both capacities he shared with that earlier director, Bridges-Adams, a quality vital to theatre administrators – the ability to perceive excellence in others, and the generosity not to resent their successes. As an actor, again, most of his colleagues and contemporaries are in agreement; he excelled as a character actor, in such roles as Falstaff, Pandarus, Mosca, Claudius, or Aaron in *Titus Andronicus*; he was less suited to the great tragic leading roles and at Stratford, bowing to the precedence of other actors, he rarely attempted them.

Quayle treated the development of the Memorial like a military manoeuvre. It needed, he believed, the presence of the greatest actors, and the *réclame* that would follow, and he dismissed with the aplomb of a Montgomery all those who said (and had been saying for years) that such actors would never agree to work at Stratford. He had, after all, persuaded Diana Wynyard and Godfrey Tearle to play there the previous season: 'All it needs,' he told a reporter in 1949, 'is for a few top-ranking actors to join hands and storm in together, and then stay for two seasons . . .' And he proved himself right. Within six years of that statement almost every major star-actor on the British stage, including Olivier, Richardson, Gielgud, Ashcroft, and Redgrave, had played at least one Stratford season, working with some of the most gifted British directors, including Brook, Guthrie, Glen Byam Shaw, and George Devine. The Memorial Theatre, just as Quayle had predicted, was transformed by their presence. Within a few years of his taking over, the pendulum, which had in the past always swung in favour of the Old Vic, had swung decisively to Stratford, and it was the Memorial that had replaced the Vic as the foremost classical theatre in the country, attracting ever-increasing audiences and publicity in the process. It was indeed, as Brook said, a success story. Thanks to the force, pragmatism, and persuasiveness of Quayle, to his wide-ranging theatrical contacts, and to his ability to pick and then work well with, a fine team of administrators – all, like him, with a wartime military background – he was able to bring about a revolution.

Quayle had an impressive range of contacts from his pre-war theatre work, which had brought him into the Gielgud 'stable'. He had acted, in a junior capacity, with Gielgud himself, with Byam Shaw, Devine, and Ashcroft, and he had worked with Guthrie at the Vic, and with some of the most talented younger actors who were to emerge in the post-war years. He had good West End management contacts, with the ageing C. B. Cochran for example, and with Binkie Beaumont of H. M. Tennent. The Tennent connection had been strengthened just after the war by Quayle's directing for them a successful adaptation of *Crime and Punishment* with Gielgud as Raskolnikov. So, although not famous, he was in his phrase, 'something of a white-haired boy' at the time, and regarded as a coming man. He was skilful enough to capitalize on that reputation, and on his contacts. It was Quayle, for instance, who manoeuvred Binkie Beaumont on to the board of Stratford governors, because he saw that Beaumont could be helpful to him. 'I needed someone like him on my side,' he considered. 'Beaumont had great influence. He could go to an actor like Gielgud, and say "There's nothing in London for you at the moment, so go off to Stratford like a good salmon, and swim in the sea".'[2] For over twenty years, of course, Gielgud had been held up by critics as the kind of actor the Memorial should be employing, and for over twenty years everyone connected with the Memorial had been saying that such exalted ideas were either impossible or undesirable. According to Gielgud no one had, however, actually asked him to go there; he was somewhat piqued at this, and when Quayle asked him to work for the company he agreed at once, without hesitation.[3] His Stratford appearances marked his first Shakespeare performances for six years and his participation first as a director, and in Quayle's second season as an actor, virtually assured Quayle's new policy of success. Where Gielgud led, others would follow.

Quayle also had one other inestimable advantage, besides his own contacts and acumen. He had a chairman of equal energy and determination, a man with whom he was swiftly on the closest terms of friendship. The relationship between Quayle and Fordham Flower was not undermined, as that of all their predecessors had been, by clashes of temperament and opinion. They were alike in manner, alike in their enthusiasm and aims, alike in their war experiences, even alike in their habitual mode of quasi-military speech. In Quayle, Fordham Flower saw a man after his own heart, not reticent and mandarin as he found Barry Jackson, but outspoken, tough, full of pep and verve – the leader he had been seeking for his company. Together the two men made a formidable team, two trouble-shooters well able to protect each other's backs and to quash the remaining dissentients among the Press and the governing board who opposed Quayle's appointment. That first season, especially, such mutual protection was necessary. Barry Jackson's friends among the Press were all too ready for Quayle's first solo season to be a disaster. Lord Iliffe was influenced by them and Fordham's opponents on the governing board were waiting for the chance to prove the new young chairman had backed the wrong man. But in the event the success of Quayle's first season silenced the critics. The praise, and the audience response, for the productions of 1949 were unprecedented. Quayle's policy of going all out with guns blazing paid off within a year. Faced at the end of it with a financial surplus, critical acclaim, and box-office records broken yet again, not even the most determined of Fordham's or Quayle's opponents were left with much ammunition.

'Damn London, let London come to us,' Quayle had told a journalist at the beginning of the season. For the first time since the foundation of the theatre seventy years before, London did. Stratford's provincialism and the old bogey of the metropolis had been scotched, it seemed, and many people believed that it had finally been killed.

According to Anthony Quayle some thirty years later, he never formed policies as such while director at Stratford. He was, he maintained, opportunistic, seizing what chances there were and making the most of them.[4] But although he distrusted the word 'policy', his years at Stratford were marked by clear intentions, achieved with great rapidity. His announced intention, when he was appointed, was simple enough: it was, he told journalists, 'to make Stratford the high-spot of Shakespearian acting and production'. 'I want it', he said, 'to be the best in the world.' His aim was qualitative. Not a man given by nature to theorizing, and preferring always the practical approach, he had little sympathy with theatres with more theoretical aims. It would be impossible to imagine

Quayle directing a theatre with a clear political and propagandist intention, such as Brecht's Berliner Ensemble (founded the same year Quayle took over at Stratford) or a theatre dedicated to exploring certain ways of performing plays, such as the Moscow Arts. He was in pursuit of excellence, and prestige, and in 1949 when the idea of an ensemble company was still foreign to English theatre, the proven and accepted way to achieve quality was to introduce into a company a roster of as many fine actors as possible. The Tennent formula of a cluster of great stars surrounded by their attendant satellites provided, as even a radical director like Brook saw, the nearest thing to an ensemble company English theatre had produced. That was the formula of the theatre Quayle had grown up with, and he had been in, or had seen, some of the finest productions that resulted from it. It was natural that he should seek to apply the formula at Stratford, and he continued to defend it as a policy throughout his time there, always maintaining that, while some continuity of companies was desirable, a wholly permanent company was 'neither desirable, nor practicable'. For the great Shakespearian roles, he believed, the greatest contemporary actors were needed, and he recognized that Stratford had no hope of persuading them to stay in a company for more than one season: financially it was too unrewarding for them. But although the policy of employing great star actors was the linchpin of his ideas for the Memorial, Quayle also mustered some fine supporting companies, many of whom returned to Stratford for several years. There was rarely the sense, in the early Fifties, that Stratford companies were, in Bridges-Adams's phrase, composed 'of a star and twenty sticks'. In so far as he was able, he tried to achieve a uniformity of excellence, extending to directors, designers, leading actors, supporting actors, even bit-part players.

Besides his unshakeable belief in the necessity of stars, Quayle held one other belief which was central to his work at Stratford and to the development of the Memorial throughout the decade of the Fifties. He believed the theatre should continue to survive, as it had always done, without subsidy. This was partly due to his innate conservatism and distrust of state aid, and partly due to his own bouncy impatience with red tape. He knew what he wanted to do with the Memorial, he thought the theatre could generate the funds to do it, and he had no wish, he said, 'to be subject to the outside influences and bureaucracy attendant on grants'.[5] Like Fordham Flower at that time, he took pride in the fact that the Memorial *was* self-supporting, and a great deal of his energy was taken up with ensuring that it should continue to be so. One way of earning money was through touring.

Stratford's commitment to tour, always one of the fundamental tenets of its existence, had fallen into abeyance for over twenty years by the time Quayle was appointed. He was to revive the idea almost immediately, taking the company on a fourteen-week tour of Australia at the end of his first season. Throughout the Fifties there were other ambitious international tours, to Australia and New Zealand again, on several occasions to Europe, to Russia, and to the provinces; there were also frequent limited seasons of the most successful Stratford productions in London, all of which generated considerable revenue. But that revenue was, as Quayle was well aware, vital to the unsubsidized Memorial, and particularly vital if the theatre was to expand its operations, as Quayle later hoped would happen. For although the Memorial still had considerable assets when Quayle took over, including a large number of property holdings in Stratford, and cash reserves of £173,000, the theatre's financial prospects were no longer as rosy as they had once seemed. There was also an inheritance of neglect, and of a financial caution that prevented the theatre from capitalizing on many of its holdings. The theatre itself, as Barry Jackson had reported, had fallen into a state of disrepair; more work was needed on it, and would continue to be needed; reserves had to be kept back for that. The properties the theatre owned in Stratford also had to be maintained, and many were in a very dilapidated condition. Some had been let by Archie Flower on extremely long leases, at extremely low rents (the Arden Hotel, for example, a flourishing hotel immediately opposite the stage door of the theatre is on lease to the year 2009, by which time the rent to the theatre will have risen to £3,500 per annum).[6] Quayle has always maintained that throughout the Fifties the Stratford theatre 'led a knife-edge existence financially', and the figures bear this out. In the past the Memorial had been able to make large surpluses each year because the companies were small, rarely more than twenty-five to thirty actors, and spending on productions and on staff was kept to an absolute minimum. Under Quayle, as under Barry Jackson, costs immediately and inevitably went up. The theatre was fully and properly staffed; companies were larger, averaging sixty actors, numbers that reflected the more ambitious scale of productions and the use of numerous walk-ons or 'supers'. Salaries were kept at the more realistic levels established by Jackson, and production budgets were increased.

The large annual surpluses that had been a feature of previous decades, and which had been achieved only by a parsimony inimical to excellence, immediately disappeared. Narrow profit margins were to be a feature of the theatre's work throughout the Fifties. Most seasons made a small surplus in the region of £2,000, sometimes slightly swollen by bar profits and catering. No season, not even the celebrated Histories season of 1951, or the 1955 season starring the Oliviers, which played to an average 95 per cent capacity, ever made a surplus even approaching those made before and during the war. If budgets were exceeded, or audiences fell back, seasons could make a substantial loss: in 1950 –1, for instance, there was a deficit of £21,105 because the theatre had been closed for repairs during the winter and had lost its revenue from touring shows. In 1958 a sharp rise in production costs contributed to a deficit of over £15,000 on the season.[7] As Quayle himself said, the theatre only needed to have three consecutive years of such losses for its position to become shaky, its reserves dangerously depleted. So, although the productions at Stratford continued to appear opulent, sumptuously dressed and set, the opulence was carefully controlled. Both Patrick Donnell (the stage director at Stratford, and later general manager) and Quayle knew the strictness of budgets; elaborate sets and clothes were produced by the workshops and the brilliant costume department under Kegan Smith, but often for a very modest outlay.

Even so, as Quayle and Fordham Flower both knew, the productions *were* wasteful, and in a sense it was difficult to alter. It was rare to revive more than one production for a second year, and this meant it was impossible to recoup the capital outlay on sets and costumes. A production could not play more than sixty performances in a season, and many played as few as thirty. So the London transfers and the international tours had another function besides introducing the company to wider audiences and adding to its prestige; they made financial sense, for they prolonged the life of a production that was, by reason of the Memorial being a festival theatre, artificially short. These financial realities did not percolate to the Press. Newspapers, seeing that box-office takings rose steadily throughout the decade, proclaimed the Memorial the 'nearest thing to a gold-mine in British theatre'. Within a year of Quayle's taking over, Richard

Findlater, the most perceptive of the younger critics then writing, noting that for the next season the Memorial was to employ artists of the calibre of Gielgud, Brook, and Guthrie, hailed the Stratford theatre as 'our nearest approach to a National Theatre'. 'Why not', he asked (stating for the first time in print the question that – with variations – was to bedevil Quayle and the Memorial for years to come) 'keep the theatre open throughout the year, with a second company playing non-Shakespearian repertory?'[8]

Quayle's work at the Memorial had a brilliant three-year start. In his first season the work included two highly balletic but exquisitely designed productions, *A Midsummer Night's Dream* and *Cymbeline*, directed by his erstwhile rival, Michael Benthall. There was a highly acclaimed production of *Henry VIII* by Guthrie, with a brilliant and innovative set by Tanya Moiseiwitsch; there were two more conventional productions (*Macbeth* and *Othello*) which served primarily as vehicles for the leading actor, Godfrey Tearle; and there was Gielgud's celebrated production of *Much Ado about Nothing*, with, that year, Quayle and Diana Wynyard as Benedick and Beatrice – the first presentation of a production that was to be frequently revived over the next six years. His second season, pinned on Gielgud, revived the *Much Ado,* with Gielgud and Ashcroft in the leading roles, and included Peter Brook's now legendary production of *Measure for Measure,* with Gielgud as Angelo and Barbara Jefford as Isabella (a production which opened to mixed reviews, and whose reputation grew later), and Gielgud's and Quayle's production of *King Lear,* with Gielgud in the title-role, and fine sets by Leslie Hurry.

The companies for these two seasons brought together a number of actors who were to return to Stratford frequently in the Fifties – not only Gielgud and Ashcroft, but also Harry Andrews, Gwen Ffrangcon-Davies, Leon Quartermaine, Robert Hardy, Barbara Jefford, and Alan Badel (the last three all young actors at the beginning of their careers who were to be brought on and given major chances at Stratford). The productions, fine though many of them were, were not put on under the easiest of circumstances. Each had four weeks rehearsal (an RSC production now has six; sometimes, particularly when Brook is directing, longer). Quayle considered that adequate, and so did most of his leading actors, many of whom had had a baptism of fire in their youth with the short rehearsal periods at the Old Vic. But there were no previews, as there are now, and the time available for technical and dress rehearsals, in highly elaborate productions, was minimal. Now, an RSC production customarily has a day of 'technicals' (when lighting, set changes, and music, are co-ordinated and rehearsed), a dress rehearsal day, and then a week or more of previews, during which time changes of a quite radical nature such as the moving of intervals, cuts, costume modifications, re-blocking, can be made. To accommodate the technicals and dress rehearsals the theatre is dark for one or two days.

When Quayle took over at Stratford the idea of the theatre's being dark for even one night was unthinkable, and he remembered his first season as a nightmare because of this. The introduction of each new production, throughout the season, had to be made in one day; this meant that he had twenty-four hours in which to strike the sets for the previous production, install the new sets, plot the lighting, dress rehearse, and open his new production to the Press. The strain was immense, on all the staff, the directors, and the actors. Having done this for five productions his first season he flatly refused to do it again, and for the second season the theatre was dark for one night before each new opening, an innovation that provoked predictable protest from the governors because of the loss of revenue, and from the town of Stratford, where the powerful hoteliers were by no means yet reconciled to the idea of staggered openings, let alone to the theatre's being closed during the season.

The climax of Quayle's initial years with the Memorial came with his third season, for Festival of Britain year, 1951. During the winter before the season began, the theatre was closed for extensive renovations. These were long overdue; some patching up had been done during Jackson's years as director of the company, but much more fundamental and expensive changes were needed. The theatre was still shabby, and much of its sound and lighting equipment was out of date. The design of the auditorium had remained unchanged since 1932. There was still the famous gulf between stage and audience, and the circle was still isolated from the stage by the flanking white walls with their fussy mahogany panelling. Both Guthrie and George Devine told Quayle how much they disliked the theatre; both considered it a white elephant. 'There it is,' Devine once said of it, 'that great lump of masonry, standing on the river-bank, imposing itself on everyone who has to work there.'[9] Guthrie's advice was terse: sink it and start again. Quayle was not happy with the theatre either. He considered it had a bad, cold atmosphere, and that no matter what tinkering was done to the stage and forestage, the gulf between it and the audience remained unbridgeable. He called in Brian O'Rorke, architect-elect of the National Theatre, and the modifications O'Rorke made in 1950 greatly improved the Memorial. Under both Peter Hall and Trevor Nunn further changes have been made, but the Stratford theatre today is still very much the result of the 1950 alterations. The circle was cantilevered forward, with side additions curving towards the stage, the stalls were re-stepped to improve sight-lines, and the proscenium arch was re-styled; the forestage was enlarged, and the entire auditorium redecorated and reseated. New lighting and sound equipment was installed, and a new wing of dressing-rooms was built. The changes were expensive (they finally totalled some £100,000, after earlier estimates of half that amount) and they reduced the theatre's reserves substantially. But the increased number of seats brought in, at 1950 prices, another £20,000 per season.[10] The benefit to the productions from the increased intimacy of the auditorium was incalculable.

The idea of mounting a sequence of history plays for Festival of Britain year was Quayle's; it was a bold plan, and it met with considerable opposition. Throughout the 1950s the repertoire at Stratford was limited to five plays, so Quayle was able to attempt only half the full cycle of the Histories, *Richard II*, the two parts of *Henry IV*, and *Henry V; The Tempest* was added to the list to fill out the season. Even so, he was attempting something entirely new. Apart from Frank Benson's highly cut and transposed history sequence in 1906 (played without *Henry V*, and with the plays out of order), no one had ever tried to present the Histories as one continuing story. It was even rare for the two *Henry IV*s to be played together; *Part I* was by far the more popular, and most frequently revived. The other two plays in the sequence, *Richard II* and *Henry V*, had become firmly categorized as 'star vehicles', the one tragic, the other heroic. This view had been strengthened by the fact that the country's two leading actors had each excelled in one of the roles: Gielgud had been hailed as the definitive Richard II, and Henry V was embodied for a generation by Olivier, first on stage, and then on film.

The argument that the four first plays of the sequence had an inner unity and a dramatic progression, as Quayle believed, was not widely held in 1951. For two centuries scholars had emphasized the distinctions between the plays rather than their unity, drawing attention to the considerable differences in the style of writing between them; Dover Wilson considered that the many links of theme and plot had been added later, to give the plays a spurious unity originally unplanned by their author. It was not until 1944, with the publication of Tillyard's *Shakespeare's History Plays,* that these arguments began to be challenged. Both the literary and the theatrical interpretation of the plays had led to their distortion. As the critic T. C. Worsley wrote,[11] the emphasis on the star actor in the title-role turned the play *Richard II* into a personal tragedy, relegating Bolingbroke to a secondary figure, and minimizing the play's political arguments. In *Henry IV* the distortions continued. The habit of viewing the two plays separately, and of sentimentalizing Falstaff had led critics like Hazlitt and Bradley to find psychological inconsistencies that disappeared when the two plays were treated as a whole. In the theatre Falstaff and Hotspur had long been regarded as the leading roles, and the progression of Prince Hal towards kingship became a secondary theme, clouded by what was often regarded as his cold and distasteful rejection of Falstaff. Even in the celebrated productions of the two plays for the Old Vic in 1945-6, with Olivier as Hotspur and Justice Shallow, and Richardson as Falstaff, this area of the plays was the least explored, and the performance of Hal generally regarded as the weakest aspect of the productions. *Henry V,* different in style and played in isolation from the preceding history plays, had been regarded as a heroical pageant for over three hundred years. Commentator after commentator remarked on its jingoistic patriotism; company after company, like Benson's, used it as an excuse for irrelevant processions and display. The actor playing the title-role was expected, above all, to be stirring: 'Make the bells ring with the speeches, like Lewis Waller,' Clement McCallin was advised when he played the part at Stratford in 1937. 'Think of yourself as England!' Olivier was counselled when he undertook the role. Olivier had, on stage, tried to explore the character's self-doubt, but he had played the part in isolation from the *Henry IV* plays, as had all the actors attempting the role before 1951.

No company had ever embarked on an exploration of all four plays, attempting to trace their continuing themes, their poetic structure, and their development of characters. The workings of Richard II's curse had never been followed through; the contrasting of three kings, one anointed, one a usurper, one attempting to merit kingship, had never been examined. Their central story, the expiation of guilt and Hal's transformation from renegade boy to the mirror of all Christian kings, had never been given by one company on one stage. The intricate sub-plots of the plays, the way in which actions throw ahead of them long shadows, the continuing revenges of sons for fathers – these could never be fully appreciated when they were played singly, or out of sequence. 'The plays' . . . full power and meaning', Quayle believed, 'only became apparent when treated as a whole'.[12] But Quayle's arguments for presenting the four plays as a sequence were not accepted by many people, including some of the theatre governors. Their opposition deepened when they learned that they were to be produced on a single permanent staging. Disaster was presaged, and had it not been for the energetic support of Fordham Flower, Quayle might have had to abandon the project. But Fordham, remembering Charles Flower's pioneering enthusiasm for a histories sequence, was in favour from the first. The project was agreed. However, Quayle was unable to do the thing he most wanted, which was to rehearse all four plays together and open them on successive first nights. There was not enough money to do that, and so the plays opened at monthly intervals. In Quayle's view the full impact of the sequence had been diffused. He believed that 'as much as anyone else, including ourselves, the critics needed to be educated about these plays, to be made to see them in a new way',[13] and the subsequent reviews proved him right.

The critics began by being resistant to the productions, finding fault with them precisely because they did not conform to traditional preconceptions. Most of the reviews for *Richard II* (the opening production) concentrated almost exclusively on Redgrave's performance as Richard, and on lengthy comparisons with previous stars who had played the part such as Gielgud and Guinness. They expressed little interest in the wider context of the play, and found Redgrave insufficiently moving and sympathetic; few questioned the degree to which Richard *should* be sympathetic. The two parts of *Henry IV* received higher praise, though again many critics baulked at an unsentimentalized portrayal; the *Guardian* complained that this Falstaff (played by Quayle) made one think, but did not make one merry. The final production, *Henry V*, was not helped by journalistic drumming-up of interest in Richard Burton, who had been highly praised as Hal. According to the *Sunday Times*, 'one question pervaded the town' of Stratford; the question was not whether the production would succeed as the final link of the cycle, but whether Burton would 'bring off' the role of Henry, and ascend at one glorious leap to the pantheon of great actors. The general consensus among critics still devoted to the idea of Henry as a bravura part was that he did not. Ivor Brown was one of the few leading critics to dissent from this view; he suggested that Burton's performance, and the production, were true to the play, and that a thorough re-examination of the text was called for from scholars and critics. Burton's restrained performance, exploring the King's insecurity and self-doubt, did not provide what many critics still sought, an actor they could greet as 'the Lewis Waller of the 1950s'.

Some critics later recanted to a degree, and modified their earlier views as the season progressed, but on the whole the criticism of the 1951 Histories reveals more about the critical prejudices of the period, and the reviewers' unwillingness to abandon tired and received ideas, than it does about the productions themselves. Few grasped at the time the significance of the productions, the freshness of their approach, and the care of their textual analysis; few acknowledged the radical and ingenious nature of Tanya Moiseiwitsch's permanent staging, which in an era of opulent and operatic sets was astonishingly and uncompromisingly plain, and which, if it lacked the poetic vision of John Bury's designs for the Hall/Barton histories sequence in the 1960s, provided something that, in 1951, was of great value – a swiftly adaptable, uncluttered platform for the plays, from which they could speak. The performances of the company received more acknowledgement, even when tempered by prejudice, and the highest praise went to those actors performing roles about which the critics had fewest preconceptions, such as Harry Andrews as a fine Bolingbroke/Henry IV, declining from the *haut formidable* rebel of *Richard II*, to the haunted old age of *Part II*. Richard Burton as Hal, a still distanced figure, 'like a man who had had a private vision of the Holy Grail', Hobson wrote, was applauded and actors playing smaller parts, such as Barbara Jefford as Lady Percy, Robert Hardy as the young Hotspur and Fluellen, and Alan Badel as Poins and the Dauphin were praised. Redgrave was acclaimed for his Northumbrian-accented Hotspur, and there was greater appreciation of his Richard II by the end of the season, but Quayle's Falstaff, going against the traditional grain and somewhat grudgingly praised, remained, T. C. Worsley considered, 'undervalued'.

Nevertheless the season was a triumphant success with audiences; it played to over 90 per cent capacity houses, and was a personal triumph for Quayle who had directed the plays (with Redgrave responsible for *Part II*) as well as playing Falstaff. And if the intentions of the season had not been clear to critics at the beginning, or if they had felt them to be misguided, its achievements were roundly acknowledged by some at the end. 'It is now possible to say', Robert Speaight wrote, 'that Shakespeare is better performed at Stratford than anywhere else in the world . . . Mr. Quayle's conception of the tetralogy is brilliantly realised: to attend these plays on successive nights is a unique and gathering experience . . . they do not simply add up, they multiply.'[14] Quayle's achievement, besides the quality of the productions, was to force a re-examination of the history plays, and his work was to have continuing influence, both among scholars and critics and in the theatre. John Barton and Peter Hall, who were both then at Cambridge (Barton at King's, Hall at St Catharine's), saw and greatly admired the productions, and were to carry Quayle's work further with their productions of all eight history plays thirteen years later. Terry Hands was to direct superb productions of the same plays between 1975 and 1980. Kenneth Tynan, who was just beginning his career as a critic in 1951 with sparkish reviews in the *Spectator,* expressed most eloquently the new insight which Quayle's productions had initiated:

I suspected it at Stratford four years ago, and now I am sure: for me the two parts of *Henry IV* are the twin summits of Shakespeare's achievement. Lime-hungry actors have led us always to the tragedies, where a single soul is spot-lit and its agony explored; but these private torments dwindle beside the Henries, great public plays in which a whole nation is under scrutiny and on trial . . . the odd irregular rhythm wherein societies die and are re-born is captured as no playwright before or since has ever captured it . . . To conceive the state of mind in which the Henries were written is to feel dizzied by the air of Olympus . . .[15]

What happened next exposed, all too cruelly, the weakness built into the system by which the Memorial operated. The Histories played out their triumphant season, and were then reluctantly dropped from the repertoire. A festival theatre like the Memorial could hardly present the same four plays two years running. The production of *The Tempest* was revived the following year (with a new cast), but the history plays had to be abandoned; only one, *Henry IV,*

Part I, was ever revived, and that was taken, in sad isolation, on tour to Australia and New Zealand in 1953. The fine company that had been at Stratford for the Histories, many of whose members had been two or three seasons with the Memorial, was disbanded, and only a few actors were able to return for 1952; some of the most promising, including Richard Burton, Robert Hardy, and Alan Badel, left. Instead of being pinned on company strength, the 1952 season was again pinned on a star actor.

Unfortunately, as Quayle was already beginning to discover, it was not that easy to find stars. For a start there were too few of them: Gielgud, Ashcroft, and Redgrave had already appeared at the Memorial, and would not return there immediately. That left as alternatives Edith Evans, Laurence Olivier, Alec Guinness, Ralph Richardson, and Paul Scofield as a contender from a younger generation. But all those actors were constantly in work, and had to be tempted to Stratford at the right moment, when they were available, with exactly the right range of parts. This could involve the artistic director at Stratford in a somewhat undignified juggling bout with plays, actors, guest directors, and designers. When it came to a final decision as to what productions should be put on it was always the choice of actor that came first. The seasons were constructed around the stars, but the system only worked when the chosen actor was well cast in the roles assigned for the season. If he or she was miscast, or off-form, then the whole edifice crumbled.

In 1952 Quayle juggled the available balls in the air, and with some jubilation announced that the company was to be led that year by Ralph Richardson, who would play Macbeth, Prospero, and Volpone. The two other plays for the season would be *Coriolanus,* with Quayle in the title-role, and *As You Like It,* with Margaret Leighton as Rosalind, Michael Hordern as Jaques, and the young Laurence Harvey as Orlando. Michael Benthall directed the revival of his 1951 *The Tempest,* Gielgud directed *Macbeth,* George Devine *Volpone,* and Glen Byam Shaw *Coriolanus* and *As You Like It.* But of what sounded an interesting and promising season, only two productions came near success. The *As You Like It* was highly praised; *Volpone* (which had been included at Richardson's suggestion) was given a romping production by Devine, with a splendid set by Malcolm Pride that used all the 1932 stage machinery and, according to the *Evening Standard,* 'ascended, dived, capered sideways – did everything, in fact, except sit up and beg'. According to all who saw it, Mosca was one of Quayle's finest performances, splendidly devious and oilily parasitical. His Coriolanus was less successful, but even so he fared a great deal better than the luckless Richardson, for whom hardly a critic had a good word all season. As Volpone, Harold Hobson in the *Sunday Times* found him 'perfunctory, lackadaisical, and slackly pitched'. There were similar comments on his Prospero, and his Macbeth ('dazed and fogbound') was universally condemned. Tynan criticized Gielgud for the unsubtlety of his production, with its black sets and 'its single message: "Background of evil, get it?"' and declared that Ralph Richardson had become 'the glass eye in the forehead of English acting'.[16] Richardson was philosophic about it all. Macbeth was, together with Othello, the part he wished to play more than any other, he said later: 'And in the bathroom I'm rather good . . . [but] I found when I came to play Macbeth ("Is this a dagger which I see before me?") I just didn't damn well see the dagger, and neither did anyone else.'[17]

Richardson never returned to Stratford after this unhappy season, and at the end of it Quayle formulated a new plan for the Memorial, one designed to shape its work over a three-year period. 'The present system', he said during 1952, 'is too cruelly wasteful to continue indefinitely . . . Stratford's best productions must have a longer lease of life.' He saw only one way to solve the Memorial's problems, the way Richard Findlater had suggested earlier: the organization must expand.

Quayle's intention was to create two Stratford companies, beginning in 1953. One would play the Stratford season and the other, led by Quayle himself, would go on a thirty-four week tour of Australia and New Zealand. If all went well, two companies would continue to play the following year, 1954, one at Stratford and one touring America. Beyond that, no detailed plans were announced, but Quayle had his own private intentions. The tours would, he hoped, generate revenue for the Memorial, and with those funds, and the advantage of having two companies in existence, he hoped to be able to lease a London theatre, where Stratford's best work could transfer, and where it might also be possible to do other work besides Shakespeare, including modern plays which, he felt, would be an inducement to young actors to stay with the company. Quayle's ambition to expand the company did not, however, spring solely from a desire to strengthen its work or to give a longer life to its productions. It sprang also from his conviction that Stratford was about to gain an unwelcome competitor: the National Theatre. Although it was to take another ten years before the National Theatre company came into being, and a further thirteen before the theatre itself opened, in 1953 Quayle had no way of knowing that the delay would be so long. For in the early Fifties the pulse of that long-delayed project quickened, and for a time it looked as if the National might finally come into existence.

The first major indication had come in 1946, when the Old Vic and the SMNT Committee joined forces to form a new joint council, with a view to the Vic's developing and flowering into the new National Theatre Company. The chairman of the new council, Oliver Lyttelton, then confidently envisaged that the National Theatre would be built, and occupied, by 1951. Progress was much slower than that, but progress was made. In February 1949 the National Theatre Bill was passed, and the government pledged that the Treasury would donate the sum of one million pounds to the National Theatre, provided the LCC supplied a suitable site for the building. The LCC had already offered a site on the South Bank and in July 1951, during the Festival of Britain celebrations, the foundation stone of the new National was laid there by Queen Elizabeth, now Queen Mother. That foundation stone was subsequently to endure many peregrinations as decisions about the location of the National changed again, and throughout the Fifties the whole project was to suffer many setbacks. But it was impossible for Quayle to foresee these, and knowing that the National had a powerful and energetic lobby behind it he feared that what had been a potential rival was rapidly becoming an actual one. He felt that if the National Theatre came into being, backed by state subsidy, the Memorial would suffer. The National would be able to offer higher salaries; its actors would be able to live at home, instead of having the difficulty and expense of moving to Stratford for a season. It would be able to offer its actors a varied diet of work – anything from modern plays to Aeschylus, as well as Shakespeare. Quayle believed that Stratford would then lose its attraction for star actors, and would decline again, just when its prestige was growing. These feelings were to haunt Stratford for another ten years, and to dictate many of the theatre's future policies. Quayle's immediate solution was similar to the one Peter Hall adopted some years later: expand the Memorial's operations to London, and quickly, before the National could open. Quayle, with his inbuilt opposition to state subsidy for Stratford, knew that such a project would be expensive, and hoped to build up the revenue for it by the tours of 1953 and 1954. He also knew that the organization, already becoming too much for one man to run, would need to be strengthened internally, but by 1952 he thought he had the solution to that problem also.

Late in 1951 there had been an extraordinary putsch at the Old Vic which was to have dire effects for that company, but to be of indirect benefit to the Memorial. In the immediate post-war period, the governors of the Old Vic made a series of what seem now to have been unaccountably foolish decisions. First, in 1948, they fired Olivier and Richardson as directors of the company, despite the fact that the two men had been responsible for some of the greatest seasons in the Vic's history. Then, in 1951, they decided to close the Vic's most promising off-shoot – the Old Vic Theatre Centre and School, which had been in existence for four years under the joint directorship of Michel Saint-Denis, Glen Byam Shaw, and George Devine. In the ugly period of recriminations and attacks that followed the announcement of the closing of the Centre, Quayle saw an opportunity for Stratford. He was a friend of both Byam Shaw and Devine; he admired their work at the Vic, and saw at once that it could be of great benefit to Stratford. He believed the Memorial needed some form of training school attached to the company to develop younger actors – there had been several attempts to set up such a school since the war, all of which had foundered. His first idea was for Stratford to take on the Centre, with its directors, and move it, lock, stock, and barrel, to the Memorial. When this idea proved impracticable (there was not enough money to fund it and Saint-Denis, exhausted by the machinations in London, had already decided to return to Europe) he decided on a more gradual approach. He invited Byam Shaw to come to Stratford as his joint director, and Devine to do a production (the *Volpone*) the next season. Byam Shaw agreed, but asked that he should work at Stratford for one year without any title, simply as a guest director; this he did in 1952. So, when Quayle announced his new three-year plan for the company at the end of that year, he already had the two other people to hand whom he considered essential to its realization. Byam Shaw duly became joint director, and it was announced that he would direct the next Stratford season while Quayle took the second company on tour to Australia. Devine, more loosely connected with the new triumvirate, would continue to direct guest productions. But Quayle wanted the triumvirate to develop into something more formal; he saw in it a way of making a London operation a practical possibility. The idea was to find a London theatre of which Devine would be the director; Byam Shaw would be responsible in the main for Stratford, and Quayle himself would be free to move between the two organizations, sometimes directing or acting at one or the other, sometimes taking a company on tour. The plan would free Quayle from some of his administrative responsibilities, under which he was beginning to chafe, and had the advantage that it would leave him more time to pursue the aspect of his career that he was beginning to feel was suffering from his role as artistic director, his acting. Quayle's move was an astute one: even if the triumvirate had, for the meantime, to remain an informal one until money had been raised and a London theatre found, he had managed to bring together three of the most talented of British directors, whose very different characters and abilities created a promising balance.

Byam Shaw, the eldest of the three, was the most experienced. He was the son of a painter and brought to his productions, according to those who worked with him, three great qualities – a superb visual sense (he generally worked with the designers Motley), immense care in preparation (which he had learned from Saint-Denis) coupled with an almost intuitive grasp of the rhythms of a play, and great ability to work with actors, perhaps because he himself had been an actor for some sixteen years. Before the war he had appeared in many of Gielgud's productions, and he had acted for Saint-Denis, both in his ill-fated *The White Guard,* and in what was generally regarded as his greatest production, *The Three Sisters,* with Gielgud and Ashcroft, in Gielgud's Queen's season of 1937– 8. A profoundly gentle man, he perhaps lacked some of the iron essential in a theatre administrator, and he disliked intensely the public demands which were made upon him as joint director. But if he lacked Quayle's entrepreneurial flair, he was a fine director, immensely loyal, and much loved both by the acting companies at Stratford and by his stage staff. Like Quayle, he had excellent contacts with leading actors many of whom were personal friends; Quayle felt that in his hands the Stratford seasons were safe, and that the theatre would continue to attract the best actors, directors, and designers.

Devine, three years older than Quayle, was the maverick of the trio, the most piratical, and the least committed to Stratford. He too had begun his career as an actor, switching to direction later, and of the three it was he who was most influenced by, and closest to, Saint-Denis, whom he regarded almost as a father, certainly as a mentor. He had worked with Saint-Denis at his first experimental English school, the London Theatre Studio, which survived from 1936 to the outbreak of war. He was deeply influenced by Saint-Denis's ideal of a permanent ensemble company and by the Saint-Denis techniques of training and developing actors through experimental group work, which had continued after the war at the Old Vic Centre. Devine was a gifted teacher as well as a gifted director, particularly of comedy, and Quayle still hoped that a Stratford training-school might emerge, of which Devine could be the director; various plans for linking the Memorial with RADA were explored, but never materialized.

Imaginative and bold though this idea of a triumvirate was, however, its success depended on the energy and commitment to it of all three men involved, and it was on that that the project was to founder. The difficulty was partly that Quayle himself remained overstretched. During 1952, when the idea of the triumvirate was first discussed, he was playing Coriolanus and Mosca, was involved in the day-to-day running of the Memorial, and by the end of the year was finalizing, and rehearsing, the ambitious tour to Australia and New Zealand, in which he was playing three major parts (Othello, Jaques, and Falstaff) and directing two of the three productions. For most of the following year, 1953, he was abroad, and although he kept closely in touch with Stratford, he was not in a position either to strengthen the new triumvirate or to push hard on the search for a London base. Byam Shaw, during the same period, was totally occupied in directing. Devine, the least committed of the three, was meanwhile pursuing projects of his own that had little connection with Stratford. During the period 1953–5 he directed five plays for the Memorial, but he also did other free-lance productions including directing for Sadler's Wells and H. M. Tennent. The evidence suggests that, although his productions for Stratford were interesting and original, his heart was not in the work. In 1952 he had met the deceptively precious and formidably ambitious Tony Richardson, then just down from Oxford, and Devine seemed to his friends to come as strongly under Richardson's influence as he had formerly been under Saint-Denis's. It was Richardson who was to lead him away from the Stratford involvement.[18]

Richardson wanted to establish a new theatre company in London which would evolve a group style of work and which would concentrate on the plays of new authors, both British and foreign. At exactly the same time that Devine was deputed to find a suitable theatre in London for Quayle, he was also trying to find a theatre for this project. When he found that it was difficult to raise backers for his writers' theatre, Devine briefly tried to combine the two projects. Like Guthrie before him, he was aware of the Memorial's tempting reserves and the possibilities they promised. He began negotiating for a lease on the Royal Court Theatre, then on lease to Alfred Esdaile, a retired music-hall comedian. Esdaile seemed agreeable, but when Quayle and Devine went to see him he named such a large figure for the transaction that the whole scheme promptly collapsed.[19] Although other theatres had been considered, none was suitable, and the negotiation with Esdaile was the closest Quayle came, during the 1950s, to finding a London base. It was, in any case, unlikely that the scheme would have been successful, for the marrying of Quayle's star-oriented classical companies with Devine's and Richardson's plans for a writers' theatre and group work would have been extremely difficult. If the merger had happened the subsequent course of English theatrical history would have been profoundly different. But it did not, and the failure of the negotiations with Esdaile marked a turning point for Stratford, although that fact did not become apparent until later.

Meanwhile, the work at Stratford from 1953 to 1955 demonstrated how difficult it was to achieve the organic growth aimed at in Quayle's three-year plan. There was continuity of direction, but apart from that the seasons were *ad hoc* affairs. Some smaller-part actors returned for successive seasons, but in the main a new company was formed each year, led by a new constellation of stars. With skill and resourcefulness the directors rang the changes: Ashcroft and Redgrave for one season; Olivier, Gielgud, for another. But these were all actors who had made their names before the war; within the canon of Shakespeare's plays there was a diminishing range of parts they could play, and it diminished further with each season they undertook. Later in the decade, in an effort to find parts for them, such actors were to undertake roles for which they were, strictly speaking, too old. Redgrave was fifty, for instance, when he played Hamlet at Stratford (and was the oldest actor to attempt the role since 1938 when it had been played by Esmé Beringer, an actress of sixty-four). Ashcroft played Rosalind at Stratford when she was fifty (and had considerable doubts about risking it).

It was also extremely difficult to persuade the star actors to play several seasons at Stratford, for their appearances there involved considerable financial sacrifice. By the mid-Fifties the top salaries had risen to £60 a week, but the seasons lasted nearly eight months and virtually precluded their undertaking outside work during that period. In the West End they could earn four or five times that figure, in films substantially more (Vivien Leigh was reportedly being paid £5,000 a week, for instance, to film *The Deep Blue Sea* in 1954, the year before she came to Stratford). Most were prepared to work on the principle that a year of West End work, or filming, could then subsidize them for a season at Stratford, but more than one season was another matter. Redgrave, who played at Stratford in 1951 for the Histories, and again in 1953, found himself at the end of that year in a difficult financial position, exacerbated by paying back tax on film-earnings during a period when he had been working for a low salary. As he pointed out to Fordham Flower, the actors were, in effect, subsidizing the Memorial.[20] This meant that it was extremely difficult to achieve any ordered progression in the work at Stratford. The stars came and went; younger actors like Richard Burton or Laurence Harvey came, made their mark, and were promptly snapped up for films. The successes, and failures, of the seasons were isolated. Neither could have much effect on the next year's work, when there was a new company in residence. Some of the younger actors in the companies found the atmosphere at the Memorial crushing and hierarchic: they termed it 'officers and other ranks', and resented what they saw as the exclusion of supporting actors from the production discussions between the directors and their leading actors. Both Quayle and Byam Shaw deny that exclusion, but both were aware that the Memorial's dependence on stars created problems, and not just in rehearsals. After being so long regarded as provincial and second-rate, the Memorial had become the Fortnum and Mason of the theatre, the place where audiences went expecting the best, and the most rare. And audiences and critics who went expecting gulls' eggs and caviare were unprepared to accept less exalted fare. Quayle and Byam Shaw were trapped in a dilemma of their own creation: any attempt to set the theatre on a new course, to abandon the line-up of stars which their administration had led people to expect, met with resistance from audiences, critics, and from the governors.

This problem manifested itself very clearly during the course of

Quayle's three-year attempt to expand and develop the company. While he was on tour in Australia during 1953, Byam Shaw mounted a highly successful and acclaimed Stratford season. The stars were Peggy Ashcroft, Michael Redgrave, and Marius Goring. All the productions, cavils apart, received good reviews. All attracted large audiences, and T. C. Worsley spoke for many critics when he wrote that the company seemed to have a new gusto, boldness, and freedom in their work. The most successful production of the season, and the one with the longest life, for it transferred to London for a limited season and then toured Europe, was *Antony and Cleopatra,* a production that, *The Times* felt, came 'nearer to perfection than any in living memory'. It was an example of the Stratford system at its best: a simple, fast-paced production that rescued the play from what Bridges-Adams had called 'the excesses of Wardour Street'. It relied little on scenic effect, and acquired power from Byam Shaw's restrained direction and use of lighting, and from the insight and daring which the leading actors brought to their performances, particularly Redgrave as Antony, and Ashcroft as a controversial Cleopatra, playing her as a 'wily Greek' with a pale skin and vivid red hair, and emphasizing not the traditional voluptuary, but Cleopatra's guile, her chameleon-like ability to transmute from the petty to the noble, from the queen to the bawd to the scold. The production was highly praised in Stratford, acclaimed in London, and packed the 1,700 seats of the Prince of Wales Theatre there for its limited season. But by the end of 1953, when that production was playing in London and Quayle had returned from the tour of Australia which had netted a substantial surplus for the Memorial's reserves, both Quayle and Byam Shaw felt that change must be attempted. For the second year of their three-year strategy for the Memorial they felt they must risk a season that was not pinned on an Ashcroft, a Redgrave, or a Gielgud, and attempt to develop a younger group of actors.

For 1954 a company was gathered with an average age of twenty-three, for what, in its singularity, became known as the 'season without stars'. Quayle himself appeared with the company, and so did a few older actors such as Leo McKern (who had been on the Australian tour), William Devlin, and Rosalind Atkinson. But most of the company were not only young, but virtually unknown. Some had worked in the Memorial companies before, such as Barbara Jefford, Keith Michell, and Laurence Harvey. Many were graduates of the Saint-Denis Old Vic School, and the directors were the triumvirate of Byam Shaw, Devine, and Quayle. It was an interesting season, uneven almost inevitably, but given considerable verve and energy by the new young company. Devine's earlier production of *The Taming of the Shrew* was noticeably improved in revival by the young cast, and his other production, *A Midsummer Night's Dream*, which was a reworking of an earlier production at the Young Vic, was highly original, with strange insect-like fairies, and a malevolent, predatory Oberon. But interesting and bold though the season was, it was a success neither financially nor critically. Attendance figures dropped, though not as sharply as some governors had feared: they fell from 96 per cent to 92 per cent capacity. The critics carped, and when, during the season, it was announced that the long-projected tour of America would not take place, it was widely assumed (wrongly) that it was this young company which had been chosen to tour, and that the project had collapsed simply because they did not come up to scratch.

Quayle felt very bitter that the season was regarded as a failure. He felt that the Press were entrenched, and that they would not support something new. 'They did not support me when I was appointed,' he said, 'and they did not support me when I attempted to change policy. All the Press were interested in was stars.'[21] It was certainly true that Press uninterest in the 1954 season was marked, but that was not the reason that the experiment with the young company was abandoned at the end of that year. The main reason was that the other developments Quayle had hoped for, and which were essential to his three-year strategy, had not materialized. By the end of 1954 his plans for a London theatre were at a standstill. Devine was by then deeply involved in the negotiations that, in March 1955, were to lead to his becoming artistic director of the newly formed English Stage Company; the American tour, which would have brought in substantial revenue, had had to be called off. So Quayle had no second theatre where some of his younger company could have been diverted, and without Devine's help and the additional revenue from the American tour, his hopes of getting that second theatre had diminished. Meanwhile, Stratford was already committed to the stars of the next season. When, during 1954, the news leaked that those stars were to be Laurence Olivier and Vivien Leigh, what remaining tenuous interest there was in the experiment with young actors disappeared completely. The 1954 season was eclipsed by the surge of interest in the Oliviers.

The 1955 season was to mark the zenith of the Memorial's prestige during the Fifties, as if Olivier, by agreeing to appear there, had set the seal on the theatre's success. The box-office was immediately besieged for tickets: 500,000 applications arrived for the 80,000 seats available in the opening weeks of the season. Before the season even began there was an avalanche of publicity. Olivier had recently been appearing in Terence Rattigan's *The Sleeping Prince* with Vivien Leigh, and had had to endure considerable criticism because of it. 'The Rattigan frolic', commented the *Evening Standard*, 'has not enhanced Olivier's reputation . . . except as a devoted husband.' There was considerable speculation that Olivier was worried by what the *Standard* called 'the shadow behind him' (the rapidly increasing reputation of Michael Redgrave) and that this had prompted his decision to go to Stratford for 'some serious acting'. Olivier's last performances in Shakespeare had been some four years before, in 1951, when he played in *Antony and Cleopatra* (also with Vivien Leigh) in the West End and in New York. But what was interesting about these gossipy speculations was that it was generally agreed that even an actor such as Olivier *could* enhance his standing by a Stratford season. Six years earlier no newspaper would have thought of suggesting such a thing.

Ironically it was just at this moment, when the Memorial seemed set for one of its most exciting seasons, that Quayle's visions for the theatre were collapsing and his own enthusiasm beginning to pall. In all the excitement about the Oliviers, no one paused to ask what had become of the three-year plan, of Quayle's hopes to expand and develop the company, or even what had happened to the previous year's experiment with a young group of actors. If the 1954 season was discussed at all, it was in terms of a temporary aberration. In the popular view, Stratford was now back on course; in the excitement which anticipated Olivier's Malvolio, Macbeth, and Titus Andronicus, and a new production by Peter Brook, no questions about Stratford's future development were asked. Quayle, Byam Shaw, and Fordham Flower, the three men at the heart of the whole great machine were, it seemed, the only ones who *had* any doubts about its future.

The 1955 season had two faces, a public and a private one. Publicly, it was a triumphant success, the greatest achievement since 1951 and the Histories. Like many Stratford seasons, it was slow to get into its stride. The first production, Gielgud's of *Twelfth Night,* was slowed and congested by complicated and somewhat dated sets which necessitated numerous changes. Most critics found Vivien Leigh's performance a coldly perfect miniature of Viola, and were disappointed by Olivier's lisping puritanical Malvolio, although expectations for the season had been pushed so high that disappointment was inevitable. The second production of the season, of the rarely performed *All's Well that Ends Well,* was judged competent and not very exciting. It was only with the third production, the notoriously unlucky *Macbeth,* that the season took fire.

Byam Shaw directed the production, one of the very few on which he did not work with Motley. The designer was Roger Furse, who produced sets of exceptional ugliness that dwarfed the actors beneath looming angular neolithic structures, and which in the England scene, as Tynan commented, needed 'only a cat and a milestone to go straight into *Dick Whittington*'. Hampered by the awkward staging dictated by the sets, and by clumsy handling of the witch scenes, it was not judged one of Byam Shaw's best productions.[22] But it had Olivier, at the height of his powers. He had played Macbeth only once before, at the Old Vic in 1937, at the age of thirty when he was only just beginning to make his reputation as a classical actor after ten years spent appearing almost exclusively in modern plays in the West End. He then took refuge behind notoriously elaborate make-up, and his Macbeth was no exception. 'You hear Macbeth's first line,' Vivien Leigh said of that performance in 1937, 'then Larry's make-up comes on, then Banquo comes on, and then Larry comes on . . . ' This time Olivier's make-up was minimal. He looked fiercely beautiful, like Masefield's conception of Macbeth as 'not a hangman . . . but an angel who has fallen'. It was a romantic portrayal, filled with moments of daring like the sudden leap on to the table in the banquet scene, or the odd convulsive gestures with which he attempted to thrust away the ghost of Banquo. It began in a low key: 'Taking up his stance', wrote Richard Findlater, 'with arms folded, he *waits* . . . he radiates a kind of brooding sinister energy, a dazzling darkness . . . one glimpses the black abysses of the general's mind, the pre-history of life at Dunsinane'. The reason for the low-key beginning was, Kenneth Tynan argued, that most actors playing Macbeth created a character who shrank as the play progressed, who began as complex and fascinating, but ended up just a cornered thug: 'Mindful of this,' he wrote, 'they let off their big guns as soon as possible, and have usually shot their bolt by the time the dagger speech is out'. Olivier paced his interpretation quite differently; his Macbeth was a man haunted by murder from the first, who greeted the air-borne dagger with a 'sad familiarity'; he was a man who had killed Duncan many times before in his mind. Once the murder had actually been accomplished, he greeted with a growing and anguished incomprehension its failure to bring him the release and serenity of power he had sought. The whole performance built to a magnificent climax, to something like Hazlitt's vision of Macbeth as 'a lion in the toils'. ' "I 'gin to be a-weary of the sun" held the very ecstacy of despair,' Tynan wrote, 'the actor swaying with grief, his voice rising like hair on the chest of a trapped animal. "Exeunt fighting" was a poor end for such a giant warrior. We wanted to see how he would die; and it was not he but Shakespeare who let us down.'[23]

Significantly, in his criticism of the production, Tynan devoted almost all his space to Olivier's performance. He added a few snappy asides about Vivien Leigh, and dismissed the rest of the cast and the production in a few lines. Most of the other critics followed suit. Tynan was the last of the major English critics to write in this way. In his reviewing he followed a tradition that had passed down from Hazlitt through Scott, Archer, and even Shaw, to Montague and Agate; like them he concentrated (in the early Fifties) on writing about performances. Indeed he later claimed that it was the 'urge to commemorate' the actors of this period, 'whose work would otherwise die with the memories of those who saw it', which turned him into a critic.[24] Because he did so we have been left with unforgettable descriptions of the great actors of the post-war period, but with a much less vivid impression of the productions they appeared in. This lacuna in the criticism of the Fifties obscured the fact that a real danger threatened the productions of the time, at Stratford and elsewhere. Performances on the scale of Olivier's Macbeth demanded direction of equal vision, and supporting companies of great strength if they were not to degenerate into one-man shows. At Stratford, where the directors' attentions were focused on the stars on whom the theatre so depended, this balance was achieved with less and less frequency as the decade progressed, and the signs of imbalance were there as early as 1955. The *Macbeth* was at one and the same time an example of the strengths and weaknesses of the Memorial. The production was praised, *en passant*, for speed and clarity, but it was conventionally staged, with none of the daring and imaginative vision of, say, Komisarjevsky's production of the play in 1933. The supporting company had a preponderance of inexperienced young actors who were eclipsed by the Olivier wattage. Most had been at Stratford for only a few months and were inexperienced at playing Shakespeare; they had had no time to achieve any company identity. The result – a diamond in pinchbeck – was the consequence not just of the director's being off-form, but of the system that created the production. But in the same year at Stratford, shortly after the *Macbeth,* came Peter Brook's production of *Titus Andronicus,* a production of such coherence and power, with both director and company in full mastery of their material, that it transcended the system.

No one at Stratford, however, could have predicted that this would be the case. Although the production brought together the country's greatest actor, and its greatest director, many people had doubts as to whether the chemistry of Brook and Olivier would work. Olivier was that paradox, the actor with pyrotechnical mastery whose every inflection was minutely examined and planned, yet who, through some mystery of his art, could suddenly achieve moments of naked power which seemed purely instinctual. He was the acknowledged leader of his profession, and while some directors found him sympathetic and easy to work with, others found he could on occasion manifest a sudden actor-manager autocracy and hauteur.

Brook on the other hand could be no mean autocrat himself. He might no longer direct actors with a Von Sternberg megaphone as he had done in the fight scenes in his Stratford *Romeo and Juliet,* but his remorseless questioning, his working and reworking of scenes were already famous, and so was his icy anger when his exacting standards were not reached. His intellectual exploration of a play was unrivalled, but to some of the actors who worked with him, including Gielgud, he seemed to have a concomitant wariness of emotion, a suspicion of actors 'letting-go', an intellectual's scepticism of precisely those moments of sudden and inexplicable power that were at the heart of Olivier's performances. The two men had worked together only once before, on Brook's first professional film, *The Beggar's Opera,* in 1953, and while making it their relationship had been stormy, punctuated by frequent disagreements.

There were other reasons for misgivings about the project, the chief of which was the play they were to work on. Brook was originally invited to Stratford to direct *Macbeth*; having a healthy regard for the superstitions of ill-luck attached to it, he absolutely refused. Nothing would make him consider it, he said; the only Shakespeare play he wanted to direct at that moment was *Titus*. This announcement astounded both Byam Shaw and Quayle. *Titus* had a history of almost total theatrical neglect. Although evidence suggests it had been popular in Shakespeare's lifetime, and it was acted a number of times between 1717 and 1725, only two subsequent revivals, both in heavily adapted texts, are recorded until 1923, when it was presented at the Old Vic by Robert Atkins, when its plethora of murders had been greeted with hearty laughter. It remained the only play in the Folio not to have been performed at the Memorial. Critics and commentators had been almost unanimous in their distaste for it; few considered it to be entirely Shakespeare's. Dr Johnson dismissed it roundly as spurious, later writers as a barbaric pageant. T. S. Eliot considered it 'one of the stupidest and most uninspiring plays ever written'. Such a chorus of disparagement was always likely to encourage and interest Brook rather than discourage him, and he dismissed it impatiently. Byam Shaw and Quayle, mindful of Brook's recent success with that other curiosity, Otway's *Venice Preserved* (a play which had been dismissed equally passionately, but more recently), agreed; so did the Oliviers.

Brook was not deterred by the play's notoriously bloodthirsty sequences, by the many ugly murders, the rape of Lavinia and the lopping off of her hands, by the Thyestean feast in the last act with Tamora's sons baked in a pie. He saw the play, he wrote, 'not as *grand guignol*, but as an austere and grim Roman tragedy, horrifying indeed, but with real primitive strength, achieving at times even a barbaric dignity'.[25] Circumspectly, however, whenever the text threatened to descend from barbaric dignity to bathos, he cut. He had wanted to direct *Titus* for many years, and had at one time considered directing it with an all-black cast. His Stratford production was meticulously prepared over an eight-month period, and he designed the sets and costumes himself, and wrote all the music. According to Brook many years later,

Titus Andronicus was a *show*; it descended in an unbroken line from the work of Komisarjevsky. I had leading actors such as he had never had, but it was the totality – the sound, the visual interpretation, everything interlocking, that made it happen. I could not have done it without Olivier and Quayle and Vivien Leigh, who were marvellous, but the rest of the company were not all strong, and so the production had to be: it could not have been born out of company work as, say, the *Midsummer Night's Dream* was in 1970.[26]

His solution to the play's extravagances was to formalize the horrors, to confine them within a ritualistic framework so that the agonies were distanced, episodes in a black progress towards greater and greater atrocity.

The set was sombre and huge, dwarfing the figures of the actors with its tall square-ribbed pillars, which later moved back to create an echoing empty space. The lighting was shadowy, smoky, flaring with the torches whose flames were contained within strange distorted cages. Brook worked with a limited palette of colours in both costumes, and set and lighting: bile green, blacks, reds and browns, and the liverish colour of dried blood. The first scenes began in an unearthly greenish darkness, with a procession accompanying Titus and the coffins of three of his sons; Brook's strange *musique concrète* boomed and breathed around the auditorium. All through the production strange music provided emphasis, alarum and counterpoint; some sounds were created by using conventional instruments, distorted by recording at different speeds, or by the use of an echo chamber, others were created with an assortment of household objects – wine glasses, a toy trumpet. The music created a sense of dislocation, threat, and unease. By the time the banquet scene had been reached the stage was bathed in an ominous blood-red light, the costumes were red, and it was as if the whole universe on the stage had been drenched with blood. With every means at his disposal Brook played on the nerve-endings of his audience, but he played subtly; in a play replete with murders there was no visible gore; when Lavinia's hands had been chopped off she came on to harp music, her wrists spouting not blood but long red velvet ribbons. Perhaps precisely because there were no attempts at laborious theatrical fakery, at blood capsules or papier mâché heads, the atrocities of the play were the more horrifying – certainly audiences did not laugh, though many among them fainted. By holding the production in this iron grip, the latent absurdities of the play were skirted, and perhaps (as Harold Hobson suggested) for post-Buchenwald generations the play's profligate brutalities no longer seemed comfortably remote, or ridiculous.

Of the grandeur of Olivier's central performance there was not one dissenting voice:

This is a performance which ushers us into the presence of one who is, pound for pound, the greatest actor alive ... As usual, he raises one's hair with the risks he takes; Titus enters, not as a beaming hero, but as a battered veteran, stubborn and shambling ... A hundred campaigns have tanned his heart to leather, and from the cracking of that heart there issues a terrible music, not untinged by madness. One hears great cries, which, like all this actor's best effects, seem to have been dredged up from an ocean-bed of fatigue. One recognised, though one had never heard it before, the noise made in its last extremity by the cornered human soul.[27]

That was Kenneth Tynan's view and Richard Findlater, writing in *Tribune,* sensed something similar. He noted the way in which Olivier received the news of his sons' death, and his own betrayal: 'He leans against a pillar, head tilted back, and his face is a tragic unforgettable mask of grinning whiteness ... "Now is the time to storm, why art thou still?" says his brother. And Titus answers with a gentle laugh ... '

At the same time that Olivier was playing at the Memorial there was also a London season, and a European tour, led by Gielgud and Ashcroft, of two productions: another revival of Gielgud's perennially fresh *Much Ado about Nothing,* and Devine's production of *Lear* with sets (and extremely wayward costumes) by the ballet designer Noguchi. The Memorial Theatre's reputation could not have been higher; it was generally acknowledged as the foremost classical theatre in the country. But behind this triumphant front the realities of the theatre's position were somewhat different. At the very moment of its greatest acclaim, the structure Quayle had created was beginning to crumble. Partly it was that the theatre in general was about to change swiftly, and radically, with one of those abrupt shifts of gear that had marked the beginning of the demise of the actor-manager and the rise of the director in the period 1912–14. The signs were already there. In 1955 Peter Hall became director of the Arts Theatre in London, and put on in the course of the year an ambitious range of plays, including O'Neill's *Mourning Becomes Electra,* and Beckett's *Waiting for Godot.* In 1956 George Devine's and Tony Richardson's English Stage Company opened at the Royal Court, and John Osborne became the first of its new young writers to be acclaimed. In 1953 Joan Littlewood's Theatre Workshop took over the derelict Theatre Royal, Stratford East, and in 1955 attracted considerable attention with its controversial production of *Richard II* and its appearances at the Paris International Theatre Festival. In 1956 the Berliner Ensemble visited Britain for the first time and enjoyed a triumphant season at the Palace Theatre – an event that was to prove as influential to British theatre as the appearance of Diaghilev's Russian Ballet in London in 1911.

These different happenings could not, obviously, point the British theatre in one single new direction, and the subsequent careers of the young tiros connected with them were later to take many different courses. But between 1955 and 1960 a remarkable number of new talents did emerge: among directors, Peter Hall, Tony Richardson, Lindsay Anderson, William Gaskill, John Dexter, and Peter Wood; among writers, John Osborne, Arnold Wesker, Brendan Behan, John Arden, Peter Shaffer, Harold Pinter, and Robert Bolt; among designers, John Bury, Sean Kenny, Jocelyn Herbert; among actors, Kenneth Haigh, Alan Bates, Joan Plowright, Dorothy Tutin, Judi Dench, Albert Finney, Robert Stephens, Richard Johnson, Frank Finlay, Peter O'Toole, and Robert Shaw. Many were, at the time, pigeon-holed into categories that were convenient but superficial: writers who had no such common sympathies were lumped together as Angry Young Men; actors from widely differing backgrounds were greeted as that fashionable new specimen, the working-class actor. But if the differences between these emerging artists were more considerable than was then acknowledged, almost all of them had one thing in common: their youth. They were nearly all part of that minority which, in 1956, Kenneth Tynan had cleverly predicted would provide the potential audience for *Look Back in Anger*. 'What matters,' he wrote, 'is the size of that minority. I estimate it at roughly 6,733,000, which is the number of people in this country between the ages of twenty and thirty.'[28] For the past decade, British theatre had been dominated by men and women who had made their reputations before the war. Between them and the new minority detected by Tynan there was almost a missing generation, those whose careers had either been ended, or interrupted, by war. Of that generation, very few emerged to positions of influence in the post-war theatre – Michael Benthall (whose later work did not fulfil its early promise) and Anthony Quayle were exceptions in this respect. It was not surprising therefore that the sudden influx of youth into the British theatre in the mid-1950s should have such a swift and profound effect. Whereas the most influential productions in the first half of the decade were almost all either of Shakespeare or classic plays, those in the second half of the decade were almost all of new work by contemporary writers.

Several of the star actors who had appeared at Stratford were quick to respond to this upsurge of new talent. Ashcroft went to the Court to appear in Brecht's *The Good Woman of Sezuan* in 1956; Olivier appeared there as Archie Rice in Osborne's *The Entertainer* in 1957. Those of the Establishment less quick to link hands with the *avant-garde* subsequently suffered temporary arrests in their reputations. Gielgud, for instance, was castigated by Tynan for appearing in a weak Noel Coward play in 1956 ('Fewer people forgave John Gielgud for appearing in *Nude with Violin* than would have forgiven him five years ago').[29] He then spent much of the late Fifties and early Sixties touring the world with his solo recital programme, *The Ages of Man*.

The Memorial, just as much as its actors, needed to respond to this new tide in the theatre; if it did not, it was in danger of being marooned on the sandbanks of the past. But it was intensely difficult for the Memorial to adapt. Devine had left; there was no London theatre, and until Quayle and Byam Shaw had a London base there was no way of tapping the new writers and the new actors who were attracted to their work. The stars who had brought Stratford its renown were ageing, and in six years the Memorial had failed to develop successors to them. These difficulties were accentuated by Quayle's personal position. He had achieved a very great deal, but his three-year plan for the Memorial had been only a partial success. Journalists continued to emphasize his seemingly undiminished vigour and authority – 'He has the energy of the cross-country runner, and the self-confidence of a judge,' one wrote in 1956 – but in private he was ready to admit how exhausting, how depleting, the work at the Memorial was. The stress was unremitting; it was almost impossible for him to have a family life for the demands on his time were constant. He could take only two weeks holiday a year, in January; his salary was £5,000 per annum which, as he was well aware, was minimal compared to what he could have earned working in London, or in films. Above all he was beginning to worry that his own career as an actor was suffering from his work at Stratford. His position as Director, and the use of stars, had forced him to consign to other actors roles he might have wished to attempt himself. And although he had achieved great success in leading character roles, as Iago for instance, or Mosca, or Pandarus, and in the 1955 season with a superb performance as Aaron in *Titus Andronicus*, he had had notably less success when he had attempted parts such as Coriolanus, or (in 1954) Othello. Friends felt that the cool response to his Othello from the critics had hurt him deeply and damaged his confidence.

What he feared was a 'falling-off' in his acting career was making him restive. Reacting to this, at the end of 1954 he formed his own limited liability company, Anthony Quayle Ltd., with a view to staging plays outside Stratford. Then in 1955 he approached the governors and asked for a period of sabbatical leave, so that he could appear as Tamburlaine at the Winter Garden, New York. This request to undertake outside work, the first he had made during his directorship, met with some opposition from the governors, and Quayle, in August 1955, offered his resignation, just as *Titus Andronicus* was opening. The governors did not take up the offer; Quayle was asked to remain and sabbatical leave granted, but not with the best of grace.[30]

The production of *Tamburlaine* opened in January 1956 and was a great success. As a result Quayle received numerous approaches for film and television work. He was playing no parts that year at Stratford, but he had agreed to return there and direct the last play of the season, *Measure for Measure*. In the meantime there was one other event that crucially affected Quayle's attitude towards the Memorial.

Because Devine was to be at the Court, and Quayle in America for the first half of the 1956 season, new directors for Stratford were needed. And unless Quayle and Byam Shaw were to abandon their schemes for a London theatre, they also needed someone to replace Devine in their informal triumvirate. Scouting around for that replacement, and for new blood for Stratford, they decided to approach Peter Hall, the twenty-four-year-old Cambridge graduate who was having a *succès d'estime* with his season at the Arts Theatre. During 1955 the three men met for the first time, over lunch at a small Soho restaurant. Both Quayle and Byam Shaw were impressed by Hall; when they left, Quayle turned to Byam Shaw and, echoing his thoughts, said, 'That's the next director of the Stratford theatre'.[31] The recollections of Hall and Quayle differ as to what happened next. Hall was invited to direct at Stratford, but remembered only vague and inconclusive discussions about a London theatre and his joining the triumvirate. Quayle recalled much more precise discussions: according to him it became clear that if Hall was to join the triumvirate its roles would need to be reassigned, with Byam Shaw remaining responsible for Stratford, but Quayle taking on London, and Hall Quayle's original role of cross-pollinator. This suggested reassigning of roles was, according to Quayle, the factor that finally convinced him he must leave the Memorial. He believed Stratford must have a London base, but the last thing he wanted to do was administer it himself. The prospect filled him with horror; he envisaged at least five more years of committees, finance battles, and a desk-job. Believing that involvement in administration blunted the edge of any creative talent, he saw himself abandoning for good all his ambitions as an actor.

While Quayle was away in America, the friendship between Byam Shaw and Peter Hall strengthened, and the older man's admiration for the younger director intensified. He considered Hall a 'genius of the theatre', and that his first impression of him at that lunch in Soho had been correct: Hall would be, and should be, the future director of the Memorial. In the meantime he did everything in his power to help Hall with *Love's Labour's Lost,* his first major Shakespearian production. Shortly after Quayle returned to England, and three weeks after that production of *Love's Labour's* opened, Quayle announced his resignation as director. Both Byam Shaw and Fordham Flower tried to dissuade him, but Quayle was adamant, and was open about the fact that he felt continuing to be director of the Memorial was affecting his career: 'Ambition and duty conflict,' he told journalists. 'It was quite a slice out of my life to devote entirely to one theatre, and one author, and I have many other ideas and ambitions unfulfilled.' He hoped, he said, to return often, both as an actor and as a producer, but that wish was not fulfilled. He was not invited to appear with the RSC, or to direct, during the years of Peter Hall's directorship, and he has worked with the company only once since then, in 1976.

Quayle's departure was to an extent eased by Byam Shaw's agreeing to remain as sole director of the company, but the theatre lost a man of acumen, panache, and vision at exactly the moment when those qualities were most urgently needed. Byam Shaw was fifty-two when he became sole director, and his health was not strong. He was not the man to effect the radical changes that each Stratford season made increasingly necessary.

Within the structure as it existed he attempted to make improvements. He tried to give chances to younger actors. He brought Alan Badel back to Stratford in 1956 to play Hamlet; he gave major roles to Richard Johnson and Dorothy Tutin in 1957 and 1958; Ian Holm, who had been with the company four seasons was finally given some major parts (Puck and the Fool in *Lear*) in 1959. He continued to invite Peter Hall to direct, and in 1958 and 1959 also brought in Tony Richardson, who had previously worked at the SMT as Devine's assistant and who had in the meantime become famous as the director of *Look Back in Anger* and *The Entertainer*; actors in the companies noted that there was considerable rivalry between the two young men. But these attempts to revivify the company were not enough. Stars continued to dominate the seasons, although Byam Shaw was forced to cast his net wider than before, to include celebrated actors with little experience of playing Shakespeare.

The increasing lifelessness of the Stratford work, the predictability of design, the marked lack of company playing, was most often noticeable in Byam Shaw's own productions, and was not lost on the new generation of theatre critics. 'The . . . production is dismal,' Tynan wrote of the 1958 Byam Shaw/Redgrave *Hamlet*. 'The courtiers line-up like mechanical waxworks . . . the music is Victorian, the costumes are fussy, and the setting . . . appears to have been inspired by the foyer of the old Paramount cinema in Birmingham.' 'There is not the slightest attempt at ensemble playing,' Alan Brien wrote, in the *Spectator,* of the same production. 'The rest of the cast freeze solid whenever a leading actor speaks . . . '

It was the productions by guest directors that were the most sparkling during this period: Peter Hall's exquisite Caroline production of *Twelfth Night* in 1958; Tony Richardson's *Pericles*, with a black, calypso-singing Gower, and all the brothel scenes intact (the girls in the brothel were not *actually* naked, as they appeared to be, it was hastily explained; they were *made-up* to look naked). There was a delightful summery production of *Much Ado about Nothing* by Douglas Seale, also in 1958; and Peter Hall directed a fresh and entrancing *Midsummer Night's Dream* in 1959, with an energetic young cast, impudent fairies, and beautiful Elizabethan sets by Lila de Nobili. These were the highpoints of the four years of Byam Shaw's directorship, and it was not perhaps surprising that his own work suffered, particularly in comparison. He was perhaps experiencing what Quayle had feared, the blunting of creative talent by excessive administrative work. Certainly by the end of the decade

Byam Shaw felt that his own contribution to the Memorial was exhausted: 'The stars policy had gone as far as it could; it had been done and overdone', he said, 'and I personally could not have gone on, not for one more season.'[32]

That the stars policy had, in fact, reached *reductio ad absurdum* was illustrated by Byam Shaw's last year as director, in 1959, which was also the Memorial's hundredth season. That year, in honour of the occasion, there was an extraordinary roster of famous names at Stratford. They included Charles Laughton, Edith Evans, Laurence Olivier, Paul Robeson, Sam Wanamaker, Angela Baddeley, Harry Andrews, Robert Hardy, and Mary Ure; promising younger actors included Ian Holm, Vanessa Redgrave, and Albert Finney. The directorial team was Tony Richardson (*Othello*); Guthrie (*All's Well*); Peter Hall (the *Dream* and *Coriolanus*); and Byam Shaw himself (*Lear*). The season was, admittedly, undermined from the first by the ill health of both Robeson, who was recovering from pneumonia, and Laughton, who had not long to live, both of whom had extremely taxing roles – Robeson was Othello, Laughton played Lear and Bottom. But even given this underlying weakness in the season, nothing could disguise the fact that from the heterogeneous collection of actors, a rag-bag of styles emerged. Not only did many of the stars produce disappointing performances, their performances remained oddly isolated within the productions; nothing jelled. This was most apparent in the production of *Othello*; Robeson was understrength vocally, but even so it was hard to understand how the combination of him, Sam Wanamaker as Iago, and Mary Ure as Desdemona – all actors from totally different traditions, and with totally different acting approaches – could possibly have worked. There were as many different acting styles on stage, critics noted, as there were tongues in the Tower of Babel.

The *Lear*, beautifully staged by Byam Shaw, had fine supporting performances, particularly from Albert Finney as Edgar and Ian Holm as the Fool, but that could not disguise Laughton's sad unevenness and lack of power in the central role. Guthrie's *All's Well* was typically iconoclastic, beginning in an Anouilh-esque château and departing to what appeared to be the African desert for the wars. It was a giddy exercise in directorial sleight of hand, and the critics divided into two camps, those who found it fun, and those who found it over-hectic. The two most interesting productions of the season were both Peter Hall's, and they demonstrated the divide the theatre had reached in that last year of the decade. His *Coriolanus* is remembered by all who saw it for Olivier's electric, arrogant performance in the title-role, with its extraordinarily daring death-fall at the end. It was not, apart from that performance, a strong production. Many of the cast were disappointing, even Edith Evans as Volumnia; it was hampered by an obtrusive staircase-set by Boris Aronson, and by conventional handling of the crowd scenes. The most interesting production of the season was Hall's of *Midsummer Night's Dream,* for it came the closest to overall coherence and evenness of style in playing. It was the only production in the season that was not overburdened with stars; apart from Laughton it had a cast of unknown, but highly promising actors.

Byam Shaw had decided several years earlier that he could not continue as director, and he had told Fordham Flower of this at the end of his first solo season in December 1957. What he had then proposed, generously, was that he should continue as director for two more seasons. It would be a caretaker regime, a period during which his successor could become familiar with the workings of the Memorial, and increase his experience as a Shakespeare director. Then, as earlier, he had no doubts that his successor should be Peter Hall. At that point Fordham and Hall knew each other only slightly, but Fordham, who was very close to Byam Shaw, was prepared to accept his advice. Between the end of 1957 and the summer of 1958, Byam Shaw and Peter Hall had long discussions about the future of the Memorial, and Hall agreed to take on the directorship. His appointment was ratified by the theatre's executive council on 9 July 1958, and the same day Fordham wrote to him formally offering him the position. Hall replied, in neat schoolboy handwriting:

At this moment I think Stratford is the most important theatre in this country, and it has been made so by the work of Tony and Glen in the last ten years. It is a marvellous heritage, and a great responsibility. Ever since Glen spoke to me about the possibility, I have been very excited. I would want to be, as Glen knows, not a revolutionary, but someone who wants to carry on a fine tradition in his own terms.[33]

Many years later Hall still saw his work at Stratford in much the same way, as being 'evolutionary' rather than 'revolutionary'.[34] That view is loyal to those he admired, and diplomatic, and there are arguments to support it. Certainly the changes Hall subsequently made could not have been achieved had it not been for the work of the previous thirteen years, the contributions of Barry Jackson, Quayle, and Byam Shaw, the companies they brought together and the reputation for excellence they had built up. Practically, the changes he made would have been impossible without the revenue which Quayle had created through touring and transfers. But the changes Hall was to make were, nonetheless, both startlingly radical and startlingly swift.

Hall's appointment became public knowledge that October, and was formally announced on 15 November 1958. He gave several interviews in the next two months, but he continued to take a diplomatic stand. He insisted that his appointment 'would not mean a revolution on the Avon', and contented himself with making a few modest suggestions, such as that productions had perhaps become a little over-decorative, that techniques of verse-speaking needed examination. He stated his belief in the need for permanent companies, but beyond such hints gave no indication as to the scale of his plans for Stratford. It may be that the reason for this was not purely diplomacy and tact, but because Hall's ideas were not yet finalized in his own mind. There is certainly no evidence that, as has frequently been suggested, he made a London off-shoot for Stratford a formal precondition of his becoming director. But a London theatre was key to his ideas, and the moment when that project and his other plans crystallized can be pin-pointed. As Hall himself has said, it was in December 1958, in Leningrad, which was also the first occasion on which his ideas were fully discussed with Fordham Flower.[35]

The two men were in Russia to accompany the Stratford actors on what became a triumphant tour – the first made by any English company since the Revolution. There, in the Hotel Astoria, in a room filled with Edwardian furniture that resembled a set for *The Cherry Orchard,* talking late into the early hours of the next morning, Fordham and Hall finally thrashed out what was to become the blueprint for the Memorial's future. Both considered that meeting crucial to all the developments that came after. What Hall was suggesting to Fordham was not only hugely radical and innovative in theatrical terms, it also represented a total overthrow of some of the most long-cherished policies of the Memorial, policies that had been upheld by Fordham, and by his father before him. Stratford would acquire a London theatre where it would mount a repertoire primarily of modern plays, with some revivals. Artists working for

the company would be put on long-term, three-year contracts –
something unheard of in British theatre. Whenever possible, they
would be part of the repertoires of both theatres, so that they might
be acting in Stratford in Shakespeare on one night, in London in a
modern play the next. The Memorial would recognize it could not
continue to be self-supporting indefinitely; the money to finance the
London theatre would come from Stratford's reserves, and when
those reserves were depleted the theatre would apply for state
subsidy. Upon subsidy, Hall believed, the future of the theatre
depended.

Fordham, as much as anybody, was aware that the end of an era
was approaching, and that fundamental change at Stratford was
necessary; in the past few years, as his wife put it, he had watched the
Memorial subsiding into the dust. Parts of Hall's plans were familiar
– a London theatre, for instance. It was not surprising Fordham
should respond to such suggestions. But what was astonishing was
that, at a time when state subsidy to the arts was minimal, and
controversial, he should respond as he did to the proposal that the
Memorial should seek state aid in the future. This was the total
reversal of a policy of self-sufficiency that had been proudly maintained for eighty years. That Fordham would accept that proposal
was, as Hall must have known, totally unlikely. That he did accept it
was both a testimony to his own daring and to Hall's now-legendary
powers of persuasion. In essence, all the changes that were effected at
Stratford in the next five years were considered that night at the
Hotel Astoria. At the end, when both men had talked themselves to a
standstill, Fordham told Hall that in his opinion they were both quite
mad, but that, nevertheless, he would back him to the hilt.

10

The Peter Hall Years (I)

There is a phrase used of Peter Hall by his present co-workers at the National Theatre: 'Peter is walking on the water', they say, referring to those occasions when Hall performs the apparently impossible with apparently nonchalant ease, when he steers the National through yet another financial crisis, or when he charms some initially hostile committee into total volte-face. It is a joke, of course, simultaneously complimentary and deflationary. It celebrates daring, but also bluff, and it embodies the twin attitudes most frequently encountered among those who know Hall and have worked with him. Oddly, Hall seems always to have been admired as much for what might appear failings as for his obvious qualities: those who celebrate his vision and charm, celebrate also his deviousness and politic cunning. Even those who most emphasize his circumspection seem to take pleasure in it, as if, being manipulated and knowing themselves to be, they nonetheless enjoy the style with which it is done. That Hall has this effect upon people accounts, in part, not for what he achieved at Stratford during his years as artistic director of the company, but for the fact that he was able to achieve it. For the Peter Hall legend, which was to create problems for him at the National in the 1970s, was created during his Stratford years. The extent of that legend, twenty years later, makes it difficult to remember and reconstruct the circumstances of his early years at the Memorial, when the legend was still in the making, and Hall himself was only twenty-nine years old.

At that time Hall's reputation rested primarily on his abilities as a director, and particularly as a director of modern plays. Like Guthrie and Brook, he began work in the theatre in that capacity, with no initial experience as an actor; this was true of most of the other new directors who emerged in the mid-1950s. He learnt to be a director while directing, as he has said, and a certain degree of bluff was needed in his early years to disguise his inexperience. He began

directing in his last year at Cambridge, and it always remain\
matter of some pride that, after going down, he was never out \
job. After a spell in reps, his work first began to attract attent. ...
when he went to the tiny Arts Theatre in London, first as assistant
director, and then, for a year, as director. His work there reflected his
interest in modern plays, particularly those by American and European authors whose writing had been little seen in England. The
production that made his name, however, was Beckett's *Waiting for
Godot* in 1955. *Godot* was a typical Hall choice, in that it was
daring, but a play not without prior reputation – it had achieved
enormous success in Europe over the past three years. It opened to
boos, and intensely hostile criticism in the daily newspapers, and was
saved by the laudatory reviews the following Sunday from Harold
Hobson and Kenneth Tynan. Hall's interest in introducing to English
audiences work which was already attracting attention on the
Continent and in America, marked in that season at the Arts, was to
continue when he went to the Memorial, and to influence strongly its
opening seasons in London.

In the years between *Godot* in 1955, and 1960 when he took over
at Stratford, Hall's reputation as a director with a multiplicity of
talents grew fast. With equal flair, it seemed, he could move from an
experimental play like *Godot* at a small theatre, to a piece of
charming West End froth such as *Gigi* (in which he directed his
future wife, Leslie Caron, at the New in 1956), or opera (*The Moon
and Sixpence,* Sadler's Wells, 1957). After leaving the Arts, and
before overtures were made to him about the directorship at
Stratford, he formed his own producing company, the International
Playwrights' Theatre, an attempt to further the production of plays
by European and American authors and to found some form of
ensemble company. But due to lack of adequate financial backing the
company did only two productions, Tennessee Williams's *Camino
Real,* and Anouilh's *Traveller without Luggage.* In those five years
Hall amassed a great deal of experience, far wider in its range than
that of the other young directors who also began making their names
during the same period, such as Tony Richardson, William Gaskill,
and Peter Wood (his successor at the Arts). But he had no experience
of administering a theatre of the size and complexity of the Memorial, and his professional experience of directing Shakespeare was
limited to the five productions he directed at Stratford between 1955
and 1959. To some who knew him then, like John Barton (who met

him at Cambridge, and who shared a flat in London with him for some years in the Fifties and later became his closest colleague at the RSC), he seemed nervous and diffident about directing Shakespeare, less sure of his ground than when working on modern plays.[1]

At Stratford, Hall was very much Byam Shaw's protégé, and his productions during this period reflected that. As a Shakespeare director he was still serving his apprenticeship, and his Fifties productions were deeply influenced by their era. With the exception of *Coriolanus* all were characterized by elaboration and beauty of setting; he chose to work with designers such as James Bailey (the designer of the 1948 Scofield/Helpmann *Hamlet*) and Lila de Nobili who were best known for their work on ballet and opera. Of the spare, Brechtian style of Shakespeare production that Hall was later to evolve with John Bury, and which became so recognizably Stratford's style in the 1960s, there was then no trace. But although Hall was virtually untried as an administrator and inexperienced as a director of Shakespeare, when he took over at Stratford in 1960 he was already famous, and his celebrity was to be a great asset to him. It was not just that he was regarded (as Quayle had been) as a coming man within theatrical circles; he was celebrated beyond them, and was swiftly to become more so. The reasons for this were largely unconnected with his obvious talents as a director, they were due to something much less definable, for which a word was to emerge in the next decade, and that was *image*. Hall seemed to provide a perfect illustration of the favourite early-Sixties myth: that swift tangible glamorous success was the prize of anyone, from any background, if they had the talent and the audacity to seek it; that a new social openness and freedom prevailed, and that the old barriers of age and class were tumbling. Beneath all the frivolity there was some truth in this: Hall was the first child of a working-class family to become Director at Stratford, even though class barriers in the theatre were supposed to be less of an obstacle than in many other professions. But the emphasis on success and youth led to remorseless trivialization: Hall, along with other idols of the 1960s, such as David Bailey, Mary Quant, and Mick Jagger, was hailed as a child of the new era. His youth, his success, his marriage to Leslie Caron and flamboyant life-style, coupled with the fact that he was also amusing, clever, and above all accessible, turned him into the journalists' dream. His years at Stratford were to be attended by more publicity –

both serious and frivolous – than those of any other director, or since.

The fame and the publicity helped Hall, and he used them as . His precocious celebrity gave him a head start: from the moment he was appointed there was a widespread assumption that his regime would bring excitement and change; the very reason Hall kept having to deny that his being director would mean 'a revolution on the Avon' was because journalists assumed automatically that it would. If Hall had been no less able, but twenty years older, his appointment would have been greeted very differently. As it was, his own image, and his plans for the Memorial, suited the frenetic expansionist spirit of the age. The man, the moment, and the method came together with perfect timing.

The single most remarkable thing about Peter Hall's initial work at Stratford was the astonishing speed with which he effected the changes that had been discussed with Fordham Flower in Leningrad. In one year, this was what he achieved: the Stratford stage was substantially redesigned, with a rake, a new false proscenium arch, and an apron stage that jutted fourteen feet into the auditorium; a second theatre in London, the Aldwych, was leased, its stage redesigned to match the new Stratford one, and a first season there launched; three-year contracts were initiated, and the first sixteen artists who would form the nucleus of Hall's new 'permanent' company signed them; a number of new playwrights, including John Arden, Robert Bolt, Peter Shaffer, and John Whiting, were commissioned to write plays for the Aldwych; and finally and symbolically, the Memorial Theatre and its company's name was changed, to the Royal Shakespeare Theatre, and the Royal Shakespeare Company – a move that allowed Hall to jettison the somewhat funereal Victorian associations of 'Memorial', and emphasize the new forward-looking policies of his company. The new title, as someone remarked to Hall, had 'practically everything going for it except God'.

For one or two of these changes to have been achieved within a year would have been remarkable; for them all to be achieved was extraordinary, particularly since they were brought about at a time when Hall was also engaged in planning his first Stratford season, of six plays, three of which he directed. Nor were the changes easy ones to make. The long-term contracts, as the Secretary General of Equity noted when welcoming the scheme, were 'revolutionary', nothing like them had been attempted before in English theatre.[2] They offered actors a security, and a guaranteed continuity of work, unheard of before, and it was not surprising that many were eager to embrace the opportunities they offered. Among the first contract artists to be signed up were Max Adrian, Peggy Ashcroft, Ian Bannen, Richard Johnson, Peter O'Toole, Eric Porter and Dorothy Tutin. But the contracts were expensive, difficult to administer and inflexible – they did not allow sufficiently for the swift changes of heart and fortune that characterize the theatre. Peter O'Toole, for instance, told journalists in 1960 that he 'was wildly enthusiastic' about the contracts, and that 'this was the way actors ought to work', but he played only one season with the new company (at Stratford in 1960) before he was offered a major film role – Lawrence of Arabia. Then, although he had been cast in the leading role of Henry II in Hall's production of *Becket* for the following year, he promptly left the RSC to make the film.

Nor was it easy, as Hall rapidly discovered, to acquire a London base for the company. West End managers by no means welcomed the idea of admitting to their enclave such a competitor. As soon as Hall's intention to acquire a London theatre became known, Binkie Beaumont resigned from the Stratford board of governors because, he wrote to Fordham Flower, he felt there was a conflict of interest.[3] In Hall's view, Beaumont then encouraged other West End managers to try and block the Stratford expansion. Suddenly and mysteriously there were no London theatres available for lease. The Aldwych was acquired only by means of a little chicanery. It was one of the theatres which most interested Hall because, although it was situated only on the fringes of the West End, it was the perfect size, seating just over one thousand people. It was nearly thirty years since the Aldwych had been famous for its farces, and the theatre had housed no major successes for some years, which made it seem possible Stratford would get it. But when the RSC applied for a lease from Prince Littler, it was refused: Littler was, with Beaumont, a director of H. M. Tennent. But Prince Littler had a brother, Emile, with whom he existed in a state of some rivalry; the RSC then applied to Emile, and secured a promise of the Cambridge Theatre. They made sure that this news filtered to Prince Littler with all possible speed; when it did, as anticipated, the Aldwych suddenly became available. Prince Littler signed a deal which seemed advantageous to the RSC. He covered the major part of the costs of renovating the theatre in

1960, and set a fairly low fixed rent for an initial period of five years. But Littler was guaranteed a high percentage of the gross – 25 per cent. This meant that even on its most successful productions the RSC cleared little. The only substantial commercial success they had during the 1960s was *Becket* (which later transferred to another theatre). But *Becket* was a large-cast, lavish production, and by the time costs and Littler's percentage had been offset against takings, the RSC was left with a tiny surplus for a production that had been a sell out.

The remarkable thing about all these initial changes was that they were almost all organizational. They had an instantaneous effect on the structure of the RSC. Suddenly there were two theatres instead of one; instead of five annual productions at Stratford there were now six, plus a further eight or nine at the Aldwych; where there had been one company of around sixty actors there were now two, totalling over one hundred. All this put an immense strain not only on the company's financial resources, but on its actors, stage staff, and managerial team. There were some, Peter Brook among them, who felt that this approach, this sudden new creation of a vast superstructure, was wrong. They felt that Hall should first have attempted to change his companies from the *inside*, beginning with a re-examination of their methods of work, training, and rehearsal, and that only as the company developed should the superstructure have become more complex. This headlong expansion of the RSC was in many ways predictable considering Hall's impetuous personality; he would always rather launch a battle than laboriously train the troops. Many who know Hall well consider this his greatest quality – that he likes to take risks, that he is a gambler rather than an investor. And Hall was taking an enormous gamble from 1960 onwards; but that he did so was not just a matter of his own nature and inclinations, it was also a straightforward matter of politics. The reason he opened a London theatre and launched a company there with such precipitate speed was – yet again – because the birth of the National Theatre seemed imminent. For the first six years of Hall's directorship at Stratford, the RSC and the National Theatre lobby were to be engaged in a complex political power struggle, which extended beyond the confines of those two bodies and involved MPs, the LCC, the Arts Council, the Old Vic, and practically every other member of the Arts Establishment in the country. The continual protestations of mutual goodwill and camaraderie which continued to be made by both sides during much of this period disguised what was always intense rivalry, and sometimes intense anger and bitterness.

On the face of it, by 1960 the National Theatre project had made little progress in the seven years since it had first seriously alarmed Anthony Quayle. No company had been created, no building work had commenced; the foundation stone laid by Queen Elizabeth, the Queen Mother, still sat in solemn isolation, and successive governments had failed to release the million pounds pledged to the creation of the National by the 1949 Act. But despite conspicuous lack of progress, influential lobbying continued, and in 1960 Lord Cottesloe, the newly appointed chairman of the Arts Council, began compiling a feasibility report on the National for the Treasury. Meanwhile the National Theatre Trustees had attempted to strengthen their position by approaching Laurence Olivier with a view to his becoming future director of the National. Olivier had been informally sounded out on this possibility by Oliver Lyttelton, chairman of the Joint Council of the National Theatre, in 1957; he had proved agreeable, and the following year was made a NT Trustee. From that year onwards Olivier became an active campaigner for the National, as well as, unofficially, its Director-designate. Peter Hall knew this. During 1958, when Hall had been offered the directorship of Stratford, but his appointment had not yet been announced, he and Olivier met in the theatre restaurant at Stratford to discuss the next year's production of *Coriolanus*. According to Hall, Olivier told him that he hoped to make the National happen, and invited Hall to join him as his second-in-command. Hall refused.[4]

During 1959 Hall's plans for a permanent company and a London theatre began to leak out within the acting profession. The reaction of the National's supporters was swift; they began to make overtures to Stratford. Informal talks were held that April at Olivier's home, Notley Abbey.[5] Present were Olivier, Lord Esher, and Oliver Lyttelton (by then Lord Chandos) all representing the National's interests, Fordham Flower and Peter Hall, representing Stratford. The subject of discussion was whether Stratford might join forces with the Old Vic and the National campaigners on the Joint Council, with a view to forming one future NT organization, one company. That it was essentially a meeting between two separate theatre factions, aiming at different things, was obscured by the fact that they were all interconnected. Olivier had worked at Stratford before, and was to work there again, in a Hall production, that year. Chandos, the son of Dame Edith Lyttelton, was, like his mother before him, a Stratford governor; he was also the cousin of Fordham's wife, and the two men were old friends. But the reasons behind this sudden attempt at an alliance were far from altruistic on either side. Chandos was trying to gather as broad a basis of support for the National Theatre as possible, and the addition of Stratford to his lobby strengthened it. Stratford possessed a prestigious theatre and substantial reserves, which were tempting. If Stratford extended its empire to London, however, this directly threatened a future National Theatre. With a London base Stratford would be able to mount the kind of repertoire that had always been seen as the National's province. Suddenly the National's territory was being invaded, and according to numerous sources, Chandos and Olivier were alarmed. Not only would the RSC provide a potential competitor, it might supersede the National altogether. No one could believe that the government would subsidize two major theatre companies dedicated to a very similar ideal. And the RSC had a head start: it had the resources to open in London almost immediately. At the most optimistic estimate then a National Theatre could not be built and occupied before 1964 (a date favoured because it was the four-hundredth anniversary of Shakespeare's birth). Until the government made up its mind about the National, and donated funds, it was impossible even to set up a company.

From Hall's and the RSC's point of view, the invitation also offered advantages. Co-operation would enable them to know exactly what the Joint Council of the National was up to. There was even a possibility that Stratford might be able to function to its advantage as part of a National Theatre federation. But if Stratford had nothing to lose from co-operation, it had everything to gain from pursuing its own plans as speedily as possible. If the RSC was slow to expand, and a National Theatre company began work *before* Hall could launch his London operation, then the whole viability of his schemes would be threatened, and the likelihood of a future subsidy diminished. As he saw it, Hall *had* to forestall the National. If he did so, then there was another possibility: that the RSC by virtue of its size and the quality of its work would be accepted as a *de facto* National Theatre with Peter Hall, not Olivier, as its director. This solution was later to be suggested by several critics, but Hall has always denied that that was a motive, and has maintained that he favoured the idea of two major companies – like Jean Vilar's Théâtre

National Populaire and the Comédie-Française in Paris – from the first.[6] But Hall was far too astute politically for this possibility to have escaped him, and the National Theatre lobby was later convinced it did not.

Under Hall the company's work had a much more tentative and uncertain beginning that it had had a decade earlier under Quayle. Partly this was due to the fact that Hall was attempting change on a much larger scale, but also, perhaps, as Peter Brook suggested, because politics took precedence over artistic policy. Certainly the RSC's work for its first two years under Hall's direction was uneven; but it was not just a matter of its having some spectacular successes, and some equally spectacular flops – that would always be inevitable in the work of any company taking risks – it was as if Hall, so certain about organizational reforms, was less certain about artistic ones, so that – initially – the company's work veered wildly in different directions.

The linchpin of Hall's artistic policy was the creation of a company: 'I was clear from the outset,' he wrote in 1964, 'that I could contribute little unless I could develop a company with a strong permanent nucleus.'[7] It was a description that could have been applied equally justly to such diverse groups as Benson's company in the 1890s, the Moscow Arts, or the Berliner Ensemble, and Hall avoided being more specific, resting his case as it were on the twin foundations of quality and continuity. This avoidance of more rigidly defined aims marked from the first the major difference between the RSC as it became and the major European companies it was to rival and sometimes surpass; unlike the Moscow Arts, unlike the Berliner (greatly though that company's work influenced the RSC stylistically for a period), doctrines, whether artistic or political, were to be avoided. Hall created a company markedly free from theoretical dogma, the evolution of whose work depended strongly upon a confederacy of individual tastes and beliefs. It was (and has remained) an organization flexible enough to contain those who in some respects fundamentally disagreed with it. In the early Sixties, for example, Peter Brook considered the RSC 'did not have an artistic policy under Hall any more than the BBC does', and believed its 'ideal was to do good things very well, the traditional target of liberal England';[8] nevertheless, Brook directed some of his own finest work, and the RSC's, under those auspices. Given that the backbone of his

Peggy Ashcroft as Katharina and Peter O'Toole as Petruchio in *The Taming of the Shrew*, 1960, John Barton's first production at Stratford.

Landmarks in the early work of the RSC: *top*, the final confrontation between Achilles (left) and Hector (Patrick Allen and Derek Godfrey) in Peter Hall and John Barton's 1960 production of *Troilus and Cressida*. Designs by Leslie Hurry. *Bottom*, Clifford Williams's superb 1962 production of *The Comedy of Errors*, with Ian Richardson (centre forestage) and Alec McCowen (far right) as the Antipholus twins, and Diana Rigg and Susan Maryott as Adriana and Luciana.

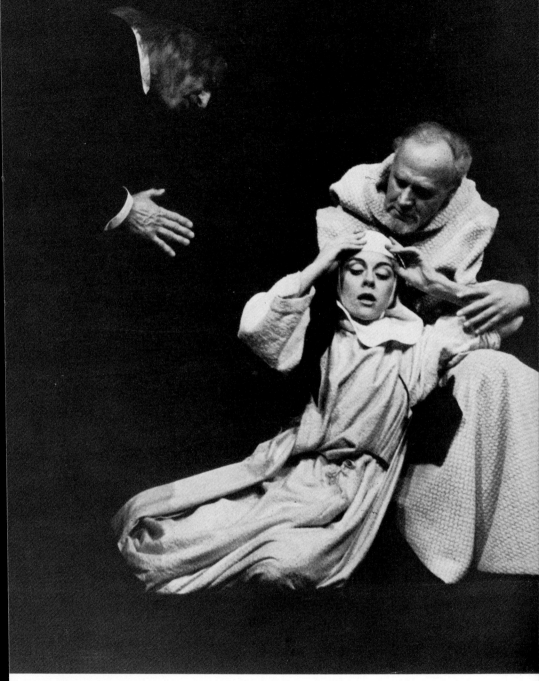

Dorothy Tutin as Sister Jeanne, Max Adrian (left) as Father Barre, and Donald Layne-Smith as Father Mignon in Peter Wood's production of John Whiting's *The Devils*, Aldwych, 1961.

The Wars of the Roses trilogy, 1963–4, directed by Peter Hall, with John Barton and Frank Evans, designed by John Bury. *Left, above* (left to right), David Warner as Henry VI, Donald Sinden as York, and Brewster Mason as Warwick; *below,* the Cade rebellion with Clive Swift (centre back) as Cade.

Above, David Warner as Henry with Peggy Ashcroft as Queen Margaret.

Right, Ian Holm as Richard III in the final play of the Histories sequence, 1964, directed by Peter Hall, with John Barton and Clifford Williams. *Below*, Patrick Magee as de Sade, Glenda Jackson as Charlotte Corday, and Ian Richardson as Marat in Peter Brook's production of Peter Weiss's *Marat/Sade*, Aldwych, 1964.

The blinding of Gloucester (Alan Webb) watched by Regan (Patience Collier) in Peter Brook's celebrated production of *King Lear*, 1962, with Paul Scofield in the title-role.

Top, *The Taming of the Shrew*, 1967. Left to right, Patrick Stewart as Grumio, Michael Williams as Petruchio, and Janet Suzman as Katharina. *Bottom*, Tourneur's *The Revenger's Tragedy*, 1966, with Ian Richardson (left) as Vendice, Alan Howard (recumbent) as Lussurioso, and Ted Valentine as a Gentleman. Both productions directed by Trevor Nunn, with designs by Christopher Morley.

company's work remained Shakespeare, Hall's concept of a flexible, artistically unconfined company was in any case perhaps inevitable. Shakespeare's protean plays, with their multiple sympathies and extraordinarily broad moral vision, do not lend themselves to a doctrinaire approach: at least, not without the kind of editing and revision practised upon them by the Berliner. However, the fact that Shakespeare's work remained central to the company's repertoire made it doubly difficult for Hall to create a company. Shakespeare's plays, unlike, say, Chekhov's, do not naturally lend themselves to ensemble work. Most of his plays, and particularly the tragedies, are hierarchic in cast terms; they contain one or two roles that remain the mountain peaks of theatre, then a range of strong supporting parts, then a large number of brilliantly observed but tiny parts. No matter how fine a company performs *King Lear,* or *Macbeth,* company strength will not totally compensate for any weakness or slightness in the central roles, yet to keep the very few actors capable of conquering them within a permanent company was exceptionally difficult. Nor was Hall by any means indifferent to, or unaware of, the prestige lent a company by stars. In his first season he planned to include Paul Scofield, Rex Harrison, and Kay Kendall. Later he could draw on actors promoted and developed within the company, such as Vanessa Redgrave, David Warner, Ian Holm, and Glenda Jackson. But such actors were likely to leave the company, often for films, just when they were becoming most valuable to it. As Hall wrote of his struggles to create a company, 'If you are lucky enough to create it, it immediately begins to disintegrate'.[9]

Hall faced another difficulty in creating the company he envisaged. It was central to his concept of the new RSC that its actors should be able to work both in Shakespeare, and in modern plays at the Aldwych. But integrating the two theatres' work was exceptionally difficult. For most of the eight years of Hall's directorship, comparatively few Stratford productions transferred to London. This meant that, apart from revivals of classic plays like *The Duchess of Malfi* which opened the Aldwych operation in December 1960, a large number of new plays had to be found each year to fill the London repertoire. Although some actors worked both in London and in Stratford in the same season, commuting between the two theatres, what generally happened at first was that the companies rotated, beginning their RSC work in Stratford, then moving to London. This meant that Hall had a company of some fifty or sixty actors to accommodate at the Aldwych in modern work, and the effect this had on the Aldwych repertoire in the first years of the company's existence was evident. Hall sought to find plays that would use a Stratford-size company, what he called 'epic plays that are not historical . . . plays written for a company with themes that require large casts'. But in seeking such plays Hall was running counter to his time. The new English playwrights who were beginning to emerge were not, in the main, writing such plays; they were writing intense intimate plays, requiring small casts. This meant that it was not until 1962, when Hall launched a season of smaller-cast plays at the Arts Theatre, that the RSC was able to begin presenting more experimental new work. Its early Aldwych seasons were dominated by large-cast, middle-brow plays such as *Ondine, Becket,* and *Curtmantle,* which were all well received. The only major new play of any lasting significance that the RSC mounted at the Aldwych in the first two years of its existence was *The Devils,* and it was not until 1963 that the problem of a two-centre operation combining Shakespeare and modern work began to be, if not resolved, rationalized.

For his first season Hall chose a theme – the development of Shakespearian comedy – and the plays ranged from early work (*Two Gentlemen of Verona*) through the middle period to late plays, the bitter *Troilus and Cressida,* and a romance play, *Winter's Tale.* Although the productions contained some fine individual performances, most notably O'Toole's Shylock, and Eric Porter's Leontes, they made little significant advance on previous work at Stratford, with the exception of the *Troilus.* That production had a brilliantly innovative set (designed, surprisingly, by Leslie Hurry) of the utmost simplicity; it consisted of a shallow octagonal box filled with white sand, backed by a cyclorama the colour of dried blood. It suited the bleakness of the play's vision, and provided a superb background for the spectacular Homeric fight sequences, brilliantly lit and using mist (dry ice) for the first time at Stratford – a device then so unfamiliar that some of the critics thought it was steam. But although the production was a breakthrough in design and in company work, it was without influence on the next Stratford season.

  By that time the majority of the 1960 company had moved to the Aldwych, and so for 1961 Hall had to begin again and try to create a second company at Stratford. This time he was far less successful: while the 1960 actors went on, in the second year of working together, to provide increasingly strong work at the Aldwych (even in somewhat disappointing plays), at Stratford the work fell apart. The company included three great stars, Edith Evans, John Gielgud, and Peggy Ashcroft; one newcomer, Christopher Plummer, brought in from Stratford Ontario; some actors from previous seasons – Dorothy Tutin and Geraldine McEwan; a contingent from the Royal Court – William Gaskill, directing *Richard III*, and Ian Bannen, who had worked at the Memorial in bit parts for four seasons in the Fifties, and who had recently been acclaimed as Serjeant Musgrave at the Court; and one promising but fairly unknown talent, Vanessa Redgrave, who was given the part of Rosalind when Dorothy Tutin fell ill. The supporting company was weaker than that of the year before. The only truly successful production of the season was the exquisite and delicate *As You Like It,* directed by Michael Elliott, and lit up by Redgrave's Rosalind. The *Much Ado* and *Richard III* were competent, but broke little new ground; the *Hamlet* was, Tynan wrote in the *Observer,* 'as paltry and undercast as any I recall from the days before Sir Barry Jackson took over the theatre' (a view widely shared by the other critics); *Romeo and Juliet,* directed by Hall, had last-minute cast changes, and suffered in comparison with Zeffirelli's famous production of the play at the Old Vic the previous year. But the production that illustrated best how far the RSC seemed to be going off-course was the final one of the season, *Othello,* a production that epitomized everything that was bad about the theatre of the 1950s, everything that the RSC was supposed to be attempting to reform.

The history of the production was simple: Hall wanted Gielgud to act at Stratford; Gielgud wanted to play Othello – a part to which he was manifestly ill-suited – and he wanted to work with the newly fashionable Zeffirelli, most of whose work before the 1960 *Romeo and Juliet* (his first English production) had been in opera, and with the film director Visconti. Zeffirelli wanted beautiful but very complex sets, which were completed late; all went well until the moment of pure horror when Gielgud and Ashcroft went into the theatre to dress rehearse, and saw the sets for the first time. Nothing so elaborate had been seen on the English stage since the heyday of Beerbohm Tree. There were pillars, grilles, and battlements to be flown in and out; huge embossed doors to be erected; vast flights of steps to be put up and dismantled. Many of the sets were painted chocolate brown, so that when Gielgud, in his Othello make-up, stood against them, his face became immediately invisible. The dress rehearsal lasted five hours, at the end of which the unfortunate actors had not even got through the whole play.[10] The first night, largely thanks to Hall's intervention, was a slight improvement, but it still lasted four and a half hours, and was punctuated by Bensonian intervals, and the sound of frantic backstage hammerings. In an ultimate gesture of folly, Zeffirelli had even placed a set-change between Iago's first soliloquy and the scene that precedes it. When the sets were finally in place, an exquisite stage-picture, superbly lit, and reminiscent of a Veronese painting was achieved – but only at the cost of the destruction of the play.[11] This fiasco gave a great opportunity to the critics to have fun at both Gielgud's and the RSC's expense, and they took it with relish: the production, which had been extremely costly, was taken off with due speed.

Failure, even on this scale, is an inevitable part of any theatre's growth, and there were some critics who, like Bernard Levin, were prepared to forgive the flops, arguing that the successes (such as Michel Saint-Denis's great production of *The Cherry Orchard* which ended the first Aldwych season) were equally as spectacular – an indication, at least, that upheaval and change on the grand scale were taking place. Others were less tolerant. Harold Hobson, writing in the *Sunday Times* at the end of the 1961 season on the need for some coherent style in a future National Theatre company, felt that no such coherence was developing at Stratford:

The unfortunate players are blown about in gales of contrary doctrine. Sometimes they have a curtain, sometimes not; sometimes they imitate the previous performances of greater players than themselves, sometimes they are built on novelty . . . often they match ducal costumes to dustbin voices . . . as a preparation for a National Theatre this is no good at all. We need a style, and Stratford ought to be able to find it for us.

The year 1962 was a key one in the development of the RSC. It was the year in which Saint-Denis, Peter Brook, and Clifford Williams joined the company as resident directors; it was the year John Bury designed his first Stratford production; the year in which the RSC was finally promised its first subsidy. It was also a year when the RSC was under intense pressure, and the moment when it found the style that was to characterize its best work under Hall's directorship. The triumphs of the next two years, of the *Wars of the Roses,* the History cycle, and the two equally superb Aldwych seasons, were forged in the furore, the fights, the overwork, and the sheer excitement of 1962. It began with the announcement, in April, that there was to be a significant change in the RSC hierarchy: Peter Brook and Michel Saint-Denis were to join Hall – Saint-Denis as general artistic adviser to the company, Brook on the directorate – the idea being that the company would be administered artistically by a triumvirate.

It is interesting that Hall, like Quayle before him, felt the need to share his responsibilities, and it was a further example of a need he seemed to feel for artistic father figures. The first had been Byam Shaw; the second, John Barton, the senior colleague from his Cambridge days, whom Hall had brought in as an associate director immediately after his own appointment. Now Hall invited to share his responsibilities the two men he most admired in English theatre – though, as it happened, they did not greatly admire each other. Saint-Denis, Hall considered, 'brought Europe into the company'. His main task was to undertake studio training-work with young actors, work which he began in 1962 but which was severely curtailed by his ill health. Brook was there because he was, Hall felt, the 'consistent revolutionary'.[12] Brook was at this time actively opposed to the continuing organizational expansion of the RSC; he was pushing for the company to become smaller, to continue to work in both Shakespeare and modern plays, but to try to find, with a small nucleus of actors, a new dynamic. But this was not the course the RSC pursued that year.

Over the next twelve months the company staged twenty-four productions, an ambitious volume of work not equalled for many years. Including staff and acting companies, it employed nearly five hundred people, and it played to over 700,000, making it at the time the largest theatre operation in the world. There was a Stratford season of seven plays, an Aldwych season of eleven plays, a season of seven plays in monthly repertory at the Arts Theatre, and a provincial tour of revivals of *The Devils* and *Troilus and Cressida*.[13] By any law of averages the company should have been overstretched; probably it was, but the sheer volume of activity, and the fact that at the same time the company was engaged in what was extensively publicized as a battle for survival, seemed to have a galvanic effect on its work.

The season at the Arts lost money, but it was both memorable and exciting, and included some exceptionally good productions, among them David Rudkin's first play, *Afore Night Come* (Clifford Williams's first production for the RSC), Gorky's *The Lower Depths,* and a strong production of the rarely performed *Women Beware Women,* with brilliant central performances from Jeanne Hepple and Nicol Williamson. At the Aldwych a much more challenging repertoire than that of the previous year was mounted, including a fine production of *The Caucasian Chalk Circle* by William Gaskill; the RSC's first production of a Pinter play (*The Collection*); a Strindberg, and another John Whiting, *A Penny for a Song.* This repertoire, which could not rely on large audiences, was bolstered by the revivals and transfers of hit Stratford productions which were assured of large houses.

At Stratford the season was the strongest the company had yet achieved, and it was notable that much less reliance was placed on senior actors. Although the company included Eric Porter, Irene Worth, Marius Goring, and Tom Fleming, and Paul Scofield joined at the end of the season to play Lear, much greater chances were given to the company's best young actors, to Judi Dench, Ian Holm, Ian Richardson, Diana Rigg, Tony Church, and Peter Jeffrey, all of whom had been with the company since at least 1960, and some longer. All the productions were strong, but what was most significant was the sense of a new coherence, as if the company had finally thrown off past conventions and found its artistic identity. This was marked in the first production of the season, *Measure for Measure,* the first RSC production to be designed by John Bury, who had worked for eight years with Joan Littlewood at Stratford East. Bury was to spearhead the revolution in design at the RSC, and his radical approach was apparent in that first production. He set *Measure* on a bare stage, out of whose dark empty spaces the characters emerged with great intensity; the eyes of the spectators were concentrated totally on the actors. The junction between scenes almost disappeared, so swift was the transference; a chair was moved, a spotlight came on, someone moved forward, the scene began. The contrast with the two revivals that followed it (of the 1959 *Dream* and the 1960 *Shrew*) was intense. Its new simplicity, which had been foreshadowed by the 1960 *Troilus,* marked all four other Stratford productions that year, the *Macbeth,* Gaskill's fine production of *Cymbeline,* and the season's two runaway successes, Clifford Williams's *Comedy of Errors* and Brook's *King Lear.*

Williams's production, his first at Stratford, was a stopgap, put on with a brief rehearsal period as a fill-in until *Lear* could open (this had had to be postponed as Scofield had been ordered to rest by his doctors). It turned out to be one of the greatest comedy productions ever mounted at Stratford. It took a farce of no great popularity and turned it into a breathtakingly fast and inventive extravaganza. It was set on three planked, raked platforms, with a few benches. At the beginning of the play the entire cast marched downstage in a solemn phalanx, all clad in uniformly grey costumes. Then the fun began: as the story spiralled into progressive absurdities of confusion, with two sets of identical twins at large, so decorative elements were added to the costumes – a scarlet feather here, a slashed jerkin there, a vivid ruff, an absurd hat, until the stage became a swirling carnival of colour. It was both anarchic and brilliantly controlled – and was a totally unpredicted, unforeseen success. It was after this production that Kenneth Tynan, for one, decided the RSC had come into its own:

The *Comedy of Errors* is unmistakably an RSC production. The statement is momentous; it means Peter Hall's troupe has developed, uniquely in Britain, a classical style of its own. How is it to be recognized? By solid Brechtian settings that emphasize wood and metal instead of paint and canvas; and by cogent deliberate verse speaking, that discards melodic cadenzas in favour of meaning and motivation . . .[14]

This fine season was crowned with Peter Brook's now legendary production of *King Lear,* which has been widely and extensively discussed elsewhere. But one of the most significant aspects of that production was that although it was unmistakably Brook's work, and contained at its heart an incomparable performance from Paul Scofield, who was not one of the RSC's contract artists, it was not an isolated artistic event. All of Brook's previous productions at Stratford, from the 1946 *Love's Labour's Lost* onwards, had been like theatrical meteors, just as Komisarjevsky's had been in the 1930s. They were the product of his revolutionary theatrical vision, unrelated to other work in the same theatre, pointing the way to new possibilities that were then never explored by other directors. That was not so of *Lear*; in the austerity and simplicity of its staging, in the severity of its costuming, the unsentimentality and rigour of its approach, it chimed with work already being done by the RSC and was afterwards, as Peter Hall said, to have a continuing influence on the company's work – an influence detectable immediately the next year in the productions of the *Wars of the Roses*. It was also the product of a strong and experienced group of actors; Scofield gave a towering performance as Lear, but the playing of the rest of the company, from the most senior actors to the most junior, had a uniform strength and audacity. In every sense this was not the fitful brilliance attained just by bringing in a great director and a great actor, but company work.

It was fortunate that the company hit form when it did. Had its work been less extensive, or as uncertain as it had been the previous year at Stratford, the subsequent events might have been very different. For during 1962 the company was operating at the eye of a storm, even if it was a storm Peter Hall assiduously prevented from abating. It was caused, inevitably, by money problems, and the continuing imbroglio with the National Theatre.

Many of the changes that continue to shape British theatre had their origins in the muddles and intrigues that marked 1962. It was the year in which British theatre was carved up, to be dominated thereafter by two major subsidized companies; it was the year the Arts Council began its evolution from tiny department to dispenser of millions of pounds of grant aid; it was the year in which the future scale of the National Theatre was determined, and the RSC's need for the Barbican theatre created; in which the disparity in subsidy and salaries between those two organizations was laid down, and their position of (comparative) centralized affluence established.

Two years before, during 1960, largely as a consequence of the previous discussions at Notley Abbey, Stratford was invited formally to join the Joint Council of the National Theatre, and accepted. The timing was not arbitrary; Lord Cottesloe was preparing his report for the Treasury on the subject of a National Theatre, and wanted the Joint Council to submit proposals. 'Things are cooking a bit over the National Theatre etc.,' Chandos wrote to Fordham Flower. 'One of the keys to the situation will, I believe, be the attitude of Stratford. Frankly my idea is that we should make a tripod of Stratford, the Old Vic and the National Theatre . . .'[15] Chandos saw no difficulties in involving Stratford in his National Theatre 'tripod'. 'Collaboration does not mean amalgamation or anything of that kind,' he reassured Fordham. 'It only means that when the National Theatre is built, we should work out how we can most usefully scratch one another's backs.'[16] Chandos was more than a little disillusioned with his dealings with the somewhat dilatory representatives from the Vic, to whom in private he referred as 'la tragédie anglaise',[17] He therefore welcomed the addition of Fordham's and Hall's administrative flair and expertise.

A new executive committee was set up to prepare the proposals for Cottesloe and the Chancellor, and it nicely balanced all the constituent factions. It was chaired by Kenneth Clark (a neutral figure in that he was not involved in theatre, though he subsequently became a member of the NT Board). Its members included Chandos and Olivier, Fordham and Hall, and from the Old Vic, Alfred Francis and Michael Benthall. They were later joined by two representatives of the commercial theatre, Prince Littler and Binkie Beaumont of H. M. Tennent. This committee had seven meetings between August 1960 and the end of that year, and an active part in the discussions was played by Peter Hall. But although numerous key topics were lengthily discussed, including costing, size of companies, organization, and design of the future National, the discussions were fatally unspecific on many details; the impression the minutes give is that numerous obstinate and obvious difficulties were bulldozed out of the way in order to arrive at a scheme which appeared to upset none of the special interests of the parties involved. One vital point which was never discussed, for instance, was the future of the RSC's activities at the Aldwych. But by the end of the year the committee had made sufficient progress to draw up a memorandum regarding the National Theatre, which was duly submitted to the Chancellor of the Exchequer, Selwyn Lloyd, on 9 December 1960. The memorandum, which was not at the time released to the Press, proposed an ambitious scheme that reflected the composition of the committee: the National Theatre would consist of a company of approximately 150 actors, who would be divided into three groups; one would appear at the new National building on the South Bank, one at Stratford, and one would tour; the Old Vic building (which was in a poor state of repair) would be retained for a young company, or experimental work. The company would be subsidized, and in the period before the new National building was complete, both the Old Vic company and the RSC would receive interim subsidy (the Vic's present subsidy being increased, the RSC's created) in order for them to build up a team of actors of suitable excellence.

This scheme begged numerous questions, the chief of which was the degree of autonomous power the Old Vic and the Stratford company (which operated under a complex Royal Charter) would retain. Hall had, however, repeatedly made it clear at the committee's meetings that Stratford envisaged losing its autonomy. 'Mr Hall said that it must be understood that upon the completion of the NT both Stratford and the Old Vic would be entirely absorbed in the overall NT organization,' the minutes record for one meeting. 'Mr Hall said that Stratford had from the outset accepted the fact that both organizations would lose their identity in a complete amalgamation, and that this had been accepted by his Governors,' they record for another.[18] But what the discussions left unclear – disastrously as it was to turn out – was exactly what was meant by 'entirely absorbed' and 'complete amalgamation'. All might, however, have proceeded smoothly, had it not been for the vacillation of Macmillan's government.

On 21 March 1961 Selwyn Lloyd, making no reference to the memorandum, announced in the House that the government had decided there would be no National Theatre. Instead it proposed to release the sum of £400,000 per annum in subsidy to the theatre, to be divided between existing organizations, namely Stratford, the Old Vic, and regional repertory companies. This announcement provoked predictable controversy. Lord Chandos said it was a public insult to the Queen Mother, who had laid the National's foundation stone ten years before. The LCC, who had ambitious plans for the South Bank, and who had been keeping the National's site there open for ten years, was outraged. The Joint Council of the National was plunged into gloom; after eighty years it looked as if the campaigning had all been fruitless. Stratford's reaction was somewhat different, although they expressed appropriate condolences, and urged the Joint Council to fight on. From the RSC's point of view, the Chancellor's decision had numerous advantages: it promised subsidy, and it meant the company need no longer fear competition from the National. During the same month Lord Cottesloe, the chairman of the Arts Council, duly wrote to Stratford asking the theatre to begin negotiations and submit figures on which a future three-year grant could be assessed.[19] In May the figures were supplied by Patrick Donnell, together with a statement from Peter Hall. They must have come as something of a shock to the Arts Council, for they revealed for the first time the scale, not to say the magniloquence, of some of Hall's plans for the RSC. The company was asking for what was then regarded as an enormous subsidy of £124,000 to cover a deficit of that amount which Hall feared the theatre might be left with that year, and to cover an increase in salaries to actors which he felt was overdue. (Salaries remained pegged at a top level of £60 a week, and he wanted to raise that to £100.) These figures later turned out to be inaccurate as predictions, for the RSC was estimating a deficit of £47,000 on the first year's operation at the Aldwych alone, and in fact the company's overall deficit that year was just under £30,000. But given that when the estimates had to be made the Aldwych had only been open for four months it was not surprising that these predictions proved wrong – the RSC had little to go on in making them. What *was* astonishing was that Hall was also coolly appealing for funds to rebuild the Stratford auditorium, to transform it into a 2,000-seat thrust-stage amphitheatre at an estimated cost of some £400,000, £350,000 of which, he suggested, might come from the Arts Council in instalments over a three-year period.[20] The RSC then went ahead with planning the rest of its 1961 and 1962 work in confident expectation of a respectable Arts Council cheque. This expectation, and its subsequent frustration, was to prove central to the complicated events that followed.

In London, meanwhile, a considerable amount of lobbying for the National Theatre was continuing, the prime movers being Isaac Hayward, Leader of the LCC, and the indefatigable Lord Chandos. On 9 June 1961 Isaac Hayward led an all-party deputation to Selwyn Lloyd on the subject of the National. Idealistic arguments having failed, Hayward tried a new gambit – money. If the government would release the £1,000,000 pledged by the National Theatre Act of 1949 then, Hayward informed the Chancellor, the LCC would provide money also – £1,300,000 levied from the rates, as a contribution to the capital costs of the building. This offer was generous enough to make Selwyn Lloyd change his mind; on 23 June he wrote to Isaac Hayward accepting his proposals in principle, and making several new suggestions. The government and the LCC should, he suggested, invite the Joint Council to submit a new scheme for the National, one that embraced not only the Old Vic and the RSC, but also Sadler's Wells; the South Bank scheme should include not only a National Theatre, but also an opera house. If the Council produced a workable scheme the government would subsidize the project to the tune of £400,000 per annum, £230,000 going to drama and £170,000 to opera and ballet. The drama subsidy was, he made clear, to cover all expenditure 'at the headquarters of the institutions concerned, including the Memorial Theatre at Stratford'. 'If', he continued, 'any one of the three organizations concerned should not participate in the scheme, any annual Government subventions would have to be reconsidered, and the Government would be under no obligation to contribute monies for the improvement of their existing premises'.[21] In other words, if the RSC did not form part of Chandos's National Theatre 'tripod' it might receive no grant, and no money to improve the Stratford theatre.

The proposals were becoming more and more unwieldy, and more and more grandiose. They now involved the Treasury, the Arts Council, the LCC, Sadler's Wells, the NT caucus, an opera house, the Memorial Theatre, an undecided number of new theatre auditoriums on the South Bank, and the Old Vic, which nobody could quite decide what to do with. This, however, did not deter Lord Chandos; he and his family had struggled for decades to get a National Theatre built, and as Fordham Flower wrote to a friend, 'You must bear in mind that Oliver is inclined to favour any scheme, regardless of its merits, and to accept any compromise, in order to get the building up, come what may'.[22]

Chandos struggled manfully to produce a workable scheme from these heterogeneous elements, and on 7 July 1961 he discussed it with Selwyn Lloyd. His plan was, in essence, unaltered from the previous year's memorandum. There would be an opera house, but the National would still embrace Stratford and the Old Vic; the company would play at Stratford, on the South Bank, and probably in the Old Vic theatre also. It would be governed by a council composed of representatives from all bodies, including Sadler's Wells, and be administered artistically by three directors (one from Stratford, one from the Vic, one from Sadler's Wells) all of whom would report to an overall director, Laurence Olivier. Again, the Aldwych was not mentioned. Selwyn Lloyd gave this scheme the go-ahead, and Arnold Goodman, from the firm of solicitors Goodman, Derrick & Co., was asked by Chandos to draft a proposed constitution that yoked all these groups together. Goodman arranged a visit to Stratford for the middle of August 1961 to consult on a constitution. But by the time Goodman visited Stratford there had been other developments that had profoundly altered Stratford's attitude to the whole project. In July, Fordham Flower had written to Lord Cottesloe: the RSC had submitted its estimates to the Arts Council in May, when could it expect to be told how much subsidy it would receive, and when could it expect the money?[23]

Cottesloe's reply was a bombshell. Although no one at the Arts Council had, it seemed, seen fit to inform the RSC of the fact, it would now *not* be receiving subsidy. The position had changed as a result of Selwyn Lloyd's new decision on the National Theatre. The £400,000 earmarked in March for Stratford, the Old Vic, and regional reps would now not be forthcoming; furthermore, no interim grants would be made to the RSC and the Old Vic to build up strength towards the establishment of a National Theatre until the whole NT scheme had been finalized and approved both by the government and the LCC. 'This process', Cottesloe wrote, 'may, of course, take some considerable time to complete.'[24]

This news arrived two days before Goodman's visit to Stratford, and not unnaturally prejudiced the outcome of that meeting. The RSC was losing money rapidly as a result of the Aldwych; its plans for the latter half of 1961 and for 1962 had been based on an expectation of subsidy.[25] Now it was to get nothing, and for an indefinite period. The meeting with Goodman did not go well. Goodman's recollection of it was that it was dominated by Stratford's desire to know who, artistically, was to be in charge – although if accurate, this was odd, as Goodman (whom no one from the RSC had met before) was there to discuss the future constitution of the NT, not its artistic administration. According to Goodman, when he ventured the opinion that Olivier would be the director (hardly news to anyone from the RSC) there 'seemed to be an immediate diminution of interest'.[26]

In the week after Goodman's visit, the situation worsened. Fordham wrote an angry letter to Cottesloe, demanding to know whether it was being implied that 'unless Stratford was part of the National Theatre scheme, when this is eventually formulated, it will not be eligible for any subvention in the future?'[27] Cottesloe's answer to this, though couched in the language of officialdom, suggested that this, indeed, was the case.[28] It was at this point that the RSC's attitude towards participation in any National Theatre scheme underwent a profound change. In Fordham's view it 'introduced an element of coercion and blackmail into the proceedings' which had 'a deplorable effect upon his colleagues'. Both he and Peter Hall became convinced that subsidy wäs being used to twist their arms: if Stratford did not agree to the complex and hastily compiled new NT scheme, then it would be left outside it, minus all subsidy.

The gathering hostility finally broke out at a meeting of the executive committee of the Joint Council of the National Theatre on 20 September, held to discuss Goodman's report on the NT's future constitution. At this meeting all the difficult details involved in a merger were at last not brushed aside, but fully discussed. The result, according to Fordham, 'was an arid and disagreeable discussion that lasted an hour and a half':

When I pressed for details it was soon apparent that the only scheme acceptable to the NT caucus(Chandos, Kenneth Clark, and Olivier) was one that meant complete integration and amalgamation, the transfer of assets and revenue to the central authority, and one large acting company under centralized control and direction. Pressed further, they agreed that this meant the abolition of existing governing bodies, and so far as we were concerned the utter revocation of our Royal Charter. I told them that this was unacceptable and (probably) legally impossible, and that in my view, Stratford could not be governed by remote control . . . The exchanges took place entirely between me and the caucus. The Vic and the Wells sat mum on the sidelines throughout.[29]

The oddity about this reaction of Fordham's was that what the 'NT caucus' was then proposing was not so very different from what Peter Hall had himself insisted upon, with Fordham's approval, in discussions the previous year – that 'upon the completion of the National Theatre both Stratford and the Old Vic would be entirely absorbed in the overall National Theatre organization'. So why had Stratford altered its position? Was it, as Lord Goodman has implied, that Hall had believed there was a possibility of his becoming the future Director of the National, and that when he realized this would not happen, he pushed for Stratford's withdrawal from the scheme because he would not work under Olivier? Hall has always denied this emphatically. Was it that the relationship had been poisoned by the negotiations and let-down over Stratford's grant, and the RSC's feeling of being pressurized into hasty agreement with the new NT scheme? Was it simply that the extremely complex details involved had never been properly discussed, and that Stratford had been encouraged to assume it would have a greater degree of both financial and artistic autonomy than was later proposed? Whatever the final reason, and perhaps all the above were factors, this meeting marked the breakdown in the RSC's participation in any joint scheme for a National Theatre. Intermittent negotiations continued until the end of 1961, and various proposals and counter-proposals were made by both sides, but the distrust was too great, and the differences too wide, for compromise. Fordham tried to get the Joint Council to accept proposals for 'a loose federation', whereby the

future National and the RSC would exist side by side, both subsidized, both independent, but co-operating with each other in
various ways, such as co-ordinating their repertoires, and fixing their
salary levels. But by this time the National scheme was gathering
momentum, and the Joint Council was prepared to make few
concessions. 'Your energetic Mr Hall', Chandos wrote to Fordham,
'has signed up as many artists as he can lay his hands on . . . we shall
have to have a certain latitude over the salaries. Financial induce-
ments are the only ones which we have to offer.'[30]

Stratford finally and formally withdrew from the joint plan in
January 1962, although the decision was not announced until some
months later. And when Chandos's final NT scheme was submitted
to the Chancellor and the LCC, the only references to Stratford were
brief and bleak: the RSC was 'to remain artistically and financially
independent of the National Theatre', and the RSC 'must make its
own arrangements with the Arts Council and the Treasury'.[31] There
the matter might have ended, just another episode in the laborious
and chequered creation of the National (though one with enormous
implications for the future of the British theatre) had it not been for
the fact that the RSC was finding it peculiarly difficult to make any
arrangement with the Arts Council or the Treasury.

In spite of the fact that the RSC had been negotiating with the Arts
Council for subsidy since April 1961, it had by the beginning of 1962
received and been promised nothing since Cottesloe's 1961 offer.
When Fordham repeated his appeal to Lord Cottesloe in January
1962, he was told that it was now too late for the company even to
receive aid for 1962–3 – estimates for that year had already been
submitted to the Treasury and only £10,000 would be available to
Stratford. The figure was mysterious since it bore no relation to the
estimated needs the RSC had submitted in 1961, it had never been
mentioned before, and it was proposed in spite of the fact that a few
months previously Cottesloe had informed Fordham that they would
probably receive no subsidy. The situation became more mysterious
the following month when, the RSC learned, the drama panel of the
Arts Council met and did not even discuss the question of subsidy to
Stratford, although over £150,000 was voted for 1962–3 to provincial theatres. In May a senior member of the Arts Council informed
Fordham (at a chance meeting in Stratford) that the Arts Council had
no official knowledge that the RSC was applying for subvention. By
this time both Fordham and Peter Hall had become convinced that

they were being deliberately blocked. The reason, as they saw it, was simple: the future National Theatre did not want a competitor across Waterloo Bridge at the Aldwych, and did not want its own negotiations regarding subsidy to the affected by the RSC's claims. In Fordham's view (and Hall's) the dice were loaded against them. Lord Cottesloe was not only chairman of the Arts Council, he was also an enthusiastic supporter of the National and was shortly to become chairman of its building committee. Both Chandos and Olivier, in Fordham's view, were also exerting their not inconsiderable influence to ensure the RSC would remain under-financed, and be forced to pull out from London. In Fordham's view the Arts Council was somewhere in the middle of all this, being leaned on from all sides:

Our guess is that what the Secretariat [of the Arts Council] would like to do would be to get us a very inadequate annual subsidy, so that we were always stretched, ever getting weaker and more dependent upon them. This would be blamed on the Treasury. The Arts Council would tell us they batted for us like mad but the Treasury turned it down. A situation would thus be created in which no artistic director would work here, and then the Arts Council would force us into the National Theatre set-up, on the latter's terms. Stratford would then be controlled by the NT caucus, who would swipe our revenue but treat us very much as a provincial second eleven. Anyway, our boys have pressed the Secretariat to declare what is their policy towards us, at which they all put on po-faces, look embarrassed and remain silent.[32]

While it was certainly true that neither Olivier nor Chandos was pleased at the existence of the Aldwych, or at the RSC's attempts to gain subsidy (they, after all, were defending their hard-won territory with the same zeal as Stratford), the attitude of the Arts Council remains more difficult to decipher. Part of the problem was that the Treasury, and therefore the Arts Council, took a conservative attitude towards subsidy in general at this time. Only a few years before – in 1960–1 for instance – the total Arts Council subsidy to drama was only £184,000. (In the same year the Comédie-Française alone received £300,000 from the French government, and state aid to theatre in West Germany amounted to £8,500,000.) The proposed government subsidy to the South Bank of £400,000 p.a. was unprecedented generosity, and both the Treasury and the Arts Council were wary about extending it. Nevertheless as early as February 1962, Peter Hall had become convinced that the only way Stratford would receive any grant for the following year, 1963–4, was by publicizing its case as much as possible. He accordingly suggested to Fordham that they should begin making approaches to the Press, prior to launching a major campaign at the beginning of April.[33] This duly happened; when Hall wanted to create a stir he had no difficulty in attracting the attention of the newspapers. Later the RSC was energetically to deny that any such campaign had been orchestrated, but that it had sprung solely from the righteous zeal of the journalists involved – but that was not exactly the case. The campaign was planned, helped along with judicious 'leaks', and with discreet luncheons, and it was a spectacular success. It began in March 1962, when Hall gave an interview to the *Daily Telegraph* in which he stated that without a grant the RSC would have to give up the Aldwych, and the organization he had created would not be able to survive. For the next six months the publicity about the RSC's plight was unremitting, and impassioned. The company's predicament became a national *cause célèbre*. On 8 July all three major Sunday newspapers contained statements by their respective theatre critics (Hobson, Tynan, and Brien) deploring the RSC's lack of subsidy. This was followed by articles in nearly every daily newspaper, in the *New Statesman* and *Tribune,* and by questions in the House. Eleven senior critics wrote a letter (published in the *Daily Telegraph*) calling on the government and the Arts Council to overcome 'bureaucratic obstacles' and ensure the continued work of the RSC in London.

At the end of July, in the *Financial Times,* T. C. Worsley hinted, for the first time in public, that the failure of the RSC to receive a grant was connected with opposition to the Aldwych from the National Theatre: 'Perhaps it is time to be blunt,' he wrote. 'There are ugly rumours about that some of those who have negotiated the National Theatre scheme would not be sorry (to put it no lower) to see Peter Hall's RSC out of London. They are said to fear the competition, and so far from wielding such influence as they have to get a grant for the RSC, they are carefully avoiding using it.' That he was referring to Olivier, among others, was made obvious further on: 'We hope', he added, 'that some of the leaders of the theatrical profession who so far have kept silent, might speak up on behalf of the RSC as well. Their intervention at this point would surely weigh in the scales.' Three days after Olivier's appointment as the first director of the National was announced, on 9 August, the *Sunday Telegraph* went even further, commenting that 'Many people in the theatre also feel that once the National Theatre is confirmed as his personal bailiwick, Sir Laurence Olivier could afford to speak out on the vexed subject of government aid to the RSC . . . ' Olivier had, in fact, already refused to do this, a refusal that further convinced the RSC he was waging a private war to get the company out of the Aldwych. Increasingly, the row was developing into a personal confrontation between Olivier, and Hall and Fordham, and this feeling intensified, later in October, when Olivier visited them at Stratford in an attempt at what he termed an 'olive-branch-bearing' mission. The meeting did not turn out like that, however; instead it increased the already acute resentment that existed between the two sides, a resentment reflected in the fact that each had a totally conflicting version of what had taken place. According to Fordham, Olivier had arrived with a request, and an offer. The request was that Peter Hall, Peter Brook, and Michel Saint-Denis should serve on the National Theatre building committee. The offer was that the National Theatre board would arrange an annual three-month season for the RSC at the National, *provided* the Aldwych was closed. Fordham wrote sharply to Olivier:

You, one of the great actors of our time, have taken on the Directorship of the National Theatre. In doing so, you stake your whole reputation on making it a success. But in your view (mistakenly, I suggest), you regard the presence of an expanding and successful Royal Shakespeare Company as a threat to your prospects of doing so. Isn't that precisely what you meant when you told me the other morning that the one thing which sticks in the gizzards of the powers that be is the Aldwych? I deduce from our talk that it is the aim and policy of the National Theatre Board to clear us out of London, apart from a limited token season in the National Theatre; a season which, if I understood you aright, is inconvenient to you anyway, and is really only being offered as an expedient.[34]

Fordham sent a copy of this letter to Lord Chandos and Lord Cottesloe (both of whom were mentioned in the course of it) and to the RSC President, Lord Avon. Olivier, replying, did likewise, and angrily protested that Fordham's version of what he had said was incorrect. His offer of an RSC season at the National, he maintained, had *not* been conditional on its withdrawing from the Aldwych, it had been made merely as a gesture of goodwill in case the request for subsidy was refused, and the Aldwych operation had to be curtailed. It was not, he wrote, the existence of the Aldwych that constituted a problem, 'but the apparent necessity of supporting it out of the all too inadequate funds' which were being made available. He had, he maintained, done his best to plead the RSC's cause privately, and 'nobody but a fool would expect to launch a National Theatre with any success or good will by deliberately killing off a company for which he had publicly expressed admiration and gratitude . . . Such an action would prejudice people against the National Theatre from the start, and result in an atmosphere of hostility and resentment from which it might well be impossible to recover.'[35]

It is difficult, at this distance, to understand how two such conflicting versions of what ensued at that meeting could both be tenable, and since then those still alive have maintained a discreet silence on the subject of this key meeting, and the other exchanges that year. But what is clear is that the Arts Council found itself suddenly able to give the RSC the information about its next year's subsidy with amazing swiftness after this exchange of letters took place. Fordham wrote on 22 October; Olivier replied on 23 October; on the same day Lord Cottesloe wrote to Fordham saying the Arts Council expected to be able to give the RSC the information about its grant 'within the next two or three weeks'. The information was furnished by the Secretary General of the Arts Council on 31 October, some two to three months in advance of its normal schedules. The company was to be given the sum of £47,000 for 1963–4, and the award of the subsidy was accompanied by a Treasury qualification to the effect that though the RSC might choose to operate on 'a National Theatre level', it must clearly understand that this would not guarantee it subsidy on that level.

By the time Olivier had made his visit to Stratford in late October, the Press publicity was subsiding. But the RSC was continuing with energetic private lobbying, via both John Profumo (MP for the Stratford-upon-Avon division of Warwickshire and an RSC governor), and Lord Avon. With their help questions were being asked at ministerial and senior Civil Service levels, and Avon had also, at the beginning of the month, written to the Prime Minister, Harold Macmillan, on the subject of the RSC's plight. Such moves naturally did not escape someone like Chandos, or the Arts Council. But the question that remains about this whole period, about the Press campaign, the lobbying, the descent of the whole matter to the level of character assassination, is how necessary it all was. The newspapers were, without exception, convinced it *was* necessary, and while it was true that their campaign on the RSC's behalf was to some extent manipulated, it would still not have happened had not admiration for the RSC's work been so widespread, and indignation at the company's apparent ill-treatment been so heartfelt. But the newspapers were not in possession of all the relevant facts, and there were others they chose not to emphasize. For one thing, and this was known, though little publicized, the National had during 1962 voluntarily renounced £100,000 of the £230,000 promised by the Chancellor, telling the Treasury that there would be appeals from Stratford. The £100,000 had conveniently been replaced by subsidy for the same amount from the LCC, but Lord Chandos maintained that the money had been *voluntarily* relinquished by the National before it learnt of the subsidy from a secondary source. But more important than that, in May 1962, at the very beginning of the whole Press campaign, Lord Cottesloe had given Fordham Flower private written assurances that the Arts Council should be able to get the RSC a subsidy of around £50,000 for the following year.[36] Lord Chandos knew of this, but at the time it was never publicly revealed. Nor did the knowledge of this assurance in any way prompt Stratford to mitigate the stridency of some of the appeals being made on its behalf. Perhaps this was because the RSC, disillusioned by Arts Council evasiveness and foot-dragging in the past, was unconvinced that this aid would ever materialize, and so allowed the propaganda campaign to continue unabated. Perhaps the RSC hoped that public outcry would win it a higher grant, for the £50,000 mentioned by Cottesloe (in a handwritten letter on his own, not Arts Council, writing paper) was far less than the company had requested and inadequate for its purposes.

Whatever the reason, although the publicity during 1962 was so extensive, and the lobbying to such influential figures, there is no evidence that it greatly influenced the Arts Council. Indeed the Council remained apparently stoically unflustered by it all, preserving throughout an air of industrious and patient bureaucracy, the Barnacle Branch of Whitehall. 'The Council fully expected the RSC to receive a full Arts Council subsidy the next year,' the Secretary General of the Council stated mildly in August, when the publicity was still at its height. As it turned out he was right, and Cottesloe had been pretty accurate in his assessment the previous May. The only hint of influence is that after Lord Avon's appeal to Macmillan and after Olivier's visit to Stratford, both the Treasury and the Arts Council suddenly found their minds so wondrously concentrated that they could give Stratford the news it wanted, and in advance of normal schedules.

So, by the end of that October, Peter Hall and Fordham Flower had won their battle. But the subsidy they had gained was small, and in pursuit of it enemies had been made. The next year the National Theatre company would be opening its first season, with a subsidy five times as large; it remained to be seen whether they had won the war.

11

The Peter Hall Years (II)

One of the main things that worried the RSC in 1962, as progress on the National Theatre continued, was the National's refusal to agree parity of salaries. This worry was exacerbated by the approaching Shakespeare quatercentenary in 1964. By that time a National Theatre company would have been formed, and there was considerable rivalry already beginning over the programmes the two theatres would mount in that year. The idea of working on a two-year programme beginning with the *Henry VI* plays and *Richard III* in 1963, and moving on to a cycle of the eight central history plays in 1964 (the first time this would ever have been attempted) was already being discussed at Stratford, but there was considerable anxiety that the National, offering higher salaries, would snaffle all the best actors and considerably weaken the RSC's plans. As it turned out, the worries were needless.

By the end of 1962 the RSC could offer actors something that proved to be equally as tempting as high salaries – the chance to be part of a strong company, producing revolutionary work. Young actors were attracted by the increasingly democratic, anti-hierarchic structure, and the opportunity for rapid promotion to major parts if they showed talent. Hall was offering idealism, and a certain puritanism; many journalists during this period were to comment upon the almost monastic atmosphere at Stratford. The companies were, for instance, deliberately classless. The old habit of printing the stars' names in larger letters above the play-title on posters and on programmes was immediately abandoned when Hall took over, and from 1963 onwards all billing became alphabetical. And although the practice of employing large numbers of walk-ons, or spear-carriers, continued under Hall, even small-part actors were encouraged to take a more active part in rehearsals. The old tendency to shape a production mainly through private discussions

between director and star was abandoned, in favour of full c
discussion. Directors would begin work on a play usually wi
company meeting, at which their ideas and approach w
explained in a directorial talk – but these talks, though often
conceptual, did not seek to define the performances. None of the
RSC directors approached a play as, say, Michel Saint-Denis did,
from a rigid framework; their approach was more indirect, and more
fluid.

Meanwhile, actors were expected to work, and work hard, at their
art. The RSC companies had before them the example of Hall
himself, and other house directors such as John Barton, who
appeared never to do anything else. The hours both men put in
became legendary, and everyone in the company, staff and actors,
was expected to do the same. There were then far less strict Equity
regulations and it was commonplace for actors to work thirteen-hour
days for months in succession, rehearsing during the day and playing
at night; in the run-up to an opening they often worked longer –
dress rehearsals might go on until two or three o'clock in the
morning, and the actors would be called again at ten. In addition to
rehearsals and performances there were singing classes, movement
classes, voice work, sonnet classes with John Barton, and studio
work with Saint-Denis. It was a discipline that, at the Stratford end
particularly, where the company was cut off from other theatres and
actors, where social life was confined to one cinema and a few pubs,
and where many actors were isolated even from their families,
intensified the atmosphere of monasticism, of a group whose waking
hours were all dedicated to one end.

Helped by the volume of work, and the increasing emphasis on
training, an RSC style began to emerge, a style critics had begun to
note in 1962, and which was clearly visible in the RSC's Stratford
productions over the next two years, the *Wars of the Roses* and the
History cycle. It was partly visual, embodied in John Bury's spare
Brechtian style of design, but it was also a style of speaking verse
which married with that design, and which Tynan was to refer to as
one of the 'Hall-marks' of an RSC production. Hall later maintained
that if he had to cite his greatest contribution during his years with
the RSC, it would be the development in verse-speaking that
occurred at that time. All three senior RSC directors described it in
the same terms. Hall considered the ideal for which they strove was

'dry, cool and intellectual'; Barton, that 'it was a kind of rational style; we stressed the pointing up of meaning'; Brook, that the style 'depended on a rational appraisal of the material, not just playing on feeling and intuition'.[1]

When Hall first went to Stratford he found that there were two most common approaches to speaking verse: one was a derivation of the old Bensonian method, intensely rhetorical and operatic, relying on beautiful musical cadenzas, often at the expense of the sense; the other, more recent approach, was the result of the fashion for method acting, and emphasized naturalism above all else. According to Hall, when he was rehearsing during the Glen Byam Shaw 1959 season at Stratford, for instance, actors in the company were being told in his rehearsals that if they did not know where the lines ended as they spoke a speech, they could not speak it properly; when they went to rehearsals with Tony Richardson, they were being told, 'Just make it *real*, like any other speech'. In Hall's view, naturalism did not work: 'Actors had forgotten that there was shape, and form,' he said. 'Shakespearian verse-speaking was *dying* of naturalism.'[2] So, in classes and in rehearsals, both Hall and John Barton tried to evolve a different approach, influenced by the fact that both men were products of the Cambridge English school and that both had worked on numerous productions there with George Rylands, the grand old man of Cambridge theatre, lecturer in English, and a Fellow of Barton's college, King's. But the two men saw the Cambridge tradition and influence on them differently. For Hall, the influence of F. R. Leavis was important, perhaps pre-eminent. Leavis had revolutionized the study of English literature, introducing a technique of cool scientific analysis that amounted almost to dissection, and for Hall the theatrical approach to a play, and to verse, was similarly analytic, beginning always from the text and searching it for meaning, symbolism, structure, and ambiguity. To that analytic, textual approach was married the influence of Rylands, and his understanding of the shape, form, and colour of verse. It was an approach that had, as Hall noted, a curious Cambridge ambivalence. 'Perhaps our ideal was to speak like Rylands, and think like Leavis.'[3]

Barton, on the other hand, was to be the prime influence on methods of verse-speaking at Stratford, and he considered that Leavis had no influence on him at all and that Rylands's influence was only partial. However, like Rylands, he insisted on the primacy of verse structure, on the importance of understanding its rhythms, and technical differences like end-stopped lines and feminine line endings. Obviously, these were only influences, communicated in rehearsals and increasingly developed as John Barton began to do more verse-speaking work, and to conduct sonnet classes with RSC actors. The influences were then transmuted and mitigated by the actors who actually spoke the lines. But they unquestionably had an effect, and for this one does not have to rely on memory. If one compares the televised version of the *Wars of the Roses* (made in 1965), with televised sequences from Terry Hands's productions of the *Henry VI* trilogy in 1977, the difference in styles, both of verse-speaking and acting, is remarkable. The Seventies approach is freer, more romantic, and more passionate; the Sixties method is very much as Hall and Barton later attempted to define it, cooler, drier, intensely rational, highly disciplined. In retrospect Hall felt that the gradual evolution of a different approach was inevitable, and that by the end of the Sixties the techniques he and Barton had pioneered were becoming too dry, that change was needed.

The first time the two men actually worked in tandem was on the *Wars of the Roses,* when the RSC began to evolve the technique of group direction which was to characterize some of its best work. The background to the productions was one of intense strain. Despite fine work the previous year, and despite playing to near capacity audiences at Stratford, the effect of the Aldwych on the company's finances was beginning to bite; there was a deficit of over £38,000 on 1962–3, and even with the Arts Council grant for 1963–4 the deficit was to rise that year to over £45,000.[4] The RSC was under-financed, and continuing to draw on falling reserves; the *Wars of the Roses* and the History cycle that developed out of them the following year were vital to the company's future, and to its attempt to increase its grant. 'These productions', Fordham Flower wrote, 'were Peter's last chance; he sank or swam by them, and the fortunes of the company depended upon them.' Hall in particular had been under great pressure, and work on the *Wars of the Roses* began at a time when his marriage was breaking down. At the end of April, when work was just beginning, Hall collapsed at rehearsals of *Richard III* and was unceremoniously bundled on to Henry VI's funeral bier. His doctors diagnosed a nervous breakdown, and told him to rest completely for six months. He was back at rehearsals after three weeks, but the opening of the productions had to be postponed.

John Barton had followed the lead of the few companies who had previously attempted these neglected plays by editing them heavily. But he had done more than that, he had condensed four Shakespeare plays (the *Henry VI* trilogy and *Richard III*) into three, which were titled *Henry VI, Edward IV,* and *Richard III,* and this had involved intensive reworking, and in some cases rewriting, of the text. From the 12,350 lines of Shakespeare's four plays only just over half remained, to which over 1,400 lines of cod-Elizabethan verse by Barton had been added.[5] Barton had had to tighten the narrative line drastically; his version reduced the complexities of the plays and heightened one aspect of them above all – the study they presented of the intricacies of political power. At the beginning of 1963 the task was still incomplete, and Barton then had to leave for a tour of his theatre concert programme, *The Hollow Crown,* in America. When he returned in March he and Hall had under two months to finalize the texts, at the same time as Hall was directing a revival of *A Midsummer Night's Dream* in London. When the actors went in to the first read-through on 25 April they were all handed voluminous folders – the text of the *Wars of the Roses,* which none of them had yet seen. But in spite of these difficulties the *Wars of the Roses* was a triumph for the RSC, and working on them forged a superb company. Only three of the actors were well known; one was Peggy Ashcroft, playing Margaret, and the other two – Donald Sinden playing York, and Michael Craig playing Suffolk – were thought of primarily as film actors at that time. David Warner, then twenty-two years old and only one year out of RADA, was playing the key role of Henry VI (Margaret's husband, creating a potentially difficult imbalance in their ages, for Ashcroft was then fifty-six). Many of the rest of the cast were actors who already had experience within the RSC, such as Ian Holm (Gloucester/Richard III), Roy Dotrice (Bedford/Edward IV), Brewster Mason (Warwick), and Janet Suzman (La Pucelle/Lady Anne). Few were completely new to the company, but several were playing their first major Shakespearian roles.

John Bury's sets were on a huge scale, and strongly schematic. The plays were about war and warring politics, as well as endless and increasingly vicious, senseless battles, and the steel-floored staging presented the very image of Armageddon. Both sets and costumes had a curiously timeless quality, suggestive not just of these wars but also of more recent combats. Certain stage images dominated the productions, the most memorable being the celebrated council table which enabled the directors to show swiftly and succinctly the fluctuations of power. The playing was sharp, unromantic, and fast, so that the narrative of the plays was propelled forward at a relentless pace; part of the excitement engendered by the productions was due to the fact that audiences and critics were (*pace* Barton's editorial interventions) watching little-known and rediscovered plays. Quite simply they did not always know the plots; it was, as one commentator suggested, a little like going to see *Hamlet* knowing only that it was about a prince ... But perhaps the productions' greatest achievement was that they restored the long neglected and disparaged *Henry VI* plays to the theatrical repertoire, re-awakened academic and critical interest in them, and through them unlocked for the first time the full possibilities of Shakespeare's astonishing eight-play History cycle. The productions took Quayle's work of 1951 a step further, and paved the way for that of Terry Hands, who would direct virtually full-text productions of all eight history plays for the RSC between 1975 and 1980. As Hall and Barton had believed they would, the plays spoke directly and powerfully to a modern sensibility, Shakespeare's understanding of the labyrinthine convolutions of political power, of the connections between council chamber and battlefield, between individual ambitions and the destiny of nations having a direct contemporary relevance to people who, as Hall pointed out, were also 'living in the middle of a blood-soaked century'.[6]

Almost everyone connected with the RSC at that time, Hall included, considered the *Wars of the Roses* the pinnacle of the company's achievements. The productions were, Bernard Levin wrote in the *Daily Mail,* 'a landmark and a beacon in the post-war English theatre, a triumphant vindication of Mr Hall's policy, as well as his power, as a producer'. The view was shared, almost without dissent, by all the critics. The productions indeed began the high-noon of the RSC's existence that decade, one of those extraordinary periods that can happen to theatres when they suddenly make a breakthrough, and everything they touch turns to gold. The National, under Olivier, was to enjoy a similar period in 1965–6, and the RSC again, under Trevor Nunn, from the late Seventies. In 1964 the company, with impresario Peter Daubeny, launched the first of what became the annual World Theatre Seasons, at which leading companies from all over the world made guest appearances. The company also stepped up its own touring programme to Europe and America, establishing that reputation for radical excellence which would make the RSC the most internationally celebrated of all European theatre companies. Both in 1963 and in 1964 the company pulled off the coup of producing fine work simultaneously in London and in Stratford – which was not an easy feat. As Hall said, balancing the two ends of the RSC operation was difficult, for they tended to see-saw; if Stratford enjoyed a distinguished season then the Aldwych often languished, and vice versa. But Hall's company was now strong enough in terms of actors and directors to respond to the challenge, and the repertoire at the Aldwych also developed rapidly during this period. While the *Wars of the Roses* and the History cycle from *Richard II* to *Richard III* played at Stratford, at the Aldwych the company mounted a succession of strong revivals, and a selection of much more daring modern plays than they had yet attempted, partly due to the influence of Brook and Clifford Williams.

In 1963 the company began to explore the work of German and Swiss dramatists whose concern with recent European history, whether their approach was documentary like Hochhuth, or metaphorical like Dürrenmatt or Weiss, chimed with the RSC's attempts to link Shakespeare's history plays to the post-war consciousness. It was as if, eighteen years after the war, the theatre could at last attempt to examine the significance of those events. Oddly, the generation who had actually served in the Second World War produced theatre totally removed from the experience; Hall's generation was the first who seemed able to come to terms with it. The 1963 season included Dürrenmatt's *The Physicists,* in a superb production by Brook, and Hochhuth's highly controversial study of the Pope's involvement with Nazi Germany, *The Representative,* in a hard-hitting production by Clifford Williams.

In 1963–4 at the LAMDA studio theatre, Peter Brook and Charles Marovitz organized a series of club performances of experimental work under the general title Theatre of Cruelty, and this led directly to the most interesting play of the Aldwych season of 1964, Brook's production of Peter Weiss's *The Persecution and Assassination of Marat as Performed by the Inmates of the Asylum of Charenton under the Direction of the Marquis de Sade* (or, mercifully, *Marat/ Sade*), and eventually to Brook's 1966 play/production about the Vietnam war with the punning title, *US.* This new radicalism in the RSC's work was in marked contrast to that of the new National Theatre (which opened at the Old Vic at the end of 1963), which with a very few exceptions concentrated its energies on star-dominated, elaborately staged, and often superb productions of a notably safe repertoire – *Hobson's Choice*, *The Master Builder*, *Hay Fever*, *The Royal Hunt of the Sun*, *The Crucible*, *Trelawny of the Wells* – with a marked tendency to excel at Restoration plays such as *The Recruiting Officer* and *Love for Love*. The different approach of the two rival organizations at that time could be summed up by the fact that whereas the RSC's quatercentenary offerings included the full History cycle in Stratford, and in London *Marat/Sade* in what came to be christened the 'Dirty Plays' season, the National's chief offerings were Olivier's *Othello* and Noel Coward's delightful production of his play *Hay Fever*. The National's only forays into more controversial territory were productions of Beckett's *Play*, Frisch's *Andorra* (both 1964), Arden's *Armstrong's Last Goodnight* (1965), and an uneasy attempt at Brecht, *Mother Courage* (also 1965).

For the first time since the creation of a theatre at Stratford, its company's work was becoming consistently provocative – and not just *theatrically* provocative (Olivier's *Othello* was certainly that), but *politically* provocative. The company was developing a radical identity which could be seen in every aspect of its existence, not just in its work, and which was the more noticeable in contrast to the company's conservative identity in the Fifties, an identity now taken on by the National. This pronounced change, which had been effected in only four years, was to have a marked influence on the company's future. Hostile reactions to it increased the strain on an organization already under financial, administrative, and artistic stress. The situation exploded, in a particularly ridiculous way, in 1964.

The row that flared up both within and without the organization had been smouldering for some while. That it would develop into public confrontation sooner or later was inevitable, and the spark proved to be the Brook/Marovitz Theatre of Cruelty plays at LAMDA.[7] The seasons had been organized partly as a showcase for experimental work which Brook was conducting with a group of twelve RSC actors, partly to highlight some of the problems the RSC, and other theatres such as the Court, had been experiencing with censorship. It sprang, above all, from Brook's growing interest in the theories of Antonin Artaud, the French actor, director, and poet who had founded the Théâtre Alfred Jarry, and who had later spent some nine years in asylums before his death in 1948. Artaud's vision of theatre was to have a profound influence on Brook's work thereafter, and it was Artaud who had coined the term Theatre of Cruelty, which he used in a specific, but somewhat confusing sense. When the RSC launched its Theatre of Cruelty experiments, the title was popularly supposed to imply cruelty of content – plays that deliberately concerned themselves with ugly events. But this was not Artaud's meaning; his vision was of a theatre that was not in the traditional sense cathartic, or draining but ennobling, but of a theatre that had the power to disturb the spectator to the depths of his being, to make him confront the ugliness and evil within himself without the uplift associated with the Aristotelian concept. 'Theatre of Cruelty', he wrote, 'means theatre that is difficult and cruel for myself first of all.'[8] It was a bleak vision, but a severely moral one, which made it all the more ironic that the RSC's attempts to explore it were to be widely and facilely greeted as immoral. It was concerned not only with the purpose of drama, but with its methods: Artaud envisaged a theatre that returned artistically to its most primitive roots and explored ritual, mime, dance, song, and music rather than language, and thus reached out much more directly to the nerves and psyches of spectators.

The influence of Artaud on RSC work could be seen as early as 1962; in Brook's production of *Lear*, for instance, in which the sympathetic comments of Shakespeare's serving men after the blinding of Gloucester were cut, and the house lights brought up on the audience as Gloucester slowly groped his way to the back of the stage. Those cuts had caused ripples of unrest at Stratford, and several influential people, including Nevill Coghill (former Professor of English at Oxford and a Stratford governor), had written to Fordham Flower to complain at this 'violation' of Shakespeare. But that small rumpus was as nothing compared to the ferment of indignation created first by the LAMDA work, and then by the Aldwych season of 1964.

The LAMDA seasons included scenes from Genet's *The Screens*, the wooing sequence between Richard Gloucester and Lady Anne from *Richard III* performed in mime; a Marovitz collage of *Hamlet*; the reading of a letter from the Lord Chamberlain that detailed the cuts he required in an RSC play; and a five-minute item called *The Public Bath*, in which the then-unknown Glenda Jackson undressed and bathed on-stage, to represent both Christine Keeler and Jacqueline Kennedy (this was not long after Kennedy's assassination) while comments from *The Times* on the Keeler trial were read out. Since these were club performances they were not subject to censorship, and so words and actions which would then never have been permitted on the stage could be used. It was very much work-in-progress which also enabled the RSC to gibe at the censor, with whom they were engaged in a running battle over their Aldwych programme.

A 1964 performance was seen by one of the RSC governors, Maurice Colbourne, who had many years earlier acted in Bridges-Adams's companies, and who was both a governor of long standing, and an old friend of Fordham Flower. Colbourne was outraged by what he saw, and particularly by the sequence in which two actors read out the Lord Chamberlain's letter which itemized the numerous four-letter words he required to be cut. Colbourne totally misunderstood this sequence (he assumed the two actors were improvising) and decided to take action. Although he was a governor, he was not a member of the inner circle, the executive council, and accordingly he wrote to someone who was – not Fordham as might have been expected, but Emile Littler. Littler repaired that omission by sending Colbourne's letter to Fordham, adding his support to it. Colbourne's arguments were forcefully expressed, and the main tenor of them was that it was a disgrace for a company with the title 'Royal Shakespeare' to present this meretricious rubbish, and further, that a company operating under Royal Charter had no right to be publicly rude about a member of the Queen's household, namely the Lord Chamberlain. Together Colbourne and Littler requested that 'Colbourne's report' should be distributed to the theatre's council, and fully discussed at the next meeting.[9] Fordham stalled; he was, as always, loyal to his directors and had no intention, he told Littler, of allowing the LAMDA work to be discussed in council unless the relevant directors could be there in person to defend it. It *was* finally discussed that July and Fordham obviously thought that the whole matter would then blow over – he was not unused to similar protestations from governors. But this was not the case; the matter dragged on for months, with both Colbourne and Littler becoming more incensed with each new play that opened at the Aldwych, where the repertoire included the revival of Rudkin's *Afore Night Come* (which contained a particularly violent ritualized murder), and *Victor,* a play by Artaud's fellow surrealist, and co-founder of the Théâtre Jarry, Roger Vitrac. *Victor* was a farce that hinged on the fact that its protagonist suffered from acute wind; whenever she farted, an RSC musician blew a loud blast on a tuba. This seemed bad enough to Littler, but when in August Brook's production of Weiss's *Marat/Sade* opened, it proved the *coup de grâce*.

Weiss was an avowed disciple of Artaud, and his own comments on his play tended to be both portentous and didactic. Yet *Marat/ Sade* was neither of those things, but an extraordinary and revolutionary play, as intricate and complex in its scheming and in its themes as a series of interlocking Chinese puzzles. Set in the bath-house of the asylum at Charenton (where de Sade had actually been imprisoned) it recorded a performance by the inmates of the asylum, directed by de Sade, of the murder of Marat by Charlotte Corday; thus the re-enactment of the killing of a political revolutionary was directed by a sexual revolutionary within the confines of a madhouse. The language was cool and reflective, the arguments between many of the characters icily philosophical; the action of the play, and of the play-within-the-play, was violent in the extreme, including the whipping of de Sade by Charlotte Corday with her own hair, a mass execution, and the final killing of Marat who sat on-stage in his bath throughout, itching and scratching at a suppurating skin disease. Weiss constantly led his audience in one direction, then steered them the opposite way; his play turned inside out, and reinvestigated notions of sanity and lunacy, of sexuality and violence, of revolution and reaction, and also notions of theatre – what was theatre for, when was someone acting? 'I always thought plays were meant to entertain,' Coulmier, the director of the asylum, says to de Sade at one point, 'but how can entertainment deal in sarcasm and violence? I always thought poets strove to achieve pure beauty, but what is beautiful about whipping and corpses?'

Brook gave the play a production that overwhelmed audiences; each actor presented a detailed study of a particular form of insanity, and the individual madnesses interacted, creating terrifying insane rituals that seemed to threaten constantly to spill off the stage and into the auditorium. Even critics who could not stomach the play acknowledged the force with which the production hit them. 'Its breadth, its totality,' Levin wrote in the *Mail*, 'its breathtakingly rapid and varied use of every imaginable technique, dramatic device, stage picture, form of movement, speech and song, make it as close as this imperfect world is ever likely to get to the "Gesamkunstwerk" of which Richard Wagner dreamed, in which every element, every force, that the theatre could provide would fuse in one overwhelming experience.' For Brook, the play fulfilled the demands of Artaud: 'A play is not there to "move" people,' Brook said, 'that is a ghastly idea ... You cry, you have a bath of sentiment, you come out saying you've had a lovely time, but you've had an emotional outlet which has left you complacent ... I prefer the notion of disturbance, which leaves you in a greater state of inquiry ...'[10] But, as rapidly became obvious, there were a great many people who did not agree with him; the Coulmier notion of theatre as beautiful and elevating died hard. Cherished notions were being turned upside down by this play and this production, and many resented it fiercely; when they wrote to newspapers or the RSC to express their feelings, it was predictably the eroticism and violence of the production they condemned. The reaction to *Marat/Sade* might have been less intense, however, had the play not been given a great deal of free publicity by Emile Littler. During August, shortly after *Marat* opened, Fordham Flower left Stratford for a visit to America. While he was away Littler suddenly decided to air his grievances publicly. He gave a newspaper interview criticizing the London RSC repertoire: 'These plays are dirt plays,' he said. 'They do not belong, or should not, to the Royal Shakespeare Company; they are entirely out of keeping with our public image, and with having the Queen as our patron.' Littler claimed that his reaction was prompted solely by righteous indignation at the sub-sidized peddling of 'filth' at the Aldwych; but it was perhaps also not unconnected with the fact that the West End commercial theatres (of whose Society of Managers he was President) were having one of their worst box-office seasons on record. Seventeen plays had already closed after a few weeks' run in the West End and *Camelot,* the big commercial musical offering of 1964, had just opened to a chorus of critical catcalls. For a man like Littler this must have been a painful experience, and he cannot have been unaware that many West End managers blamed the poor season not on the quality of plays they offered, but on the presence in London of two subsidized companies – the RSC and the National.

From Littler's interview there developed an amazing theatrical brawl; both Hall and Fordham were incensed that an RSC governor should make a public attack of this kind on the company's policies. Had Littler remained the sole protestor the whole scandal might have died down quite quickly, but he found supporters. As had happened at Stratford during the Barry Jackson years, when Cunningham-Reid had provided a focus for dissent, several other governors whose major objections to RSC policy were quite different from Littler's, jumped on the bandwagon. Chief among them was Sir Denis Lowson, businessman, ex-Mayor of London, and member of the RSC's executive council. (This was some years before Lowson's subsequent prosecution in one of the major City scandals of the century.) Lowson wrote a letter to the Evening News (which he subsequently denied writing) agreeing with Littler. But as his correspondence with Fordham showed, Lowson was really objecting not to the kind of plays the RSC put on, but to the fact that plays were put on in London at all. He considered the Aldwych operation would lead the RSC to bankruptcy, and that the company's true financial position was being hidden from the governing board. Lowson and Littler provided a rallying-point for those governors who considered that the RSC belonged in Stratford, presenting Shakespeare, where it could continue to be self-supporting, and that the sooner it got back there the better.

Fordham handled the whole affair, which brought him close to resignation, with consummate skill; it was, sadly, the last time he was able to steer the company through a crisis, and the last major imbroglio he was involved in. His office was deluged with letters from people endorsing Littler's views; every letter was answered with a disarmingly polite acknowledgement and a request that the writer fill in a short questionnaire. The first question on it was: 'Which of the Theatre of Cruelty/Aldwych repertoire plays have you seen?' Most of the correspondents replied; very few, it turned out, had seen any of the productions they were so roundly condemning, and many expressed horror and outrage at the assumption that they might have done.[11]

Meanwhile the RSC actors and directors sent a letter of support for Hall and his policies to Fordham, and asked that a deputation of actors be allowed to meet Lowson and Littler to put their side of the case. The meeting was duly arranged, and a deputation of four actors led by Dame Peggy Ashcroft arrived. The meeting was not a success; Littler hardly spoke; Lowson glowered at England's most celebrated classical actress and said that he was not in the habit of discussing his companies' policies with his employees.[12] Shortly afterwards Lowson chose not to submit his name for re-election to the council; Littler, according to Fordham, more or less apologized, and the whole affair died down. It had not just been one of the last convulsions of the old guard, however, as it might have seemed, one of the last major battles to precede the abolition of censorship that finally came in 1968. Nor was it simply a clash of theatrical tastes between men like Brook who were trying to find a new purpose in theatre, and men like Littler who continued to believe that theatre should be entertainment, and family entertainment at that. It was an instance of the degree of opposition, from many different quarters, to Hall's most fundamental RSC policy – that his company should work on modern plays, in London. The opposition from within the National Theatre itself might be gradually diminishing (and both Olivier and Kenneth Tynan, the National's Literary Manager, gave the RSC valuable support during the 'Dirty plays' controversy), but Hall still felt that within the Arts Council there were many who, because they supported the National, would have preferred to see the RSC forced out of London. The Aldwych was unpopular with West End managers, unpopular with a section of the governors, and still – in spite of the quality of its work – not popular enough with audiences.

Lowson, for all his faults, had been right about RSC finances; they were approaching crisis point. For 1964, the year of *Marat/Sade*, the RSC received a larger subsidy (£85,000), but it was still insufficient and the company made its biggest deficit yet, of £65,643.[13] Partly this was because the Aldwych, not designed to cope with repertoire theatre, was costly to run. But the main reason was that, in the urgent pursuit of opportunities to present modern work, a realistic policy for the Aldwych had never been evolved. Comparatively few Stratford productions transferred there, so the RSC's Shakespeare work remained wasteful in exactly the same sense it had been in the Fifties; many of the Shakespeare productions played only at Stratford for as few as twenty to thirty performances and were then taken off. New plays that would have filled a smaller theatre, at the Aldwych played to under 60 per cent capacity. The three-year contract system was also proving expensive and increasingly unwieldy, as it became progressively difficult to find enough large-cast plays for the London end. When parts could not be found for contract artists 75 per cent of their salaries still had to be paid unless they found other work. With increasing frequency the London plays had *ad hoc* casts, composed partly of RSC actors, and partly of outsiders who might work on only one production – a negation of Hall's original policy.

By the beginning of 1965 the outlook for the company was bleak. George Farmer, the chairman of the RSC's finance committee, asked for a special meeting with the Arts Council to discuss the gravity of the RSC's financial position. He and Patrick Donnell told the Council that by the autumn of that year the RSC's own reserves would be exhausted. The Arts Council's reply was that the £90,000 already earmarked for the RSC for 1965– 6 could not be substantially increased, but that for the following year a subsidy of £150,000 might be possible.[14] Farmer replied that such an increase would still leave the RSC with substantial deficits, and that the only way of avoiding them would be 'a drastic curtailment of present policy' – by which he meant closing the Aldwych. This, he told the Council, would almost certainly bring about the resignation of the present 'management', in other words, certainly the resignation of Peter Hall whose title was Managing Director, and probably Fordham's as well.[15] The Arts Council was sympathetic but immovable, and the situation was left unresolved although a further meeting was planned between Fordham, Peter Hall, and the incoming chairman of the Arts Council who was to take over from Lord Cottesloe that May, Arnold Goodman.

There was only one ray of hope. In February 1965 the City of London Court of Common Council agreed that they should build a new theatre in their planned Arts Centre in the Barbican development, and that it should be leased to a resident company, the RSC. The City would fund the building of the theatre, and planned to lease it on terms advantageous to the RSC at a rent equivalent to 3½ per cent of the then estimated costs of the building (£1,250,000), or roughly £45,000 a year, the City subsidizing the theatre by a similar amount through its rates – the first time in history that City rates had been directed to support of the arts. It was thought that the theatre could be completed in five years, and that the RSC would be able to occupy it in 1970. Peter Hall considered the Barbican the most important thing that had happened to the company since the first theatre had been founded in 1879. Certainly it seemed to offer everything the RSC needed; it would give the company a secure London base; a theatre more economical to run than the Aldwych, designed to RSC specifications to suit RSC needs, with the most modern and advanced technical equipment. Once in the Barbican, Hall felt, then the arguments about whether or not the RSC should continue with modern work outside Stratford would be settled for good.[16]

In 1965 no one appreciated how unrealistic the five-year building schedule was, nor how often the estimated rental would subsequently need revision. The Barbican looked like the answer to Hall's prayers. The only problem was, could the company remain in London, and survive financially, until it opened?

From 1965 onwards the work of the RSC under Hall began to decline, slowly at first, then more rapidly. Peter Brook felt that the company had peaked, that too much had been achieved too soon. 'The artistic aims were fulfilled by the *Wars of the Roses*,' he said. 'After that the company had no target ahead of it.'[17] The company could surely have developed further, however, Brook's own work at LAMDA and on *Marat/Sade* had suggested that, and there were new young recruits who would begin work with the RSC that year and the next who were to suggest new directions, and bring in new energy. But it was as if Hall had built a glittering castle of achievement over a crevasse of financial uncertainty, and that uncertainty, coupled with over-hasty decisions about how the two-theatre system could be made to work, eventually undermined what he had created. He had taken many gambles, not least that he personally could withstand the strains of overseeing the whole undertaking. On Hall, and on his strange paradoxical personality, the company depended. He was the driving force of the RSC, and he could not falter. In a sense, one of the greatest strains on him must have been the one he created – his own reputation for being invincible. Just when Hall's energy and confidence were most needed, in the crisis period of 1965– 6, he began to flag, as Quayle had done ten years before. The one man who might perhaps have helped was Fordham, on whose support the company also depended. But Fordham was already ill, though it was not then known how seriously.

In 1965 the company's work held, helped by the fact that it had a large number of strong productions which could be revived. At Stratford there were fine productions of two rarely performed plays, Clifford Williams's of Marlowe's *The Jew of Malta* (in tandem with *The Merchant of Venice*), and John Schlesinger's of *Timon of Athens*, with Scofield in the title-role. The same year Hall directed two of his best productions, *Hamlet* at Stratford, and Pinter's *The Homecoming* at the Aldwych.

The *Hamlet* was (like the History productions before it) strongly influenced by the work of Jan Kott, author of *Shakespeare Our Contemporary*. The production emphasized the Machiavellian intrigues of the Elsinore court, the workings of its power politics. It also revealed once more Hall's skill (which some found dubious) at sensing the mood of his own time, and relating that to his Shakespeare productions. Certain scholars found Kott's views cheap and meretricious: in Helen Gardner's opinion, for instance, Shakespeare should not be considered as 'our contemporary', but as an Elizabethan; Kott's views, to her, seemed 'outrageous arrogance'. Hall's attempts to relate the plays to his own era similarly struck some critics as belittling the plays, and spuriously journalistic. But in Hall's view he had no option but to interpret Shakespeare in the light of a modern sensibility, and it was precisely because the plays could be interpreted so differently by different ages that they continued, uniquely in the work of any dramatist, to be performed, season after season, over three hundred years after the death of their author. Kott had seen Hamlet as an eternal figure, a young student, a 'poor boy with a book in his hands', and had posed the question, what book was he reading? In an Elizabethan production, Montaigne, he thought; by the turn of the nineteenth century, the European romantic poets and Nietzsche; by the early 1960s, perhaps Sartre, or Camus, or Kafka. '*Hamlet*', he wrote, 'is like a sponge ... it immediately absorbs all the problems of our time.'[18]

Hall's production had a superb cast, and a marvellous, implacable, black set by John Bury. Constructed from shiny Formica, it consisted of one large room, and two ante-rooms off it; a neutral, but forbidding background to the plottings of the characters, the arena of politics laid bare. Brewster Mason was a huge, corrupt, devious and dangerous Claudius; Elizabeth Spriggs a blowsy, morally weak Gertrude; Tony Church played Polonius not as a foolish dotard, but as a cunning and formidable politician. There was also an interesting Ophelia (Glenda Jackson) who was played against the traditional grain as a rebellious daughter, repressed into the refuge of madness by the cruelty and hypocrisy of the court and her family, the bawdiness of the mad scenes presaged by hints of sexual experience. But it was not over these performances, or over the emphasis on politicking within the Elsinore court that the controversy arose. It was over David Warner's performance as Hamlet. Warner, as Hall had been quick to see, possessed a direct and contemporary appeal. He looked like no other actor who had played Hamlet this century, and he made no attempt (as some earlier actors, such as Wolfit, had done) to conform to traditional physical concepts of the character. Far from looking like the Renaissance prince some critics still required, he looked like a disaffected, mid-Sixties teenager, or possibly a rock star. As an actor he emanated a bewildered gentleness that had been harnessed to great effect as Henry VI, but which had been less adequate to the demands of Richard II. This quality was intensified by his manner of speaking, which was intensely unrhetorical. Occasionally it tended towards a monotonous mumbling, but it could be effective on stage, a pool of quiet surrounded by the more pointed attack of other actors. If this Hamlet were reading a book it would have been by Marcuse, or perhaps Timothy Leary; there was the possibility he would kill Claudius, there was also the possibility he would just drop out.

Certain critics were infuriated by his performance, particularly traditionalists like Gareth Lloyd Evans of the *Guardian*. J. C. Trewin sensed a generation gap: 'Young people in last night's Stratford audience', he wrote, 'showed by their overwhelming cheers at the close that David Warner was the Hamlet of their imagination and their heart. Many of their elders will, I think, hesitate . . .' The phenomen on Trewin noted at the first night was to be manifested throughout the season; Warner's performance proved magnetic to the young, and there was no doubt about their fiercely partisan reaction to his Hamlet; queues of teenagers lined up for balcony seats, and many came, night after night, to stand at the back of the auditorium.

Hall's other major production that year, *The Homecoming*, was the most interesting new offering in an Aldwych season given strength mainly by revivals. It was Pinter's first new full-length play since *The Caretaker*, and Hall gave it a beautifully orchestrated production of icy threat, helped by some very fine performances – particularly from Ian Holm as the spiv Lenny, and Paul Rogers as Max. Holm's performance, coming so shortly after his highly acclaimed Richard III, and Hal/Henry V in the Histories sequence, illustrated how much and how quickly the RSC had been able to bring on its best young actors.

By the end of 1965 the company's problems were every bit as acute as George Farmer had warned the Arts Council they would be. Fordham and Hall had had their meeting with Arnold Goodman, and he had been apparently sympathetic, but adamant. For the following year, 1966, the Arts Council subsidy would be increased, as had been indicated, to £150,000 (a substantial increase of £55,000 on the previous year) but that was the limit. The RSC calculated that, even with subsidy at that level, the 1966 season would produce a substantial deficit, exhaust the company's private reserves totally, and leave the RSC unable to pay its creditors – in effect, bankrupt. There seemed only one solution, and that was either to curtail, or close, the operation at the Aldwych. As both Fordham and Hall knew, Goodman had been privately lobbied by RSC governors who had been urging him to use his influence to force the RSC to do just that. Goodman told them waspishly that such things must be expected in democratic institutions, but that they would not influence his decision.[19] Hall, however, became convinced that Goodman and Jennie Lee, the Minister for the Arts, *did* support the National's claim to be the sole subsidized company in London, and did want the RSC out. He had what he described as a 'hellish' fight with Goodman, and he wrote a letter of private appeal to Jennie Lee – both to no avail. There is also evidence to suggest that the Arts Council's firm attitude towards the RSC was not solely connected with the National as Hall believed, but with the political nature of some of its productions. It was Goodman who, as chairman of the Arts Council, questioned whether it was the duty of the state actually to subsidize those who were working to overthrow it, and while no one would have suggested that the RSC was that far Left, its anti-Establishment tone and its deliberate attacks on the Lord Chamberlain, not to mention its prolonged anti-Arts Council publicity campaign of 1962, had not gone unremarked. The following year the company was heavily leaned on, by Lord Chandos and others, not to mount Brook's production about Vietnam, *US*, because of its use of obscenities, and because Chandos (a former MP and Secretary of State for the Colonies) feared its anti-American tone 'might endanger the special relationship with our allies'.[20]

By now Hall was under pressure not just from the Arts Council, but also from within the RSC, from Patrick Donnell and George Farmer who argued that there could be no more gambling, no more trusting that public outcry might yet save the RSC – economies of a major kind had to be made. Hall eventually agreed, but with bitterness, and the decision marked a rift in his relationship with Donnell, who had been the key to the company's administrative development in the Sixties.[21] The nature of Hall's compromise was perhaps indicative of where his major sympathies lay in terms of RSC work. The obvious place to make economies was the Aldwych, the side of the operation that was losing the company money. That Hall refused to do. Instead he made cut-backs at Stratford, announcing that the 1966 season would consist of only one new production, *Twelfth Night,* and four revivals. The Aldwych programme, in contrast, was defiant: it consisted of nine productions of which eight, an unprecedented number, were new. It included only two productions with much chance of box-office appeal, *The Government Inspector,* with Scofield in the title-role, and Brook's *US* (a production devised with the actors). Several of the other plays put on were weak and several, as Hall must have known, had virtually no chance of filling a theatre the size of the Aldwych; they included *Tango* (by a Polish author, Mrozek, almost unknown in England, and on the strength of that play likely to remain so); Marguerite Duras's *Days in the Trees,* a novelist's play that remained obstinately novelistic; and Charles Dyer's whimsical *Staircase.* Even so, Hall later said that the compromise broke his heart, and that it marked the moment when he began to consider resignation. Looking ahead he saw only endless struggles with Goodman and the Arts Council, endless fights to get an adequate subsidy.

Hall's disillusionment at the prospect of such struggles was marked in a very similar way to Quayle's, ten years before. He began to look for new stimulus outside the RSC, to work where he would be free of constant administrative and financial worries. During 1965 he had undertaken his first work outside the company since 1960, directing *Moses and Aaron* at Covent Garden. During 1966 he undertook further outside work, and directed *The Magic Flute* (also for Covent Garden). Patrick Donnell, trying to contact him about numerous problems with the Stratford season, found it was difficult, sometimes impossible, to reach him for decisions.[22] Both the Aldwych and the Stratford seasons were on the whole disappointing. With the exception of one last minute, additional production the work at Stratford broke no new ground and at the Aldwych, with the exception of *The Government Inspector* and *US,* the work also sagged.

During this sad, dispiriting season, Fordham Flower died of cancer at St Mary's Hospital, Paddington, on 9 July. Although he had clearly been unwell for some time his final decline was rapid, and his death sudden. With it the theatre lost the man who had guided its fortunes for twenty years, who had known and loved it since he was a boy, and who had been one of those most responsible for its post-war development and achievements. Without his passion, and his vision, neither Quayle nor Hall could have contributed to the theatre as they did, and it was characteristic of him that his vision of the company should have involved a gradual reduction in the power of his own role; part of the inheritance he left the RSC was the artistic independence enjoyed by Quayle, Hall, and their successors. His death brought great change to the theatre. For the first time since its creation it would no longer have a member of the Flower family as the executive head of its governing body, and the implications of that were considerable. Fordham, like his father and great-uncle before him, had had a personal involvement with the RSC. He lived in Stratford, was friends with, and saw constantly, all the people who were responsible for the day-to-day running of the theatre. He was succeeded first by L.T.G. (later Sir George) Farmer, and then by Sir Kenneth Cork, both of whom brought great experience and financial expertise to the company, but the relationship between the head of the governors and the directors was never again the close one it had been; it was more distanced, and more formal. Fordham and Hall had great affection and respect for each other – Hall once said that he thought of him as a second father – and his sudden death may perhaps have influenced Hall in the decision he reached a year later, to leave the company.

His decision was undoubtedly accelerated by the events of 1967. During that year Hall learned that the Barbican would be delayed in opening until at least 1972. The prospect of struggling on under-financed until then, dismayed him. He began work on his first film, *Work is a Four Letter Word,* frequently commuting between London and Stratford. He undertook only one production for the RSC that year, *Macbeth.* His friends considered the highly publicized failure of that production finally convinced him to leave. During rehearsals Hall became seriously ill with shingles and nearly lost the sight of one eye. When he returned actors found him debilitated and uncharacteristically depressed; somehow the production never took fire, and it opened to considerable critical abuse. Later the same year Hall began another film, *A Midsummer Night's Dream,* shot in mid-winter Warwickshire. During shooting fellow RSC directors would come up from London and trudge around the fields of Compton Verney in wellington boots and thick coats, talking RSC policy between shots. By then, although he was discussing the planning of the next season (which, for the Aldwych, was both chaotic and late), it was already known that Hall wanted to leave, though most of his colleagues believed he could be persuaded to stay on.

By the time filming ended he was exhausted, and at the end of the year he resigned, another director who had come close to personal destruction through the work at Stratford and the demands it made. As Bridges-Adams had done so many years before, he took a last formal look at the building before he left and went, promising himself that he would never, under any circumstances, direct a theatre again. But before he departed he had found someone who he believed was right to succeed him, another young director of great talent and promise, Trevor Nunn. Nunn was just twenty-eight – a year younger than Hall had been when, eight years before, he took on the job in such a different spirit from that in which he left it.

12

A Clean Sheet

When Trevor Nunn was appointed artistic director of the RSC there were many within the company who doubted his capacity to cope with the job – not least Trevor Nunn himself. As he pointed out, he did not know how to read a balance sheet, had never chaired a committee, had never given an interview to the Press. He had, he considered, just about learnt how to run an RSC rehearsal when he committed himself to running the entire company. Reactions to his appointment were sharply divided: those who had worked with Nunn recently greeted the news with elation and optimism; others – both within and without the company – regarded the appointment as a disaster, the end of an era. Nunn's major handicap was not solely his relative inexperience; it was that he had to follow Hall, a task daunting enough for anyone. For Nunn, apparently a very different man from Hall, it was particularly hard, and he was greatly underestimated at the time of his appointment. Within an organization the size of the RSC there were many who scarcely knew him; he was judged, superficially, on the basis of first impressions, and felt to lack the Hall charisma; people looked back at his past record with the company and remained doubtful. He had the master's imprimatur, of course, in that Hall had selected him, but to many it remained a strange decision, at best one of Hall's gambles, at worst incomprehensible.

In certain respects there were, in fact, many similarities between the two men. Both came from Suffolk, both came from somewhat puritanical, hard-working backgrounds. Nunn went to Cambridge straight from Northgate Grammar School in Ipswich. If anything he had shown even more signs of being a fledgling impresario/director there than Hall had done, neglecting his academic work for theatre, and in his three years at Downing directing over thirty-four productions and taking an ambitious package of plays and revues to the Edinburgh Festival. In the highly competitive world of university theatre he had been regarded as formidable, predictably one of the Cambridge graduates who would move straight from university to success in the theatre in the manner of such predecessors as Hall, Peter Wood, Peter Cook, and numerous others. From Cambridge he had gone to the Belgrade, Coventry, first as an assistant, and then as director, and his work there had shown sufficient promise for him to be offered a job with the RSC within a year. (Nunn turned down the first offer, of an assistant directorship, but accepted Hall's next offer a year later of an associate directorship, although he was not formally granted that title until he had been with the company some nine months.) But once Nunn had joined the RSC a curious transformation took place and the rapid progress of his career suffered, almost immediately, a considerable set-back. Much of the pessimism expressed at the time of his appointment stemmed from the impression he created in his first eighteen months with the RSC – a period that was little short of disastrous.

Of the ambitious, clever, and gifted young director of Cambridge and Coventry there appeared little trace. Nunn struck his colleagues as nervous, lacking in confidence and authority. He was slightly built, dressed somewhat scruffily, and appeared considerably younger than his years. He favoured a Beatle haircut, and looked – one of his fellow directors acidly remarked – like 'every Vietnamese waiter in the world'. But it was not just that Nunn *appeared* ineffectual, he behaved ineffectually too. According to a fellow director, when Nunn entered a rehearsal room it took actors a good ten minutes to notice he was there. He experienced great difficulty in imposing any order into his rehearsals which became notorious in those early days for degenerating into anarchy. Each project Nunn was given turned to dust and ashes in his hands. His work as a co-director (on *Henry IV* and *Henry V* in 1965–6) was largely unpicked by senior colleagues. His first two solo productions, of *The Thwarting of Baron Bolligrew* and *Tango* (neither very promising material) were dogged with ill luck and Nunn himself considered them lacklustre and unsuccessful. The progress – or lack of progress – of a production called *Strike* provided a typical example of the kind of course Nunn's early work with the RSC took. *Strike* (about the General Strike of 1926) was to be partly scripted, and partly evolved in rehearsal, rather in the manner of *US*, and it was the most interesting project Nunn was given to work on in his first year and a half with the company. But the rehearsals degenerated into generalized argument and chaos. At the end of a month Nunn became ill and Clifford Williams was brought in to watch a run-through and report on progress. The actors ran the first half, and Williams expressed cautious interest. Might he perhaps see the second half? The actors pointed out there was no second half. *Strike* was scrapped. By this time Nunn's work had consisted of a chain of such disasters that he lived in daily expectation of dismissal.[1] But the expected summons to Peter Hall's office, and the expected charge of incompetence, never came. Instead, in 1966, Nunn was finally given the production that changed the course of his career, and which marked his first step towards the directorship of the RSC.

The chosen play was a little-known Jacobean drama, Tourneur's *The Revenger's Tragedy*, and the production came at the end of the depressing, low-energy Stratford season of 1966. The choice was Nunn's, and it was his first solo Stratford production, mounted under conditions of financial stringency. Its budget was minimal, and it made use of the existing *Hamlet* set. None of the established RSC stars of the 1966 season, who included Ian Holm, Brewster Mason, and Diana Rigg, appeared in it. The two leading roles, of Vendice, the revenger of the title, and Lussurioso, were assigned to Ian Richardson (the only well-known RSC actor in the production), and to Alan Howard, who was new to the company that season. Many of the rest of the cast were also new to the RSC, including John Kane, Norman Rodway, and Patrick Stewart, and to design the play Nunn brought in Christopher Morley, with whom he had worked at Coventry. The play Nunn had chosen was a strange and difficult piece, which had been subject to almost total critical and theatrical neglect. It contained some notoriously lurid scenes, including a splendidly murderous dénouement which left some twelve corpses on stage. Nunn saw it as a black and brilliant comedy of manners, that both satirized and celebrated decadence, and he felt its ambivalence of moral tone had particular relevance to late-Sixties society. He rehearsed it very freely, making use of games and improvisation; the company responded to the play's ambiguities, to its lightning shifts of mood and the challenge of its apparent excesses.[2]

When *The Revenger's Tragedy* opened it met almost unanimous acclaim; it was hailed as one of the greatest productions of the decade, and was afterwards frequently cited as one of the finest productions of a Jacobean play ever mounted. 'Lord Goodman', wrote Ronald Bryden in the *Observer*, 'may yet go down as a back-handed benefactor to the Royal Shakespeare Company. Every time the Arts Council tightens the screws on the company's subsidy, arguing that one National Theatre is enough, the RSC bounces back with some victory of sheer theatrical resource over economics, so brilliant as to suggest that it works best with its back to the wall. The new Stratford production of *The Revenger's Tragedy* is one of the finest things Peter Hall's regime has accomplished.'[3]

What few critics remarked upon, however, was that *Revenger's* was not simply a great production, it was also a revolutionary one. In terms of acting, design, and staging it marked a significant break with what had become, by 1966, the accepted RSC approach. None of the 'Hall-marks' of RSC work that a critic like Tynan had remarked upon as early as 1962 applied to this piece of work. The Brechtian neo-realism of John Bury sets, for instance; the carefully broken-down costumes and props customary in RSC productions at Stratford; the measured, rational, somewhat down-beat style of speaking verse which the RSC had pioneered – all these were absent; *The Revenger's Tragedy* was flamboyantly theatrical, anti-naturalistic – the pitch of the glittering performances central to it was not down, but up. It was also, in essence, very simple: the set was a circle of bright silver painted on the floor of the stage, the costumes monochromatic – black and silver. The image of moths drawn to a flame was the inspiration for Morley's design: those in the play closest to the epicentre of power clung to the centre of the circle, decked in silver and bathed in light. Made-up to an unnatural pallor, they were at once incandescent and grub-like. Nunn orchestrated the whole production with immense finesse. Its progress was like that of a highly formal elaborate dance of death (an impression heightened by Guy Woolfenden's brilliant, eerily rhythmic music for the production), and it ended with an actual dance of death, a skull-masked saraband in which the abrupt demise of some twelve characters skirted the ridiculous and acquired a dreamlike, sickening compulsion, the death-throes of a diseased society.

If the critics, knocked back by the power of the production, failed to note how radical a departure it was from the RSC approach, that was not the case among directors in the company. Peter Hall, after the dress rehearsal, told the assembled company that this marked the most exciting directorial debut in the Stratford theatre since his own. But Hall then left Stratford, leaving John Barton to nurse the production through to its opening. And Barton immediately began to press for changes. In the view of both Trevor Nunn and the company's other young resident director, Terry Hands, Barton disliked the very things that flouted the customary RSC style and gave the production its strength. The three-day row that ensued was nicknamed the 'Moss on the Tomb' scandal, because Barton found the stylization of the production anathema. He objected to the monochromatic colour scheme; he objected to the lack of naturalism in costumes and props. In Hands's view 'Berliner Ensemble naturalism' had, by 1966, become 'the watchword of the company': if a messenger came on from a presumed journey then he must have conspicuous mud on his boots. Suddenly here was a production with thematic costumes, schematic staging; there was a tomb, Barton pointed out – why was there no moss on it?[4]

Such criticism of productions from other directors, and subsequent changings and unpickings were common then in the period between the first dress rehearsal and the opening night – not for nothing was the actors' nickname for a dress rehearsal 'The Night of the Long Knives'. Trevor Nunn and his company had to fight hard to preserve the production; it was a fierce battle whose ultimate victory marked an artistic turning-point for the company. A radically different approach to staging a classic play had been found. With Alan Howard, Ian Richardson, Norman Rodway, Patrick Stewart, and later (in revival) Helen Mirren, a group who would become the nucleus of a new generation of RSC actors had been brought to the fore. The company had gained a gifted and original designer in Christopher Morley, and all doubts about Trevor Nunn's potential as a director had been removed. Nunn followed *Revenger's* with a string of fine productions including, the next year, a memorable *Taming of the Shrew* with Janet Suzman (Nunn's future wife) and Michael Williams, and *The Relapse,* which used many of the *Revenger's* actors. His confidence seemed suddenly to have returned; the company was revitalized. By the end of 1967 Peter Hall had no doubt that Nunn was the right person to succeed him. He considered him a highly talented director, in a tradition he understood and respected – 'an English classicist to the core, but sceptical and pragmatic; an emotional intellectual'. It did not occur to him, he maintained, that he should back someone of his own generation, with more experience. 'I felt', Hall said, 'that there was a simple rule of thumb. My successor had to belong to the next generation. It had to be someone who would challenge what I and my colleagues had done.'[5] So, just over a year after *The Revenger's Tragedy* opened, Hall asked Trevor Nunn to take over from him; Nunn, with trepidation, agreed, and Hall left the company as director in much the same way he had come to it – taking risks.

Nunn was, in a sense, Peter Hall's protégé, just as Hall had been Byam Shaw's ten years earlier. But he did not have, as Hall had had in the late Fifties, a long period of nurturing before he took over, or the benefit of wide experience in the theatre and the beginnings of an international reputation. The difficulties he faced in having within a few weeks to adjust from being a junior director to overall controller of the RSC were compounded by the company's reputation. The prestige of the RSC was still so considerable that few commentators could conceive of any role for Nunn other than that of a caretaker figure, someone who would maintain the excellence that had gone before. When Peter Hall had become artistic director change had been required, and the need for it widely acknowledged by critics and journalists. When Nunn became director, change was also vitally needed – but that fact was not immediately evident to those outside the RSC.

That the company was in a state of financial crisis *was* acknowledged – but then the company had weathered so many financial crises during the 1960s that the condition tended to be ignored. The retrenchment of 1966 had achieved something: that year the company's deficit had shrunk back to a mere £444. But the following year, 1967–8, the last year of the Hall regime, it was up again to over £32,000, and for 1968–9, the first year Nunn was responsible for the company, it swelled to a record £161,126, largely due to a disastrous and late-planned season at the Aldwych which Nunn had partly inherited. By the time he began work on the first season for which he was fully responsible as artistic director, in 1969, the RSC's private resources were totally exhausted; the company was dependent on generating its own revenue, and on its Arts Council grant, which was inching its way forward to the quarter million mark. But although the company's financial difficulties were acknowledged, they were no longer news. The RSC had pleaded threatened extinction twice in recent years, once in 1962, during the great year of confrontation with the infant National Theatre, and once in 1966. By the time Trevor Nunn became director the continuing pleas aroused less Press interest. Of the other internal problems Nunn faced there was even less acknowledgement.

Nunn inherited a structure that had been invented at speed, that was already breaking apart under strain, and that urgently needed change. The central problem, as always, was the Aldwych. Hall's insistence that the prime function of the London theatre was to house productions of new plays needed urgent reappraisal. The last great Aldwych season had been the notorious 'Dirty Plays' season of 1964. Since then, with the exception of *US, The Homecoming,* and the work of David Mercer, the new plays on offer at the Aldwych had been disappointing and second-rate. They attracted small audiences, and when Nunn took over were being budgeted on the basis of 45–50 per cent capacity houses. The policy for the Aldwych had become self-defeating as well as hugely costly, and there remained voluble opponents to it on the RSC board of governors. To make matters worse, the RSC in London now had a rival across the Waterloo Bridge, at the Old Vic – the National Theatre, and from the end of 1965 onwards, with its famous production of *Love for Love,* the National had hit form. Production after production had received rapturous praise – *A Flea in Her Ear, Black Comedy, The Dance of Death, Three Sisters, Rosencrantz and Guildenstern are Dead,* the all-male *As You Like It,* and Seneca's *Oedipus* (the last two productions being directed by RSC directors, Clifford Williams and Peter Brook respectively) – all these had been mounted in the years 1966–8 when, excluding revivals, the RSC work at the Aldwych had been uneven and disappointing, and the major successes – *US, The Government Inspector, The Relapse* – comparatively few. It was additionally hard that the RSC, which was supposed to be pursuing a new play policy, should lose two outstanding new plays of that period – *Black Comedy* and *Rosencrantz and Guildenstern* – to its rival. Clearly, if the RSC was to be able convincingly to argue its case for a London theatre it had to come up with stronger work, and it had to find a way of rationalizing its two-theatre operation. Given that the opening date for the Barbican theatre looked ever more distant, and given the company's continuing financial predicament, reforms were needed, and needed fast.

During 1968, when Nunn first had to come to grips with these problems, he was having to supervise seasons he had not entirely planned but which had been hastily cobbled together at the end of 1967 when Hall was filming the *Dream.* He was also directing two new productions – a bold attempt at *Lear* with Eric Porter in the title-role, and a more uneven *Much Ado*, with Janet Suzman and Alan Howard as Beatrice and Benedick, which was to improve on revival at the Aldwych. He needed all the help he could get from both his directorial and administrative teams, but both, in 1968, had been weakened by recent changes. On the administrative side there had been a reshuffle at the time of Hall's departure, when a new senior managerial post had been created – that of administrative director, a position held by Derek Hornby. Hornby's appointment had been designed to lift managerial responsibility from Nunn's shoulders, and reflected the need both George Farmer and Peter Hall felt the RSC had for a senior manager with proven business acumen and commercial skills. Hornby was chosen for the RSC by a top London management selection firm, and came to the company without benefit of any prior experience in theatre management, his previous job having been with Texas Instruments. Immediately under him Hornby had David Brierley as general manager, and William Wilkinson as financial controller. Of these three, Brierley was the only one with general experience of theatre, and specific knowledge of the workings of the RSC. Brierley knew the organization inside out; he had joined the company in 1961, a year after John Barton with whom he had worked on numerous productions at Cambridge. Since then he had held a variety of positions from assistant stage manager to general stage manager to administrative assistant to Peter Hall. Wilkinson, although passionately interested in theatre, had worked primarily in films, including a period as financial director of MGM England; he was hired in mid-1968 by Hornby.

Aside from these three, Nunn did have the support and assistance of several people with years of RSC experience. Maurice Daniels, the company's planning controller; John Goodwin, the formidable head of publicity; Desmond Hall, the general production manager, and Guy Woolfenden, the company's brilliant music director, all remained. But still, the fact remained that just when Nunn needed administrative backing to counterbalance his own inexperience he had a senior team which – with the exception of Brierley – was as unfamiliar with the managerial workings of the RSC as he was. The situation was exacerbated by the fact that Hornby's period with the RSC was eventful but brief. After the company became involved in contractual tangles and double-booking, when Barton's production of *Troilus and Cressida* was contracted to tour Europe and appear at the Aldwych at the same time, Hornby resigned. Brierley and Wilkinson remained, and were to contribute greatly to the future development of the RSC. Trevor Nunn added the corollary 'chief executive' to his title of artistic director, and assumed overall responsibility for the administrative, as well as the artistic organization of the company. But these alarums and excursions – Hornby's resignation came at the beginning of Nunn's first full season, 1969 – were not exactly conducive to smooth administration, and did not facilitate the pressing reforms which Nunn felt were needed within the RSC.

Nunn's strongest inherited assets were the RSC's formidable roster of actors and its team of resident directors. Although certain RSC stars from the mid-Sixties such as Glenda Jackson and David Warner were already working elsewhere by the time Nunn became director, and others, such as Ian Holm and Paul Scofield, left the company at the end of 1967, the range of actors associated with the RSC whom Nunn could call upon was still enviable. Among those connected with the company for some time were Peggy Ashcroft, Judi Dench, Brewster Mason, Eric Porter, Ian Richardson, Donald Sinden, Janet Suzman, and Michael Williams. Among those who had joined the company more recently were Susan Fleetwood, Alan Howard, Emrys James, Estelle Kohler, Helen Mirren, Norman Rodway, and Patrick Stewart. The company had not lost its ability to attract new actors, or its ability to develop them, and – less hierarchic and star-oriented than the National – it was to continue to do so with unrivalled success throughout the Seventies.

The company's team of directors was at a point of change. Hall was to continue to direct some productions until he became director of the National Theatre in 1973; Michel Saint-Denis had already left because of ill health. Brook, the third member of Hall's triumvirate, was involved in filming *US* and *Lear* at the time when Nunn became director, and over the next decade his ties with the RSC were to become looser as he became involved with his own theatre company in Paris.[6] In the next ten years he would direct only two productions for the RSC, in 1970 and 1978, although one of them was to prove to be perhaps the most influential Shakespeare production of the post-war theatre. John Barton remained, now the elder statesman of the company, and the major link between Hall's regime and Nunn's. Other directors such as Clifford Williams, who had worked frequently with the RSC in the past, were to continue to work for the company, although Williams was much in demand in the commercial theatre, and in the period 1966–7 was being energetically wooed by the National. That left, apart from Trevor Nunn himself, two directors, both of whom were relatively new to the RSC. There was David Jones, a television director who had first worked for the RSC in the Arts Theatre season of 1962, and who had been brought into the company primarily in an administrative capacity; the other was Terry Hands. Hands was a year younger than Nunn, and had joined the RSC from the Liverpool Everyman (which he founded) a year after him to run Theatregoround, the company's small-scale touring unit. Between Nunn and Hands, the two youngest directors in the company, there existed friendship tinged with rivalry, and affection tempered by sporadic exasperation. It was an odd, symbiotic relationship, which became progressively central to the artistic development of the RSC. At the time Nunn became Director the difference in their personalities, and in their approach as directors, was marked. Hands was overtly ambitious, abrasive, and unquenchably articulate. In rehearsal he could be condescending and autocratic in the extreme. 'Actors are like racehorses,' he once told Ian Richardson, 'you just rein them in or whip them on, and make sure you give them a lump of sugar if they do well.'[7] The company name for him (he is half-German) was Gauleiter Hands.

Hands's work with the RSC had suffered similar disasters to Trevor Nunn's in his first period with the company, but his work on Theatregoround had been of immense value. He had developed it with great speed, so that within six months of his taking over it had twelve shows on the road. It played in schools, factories, small church halls, and had a wide variety of programmes ranging from those aimed at children to actors' workshop courses and small-scale productions like *Agincourt*, created for the RSC by John Barton. It was partly from these early small-tour operations, on which Buzz Goodbody, the future director of the RSC's first small theatre, The Other Place, worked as an assistant, that the RSC's later small-auditorium work developed. Theatregoround gave opportunities to young bit-part players, as well as (gradually) to more senior actors, and in Hands's view it helped to create a new work ethic, one that placed emphasis on cheapness and minimal scenic effect: the TGR budget was tiny, and everything for its shows had to be packed in small transit vans.

The quartet of Nunn, Barton, Jones, and Hands was to become the key to the fortunes of the RSC over the next decade. They were to be responsible for the bulk of RSC productions, and primarily for the formulation of the company's artistic policies. Reversing a recent decision of Peter Hall's, Nunn made David Jones the administrator/ director of the Aldwych, and freed Hands (who had briefly held that post) from a desk job so that he could undertake more productions, beginning with his debut at Stratford, the highly successful *Merry Wives* in 1968. The decision did not improve the relationship between Hands and Jones which was already hostile, but it was of immense benefit to the RSC. In David Jones the company gained a stable, calm administrator who did much to put the Aldwych back on its feet; in Hands, someone who was to emerge as one of its finest and most original directors.

The 1969 season began with an unconsciously symbolic gesture on Trevor Nunn's part. He asked for a new stage-cloth for the floor of the conference hall where most Stratford rehearsals took place. The old cloth was stained with coffee, burned by cigarettes, and generally shabby. Nunn wanted to create a rehearsal room with a very different atmosphere, a room that might function as a chapel would within a monastery, a place of serenity in which notices requesting quiet would be superfluous, where actors could practise their art with a priestly dedication. The new stage-cloth duly arrived and was laid; Nunn was delighted. It was pristine white; he asked actors to take their shoes off when rehearsing; there was to be no smoking in the room and no coffee drinking. The emphasis was to be on self-improvement: the actors were asked to come in early, in tracksuits, for exercise sessions. The old company learning ideals were re-emphasized, and the noticeboards bristled with rosters for classes – singing classes, movement classes, voice classes, sonnet classes. It was to be, literally, a clean sheet, a fresh start.

All went well, and the conference hall remained a temple of artistic dedication, until John Barton began rehearsals there for *Twelfth Night*. Two weeks later Nunn went in to be confronted by a room that had swiftly reverted to its original state. The new stage-cloth was scarred with cigarette burns and tacky with paint; dirty paper-cups were everywhere. Barton was serenely oblivious to the defacing of the temple. At this point Nunn realized he had just suffered one of his acute bouts of puritanism. He gave in gracefully.[8] But the impulse that had manifested itself in that new stage-cloth could be seen elsewhere, both within the organization of the RSC, and in the 1969 productions. The fresh start began with planning, and it tackled head-on the central problem Nunn had had to face when he became director – how to deal with the Aldwych? A new system had been evolved, designed to streamline and tighten up the RSC's work. It relied on having smaller companies, both at Stratford and London, numbering a maximum of about thirty-five to forty actors at each end. The actors would be on two, not three-year contracts, a rationalization of what was to be a two-year cycle of work. In theory each company would play a Stratford season and then move on to London (if possible with a short interim tour) and then play a season there. The policy for the Aldwych was to change radically. Instead of concentrating on new work the emphasis was to be placed on revivals of large-cast, often little-known or rarely performed classic plays, such as *Bartholomew Fair* (1969), *London Assurance* (1970), or the plays of Gorky which – thanks largely to the work of David Jones – the company began to explore in 1971. These London seasons would be bolstered by more transfers from Stratford of the company's best work from the previous year (always reliable at the box-office). Thus more Stratford productions would have a minimum two years of life, and be assured of a London audience; the RSC companies would have the benefit of two years uninterrupted work together.

In retrospect this solution has the obvious simplicity of all good ideas, and it was to give the RSC a continuity and structure in its two-theatre work that had been lacking; some great productions were to be the direct result of that continuity and the ensemble confidence it gave to actors. But the solution was not without problems: it was logistically difficult, because of the long gap between the end of the Stratford season, and the beginning of the London one. It involved, for the time being, a drastic reduction in the new work the company could mount, and placed it in the dangerous position of becoming a company solely concentrating on classical work, cut off from the vision of contemporary writers. It meant that the RSC had to come up with sufficient neglected plays for revival, in which field they were in hot competition with the National. Finally there was the problem of the increased emphasis on transfers. During the Hall regime there had been relatively few Stratford transfers; there were three in 1963 and 1964, two in 1965, none in 1966, two in 1967. Certain major Stratford productions had either played only briefly in London (the Brook/Scofield *Lear* for instance) or not at all (the complete History cycle of 1964). To give more Stratford productions a longer lease of life clearly made both artistic and financial sense, but the choice of which productions was an invidious one. Once the expectation of transfer had been established as a norm rather than an exception it provoked predictable anger, both from directors and actors, when it was not fulfilled. Later this policy was to regulate itself, but in the early years of Nunn's directorship it was sometimes to prove divisive and controversial.

In this context of considerable change two companies came into being during 1969, which the actors dubbed the 'heavy' and the 'light' brigade. The heavy brigade was at Stratford, and earned its title by virtue of the experience and prestige of its leading actors, who included Peggy Ashcroft, Judi Dench, Richard Pasco, and Donald Sinden; the light brigade provided part of the repertoire at the Aldwych. It was led by a younger, less established group of actors, which included Alan Howard, Ben Kingsley, Helen Mirren, Norman Rodway, Patrick Stewart, and Janet Suzman. This group was to provide the nucleus for the following season at Stratford in 1970, while the heavy brigade moved to the Aldwych in a repertoire that reflected for the first time the new policies for London. Since the light brigade was employed mainly on triumphant revivals of some of the best recent RSC work, including John Barton's superb and influential *Troilus and Cressida,* and Nunn's *Revenger's Tragedy,* it was the work of the heavy brigade at Stratford that best illustrated the most important new beginning of all – the new artistic direction of the company.

Feeling that the reputation of the RSC in the mid-Sixties had been bound up with its exploration of the history plays, Nunn and his fellow directors decided to investigate a very different area of Shakespeare's work, the late plays, of which three were planned, *Pericles, The Winter's Tale,* and (a somewhat odd choice) *Henry VIII.* Two earlier, but thematically linked plays were included, *Merry Wives* (in revival) and *Twelfth Night.* The season was completed with Middleton's *Women Beware Women.* The juxtapositioning of the plays was an interesting one that gave new resonance to some of the productions, and the two plays most obviously important to that juxtaposition, but excluded – *The Tempest* and *Measure for Measure* – were included in the repertoire the following year. It was the first time since 1960 that a thematic approach had been applied to a Stratford season (for the Histories had additional, and more obvious links), and given the difficulty and comparative unpopularity of *Merry Wives, Pericles,* and *Winter's Tale* it was a bold decision.

As it turned out, the staging of the plays was to be equally bold, and to cause some offence to the more conservative critics. Both Trevor Nunn and Terry Hands in particular were concerned to scale down Stratford productions, to try and move towards what they felt was a much-needed new simplicity of staging. Christopher Morley created a new permanent set that, with adaptations, was used for all the plays. It was a conscious stripping away of everything extraneous, creating a stage that was like a great empty box, white for *Winter's Tale,* blue for *Pericles.* It was lit from above by a huge cone of lights, poised like a lamp over a billiard table, which could irradiate the stage or be used directorially to pinpoint tiny areas of the stage or individual actors. At times, as in Komisarjevsky's work in the Thirties, light played a major role in the productions – abruptly dimmed and strengthened, for instance, in the opening scene of *Winter's Tale* to underline the hallucinatory nature of Leontes' jealousy. Music and sound played equally strong roles, heightening mood, being used as leitmotiv in *Pericles* and *Winter's Tale,* and to unforgettable effect in John Barton's *Twelfth Night.*

It was a brave and innovatory season, of which the directors were justifiably proud, and in its exploration of the elements of space, sound, and light it marked a seemingly decisive break with the naturalistic approach which had dominated the Sixties RSC work. It suggested a company moving towards clear and unborrowed objectives – and it was to have a palpable influence next year on what was to become the most celebrated of all RSC productions, Peter Brook's of *A Midsummer Night's Dream.*

When 1970 began the company had reached its financial nadir. The reserves had been used up, and the previous season, despite high attendance figures, had left the company at the end of the year with another large deficit, of £71,307. The acute state of the company's finances was recognized by the Arts Council and that year the RSC grant was increased by over £40,000 to £280,670, the largest annual increase in subsidy since 1966. In an effort to generate funds and to keep companies together between seasons, a heavy touring schedule had been maintained including, in the period 1968–70, two visits to America, two to Europe, and one to Australia and Japan. But the governors were, understandably, pressing for all possible cut-backs, and one of the first activities threatened by the crisis was Theatre-goround. Theatregoround received no special grant from the Arts Council; it was funded by the company and then cost in the region of £17,000 per annum. It was in an effort to save TGR that further company reforms were introduced in 1970. For the first time TGR productions were more closely integrated with Stratford work; leading actors appearing in the main house also worked in TGR productions, and those productions played one performance in the Stratford theatre each week, increasing the weekly repertoire from eight to nine plays; the extra performance would, it was hoped, subsidize the entire TGR operation. And the plays were not only taken to normal TGR venues, they also went to regional theatres, including the Oxford Playhouse and the Abbey Theatre, Dublin, in an effort to generate further revenue. The two TGR productions that season were *Dr Faustus,* directed by the then head of TGR, Gareth Morgan, and *King John,* directed by the young Buzz Goodbody, who became the RSC's first woman director.

Trevor Nunn was also anxious to take his reforms of the previous year a stage further, and with his new smaller companies create an even tighter ensemble. So that year, in the manner of the Meiningen Company which Charles Flower had upheld as an ideal so many years before, leading actors played, in addition to their major roles, minor ones in other productions; they also understudied and in some cases toured with TGR productions. Nunn then believed that such a way of working was the essence of true ensemble, and he was somewhat embittered to discover that it met with continual opposition and complaint from his actors. The reasons for these complaints were various: some actors resented the request for reasons of status, more complained of overwork, particularly those involved in TGR touring. Unforeseen problems – like the underbudgeting of *Faustus,* which was a poor production requiring extensive last-minute rescue work – intensified this feeling.

The season was evenly balanced (apart from the TGR productions) between two later plays, *Measure for Measure* and *The Tempest,* both directed by John Barton; two tragedies, *Richard III* directed by Terry Hands, and *Hamlet* directed by Trevor Nunn; and two comedies, *Two Gentlemen of Verona* directed by Robin Phillips, and the *Dream* – the penultimate production of the season. After the innovatory work of the year before, expectations were high, but as the season advanced they were, at least in the view of the majority of critics, disappointed. The company was predominantly a young one: Ian Richardson (Angelo, Buckingham, Proteus, Marcellus, Prospero), Norman Rodway (Richard III, the Bastard, Snout, Trinculo), Alan Howard (Hamlet, Mephistophilis, Theseus/Oberon, Ceres) and Helen Mirren (Lady Anne, Ophelia, Julia) not only had their most exacting range of roles to date, they also faced exceptionally heavy schedules, particularly as the season progressed.

Both Barton's productions were curiously dull, the more disappointing after the beautiful *Twelfth Night* of the year before. *Richard III* and *Hamlet* contained interesting performances, and moments of powerful insight, but they both suffered badly from intrusive pre-emptive design. *Richard III* was so overlaid with Gothicisms that the cast and the play eventually disappeared beneath their weight. *Hamlet* was staged by Christopher Morley in an oppressive chamber set, roofed and walled with venetian blinds which could, theoretically, convert the entire staging from white to black in the twinkling of an eye, but which proved either to stick or merrily revolve to the accompaniment of loud mechanical whirrings. Nunn had intended a plain, anti-illusionistic production which – like those of the previous season – concentrated the attention on the actors and the words. What he got, as he was bitterly aware, was deeply distracting and apparently appallingly simplistic, a set that brandished the play's moral extremes in the audience's face. The production received very mixed reviews, of which Ronald Bryden's was the most sympathetic (he had attended rehearsals) and Harold Hobson's (disgusted by a Hamlet who had long hair and appeared unwashed) the most hostile. *Hamlet* was followed by Robin Phillips's frivolous modern-dress *Two Gentlemen,* a production that at least made anachronism amusing, and which pleased the critics. Then, towards the end of a season when the confidence of the RSC's young directors had taken some hard knocks, came the *Dream.*

Purely in terms of audience and critical response to it, the *Dream* was an extraordinary phenomenon. At the first night in Stratford, the audience stood and applauded at the interval – an unheard-of occurrence – and the triumphant progress of the production, from Stratford to New York, from New York to London, continued from that moment. It received a mounting chorus of critical approbation: 'More than refreshing, magnificent, the sort of thing one sees only once in a lifetime, and then only from a man of genius . . . ' (Harold Hobson); 'Without any equivocation whatsoever the greatest

Shakespearian production of Shakespeare I have seen in my life . . .'
(Clive Barnes); 'The fame of Peter Brook's production of *A Midsummer Night's Dream* has been rumbling around the world, growing in
volume . . . Everywhere the word was the same. Peter Brook had
surpassed his *King Lear*, his *Marat/Sade*, pointed the theatre's nose in
a new direction for the next decade, and was one of the greatest,
most imaginative directors in the modern theatre . . . ' (Ronald
Bryden, writing in 1971). There were, it was true, a few dissenters.
Benedict Nightingale writing in the *New Statesman* disliked it, and
considered Brook had not reclaimed the play, as most critics felt, but
had 'remoulded it, with the help of Billy Smart, Walt Disney, J. G.
Ballard, Meyerhold and . . . his own sleeping, hallucinating self . . . '
John Simon, perhaps the most formidable, and certainly the most
feared, of New York critics, damned it. 'We are merely tickled by the
strange discords, the cunning weirdness, the *dépaysement* of it all,' he
wrote. 'Instead of being allowed to savour Shakespeare's genius, we
are forced to admire Brook's cleverness . . . ' But such dissent was
swept aside in the general chorus of critical acclaim. The production
sold out at Stratford, sold out on Broadway, sold out in revival at the
Aldwych. From August 1972 to August 1973 it was revived again,
and went on a triumphant world tour: it played to packed houses in
Paris, Sophia, Venice, Berlin, San Francisco, Tokyo, Sydney . . . It
became the most discussed, most written about, most analysed, and
most imitated Shakespearian production of the century, and – not
surprisingly – the comparative failures and achievements of the other
RSC work that year were obliterated by the attention paid to this one
production. It earned the RSC a considerable amount – over £70,000
on its Broadway season alone – and it was primarily due to the
Dream that the RSC ended the financial year of 1970–1 with a
surplus, the first surplus the company had made since its creation in
1960, ten years before.[9]

The first overwhelming impression the *Dream* gave was of vitality.
It pulsed with energy from the moment when the battery of lights
came full up on the white set, dazzling the eyes, and the entire cast,
capes swirling, burst on to the stage, to the solemn ritualistic close
and the moment when the actors poured down from the stage and
into the auditorium, clasping the audience's hands. It was, of course,
in the historical sense, a revolutionary production. There were no
pretty lights, no gauze-winged fairies, no painted trees, none of the
pantomime devices which had so obstinately attached themselves to

the play. The set was a white box with two doors and a gallery above with ladders to it. Titania's bower was a huge scarlet feather; Oberon and Puck swung on trapezes, as did the large and decidedly lumpen fairies (or audio-visuals as Brook termed them) who acted as somewhat aggressive, and occasionally distinctly surly stage-hands to the action. The costumes were influenced by those of Chinese acrobats, and were made of satin in brilliant yellows, purples, and greens. The lovers displayed an athleticism in love that gymnasts might have envied, leaping on each other's shoulders, and Hermia achieved the considerable feat of flinging herself horizontally in front of a door. There was no Mendelssohn, except as an ironic counter-point to Titania's lustful embracement of an ass at the end of the first half; instead there were unearthly noises, hummings and keenings, strange assonant chantings, or speeches suddenly sung. Much of the music was the result of a collaboration between Richard Peaslee (the composer) and the actors, improvising. The production made, in short, no attempt to re-create the pastoral images of the text; if anything its hard-edged visual clarity ran counter to them. For a few critics this was wilful and ultimately destructive contrariness but for most, by freeing the play from conventions the text was freed. Areas of eroticism and cruelty were revealed in a work traditionally thought of as a vernal comedy; there was a nightmare inherent in this dream. The characters took a necessarily painful (as well as a comic) journey, and found resolution only at the end, in the play-within-a-play scene, in which the barriers between them began to tumble ('The wall is down that parted their fathers') and Theseus and his court found they could learn from theatre – even the somewhat inept theatre of the mechanicals.

From the way in which Brook spoke of the *Dream* it seemed to be the production of a long creative journey, stemming partly from his interest in Artaud and Grotowski, from work of his as far back as the 1962 *Lear*, and the 1964 Theatre of Cruelty season. All trace of the autocratic young director of the 1940s and early Fifties seemed to have disappeared – though some of his actors might have questioned whether it had disappeared altogether. The director whose early Stratford work had been strongly conceptualized was decisively moving away from that approach. In Brook's view, the history of Shakespearian production was a reductive one. Actors, directors, and designers, he considered, had all been guilty of gearing productions to simplistic concepts, of saying, as it were, 'This play is about greed, sex, money, love, man's inhumanity to man, failure of communication, or whatever':[10]

To approach Shakespeare and produce either 'style' or clarity of certain ideas is only a reduction of the play. It is not possible for any of us, no matter how hard we try, to reveal the complete play. What we will do will always be a restriction . . . but we can try to capture in our net the richest amount of the contradictory . . . discordant elements that criss-cross these plays . . . in all our work we can try to replace 'either/or' with a greedy 'both'.[11]

Although Brook did not say so, his statements were, as he must have known, an implicit criticism of much of the past work at Stratford, including his own, and it was interesting that he chose to voice these opinions at a time when the younger directors and actors were already (before the *Dream*) attempting to move towards a freer, less conceptualized approach, with greater emphasis on exploration and collaboration.

The actors who worked on the 1970 *Dream* were an odd, powerful, and somewhat anarchic group. Many of them had been together in the RSC for some years. Others, newer to the group, had had the experience of being forged into a tight-knit company by the tough season and the exigencies of TGR touring. Several of the youngest actors in the cast could appear inadequate and inexperienced in other productions that year, but had an immense ingenuity and inventiveness in rehearsal, which was used to the full in the preparations for the *Dream*, in its eight weeks of games, exercises, improvisations and experiments. They fired each other as a group, and Brook was able to take their explorations further. Some found the process unfamiliar and difficult; John Kane (Puck), for instance, considered that at Stratford the customary feeling among directors and actors was that they 'did something' to a play, they attempted to make it fit their 'rational concept' of it. Brook, he felt, was asking for the opposite, he wanted the play to do things to them: 'You must act as a medium for the words,' Brook told him. 'If you consciously colour them, you are wasting your time. The words must be able to colour you.'[12] Brook's critics maintained that if ever a production bore the unmistakable stamp of its director it was the *Dream*. What could be more of a conceptual imposition than to set a play – much of which takes place in a wood – in what appeared to be a circus or a gymnasium? But such arguments had their roots in exactly the kind of assumption that Brook was rebelling against; they assumed that the set for the *Dream* must represent something, no matter how often Brook patiently reiterated that it was simply a stage, an empty space to provide 'a nothingness around the work'.[13] And they also assumed that whole sequences of the production which had been born in rehearsal, and derived from the actors' participation, were born in the fertile mind of Peter Brook.

Obviously, in theatre, no one production – however great – can be a blueprint for others. Nothing was sadder than the imitations of the *Dream*, the rash of derivative Shakespeare-in-a-circus productions that immediately commenced in Europe and America and were still continuing, amazingly, in the late Seventies. But if the *Dream* could not have been, and should not have been, a blueprint, it was in essence a challenging production. Its dazzling technical proficiency (and the simple fact that its director was not an unheralded youngster, but Peter Brook) disguised the fact that the production called in question theatrical values held sacrosanct for the last thirty years. 'Director's theatre' had, by 1970, become a cliché, its implications extraordinarily unquestioned. In Britain the most acclaimed directors of the twentieth century – Granville-Barker, Guthrie, Saint-Denis, Brook, Hall – were those who had put an immediately recognizable stamp upon their work; the most celebrated European companies – the Compagnie des Quinze, the Moscow Arts, the Berliner Ensemble – were those who had achieved, as Brook said, a demonstrably recognizable style. In the past the RSC had been first castigated by critics for *not* possessing such a style, and then lauded – by critics like Tynan – for achieving one in the 1960s under Peter Hall. And now Brook, generally regarded as the greatest director of his era, was rejecting that dominance. The course Brook was taking was directly contrary to that which would be taken in the next decade by some of the most celebrated European directors such as Georgio Strehler and Peter Stein. It presented its most direct challenge to the company that had given birth to the *Dream,* the RSC.

Towards the end of the 1970 season the RSC organized an event that received little publicity, and none of the attention that had been lavished on the *Dream,* but which was, in a sense, equally important for the company. A Theatregoround Festival was held at the Roundhouse, and included with the TGR work were three productions from Stratford, *Hamlet, Richard III,* and the *Dream.* They were given without décor, and in rehearsal clothes, and both *Hamlet* and *Richard III* emerged with a startling new clarity, sensed immediately by those who worked on them. Freed from the constrictions of their staging they gained new truth and power. 'It was', Trevor Nunn said, 'the experience that gave me the greatest pleasure of the whole year, forgetting about design and presentation altogether. The *Hamlet* was free; it was thrilling.'[14]

The *Dream* came precisely at the divide between two decades, at a point when British theatre was just beginning to change radically. By then a process of polarization had begun, visible from the very beginning of the decade, but most apparent in the middle of it, in the years 1975– 6. On one side British theatre was dominated by those products of the 1960s, the National and the RSC, two companies which owed their continued existence to increasingly massive state aid. Both these companies were supposed, during the Seventies, to move into new theatre buildings, on the South Bank and in the Barbican, and the design and evolution of those two new buildings had been influenced by an overlapping group of people. Both buildings had been conceived, just as the Memorial had in the late Twenties, as instruments which would help to revolutionize the practice of theatre. Both were the ultimate products of the previous decade's obsession with new prestige buildings in general, and new theatre buildings in particular. At the other end of the theatrical spectrum was the fringe, or alternative theatre, which burst forth in the late Sixties, given added impetus by the revolutionary events of the year 1968. Alternative theatre was an umbrella term, covering groups that ranged from the amiably anarchic Ken Campbell Road-shows to the Marxist community-oriented 7.84 companies. But different though the groups were they shared certain common factors and qualities: almost all were small and impecunious, and existed by hand-to-mouth touring; they played in venues similar to those in which the RSC Theatregoround units had played – church halls, schools, community centres, factories, the streets, or tiny, ill-equip-ped theatres. They attempted to reach an audience who might never visit their local rep let alone a metropolitan theatre, and the essence of their work was that it was mounted cheaply, with the minimum of equipment, and involved the close participation of all who were engaged in it. With very few exceptions all the groups devoted themselves to producing new plays, and they were to throw up a great many new writers, including Howard Barker, Howard Bren-ton, David Edgar, David Hare, Barrie Keefe, and Snoo Wilson, as

Enemies, by Maxim Gorky, directed by David Jones, Aldwych, 1971. Left to right, Patrick Stewart (Mikhail), Alan Howard (Nikolai), Brenda Bruce (Paulina), Lila Kaye (Agrafena), Philip Locke (Zakhar Bardin), and John Wood (Yakov).

Peter Brook's production of *A Midsummer Night's Dream*, 1970. Here, the wedding march sequence which closed the first half of the production, with David Waller (on shoulders) as Bottom, and Sara Kestelman (foreground) as Titania.

Top, the duel scene from Trevor Nunn's production of *Hamlet*, 1970, with Alan Howard (right) in the title-role, Christopher Gable (left) as Laertes, and Peter Egan (centre) as Osric. *Bottom*, the opening scenes of Trevor Nunn's 1969 production of *The Winter's Tale*, with Judi Dench as Hermione and Barrie Ingham as Leontes. Both productions designed by Christopher Morley.

The season of Roman plays, 1972: *left*, Ian Hogg as Coriolanus; *below*, the assassination of Julius Caesar (Mark Dignam), with Patrick Stewart as Cassius, Philip Locke as Casca (both to the right of Caesar), and John Wood (foreground, right) as Brutus. *Coriolanus* directed by Trevor Nunn with Buzz Goodbody; *Julius Caesar* by Trevor Nunn, Buzz Goodbody, and Euan Smith. Both productions designed by Christopher Morley and Ann Curtis.

Right, *above*, John Barton's 1973 production of *Richard II*. Ian Richardson (left, here as Bolingbroke) and Richard Pasco (King Richard) doubled the leading roles, playing them on alternate nights. *Below*, Emrys James as York and Helen Mirren as Queen Margaret in *Part III* of Terry Hands's acclaimed 1977 productions of the *Henry VI* trilogy, designed by Farrah.

Buzz Goodbody's production of *Hamlet*, The Other Place, 1975, with Ben Kingsley (left) in the title-role, and George Baker (right) as Claudius.

Top, the bridge scene from Terry Hands's 1975 production of *Henry V*, with Oliver Ford-Davies (centre left) as Montjoy and Alan Howard (front right) as the King. Designs by Farrah. *Bottom*, Trevor Nunn's acclaimed 1976 production of *Macbeth*, The Other Place, 1976, designed by John Napier. Roger Rees (centre left) as Malcolm, Griffith Jones (centre right) as Duncan, and Ian McKellen (kneeling) as Macbeth.

Nicholas Nickleby, Aldwych, 1980, adaptation by David Edgar, directed by Trevor Nunn and John Caird. Designed by John Napier and Dermot Hayes. Here, David Threlfall (left) as Smike, Roger Rees (centre) as Nicholas.

well as involving writers from an older generation such as John Arden and Margaretta D'Arcy, Edward Bond, John McGrath and – more marginally – Trevor Griffiths. All these writers were socialist, some Marxist, and their work strongly reflected their political militancy.

Given all these factors it was not surprising that these groups should conceive of themselves as, literally, an alternative theatre; it was the first time that writers, directors, and actors had attempted to set up their own theatrical infrastructure rather than being assimilated directly into the mainstream of theatre as, say, the writers who emerged in the late Fifties had been. It was no less surprising, since alternative theatre groups were as susceptible to cant as anyone else, that certain of the groups, certain of the writers, and certain of the critics connected with them should dismiss mainstream theatre as 'official' or 'bourgeois' – blanket terms covering everything from a play such as *No Sex Please We're British* to the activities of the major subsidized companies. This antipathy to, and suspicion of, the National and the RSC was to intensify as the decade progressed, reaching its peak in the years 1975–6 which led up to the opening of the National's long delayed new theatre. One of the main reasons for this intensification – which spread beyond those directly working within alternative theatre – was money. For the alternative theatre groups were like the RSC and the National in one important respect: they too depended for their existence on Arts Council subsidy, an irony lost neither on the Arts Council nor on the theatres concerned. That subsidy was to increase rapidly during the decade. In 1968 there were around a dozen part-time new companies, many subsisting partly on dole payments, partly on meagre box-office takings. The following year, 1969–70, the Arts Council gave its first subsidy to alternative theatre groups, totalling £15,000. By the end of the decade there were around sixty full-time alternative theatre companies, receiving subsidy in excess of £2 million. This was a dramatic increase, but there was also a dramatic increase in subsidy levels at the other end of the theatrical spectrum, particularly at the National Theatre. In 1972–3, for instance, the National received roughly one eighth of the whole drama budget of the Arts Council; by 1975–6, at the end of which year the Lyttelton Theatre opened, that proportion had risen to one quarter. Although no money was docked from other theatre operations in order to provide this sum, it did mean that what critic John Elsom called the 'gap in privilege' between the National and the RSC, and between those two companies and the rest of the subsidized theatre system, was widening.[15]

This fact was not lost on alternative theatre groups, and it contributed to the remarkable outbreak of hostility that marked the lead-up to the opening of the National. But it was not just the large subsidy required to run the National that caused hostility, it was also the scale and magnificence of its new building, the nature of its repertoire, and the nature of its audience. There could have been no clearer statement of the polarization that was occurring in British theatre than the press release put out by the alternative theatre groups belonging to ITC and TACT (the Independent Theatre Council, and The Association of Community Theatres) in 1976. There were, they claimed, *two* National Theatres: 'One stands on the South Bank . . . cost £16 million to build, is subsidized to the tune of £2 million per year and will eventually employ 500 staff and just over 100 actors. The other exists in workshops, community centres and short-life premises all over the country. It performs everywhere and anywhere . . . is subsidized to the tune of £700,000, employs over 1,000 people and is still expanding.'[16] This kind of attack placed not just the National, but also the RSC, in a very vulnerable position. In the Sixties the RSC's identity had been clear; incontestably it had been a radical company, and many of the battles it had fought – over subsidy and censorship, for instance – now benefited alternative theatre groups. Suddenly, with the advent of the Seventies, the alignment of British theatre was changing, and the company that had fought the Establishment now found itself being regarded *as* the Establishment by some of the young writers, actors, and directors then emerging. Tactically speaking, the RSC had one great stroke of luck in the Seventies, and that was that the opening date for the Barbican was delayed again and again; this meant that the National, not the RSC, drew most of the fire. But nonetheless, as became clearer during the course of the decade, the existence of alternative theatre, the quality of some of its productions, the undoubted gifts of many connected with it, meant that the RSC had fundamentally to re-examine the nature of its own work.

For one thing, the RSC needed to resolve its touring problem. Although its audiences had grown steadily and although it had placed increasing stress on international touring, the company's touring activities in Britain were in sharp decline. By the beginning of the Seventies the RSC, like many other theatre companies, was finding that traditional-style touring where large-scale productions were taken to large regional theatres was unsatisfactory and expensive. In 1971 David Brierley admitted that because of this it was through Theatregoround mainly that they maintained 'an RSC presence in the provinces', but Theatregoround had to be abandoned later the same year.[17] It was clearly unsatisfactory that a theatre which received a large state subsidy, and which had in principle been committed to touring since the 1930s, should now be defeated by economics and logistics – the more so when the new small-theatre groups, with meagre funds, were able to tour and to seek out new audiences.

Then there was the problem of new writing. The RSC had been created in the belief that its companies should work on both classic and contemporary plays, the work on one informing the work on the other. If it reverted to concentrating solely on classical work it was in danger of petrification, and everyone concerned with the RSC knew that. But at the beginning of the new decade the RSC possessed no theatre suitable for mounting new work, the Aldwych being too large and the economics of presenting such plays there too risky. Even the Royal Court, a theatre smaller than the Aldwych (seating 400 as opposed to 1,024), had recognized this difficulty and had opened a new, small off-shoot – the Theatre Upstairs – in 1969. If the RSC was not to be cut off from the work of new writers it needed something similar, a small third theatre – not a plea likely to receive much financial encouragement from the Arts Council.

Small theatres were, of course, to dominate theatrical thinking over the next decade, and not just because of the obvious and straightforward advantages they offered. A theatre small enough to risk new work, in which actors could re-examine their work methods and create a different relationship with their audiences, in which seat prices could be kept down, and spending on staging reduced – obviously such a theatre offered the RSC an opportunity for the same kind of stimulus which had occurred, a decade earlier, when its London seasons were launched. But small theatres were not simply theatres: a whole ideology was being erected around them by their apostles who, in many ways, resembled an earlier generation of theatrical puritans, the 'Elizabethan Methodists' who supported the views of William Poel. To these advocates small theatres became more than playing spaces, they became a cause: they were seen as classless and egalitarian; they were believed to banish rhetoric (*the* fashionable pejorative of the 1970s) and to promote close-range naturalistic truth (the most acceptable kind, perhaps, in a television age). Partly through sentiment, partly through wish-fulfilment, they became annexed to the post-1968 Socialist aspirations so strongly felt in British theatre, and evangelistic belief in their virtues deepened the divide already so apparent. This somewhat confused ideology needed to be questioned and challenged, a task that rested with the RSC (and the National), the two major subsidized companies.

Small theatres had one obvious drawback. They were themselves élitist, in that they severely restricted the size of their audiences; they could never form the basis for the 'popular' theatre which had been Hall's ideal in the Sixties, and which remained central to the identity of the RSC. The RSC began the new decade with a production – the *Dream* – that was a triumphant affirmation of both the power and the popularity of large-auditorium work. That ideal was to be constantly threatened over the next ten years by underfunding, inflation, rising seat prices and VAT; but it was also threatened by the new and automatic suspicion of any theatre that seated more than two hundred people.

13

Towards a New Theatre

The RSC first tackled its need for a small auditorium in 1971. At Nunn's urging, the company hired The Place, the headquarters of the Contemporary Dance Theatre off the Euston Road, and there constructed their own theatre space, seating 330 people, for a limited nine-week season. The audience sat on tiers of wooden benches, perched above the acting space rather like students in a medical theatre watching the demonstration of an operation. Three plays were given, none of which could have been risked at the Aldwych: *Occupations,* concerning the 1920 occupation of the Turin Fiat factories by the workers, a fine play by the then little-known Trevor Griffiths, directed by Buzz Goodbody; *Subject to Fits,* Robert Montgomery's play loosely based on Dostoevsky's *The Idiot;* and Strindberg's *Miss Julie.* All three productions were strong, and the performances of the actors central to them, such as Heather Canning, John Kane, Ben Kingsley, Helen Mirren, and Patrick Stewart, showed decisively that RSC actors could adapt to the demands of a small, intimate theatre, producing powerful, controlled, and immensely versatile work. Elsewhere, it was apparent that the see-saw syndrome in its two-centre work was once more besetting the company. The Aldwych season was superb; using the 1970 Stratford company in an ambitious repertoire, it included David Jones's first Gorky production, *Enemies,* and Terry Hands's productions of Genet's *The Balcony,* and the late-Restoration *Man of Mode.* But at Stratford the Shakespeare work was disappointing, although the company there – the nucleus of the old heavy brigade, with some new recruits – was a strong one, with many of the actors in their third year of working together. The outstanding production was John Barton's *Othello*, set in a nineteenth-century barracks, the RSC's first attempt at that play for ten years, and one remarkable for the strength of its ensemble playing, with a particularly fine Iago from Emrys James.

By the end of 1971, even though the Stratford season had been disappointing, it was clear that Trevor Nunn's initial strategy for the RSC was beginning to pay off. He had in existence two fine companies. The Aldwych seasons of 1970–1 had not just produced a string of fine productions, they had also attracted much larger audiences (up to an average 82 per cent capacity, for instance). When his plans for 1972 began to leak out within the company, therefore, they were greeted with some shock, for it seemed that Nunn was proposing to disband one of the companies it had taken over three years to create. The result was that the end of 1971 was an extraordinary period of rumour and counter-rumour, much misinformation, and some malice within the RSC. It was alleged that Nunn intended to direct a blockbuster season at Stratford modelled upon the *Wars of the Roses* season of 1963, for which he intended to install an elaborate and costly new stage, and create virtually a new company. The facts were these: for the 1972 Stratford season Nunn announced a thematic season of Shakespeare's four Roman plays, *Coriolanus, Julius Caesar, Antony and Cleopatra,* and *Titus Andronicus,* with a revival of Clifford Williams's celebrated Sixties production of *Comedy of Errors* completing the repertoire. All four new productions were to be directed by Trevor Nunn, with two junior directors, Euan Smith and Buzz Goodbody, as co-directors, other more experienced RSC directors having declined to be involved in the project. The four plays were produced under a joint title, *The Romans,* but Nunn repeatedly made clear in interviews both at the time and later that he did not conceive of the plays as a 'cycle'. He did, however, allow the programmes and posters produced for the season to suggest that the RSC *was* attempting a classical cycle, and he used certain directorial devices in the productions to provide cyclic and thematic links between them. A new stage *was* installed at Stratford, to the design of Christopher Morley, the designer for the season. It cost not £250,000 as was suggested then, but some £25,000, and served all four new productions, its cost being roughly equal to a four-production budget combined. The further sum of £90,000 was also spent enlarging the number of seats in the Stratford auditorium, money which had been earned from foreign tours and which was quickly recouped by increased seat revenue.[1] But if the charges of extravagance, and of deliberately emulating the *Wars of the Roses* cycle were unfair, it still seemed that the *Romans* season represented on Nunn's part a curious and sudden artistic volte face;

in several respects the *Romans* appeared to be not just a break with the principles Nunn had been at pains to establish, but a defiant reversal of them.

The strong Aldwych company, which included Brenda Bruce, Frances de la Tour, Patrick Godfrey, Alan Howard, Sara Kestelman, Ben Kingsley, Philip Locke, Helen Mirren, and David Waller, was allowed to disperse. The *Romans* company was led by Colin Blakely, Ian Hogg, Richard Johnson, Corin Redgrave, Patrick Stewart, Janet Suzman, Margaret Tyzack, and John Wood. Of these only the last three had worked recently for the RSC (Stewart and Wood came from the 1971 Aldwych company) and only they were to work for it again that decade. The company was also larger; walk-ons were reintroduced; the unpopular attempt to persuade leading actors to understudy or play small roles was abandoned.[2] The new stage, designed at that time to duplicate equipment at the Barbican, operated on a complex system of hydraulics. It proved a technical *tour de force*, and an actor's nightmare. The company nicknamed it 'the actor trap'; the *Sunday Times* described its cavortings as 'a succession of miniature earthquakes'. Nunn himself was quickly disillusioned with it, and in fact used it extensively only in the first two of his productions. Thereafter, like its predecessor, the rolling stages of 1932, it was to languish, its machinery scarcely used, for the rest of the decade, a strange aberration from a director so recently in search of simplicity, of staging that would focus attention on 'the actors and the words'.[3]

Nor was the extravagance of the staging of the *Romans* confined to the technical antics of the new machines; all four productions at Stratford were notable for their operaticism. All four began with elaborate processional scenes not textually indicated, which seemed both an attempt to link all four plays, and to make a quick preliminary directorial statement about the societies the plays examined. *Coriolanus* and *Julius Caesar*, for instance, began with assertive demonstrations of repressive authoritarianism; *Antony and Cleopatra* with an opulent pageant showing the lovers dressed as Egyptian god-monarchs, and revelling in their wealth and *folie à deux*; *Titus* with a preliminary sequence of Fellini-esque decadence. This emphasis on epic spectacle was not confined to the opening sequences either; it recurred throughout the plays. In the banishment scene in *Coriolanus* the 'trades of Rome' were equipped with braziers – for the sole purpose, it seemed, of then being able to throw smoking rags at the departing back of Caius Marcius. *Titus* included a Byzantine orgy (complete with transvestite dancers) that was reminiscent of the bare-breasted excesses of Peter Hall's Covent Garden production of *Moses and Aaron*. Several critics objected to all this; Robert Brustein of the *Observer* (reviewing only *Titus*) felt that the production was characterized by 'an opulence which subordinates sense to spectacle'. Brustein was, however, a committed and somewhat myopic Brechtian, and his distaste was perhaps predictable; certain other critics enjoyed the spectacular staging. But as Irving Wardle of *The Times* pointed out, it was not just a question of whether much of the spectacle was superfluous, it was that the spectacle was used didactically, wrenching the plays into a simplistic pattern to show the evolution of a society from tribalism to authoritarianism, to colonialism, to decadence – a four-play decline and fall. This, while it was a view that might be pleasing to a radical modern sensibility, was one hardly justified by the texts of the plays concerned. It exemplified precisely the kind of conceptual bias which Brook had identified as beleaguering the history of Shakespearian production, an approach that Nunn and the RSC had seemed poised to discard.

In later years the *Romans* came to be treated dismissively, yet in terms of critical response and size of audiences, the *Romans* were failures neither at Stratford nor in London. The critics may have quibbled, but on the whole they praised. Nunn's televised version of *Antony and Cleopatra* was a breakthrough in the transmission of Shakespeare on the small screen, and was highly acclaimed; and helped by the increased number of seats the productions played to record audiences in Stratford, and large audiences in London. They may have lacked overall company strength, but they contained some exceptionally fine performances, particularly from John Wood, who as Brutus gave what Michael Billington described as 'the best indictment of smug and boneless liberalism' he had ever seen on the stage, and from Janet Suzman, who came closer to re-creating Cleopatra than any other actress in recent memory, combining an intense and capricious sexuality with a predatory intellect, and passion with a shrewd instinct for survival.

If the productions revealed some of Nunn's weaknesses as a director, such as a certain tabloid taste for hammering home facile points, they also revealed two of his chief gifts – his ability to orchestrate the sweep of a big scene (the funeral orations to the crowd in *Caesar,* to give just one example, were brilliantly staged) and his gift of psychological penetration, so that the shifts and progress of the individual characters were sharply marked. In *Caesar* and *Antony and Cleopatra,* in particular, the interplay of huge events and individual sensibilities was caught with the same nicety that would mark later productions such as his 1976 *Macbeth,* and with a responsiveness to the hidden nuances of the text that made the sledgehammer effects (such as the Fascistic accoutrements of Caesar's entourage) doubly curious. The productions appeared, in short, the work of a divided man working in a theatre which had reached an artistic divide. It was an impression reinforced when they transferred to the Aldwych and were radically altered. Here Nunn's directorial incertitude was marked by changes to all four productions, which inevitably were much more simply staged. It was most marked in the production of *Coriolanus,* in which the whole shift of the production was altered from a Sixties approach to a Fifties one. Ian Hogg was replaced in the title-role by a star from outside the RSC, Nicol Williamson, and the production's previous emphasis on the upheavals of a tribal society changed to a Bradleian emphasis on the personal tragedy of the hero. Williamson's performance was powerful and received great praise; the *Observer* thankfully greeted the return of the star actor to the 'under-cast' ranks of the RSC; few critics noted that a production which could be so radically realigned in the space of the year must surely have been the product of more than usual directorial turmoil.

By the time the *Romans* reached London Trevor Nunn was ill, close to breakdown and plagued with acute migraines. The stress of his continuing administrative responsibilities and of directing four new productions, of months of exhausting and unremitting work, had clearly taken its toll. He directed no new productions in 1973, only one – *Macbeth* – the following year, and only one – *Hedda Gabler* – the year after.

The work of the company apart from the revivals of the *Romans* was, in 1973 and 1974, notably weaker than it had been for some years. The impetus of Nunn's first years seemed to have been lost, and the organization itself seemed in some disarray. Terry Hands's work, like Nunn's, was going through a period of readjustment following the failure of *Richard III* in 1970. The RSC, then and now, depended on the unflagging energy and continuing vision of only a very small group of directors, and with both Hands and Nunn contributing so few productions it was inevitable that the company's work would suffer. The onus was thrown upon David Jones and John Barton, and had it not been for the contribution of these two older directors, the company's fortunes would indeed have been low. The 1973 Stratford season was remarkable for only two productions, Jones's of *Love's Labour's Lost,* and Barton's much praised imagistic production of *Richard II,* with Richard Pasco and Ian Richardson in brilliant form doubling the roles of Bolingbroke and the King. In 1974 the Stratford work hit its lowest point for many years, with a season unhappily split between the work of two different companies. In these years an attempt was apparently being made to graft star actors (Eileen Atkins, Alan Bates, Timothy Dalton) and new directors (Peter Gill and Keith Hack) into the company. The graft could not be said to have taken – an indication of how difficult it was for the RSC to import actors and directors with established methods of work and established reputations, and of how necessary it was for the company, as it had done in the Sixties, to develop its own talent from within.[4]

The work of the RSC at the Aldwych during this time was more successful, but its policies for that theatre had become somewhat diluted. In 1973 the *Romans* provided the bulk of the Aldwych repertoire, and the *Romans* company was seen in new work not at the Aldwych but at The Place, hired for a second season which proved much less successful than the first. In 1974 the Aldwych season was much stronger, and the success of productions such as *Sherlock Holmes, Summerfolk,* and *The Marquis of Keith* disguised somewhat the fact that the Aldwych strategy was by this time in tatters, with at least four different groups of actors working on the season, some from the *Romans* company, some from the 1973 Stratford company, some returning after a gap away, and some new. The two-year pattern of work and the steady growth of an ensemble which had been so remarkable in the pre-*Romans* seasons of 1970 and 1971 had been lost. And it was notable that the most acclaimed production of the season, of Tom Stoppard's *Travesties,* was essentially a West End production inserted into the RSC repertoire. Its leading actor, John Wood, was in his fourth year with the RSC, but its director and designer, and the rest of its cast, came from outside the company. It earned the RSC high praise and substantial revenue, but it had little to do with the RSC's principles of company work.

However, these tinkerings and adjustments to the Aldwych policy in 1973–4 reflected the fact that the company was going through a period of some structural upheaval. Changes in the organization of the RSC were being made which would ultimately prove central to the company's renaissance in the second half of the decade.

The first major change concerned the duration of the Stratford seasons, which prior to 1974 had always ended before Christmas, usually in early December. There had then always been a difficult gap to bridge before the Stratford company could move to the Aldwych, where the programme of RSC work was halted to accommodate the Daubeny World Theatre Seasons which lasted some eight weeks and generally began in late March. In 1974 (when there was no World Theatre Season at the Aldwych) Nunn and Brierley decided to risk extending the Stratford season over the Christmas period and into January. The risk paid off; the productions played to large houses and brought increased revenue to the company. But most importantly the gap between the two seasons had been substantially reduced and the possibility of a smooth and uninterrupted transfer from one theatre to the other became more likely. It took the RSC some while to streamline the operation; the Stratford season of 1974 with its two-company system, and the different groups of actors working at the Aldwych in the same year reflected the difficulties the RSC experienced initially. But it was a change that was to be of immense importance for the company. When the World Theatre Seasons finally came to an end (the last was in 1975) it was an undoubted loss to British theatre, but for the RSC it did have one advantage: rotation of companies became truly practicable and the benefits of that were immediately apparent, in the Stratford 1975/Aldwych 1976 seasons.

The other major change was the rapid development of the RSC's small-theatre work, a development that had become more urgent since the company had – reluctantly – abandoned the costly and difficult business of integrating Theatregoround into its other work. Trevor Nunn was anxious that the discoveries the company had made by investigating classic texts for TGR productions should not be abandoned. He also wanted the RSC to continue presenting new plays of the kind that could not be risked financially at the Aldwych. This desire to find some alternative to TGR had led to the two seasons at The Place, but both had lost money. At the end of 1973 Nunn realized that the RSC was sitting on an unexploited asset – a building the company owned in Stratford which might convert into its own small theatre. The building was a small corrugated-iron hut, originally built to house Saint-Denis's studio work in the Sixties. Since then it had served as headquarters for TGR, and as a rehearsal room. The studio possessed a leaking roof and few obvious advantages other than an out-of-tune piano. During 1973 Nunn persuaded the RSC governors to allow him to test out this building for a studio theatre; rough benches to seat 180 people were installed, and three shows were put on the same year. They all sold out. At the end of 1973 Nunn decided to continue the studio's operations for at least another year. He invited Buzz Goodbody to be the artistic director of the new theatre, and asked her to draw up plans for the way in which it might operate.

Goodbody was the most promising young RSC director; she was also the one person within the company who in background and experience bridged the polarities of Seventies theatre. She had been educated at Roedean and Sussex, and had joined the RSC in 1967, aged twenty, as John Barton's personal assistant. Barton had seen and admired a production she directed while at university. Like her fellow male directors she was deeply interested in working on classical texts, and gained experience within the RSC working on both TGR and large-theatre Shakespeare. She was also a Communist and a committed feminist; she had sympathy and connections with alternative theatre work, and in 1971 had helped to start the first feminist theatre company, the Women's Street Theatre Group. Goodbody's appointment ensured that the company's small-theatre work would be integrated with its other work, that it would degenerate neither into a repository solely for classical work, nor an artistic ghetto confined entirely to new work, cut off from the RSC's wider identity. The document she drew up for the studio theatre in December 1973, and for that theatre's first and highly successful season in 1974, reflected the breadth of her commitments, and her concern that the RSC should extend not just its methods of working and its repertoire, but also its audiences, choosing some plays of local relevance, mounting Shakespeare plays that were on local school syllabuses, and keeping seat prices low. The new theatre was christened The Other Place, a name favoured within the RSC for numerous reasons, not least because it implied an alternative theatre to the large one, and because it was a quotation from *Hamlet* (IV, iii). Its administrator then and for the duration of the decade was Jean

Moore, who proved as important to the theatre's success as Good-body.[5]

The theatre was equipped, the seating redesigned, and communal dressing-rooms built, in under four months, on a shoe-string budget. The new space seated 140 people, with all tickets priced at 60p. None of the productions that first season had a budget over £200, and several were substantially lower. There was considerable Arts Council opposition to the project and it was determined that the theatre must be 'self-financing', which, roughly speaking, meant that box-office revenue had as far as possible to cover costs incurred only because of The Other Place's existence. The use of existing RSC resources – workshops, actors, directors, administrative staff and so on – was not counted. Any gains or losses made by the new theatre would be absorbed into the RSC's overall budget, but spending was closely watched so that if losses were incurred they would be minimal. Thus in its very structure The Other Place became an organic part of the RSC, its success very much dependent on the company's ability to deploy existing resources, whether of personnel, equipment, or finance. No new staff were taken on to run the new theatre, and few actors employed solely for its productions – although cross-casting with the large theatre was to become tighter in later seasons.

That first season consisted of productions of *Lear, The Tempest, Uncle Vanya*, a revival of Rudkin's *Afore Night Come,* and an improvised play, *Babies Grow Old,* directed by Mike Leigh. It brought in two young directors important to later RSC work, Howard Davies and Ron Daniels. Almost all the productions sold out, and there was a vigour, freedom, and vitality about The Other Place work that first season notably lacking in the new large-theatre productions. So, although the RSC ended the financial year with a small deficit, and although in the face of growing inflation it was being urged by the Arts Council to cut back rather than expand, the company went ahead with The Other Place work, and a second season for 1975 was planned. But although the company's structural reforms were promising, and although the creation of The Other Place indicated a continuing ability to take risks, to experiment, and to renew itself, the RSC by mid-decade was still at a fairly low ebb. It had two enervated Stratford seasons behind it; its continuity of work had been undermined; its continuing belief in the company principle appeared intermittent, and its tendency to go for the sure-fire one-off hit, or the instant prestige of the big-name star had become more marked. Above all its confidence in its large-theatre Shakespeare work, the foundation for the entire edifice of the RSC, seemed fitful. In the wake of the clarity, lucidity, and daring of Brook's *Dream* the company appeared to be floundering, relying too often on the hard-hitting but narrowly conceptual approach, or on décor and display. With the exception of Barton none of the directors appeared very confident with the Stratford stage, as if the increasingly unfashion-able large proscenium theatres had undermined all assurance in the new theatrical language of space and light which the company had explored so productively in the late Sixties. Hands's Stratford productions continued to downgrade the role of actor and rely on imposed production effects; Nunn, after experimenting with mechanistic effects in 1972, seemed in his next Shakespeare produc-tion (*Macbeth*, 1974) to be attempting to confine the awesome spaces of the Stratford stage, producing, as he recognized, 'a chamber stage within the proscenium'.[6] Both directors had, significantly, switched designers: in 1974 Nunn began his fruitful partnership with John Napier (having until that time worked exclusively with Christopher Morley), and Hands, who had previously worked mainly with the team of Timothy O'Brien and Tazeena Firth, cemented his partner-ship with Farrah.

By mid-decade it had become essential for the RSC to regain confidence in its Shakespeare work, and in the language of large-scale theatre. In 1975 the new National Theatre was at last scheduled to open under its new director, Peter Hall. The imminence of its opening was the cue for increasingly vicious attacks on large-scale theatre buildings in general and the new National in particular – attacks which proliferated and intensified throughout 1974. Opulent scenic effects and lavish expenditure on sets and costumes came under similar attack, in some cases with specific reference to the RSC. One of the company's leading actresses, Helen Mirren, who was appearing in Nunn's *Macbeth*, attacked both the National and the RSC for their production expenditure in a highly publicized letter to the *Guardian*, declaring it 'unnecessary and destructive to the art of the Theatre'. 'The realms of truth, emotion and imagination reached for in acting a great play', she wrote, 'have become more and more remote, often totally *un*reachable across an abyss of costume and technicalities . . .'[7] Some of the figures Mirren quoted to support her argument were shaky, and RSC management was able to point out

that production costs represented only a small percentage
outlay, 65 per cent of its budget alone going to staff and to r
its theatres. But Mirren was only stating publicly what ma
actors had been saying in private to the directors for some years, and
however questionable the mathematics the arguments contained an
underlying truth.

Planning for the 1975 Stratford season was finalized in July 1974.
The RSC was facing its worst financial crisis since Trevor Nunn's
appointment, a crisis it shared with most other theatres in the
country. Although its next year's grant had not been confirmed by
the Arts Council, the company had a clear indication that it would be
insufficient to keep pace with inflation which exceeded a rate of 20
per cent throughout 1974. The company faced a projected shortfall
on the next year's operation of some £200,000. It also faced major
repair bills; the heating and ventilation system to the theatre had
finally been declared unsafe, and replacing it would cost in the region
of £160,000. Cut-backs clearly had to be made. At the Aldwych
productions were switched to repertory playing rather than repertoire in order to save costs and keep the theatre open. For the large
theatre at Stratford the smallest repertoire of plays since 1879 was
announced – with some irony in view of the fact that 1975 was, after
a fashion, the centenary of the company, exactly one hundred years
since Charles Flower had formed the Shakespeare Memorial Association and launched his appeal for the Memorial Theatre. There were
to be just four productions, three new – *Henry IV, Parts 1* and *II*,
and *Henry V* – and one revival, of Hands's *Merry Wives*. Several
productions for The Other Place were planned, it was true, but that
theatre could not bring in the audiences upon which the RSC
depended. Even with these cut-backs the RSC still faced the prospect
of a large deficit at the close of the next financial year; a Centenary
Appeal was launched.

The RSC faced a year of stringency and possible insolvency;
numerous regional theatres faced immediate closure. The National,
however, as had been rumoured earlier in the year, faced a rather
different prospect. With the passing of a new National Theatre Bill in
parliament on 7 November 1974 the statutory ceiling previously
imposed on the government's contribution to the NT building, the
costs of which had already escalated above £10,500,000, was
removed. During the debate on the Bill it was estimated that the

annual running costs of the National, just for building maintenance, would be £1.15 million. Its future grant for artistic work (i.e. everything not concerned just with keeping the building open) was estimated at £1.35 million (more than three times the grant received by the RSC in 1974–5). There was widespread anxiety in the theatre that these running costs, even if they escalated, would be met at the expense of grants to other theatres, a suspicion that intensified when it was learnt that Sir Max Rayne (who had succeeded Lord Chandos as chairman of the National Theatre Board in 1971) was pressing for the NT to be funded in a different way from all other British theatres, its maintenance grant coming not from the Arts Council, but from the Department of the Environment or the GLC – a device transparently aimed at minimizing the growing disparity between grants to the NT and those to other theatres.

The RSC took no part in the attacks which were mounted on the National during 1974 by many different sections of the theatre and Press. Nevertheless the plans for the National did not exactly enhance the company's own position. When the arrangements for Stratford 1975 were completed in July, the National was still due to open the following April; at a time when Stratford had to cut back to a repertoire of four large-house plays, the National would be receiving a record grant. It was already able to offer leading actors and directors salaries far in excess of anything the RSC could afford – just as Fordham Flower had foreseen and feared in the early Sixties. At a time when the RSC's top salary to an actor was under £200 a week for a heavy rehearsal/performance schedule, the National's top rate was more than double, £500 per week, and that sometimes, as NT director Michael Blakemore pointed out, for one or two performances a week.[8] As it happened, the National's plans to open in April 1975 had to be cancelled in September 1974, and the opening of its two large auditoria, the Olivier and the Lyttelton, was delayed until 1976. But no one at the RSC knew that when the 1975 Stratford season was being put together. Like it or not, regardless of its rival, the RSC now had no alternative but to submit to the austerity its left-wing critics had been demanding.

It could well be argued that that austerity proved the saving of the RSC, just as the comparative affluence of the National contributed to its marked artistic incoherence in the mid Seventies. This is not an argument that appeals greatly to subsidized theatre companies struggling to develop in a period of inflation and recession, and bitterly aware of the far greater state funding of drama in Germany or France. But it did have two immediate effects: first, it placed the RSC in the position of underdog (to the National's top-dog). This protected it to some degree from attacks by the Left (it was further protected by its development of small-theatre work), and it inclined the Press in its favour. From the public relations viewpoint, therefore, since the new stringency at the RSC chimed with the tendency of public opinion, the RSC benefited. This was not as unimportant as it might have seemed, for it earned the RSC the kind of benevolent encouragement from critics that can be actively beneficial to a company; the National, attacked on all sides (often unfairly, for it was locked into an unfortunate chain of circumstance with a long history), received little or no such encouragement. Above all, however, the need for stringency had an immediate and powerfully restorative effect on the company's work. Quite suddenly it took off, and in 1975 the RSC found itself in one of those extraordinary golden periods of work in which, intoxicatingly, everything goes right.

For the first time the entire RST season was to be directed by one man, Terry Hands, and Hands, rather in the manner of Brook before him, appeared to have changed radically his directorial approach. Few traces of the autocratic 'Gauleiter Hands' of the late Sixties and early Seventies remained; from the first he insisted that production work must be collaborative, that he did not wish to impose a shape on the history plays but wanted one to evolve in rehearsal. And by and large that was what happened.

It was the RSC's first new attempt at the central history plays since the celebrated Hall/Barton seasons of 1963–4, and for 1975 the company decided to open the season with *Henry V*. This was, on the face of it, an odd decision. Since Quayle's first Histories season of 1951 understanding of the stature of the cycle had been growing; it had become the norm to mount the plays in chronological order. That method, obviously, had much to recommend it, and one of its side benefits was that it made one play in particular – *Henry V* – greatly more palatable to a modern audience. Seen as the third part of a trilogy, or as the fourth of a quartet of plays commencing with *Richard II, Henry V* took on new resonances. It could be seen to show the expiation of a curse, the continuing education of a prince, the story of a nation achieving unity after civil dissension. A deliberately downbeat neo-Brechtian production such as that of 1964, with its fine central performance from Ian Holm, also helped in that it avoided the superfluous pageantry and skirted the jingoism that had been associated with the play. Nevertheless, the play was still weighted down and obscured by those associations.

Henry V had so often been mounted as propaganda that it was no surprise it should be judged propagandist; and so it had been by twentieth-century critics who regarded it with mounting distaste. Yeats considered Henry a 'ripened Fortinbras', speaking the language of a newspaper editorial; Shaw dismissed him as 'a jingo hero . . . an able young philistine'; their attitudes were echoed by numerous other critics and commentators of distinction. Two world wars had made a play which was judged to glorify war unacceptable, and that productions such as those of 1951 or 1964 had not been able to dislodge this accumulated inheritance of prejudice was marked in the first reactions to the 1975 production, which was frequently to be praised for the wrong reasons. Coming at a time of national economic crisis, the play was again interpreted as a timely piece of nationalistic revivalism: it was variously described as 'patriotic tubthumping' (*The Times*); as glorying 'in being English' (*Sunday Times*); and 'rabble-rousing . . . a reminder of national greatness' (*Daily Express*). All of which went to show that while *all* Shakespeare's plays need reappraisal constantly, some need it more urgently than others. *Henry V*, which had been subject to critical stagnation for so long, needed it very urgently and the 1975 company's reclamation of the play was as important a theatrical breakthrough as the *Dream* had been five years before.

Hands wanted to open the season with *Henry V* partly because he believed that to confront the play singly rather than sequentially might aid reappraisal of it (in which aim he was only very gradually successful), and chiefly because he believed that the first Chorus speech of the play provided the company with an artistic 'dictionary', not just for that production, but for the whole season – perhaps even for the RSC's future work.[9] In that first speech the Chorus describes two kinds of theatre, the literal and the ideal; his speech is an apologia and a plea. He describes an actual stage (the 'wooden O') and apologizes for its scenic inadequacy. But he also describes another kind of theatre, the theatre of the mind and the imagination. The first may be inadequate, but if the audience can be engaged, the second – in which anything is possible – may occur. It is a direct, and quintessential, definition of theatre, and one that happened to be well suited to an organization pledged to austerity. It posited the kind of theatrical experience that a new generation, evangelically devoted to close-range naturalism, doubted could properly occur in a large proscenium-arch auditorium. From both points of view the RSC could not have chosen a play that was more timely and potentially more controversial.

Hands used the speech like a blueprint, in the process taking the company back to many of the ideals of the 1968 –70 period, ideals which had been eroded since then. The cast for *Henry V* numbered twenty-five. (In 1964 it had numbered nearly fifty, many of them walk-ons.) This time there were no spear-carriers; the English army consisted of seven men, the four captains and three soldiers who actually speak. As the cast was stripped back so, literally, was the theatre. Everything extraneous was stripped away. Farrah designed not a set but a superb stage, which was to serve for all four productions: a black platform, bare of adornment, it jutted out towards the audience with all its working trimmings clearly visible. No masking was used, so the great batteries of lights, the bridges, the wires that supported the canopies in *Henry V* – all these could be seen. It was no box of illusions but a place where the mechanics of theatrical performance were always visible. The stage itself, a wooden rectangle rather than a wooden O, had a steep 1 in 12 rake, and resembled the deck of a great aircraft carrier. It threw the actors into sharp relief and had the effect of propelling the action out towards the audience. Into this empty space Hands introduced one other element vital to the production: light. All Hands's work was remarkable for his use of light, and his techniques were central to his mastery of the difficult Stratford stage. In *Henry V* he used light to underline textual mood; to compress and speed up action; to heighten the often ironic Shakespearian juxtapositioning of scenes, which succeeded each other with cinematic celerity. Above all he used it to confine stage space and concentrate the attention, so that the audience's vision of the play was as controllable as the lens of a camera, constantly switching from wide-angle to close focus. In *Henry V* the interaction of light, music, and action was to contribute to some of the production's unforgettable *coups de théâtre*, but it also contributed to its intimacy, making it possible for actors to convey duality (emotion at variance with speech, as in Henry's address to the people of Harfleur) to the back of the theatre, and with total economy, using only the interplay of voice and feature.

The play was staged very simply. The costumes were period to some extent, but the ordinary soldiers in particular appeared time- less. As they woke to grey light on the morning of Agincourt, hunched on the ground with kit-bags for pillows, to the reveille of a ladle banged on a soup pot, they took on an eternal quality: all soldiers, before battle, must look much as they did. That scene, like many others involving the English army, was rehearsed through improvisation, after long discussion about the realities of soldiering. Its detail and unsentimental precision was typical of the production, and one of the elements that gave it its peculiar strength; this ragged and tiny army, rent with internal dissension, at times near to mutiny, and led by a king who was himself wracked with self-doubts, provided a constant corrective to the rhetoric of the Chorus speeches. What began to emerge, reinforced by the symbolism inherent in Hands's and Farrah's staging, was the odd contrapuntal nature of this play so long judged to be a simple hymn to English imperialistic impulses. The narrator, the Chorus, might present a glorious account of an unhindered and noble progress towards English victory; the dramatic action showed a very different story. As the English embarked for war the stage was tented by a great billowing heraldic canopy; as they began the long retreat back through France, to be halted and forced to fight at Agincourt, that canopy sank to the floor; reverse side up it looked like an endless sea of mud. The battle itself became not the jingoistic vanquishing of the French, but the victory of a united group of men over a hierarchic and entrenched society; when the French died, trapped in Farrah's glorious golden armour, they died visibly imprisoned in the symbol of a way of life and set of assumptions that they – unlike the English – had been unable to escape. Montjoy (Oliver Ford-Davies) became not just a diplomat negotiating between two armies, but a sensitive man trying to mediate between two ethics. Above all the king emerged, not as the first cousin to Tamburlaine decried by so many commentators, but as a revolutionary, a man willing to change himself and willing to change the rules of war, and therefore able to find, at last, a unity with his army.[10] The key St Crispin's Day speech was played quietly, and without bombast, and in that moment and in the almost music-hall elation of the subsequent scene the gulf between ranks closed. It was the production's greatest distinction that it made this moment of unification completely convincing; it was the visible welling-up of an *esprit de corps* that was closer to the vision of a Fanon than a Kitchener. It was, as the critic of the *Sunday Times* wrote, a production packed with brilliancies, marked by the power of its ensemble playing, and containing at its centre a revelatory and much praised performance from Alan Howard as Henry, the first of the four Shakespearian kings he was to play for the RSC over the next five years.

The production played a record number of performances (over one hundred) at Stratford that year alone; it was revived three times, and played extensively in Britain, New York, and Europe to a mounting chorus of critical acclaim. Its success was of crucial importance to the RSC, not just because of the production's popularity, but because it resolved many of the difficulties that had beleaguered the company's Shakespeare work since 1970. It held the large stage with confidence and released to the full the latent power of a huge playing space; it combined simplicity and economy of staging with images of stunning poetic power but it also held, in fine balance, the contribution of director, designer, and actor. Above all it showed the power of a great production to new-mint an audience's vision of a great play, a power that must remain the ultimate vindication of a company such as the RSC.

The other work in the large theatre that year was not of the same order, but it was strong, with *Henry IV, Part II* achieving a poise and authority lacking in the more uneven *Part I*. But in this fine and exciting season there was one event of great sadness. Buzz Goodbody had planned an interesting second season for The Other Place, including *Hamlet*, Jonson's rarely performed *Epicene*, (both of which she was to direct), and Brecht's *Man is Man*, directed by one of her strongest recruits, Howard Davies. *Hamlet* opened to considerable critical acclaim on 8 April 1975, and proved to be the RSC's strongest production of the play that decade, a brilliant re-examination of it in the context of a tiny playing space. Cross-cast with the large-theatre company, and with Ben Kingsley in the title-role, it was played in modern dress on a shallow platform against plain white screens. It was remarkable for the originality of its performances, which gained in intensity from being pitched naturalistically low to suit the playing space. Like *Henry V* it was a production of great fluency, scene overlapping scene with speed. Like the large-theatre productions it rewardingly investigated the complexity of personal and family relationships in the play, indicating that the RSC was now moving away from the epic style of the Sixties, with its emphasis on relationships of state, to the interior world of the plays, to the network of cousins, brothers, fathers, daughters, and sons which provides a focus for the wider events. It was a course paralleled by the discernible shift in RSC acting styles. *Hamlet* was a breakthrough in the RSC's pioneering work with classic plays in small theatres. It was a production which was to have many and lasting effects within the RSC, and to lead directly to some of its finest work.

On 12 April, just four days after the production opened, Buzz Goodbody committed suicide in London, her action coming as a total surprise to those she had been working with. Apart from the great sense of personal loss, the company lost its most promising young director, the person who had pioneered its small-theatre work, and the person most responsible for forging the vital link between the RSC and a new generation of writers, actors, and directors. Trevor Nunn returned from Los Angeles, where his production of *Hedda Gabler* was touring, to oversee *Hamlet* for its run; another young RSC director, Barry Kyle, took on responsibility for the rest of The Other Place season – a season that inevitably suffered from the shock of Goodbody's death, although Howard Davies's production of *Man is Man* was the company's strongest attempt at Brecht for many years.

Buzz Goodbody's death had a deep and lasting effect on those who had worked with her, and it might well have resulted in the disintegration of all she had worked for – The Other Place had depended strongly on her vision, energy, and commitment. In fact, the opposite happened. Because of her death the company's commitment to small-theatre work intensified. Her influence had an immediate effect on Trevor Nunn. Working on *Hamlet* in 1975 (and again in 1976 when it played at the Roundhouse in tandem with *Man is Man*), he discovered to what extent, as he put it, he had been 'yearning to do small-theatre productions'.[11] In 1976 Trevor Nunn found himself again as a director and his work in the second half of the decade was to be remarkable for its versatility and regained authority. It was also prolific. The director who had cut back to only one new production a year since the *Romans* worked on five new productions in 1976.

With two of its central team of directors, Hands and Nunn, both hitting form, with strong new directors developing such as Ron Daniels, Howard Davies, and Barry Kyle, with two exceptionally fine companies in existence, it was almost inevitable that the work of the

RSC would continue the upturn it had begun with *Henry V* and *Hamlet*. And it did; as several critics remarked, the years 1975–7 were the *anni mirabili* for the company.

The RSC began 1976 in a much more secure position financially than had been feared a year earlier. At the eleventh hour (in fact in March 1976, just before the close of the financial year) the Arts Council found itself able to give the RSC a supplementary grant of some £35,000. With this money, and with the help of the cut-backs, the benefit of revenue from *Sherlock Holmes* on Broadway, and the funds raised by the Centenary Appeal, the RSC ended the financial year 1975–6 not with a massive deficit, but with a small surplus of £794.

The company was naturally relieved at this reprieve, but it highlighted a difficulty which was to recur later in the decade. A year before the company had pleaded threatened bankruptcy; within twelve months it contrived to balance its books. Such reversals – particularly since the Arts Council was anxious not to have the granting of supplementary funds widely advertised – created a dangerous credibility gap for the RSC. It made each subsequent claim of imminent financial crisis (the next major one came in 1979) more difficult for journalists and critics to accept. For this reason, apart from any other, it was not the most tactful move to dismantle Farrah's 1975 staging at Stratford, and construct in its stead a new and elaborate permanent staging for the very next season. John Napier and Chris Dyer were responsible for its design, and one of its chief objects was to create a chamber intimacy in the notoriously difficult Stratford auditorium; the design was clearly influenced by the company's experience of intimate playing space in its small theatre. The new designs created a *trompe-l'oeil* effect: the two tiers of circle and balcony seats appeared to pass right through the proscenium arch, linking up with two tier balconies behind it. On these balconies behind the stage members of the audience could sit. The whole thing, sturdily constructed of timber, was a clever facsimile of an Elizabethan inn-yard theatre with an apron stage, and the closest Stratford had come to translating an obstinate proscenium stage into a sixteenth-century playing space since the experiments of Iden Payne. The critics were sharply divided on its merits; its somewhat coy fussiness certainly came as a shock after the bareness of the staging the previous year. That it was destined to be another of the RSC's unfruitful tinkerings with the Stratford stage became apparent when it was dismantled at the end of the year and never rebuilt.

There were six RST productions that season, all directed by John Barton, Trevor Nunn, and Barry Kyle either individually or in various combinations, and only two, *Romeo and Juliet* and *The Winter's Tale,* were disappointments. A strong company had been formed, dominated by actors with many years of experience and familiarity with the RSC. Led by Francesca Annis, Judi Dench, Ian McKellen, Donald Sinden, and Michael Williams, it included a number of the RSC's most promising young actors, Mike Gwilym, Ian McDiarmid, Robert Peck, Michael Pennington, and Roger Rees. It was a season remarkable for the versatility both of its acting and of its production approach, with John Barton's ingenious Indian Empire *Much Ado* irradiated by Judi Dench's sad and funny portrait of a spinsterish Beatrice, and his third attempt at *Troilus and Cressida,* which missed the brilliance of his 1968 production. There was a strong attempt at *Lear* in which Sinden gave an acclaimed performance, and a highly popular musical version of *The Comedy of Errors,* directed by Trevor Nunn (who also wrote the lyrics). Played in modern dress, with Ephesus a Mediterranean tourist trap it was cheeky, effervescent, and fun. To see RSC actors and directors able to switch from such broad satire, from choreographed dance routines and superbly manipulated farce to the sombre world of *Lear* or the season's outstanding success, The Other Place production of *Macbeth,* was to see a company at work whose virtuosity was unrivalled in Britain. The RSC was visibly stretching its actors, just as it was stretching its resources, never allowing them to settle into one pattern – the trap that had been so destructive to classical actors like Baliol Holloway in the past.

In fact 1976 was the first Stratford season in which the company achieved equally strong work both in its large and small theatres. The Other Place season (for which Trevor Nunn had overall responsibility) consisted of five productions, all memorable. It included the best new political play of the decade, David Edgar's study of the evolution of a National Front–style party, *Destiny* (strongly directed by Ron Daniels, it later transferred successfully to the large stage at the Aldwych); a revival of Bond's play about Shakespeare, *Bingo*; and Trevor Nunn's production of *Macbeth,* a production that grew directly out of Nunn's experiences in working on Buzz Goodbody's

Hamlet the previous year. *Macbeth* was important not just because it was a fine production widely praised, but because it illustrated the creative interaction of the company's large and small-theatre work. The 1976 production was Nunn's third battle with the play; his two previous attempts had illustrated his increasing uneasiness with Shakespeare on the large stage – and that was odd in the work of a director whose mastery of the large stage in non-Shakespeare productions such as *Once in a Lifetime, Nicholas Nickleby* and *Juno and the Paycock* (all at the Aldwych later that decade) was total.

Nunn's two previous attempts at *Macbeth*, at Stratford in 1974 and in revival at the Aldwych in 1975, had gone through a process similar to that of his *Romans* productions. Elaborately and ritualistically staged inside a huge chancel structure at Stratford, the play was scaled down and stripped back at the Aldwych. When he came to work on the play for a third time, at The Other Place, Nunn found himself totally freed; he had found the medium – the space – he had unconsciously been seeking. With relief he found that the kind of production he had wanted to do as early as 1970, eschewing spectacle and illusion as he had intended with his *Hamlet*, was, at The Other Place, more or less inevitable. Nunn used a device in his staging similar to one he had used many years before in *The Revenger's Tragedy*, one that tightened and contained the action. Inside the square playing space, a circle outlined in black was painted on the floor. Around its circumference were a few props – a king's robes, a thunder sheet – and some upturned wooden boxes. The cast consisted of only sixteen actors, and during the action of the play which took place inside the (magic) circle those not on might watch the scenes from the sidelines, rather as the actors had watched the course of the play from the galleries in Brook's *Dream*. The choice of those who watched was not haphazard: the witches observed Macbeth as he damned himself; Macduff stood on the edge of the circle, as inside it his family was murdered. The device heightened the sense that one was watching a theatrical performance; an actor could not participate in that performance until he stepped over the edge of the circle. And it increased the claustrophobia inherent in the play, the sense that the characters were locked inside a sequence of events, a tiny cosmos in which powerful emotions had apocalyptic consequences. In such a stylized production no tricks were needed for the witches to vanish into the air; they simply stepped outside the circle, and one accepted at once the convention that those outside were invisible to those still trapped within its circumference. Nunn had not made the mistake – a tempting one in that auditorium – of pursuing a naturalistic *Macbeth*; the whole production was as carefully controlled as the playing space was confined. What it unavoidably lacked in physical scale was replaced by intensity, and it became a play of tortured minds, as vivid as an hallucination.

The group who worked on it was a close one, and the production contained fine performances throughout, particularly from Ian McDiarmid as Ross, from Roger Rees as Malcolm, and from Robert Peck as Macduff. From Judi Dench and Ian McKellen, as Lady Macbeth and Macbeth, it produced two unforgettable performances.

To have two such productions as this *Macbeth* and the previous year's *Henry V* in its repertoire in the same year, the one in Stratford, the other now in London, was indicative of the breakthrough the company had made in its classical work; but to have them backed by other work covering an immense range, and of a uniformly high quality, was a triumph for the company. That year it mounted twenty-five productions, a level of repertoire that meant everyone in the organization was working at full stretch. Instead of calling a breathing space, however, in 1977 plans for further expansion were announced.

In December 1976 Trevor Nunn asked Ron Daniels to become the new artistic director of The Other Place; by January 1977, after long discussions, it was also agreed that that year the RSC would open a new small theatre in London, which would be run by Howard Davies. It was agreed that this theatre would open by July 1977, although at the time the decision was reached the company had no suitable London building. There was opposition to the scheme from the Arts Council, and the financial dangers were obvious to RSC management. Whereas The Other Place was owned by the RSC, for a new London theatre the company would have to pay rent and rates. The Other Place could use existing Stratford workshops, the new London theatre would have to put set construction out to contract; clearly its overheads would be much higher and its potential losses more biting. If the scheme had not had strong support it would certainly never have been pushed through, although to balance its potential drawbacks it offered the company numerous advantages. It meant, in the first place, that more of the RSC's Other Place productions could have, like the large-theatre work, a two-year lease of life, which they patently deserved. It meant that the company would be able to undertake more new work, and Davies was committed to the belief that the new theatre must provide a platform for new British playwrights. Not least the two appointments meant that the RSC retained the services of two of its best young directors, something which it might otherwise have been unable to do.

At the time of their appointment both Daniels and Davies were in their thirties, and they provided an interesting example of the differences between their generation of theatre directors, and those just older than them such as Terry Hands and Trevor Nunn. Hands and Nunn had both joined the RSC in their early twenties; by the time they were thirty Nunn was running the company and both had had considerable experience of working on modern and classical plays and on Shakespeare. They both followed a course – university, regional theatre, major subsidized company – very similar to that taken by Peter Hall. But the majority of directors of the next generation, the directors who began work in the late Sixties, had taken a very different course. Daniels and Davies, like many of their contemporaries such as Chris Parr or Max Stafford-Clark, had worked primarily with alternative theatre groups and regional theatres, working closely with new writers and directing comparatively few classical plays and little Shakespeare. Ron Daniels was less typical of his generation in this respect; born and brought up in Brazil (of English parents) he had founded and helped to build his own theatre before coming to England on a drama scholarship and working first as an actor. He had had some six years of frequent work as actor and director with Peter Cheeseman's company at Stoke where he directed work ranging from Greek plays to Shaw and Shakespeare. But he was closely associated with a number of British writers, including David Rudkin, Paul Thompson, Steve Gooch, and David Edgar, and although he was to direct two exceptionally fine Shakespeare productions for the RSC at The Other Place (*Pericles* and *Timon of Athens*), he faced the prospect of Shakespeare on the large stage with considerable trepidation, undertaking no large-house productions until 1980 when he directed *Romeo and Juliet* at Stratford.

Howard Davies had worked as artistic director at the Bristol Old Vic Studio after taking a director's course at Bristol University. He concentrated on modern work, particularly the plays of Edward Bond, and worked with a Bristol alternative theatre group, Avon Touring. Buzz Goodbody had brought him to the RSC on a free-lance basis, and he had been at first extremely suspicious of the company; he found himself 'uncomfortable amongst people who were Oxbridge trained', who constantly seemed to be quoting Shakespeare to each other.[12] Unlike Goodbody, Davies then had no wish to re-examine Shakespeare in a smaller space, was strongly resistant to the idea of directing Shakespeare in the large theatre, and wanted to work primarily with new playwrights – all of which made him doubt whether he was the right person to be an RSC director at all.

When the plans for the new London theatre were finally agreed in January 1977, Davies had three good Other Place productions to his credit (including two Brecht plays) and had directed a very strong production of *The Iceman Cometh* at the Aldwych. Daniels had directed the fine 1974 revival of Rudkin's *Afore Night Come* and had been responsible for persuading the company to put on Edgar's *Destiny,* a play previously turned down by numerous theatres including the National and the RSC. But neither man could have been brought into the RSC in the manner that Hands and Nunn had been before them, moving rapidly after an apprentice period to large-house work: British theatre in general and the RSC in particular had by the late Seventies changed too radically for that. By giving Daniels and Davies a free hand in the form of their own theatres (although integrated with the rest of the company work) the RSC was able to retain them, and to hold on to a number of other young directors such as Bill Alexander, John Caird, and Barry Kyle. (Kyle, however, had worked in both small and large theatres from the first and was less resistant to such flexibility.) The RSC was therefore able to bring on a new generation of directors more successfully than the National, for instance, which lacked a space equivalent to The Other Place or the new RSC London theatre, the Warehouse. It had a beautifully designed and splendidly equipped studio theatre in the Cottesloe, but the Cottesloe had been *planned*, it had not evolved, and it lacked the rough and ready improvisational ambience of the RSC's two small theatres – an ambience that reflected the small-theatre ethic and was greatly contributory to their success.

It was by no means easy for the RSC to find a suitable new London theatre, especially since its geographic range was limited. The new space *had* to be in the Covent Garden area, near to the Aldwych and near to the company's rehearsal rooms in Floral Street, partly so that it could be seen to be an integral part of the RSC and mainly because the difficulties of moving a company of some fifty actors between theatres and rehearsal rooms, with all their work tightly scheduled, demanded a new theatre within easy travelling distance. The building finally selected was the Donmar rehearsal rooms where Brook and Marovitz had staged Genet's *The Screens,* part of their 1964 Theatre of Cruelty experiments. It was rechristened, converted, and equipped at immense speed. The first show put on there, a transfer of *Schweyk in the Second World War* from The Other Place, opened on 18 July 1977; the electricity for the theatre was turned on just half an hour before curtain up, and the concrete steps up to the theatre were still wet.

The Warehouse's first season of nine plays was evenly balanced between four revivals from Stratford and five new plays: *That Good Between Us* by Howard Barker (whose plays had previously been mounted mainly at the Royal Court); *Bandits,* by the Scots playwright C. P. Taylor (a fine and prolific writer whose work had been little seen in London); *Frozen Assets* by Barrie Keefe, who with plays such as *Gimme Shelter* had emerged as the spokesman of angry dispossessed youth; *Factory Birds* by the almost unknown James Robson, which won the *Evening Standard* Best New Play Award; and *The Bundle,* a play specially written for the Warehouse by Edward Bond. Keefe's play was commissioned and Robson's substantially reworked before production; Davies was anxious that this close relationship with writers should continue: he wanted to encourage new work by commissioning rather than buying in, and to encourage writers to be part of the rehearsal process, so that plays might be considerably changed by rehearsal discoveries and the editorial judgement of directors. It was, in effect, a kind of journalistic process adapted to theatre, and it placed more emphasis on the development of writers than on the mounting of totally achieved and successful work. The Warehouse was to be a workshop as much as a showcase, and this first season was remarkably innovative, especially in view of the speed with which it was mounted. It was an unapologetically Socialist season of new work that was a considerable break with anything the RSC had attempted in the past, and admirable in the encouragement it gave not to the big names of the fringe – Brenton, Hare, Edgar – but to less well-known writers.

The opening of the Warehouse in 1977 coincided with an explosion of vitality in the RSC's work. That year it mounted an astonishing body of productions, eight at Stratford, eleven at the Aldwych, five at The Other Place, nine at the Warehouse. In March it inaugurated its now annual seasons in Newcastle, taking eight productions there for a five-week season that was a sell-out. Two of the Aldwych productions, Clifford Williams's of *Wild Oats* (a late eighteenth-century play that had languished in total neglect for over a century and which gave the RSC one of its greatest comedy productions that decade), and Michael Blakemore's of Peter Nichols's *Privates on Parade* transferred to extremely successful seasons in the West End. Nunn's production of *Macbeth* transferred to the Young Vic for a two-month season after playing to full houses at the Warehouse, and a contract was signed with Thames Television to record both it and *The Comedy of Errors*. The company's output had roughly doubled in four years, and the contribution of David Brierley, William Wilkinson, and the RSC's new planning controller, Genista McIntosh (the person with the unenviable but vital job of dovetailing rehearsal and performance schedules) was crucial to this expansion. They and their staffs were the people who made it possible, and they did so not by expanding the RSC administration but primarily by redeployment and streamlining. As its workload increased the RSC did not become administratively top-heavy. By the end of the decade it was employing between 600 and 700 people, including actors, a modest and gradual increase over the past twenty years. Both Brierley and Wilkinson believed that in this smallness lay the company's strength: Brierley's rule-of-thumb definition for when the RSC grew too large was the moment when it had to employ a personnel director. By the end of the decade Wilkinson was still employing only five people (plus a computer system he masterminded) to control every aspect of the RSC's finances. That the RSC remained a small organization, with its decision-making powers concentrated in the hands of the remarkably few people who formed its executive planning committee, contributed to its flexibility and unusual character. Far from becoming the 'ICI of British theatre' that Hall had once envisaged, the RSC continued to resemble a family unit, patriarchal, tolerant of personal vagaries, sometimes riven by enmity and dissent but closing ranks and maintaining face in public, its cement not bureaucratic procedures but personal relationships and loyalties.

While the 1976 Stratford company brought new productions and past successes to the Aldwych, Terry Hands and a large section of the 1975–6 company returned to Stratford to revive *Henry V*, to mount new productions of the *Henry VI* trilogy and, at the end of the long season, of *Coriolanus*. All four new productions were landmarks in the history of the RSC and post-war British theatre, and the *Henry VI* trilogy in particular was a fascinating undertaking, demonstrating the ways in which the RSC had changed and developed in the past decade. The productions were, in effect, premières: the first performances of the unadapted texts since Shakespeare's lifetime. What they showed above all else was the confidence that the RSC now had in its central author.[13] Hands and the company were prepared to play the trilogy as written, with very few cuts and virtually no editing, trusting that what might seem inconsistent or awkward on the page would prove to be dramatically justified; that what read as inchoate would work on a stage. This was a great step forward, incidentally a testament to the virtues of subsidized theatre and the growing loyalty of the RSC's audience. In 1962, when John Barton had worked on the plays to produce the celebrated *Wars of the Roses* sequence, he had been told that the company could not possibly risk three productions of the *Henry VI* plays. So Barton's version was in essence an artistic compromise between company interest and what was felt to be public taste. As the *Observer* pointed out (reviewing Hands's productions) Barton had not just edited (and rewritten) he had *editorialized*. His weighted approach undoubtedly streamlined the plays, ironing out many of their problems, and contributing to their drive in the theatre; it illustrated both the strengths and the weaknesses inherent in the RSC's approach in the Sixties. Hands and his company were attempting a more difficult, but also perhaps more rewarding task, honouring what had been written in its totality. In short (and disregarding the multitudinous arguments about the authorship of *Henry VI*) they were, as Hands put it, 'prepared to trust Shakespeare'.

Ultimately they were vindicated; triumphantly so. But it was not an easy progress. The evolution of the *Henry VI* plays was marked by acute stress and punctuated by some critical hesitancy – for the critics, most of whom remembered *Wars of the Roses* vividly, were being asked as much as everyone else to make readjustments in their thinking. They, like the actors, had to abandon prejudice and resist the temptation to judge these productions against their memories of a previous theatrical era. Because the plays were so little known they created numerous problems for the company. They were difficult to cast for many actors and their agents had neither seen them, nor read them, and key roles took months to fill. Several parts were finally cast only days before the company went into rehearsal, and there remained weaknesses in the casting from which the productions suffered. When the company began work on the plays, which were rehearsed concurrently (in itself a massive undertaking), the actors found they had nothing to go on, none of the landmarks provided by past productions which customarily help a company chart its way through a play. And the plays were hard; actors used to Shakespeare's mature style found much of this text difficult in its comparative rhythmic simplicity; the structure of the plays was dense, the narrative swift, with huge events telescoped into a series of tight scenes. The characterization was similarly compressed, almost expressionistic, with some of the relationships (for instance that of Henry and Margaret) left ambiguous. The plays hinged on sequences of alliances – political, military, sexual – which were forged and broken with astonishing speed, often with little naturalistic explanation. Their plots and their patternings (such as the father/son relationships that dominate their structure) were complex, and they were punctuated by increasingly frequent battles, which on the page seemed alarmingly repetitive.

There was not enough time. Hands, convinced of the trilogy's unity of conception and structure, had rehearsed the three plays as one, with the scenes numbered straight through from one to seventy-nine. He insisted that they must open on consecutive nights within one week to emphasize this unity. But the RSC was geared to at least one week in which to open a single production, and the consecutive openings created a log-jam of intense work immediately prior to the openings. Hands himself worked an increasingly impossible schedule – forty-eight hours on to six hours off – to get them open. By the time of the first nights everyone – directors, actors, technicians, stage-hands – was near exhaustion. It could not have been done had not the productions been staged with the utmost simplicity; the lessons of *Henry V* had been carried through. Even so, fine though the productions were when they opened at Stratford they had inevitably not had time to settle or be fully played in, which of course contributed to the tone of the critics' first reviews. As *The Times* remarked the following year, they read rather like reports from a battlefield. There was sharp disagreement over which of the three plays worked best, and Irving Wardle of *The Times* openly stated what several other critics went on to imply – that he 'pined' for the editorial work which had shaped these plays in the *Wars of the Roses* cycle. The next year when the productions opened at the Aldwych, immeasurably strengthened by performance, the critics saw them in one day and the tone of their reviews changed considerably. The company's belief in what Billington called 'Shakespeare's dance to the broken music of time', was vindicated, and unanimously acclaimed. Bernard Levin in the *Sunday Times* spoke for many critics when, despite some reservations, he declared the productions to be 'one of the most important, as well as the most magnificent, theatrical presentations we have seen for a good many years'.

The productions' single greatest achievement was their staging. Without pre-emption or directorial bias Hands kept the plays in an iron grip, never losing his control on their overall span by allowing episodic structure to disintegrate into muddle. As in *Henry V* there were no spear-carriers; in three plays dominated by battles only those who spoke fought. There were no sets, simply an immensely deep black platform, similar to that used in 1975. What scenic elements there were – a great bridge in *Part I*, a grassy carpet in *Part II* – were minimal. The plays ended with two unforgettable images typical of Hands's production approach: for the murder of Henry VI by Richard Gloucester the front of the stage reared up, creating suddenly a huge steel rat-trap, incandescently lit from below, in which the King, tethered in chains, goaded Richard to take the action of three plays to its inevitable conclusion – regicide. As Henry died the trap sank back; Richard twisted up and out of it, on to the stage and into his brother's new court. In a second one had been taken from a dungeon to a throne-room: the birth of Edward IV's son was being celebrated, and the new king called for music and dancing. But these musicians, and these characters, had forgotten such measures. Battle music brayed; the men instinctively reached for their swords; when the gentler music began Hands held the lighting in a slow long fade and the tiny group of survivors shufflingly, awkwardly, tried to dance. Such ellipsis and compression, depending on the interplay of space, sound, light, and the actors' abilities, formed the language of the production and the means by which Hands controlled the flow of the work and contained its geographic and spiritual sprawl.

The productions contained some revelatory performances that showed, even more than *Wars of the Roses* had done, what great roles awaited discovery and exploration in these neglected plays. It was fascinating to compare the 1977 performances with those of the Barton/Hall productions of thirteen years earlier for it was not just, as several critics noted, that certain of the characters emerged quite differently in the full text than they had done in the truncated version, it was that the playing made apparent the already discernible shift in the RSC acting approach. What had been a company with a predominantly classical approach had become a romantic one. Before RSC actors had been remarkable for poise, balance, weight, rationality; now, although the insistence on communicating the sense of the text remained unchanged, the approach was very different. Its characteristics were unpredictability, the permitting of inconsistency, the relish of ambiguity, the willingness to take risks; it was rather as if a generation of high-wire walkers had taken over from a team of superb civil engineers. So Emrys James, for instance, as York, was not a consummate political animal gnawed with ambition but a narcissistic unbalanced man, obsessed with the crown but thrown into confusion and uncertainty when he got it. Helen Mirren, as Margaret, was not the venomous schemer, the she-wolf of France York describes (and many critics apparently wanted, for her per-formance was controversial); she was voluptuous and child-like, loving and yet fickle, her eroticism, ambition, and cruelty charging each other so that the final killing of York took on more complex resonances than pure revenge. Alan Howard, as Henry, gave a performance that altered the perspective of the trilogy; his Henry provided, as the *Guardian* put it, the 'moral binoculars' for the three plays. He was not simply a holy idiot, a weak man surrounded by the strong, he was the plays' true visionary, who went to prison with a sardonic relish for the absurdity of the world. His death was devoid of the gentleness given it by David Warner in 1963; it became a willed self-sacrifice, the means of freeing himself and (disturbingly) of damning his killer. And as that killer Richard Gloucester, an actor straight from RADA, Anton Lesser, gave an astonishingly assured performance: no Machiavell, despite his claims, but a little yelping crookbacked kid, constantly in pain, constantly itching to inflict it, the last twisted product of a deformed and sick society.

    After this monumental and exhausting undertaking it was extra-ordinary to see the company summon up further energy and move from the earliest plays to the last tragedy, *Coriolanus*, and give that notoriously difficult play its most thrilling production in recent memory. It honoured the fine moral and political shading of the text, allowing neither the protagonist nor the play's factions of family, patricians, plebians, or tribunes extraneous sympathy or weight. The result was a deeply disturbing production of concentrated poetic power, which throughout resolutely refused to reduce complexities to simplistics. It received great acclaim in England and, during its tour of Europe in 1978, also in France and Germany (where it aroused considerable controversy).[14] With work of this calibre at Stratford, and fine seasons in all three of its other theatres, it was no surprise that the RSC should reap the rewards. In 1977 and 1978 the company made almost a clean sweep of all the major theatre awards (*Plays and Players*; the *Evening Standard*; and SWET – the Society of West End Theatre). Acting awards went to Judi Dench, Nigel Hawthorne, Alan Howard, Ian McKellen, Donald Sinden, David Threlfall (one of the company's most promising young actors), and Denis Quilley; other awards went to Terry Hands, Trevor Nunn, and Clifford Williams. Indeed in 1977 the commercial theatre was faced with the embarrassing spectacle of a subsidized company taking no less than eight of the major SWET awards, including Best Musical of the Year for *The Comedy of Errors*.

Several critics, praising the RSC's achievements and contrasting them with what the *Guardian* termed 'hit-or-missery' at the National, put it all down to careful planned development. The company was a little less sanguine in its own assessment of the years 1975–7. There was, indeed, 'planned development', but to those familiar with the course of planning meetings within the RSC the phrase had a wry note to it. Planning meetings, as they were well aware, were frequently scrambled affairs, often set up dangerously late because directors or administrators were tied up with work, and just getting everyone around one table at the same time was a considerable achievement. Key decisions were just as likely to take place in the back of a taxi between Stratford and Coventry station, as in ordered discussion well in advance at a properly convened meeting. And at the meetings themselves planning rarely proceeded smoothly, for it depended on too many factors. As the directors of the company acknowledged, luck played a part too in the flowering of the company's work. Trevor Nunn found the experience of these years exciting but unnerving. He could list reasons for the sudden breakthrough: the beneficent encouragement of the Press; the continuity of management and direction; the stimulus of two new theatres and of younger directors; the anchoring of the RSC's two companies with the two actors he considered led their generation, Alan Howard and Ian McKellen; the company's continuing ability to attract fine young actors; the fact that as the RSC's work-rate went up, so – as he put it –

did its 'artistic pulse-rate'. 'But in any theatrical success', he said, 'there is always the element of the miraculous, the unplanned, and the inexplicable. Suddenly there will be no last-minute hitches, casting will hold firm, the productions that work in the rehearsal room transfer to the stage and you find they work there . . . the most careful planning in the world may help you to achieve all that, but it will never ensure it.'[15] And indeed, and of course, luck does not hold; as had happened to the RSC in the post-1963–4 period, the company's work fell off somewhat in 1978–9. Both Stratford seasons were disappointing. Even the eagerly anticipated 1978 *Antony and Cleopatra,* which marked the return of Peter Brook and Glenda Jackson to the company, called forth a generally muted response from the critics, and never totally succeeded in taking fire.

The work at the Aldwych in these two years was much stronger although, affected by the impending departure of David Jones (who was going to the Brooklyn Academy in New York to found a resident company modelled on the RSC), the second half of the 1978 season plummeted disastrously, not helped by a very injudicious selection of new plays, including the dire *Women Pirates* which was rapidly abandoned. The second Warehouse season was also a disappointment after the first. It caused controversy within the acting company, some of whom were unsympathetic to a repertoire which showed signs of a certain defiant unilateralism, particularly in the large number of plays commissioned. In 1978–9 its productions were subjected to a rising crescendo of attacks from the critics, and although the choice of plays remained bravely committed to young authors, it was surprisingly narrow, eschewing experimental form, ruling out contemporary foreign writers, and concentrating on predominantly naturalistic plays by authors of a single political persuasion. If the plays themselves had been stronger this might have been defensible, but several were irredeemably thin.

Despite the difficulties the company was experiencing, however, the centre held. The 1979 Aldwych season was strong and the work at The Other Place under Ron Daniels was very fine. It included a splendid production by Barry Kyle of Howard Brenton's best play, *The Churchill Play,* two strong small-space Shakespeares, Barton's *Merchant of Venice* and Ron Daniels's *Pericles,* new work by Peter Whelan, David Edgar, and David Rudkin, and revivals of several rarely performed plays – Erdman's *The Suicide,* Brecht's *Baal,* and O'Neill's *Anna Christie.* In 1978, largely at the urging of actors within the company led by Ian McKellen, the RSC had launched yet another new activity – a small-scale tour of twenty-six towns in England and Scotland, lasting from July to October and playing in a wide variety of venues. It took two productions, *Twelfth Night* and *Three Sisters,* minimal scenery, and a portable platform stage, and marked the RSC's first major attempt since the dismantling of Theatregoround to reach audiences remote from its large theatres.

The tour was a great success and it earned the RSC its first commercial sponsorship, £12,000 from Hallmark cards. Hallmark supported similar tours in 1979 and 1980, donating £25,000 the second year and £45,000 the third. In 1981, however, their withdrawal from the scheme coupled with Arts Council cuts to the RSC's touring subsidy forced the company to abandon plans for a fourth tour.

That first tour threw up one of the three outstanding productions of the 1978–9 period, a beautifully paced and observed *Three Sisters,* directed by Trevor Nunn. Jane Lapotaire gave an electric performance in *Piaf,* directed by Howard Davies, and the Hart/Kaufman comedy *Once in a Lifetime,* also directed by Nunn, was the third production to prove the RSC's continued versatility and vitality. With work such as this in evidence, it was clear that although the RSC might have had to face some setbacks it was far from in decline. This was confirmed when, on the edge of a new decade, the company's work gathered strength once more. 1980 saw a much stronger Stratford season, with three fine productions from Terry Hands (*As You Like It,* with Susan Fleetwood as Rosalind, *Richard II,* and *Richard III* – the two latter productions completing Hands's five-year assault on the full History cycle). There was a much acclaimed *Timon,* with Richard Pasco in the title-role, directed by Ron Daniels at The Other Place. There was an explosion of fine work at the Aldwych, with Norman Rodway and Judi Dench giving marvellous performances in Nunn's production of O'Casey's *Juno and the Paycock.* But the season was dominated by two audacious marathon undertakings: John Barton's production/adaptation of ten plays centring on the Oresteia legend, *The Greeks,* and Trevor Nunn's and John Caird's production of David Edgar's eight-hour adaptation of *Nicholas Nickleby.* Both projects were daunting undertakings, planned at a time of renewed financial crisis, and both proved remarkably successful, *Nickleby* (which transferred to Broadway) displaying some of the RSC's greatest, most inventive work.

With productions such as these, building on the achievements and discoveries of the Seventies, the RSC seemed well poised for whatever exigencies the next decade might bring. But in that decade, and in a period of acute recession and record unemployment, the company would have to face its most difficult test for twenty years: the long delayed move to the Barbican theatre.

The RSC had, throughout the Seventies, kept assiduously quiet about the Barbican theatre; its delays had been silently blessed by many within the company. This feeling was partly due to the uproar that surrounded the opening of the National, which made the RSC very nervous indeed; partly to the company's own questioning of the need for expensive new theatre buildings; partly to the fact that the Barbican remained very much an unknown quantity. The building itself augured well; less grandiose in conception than the National, despite its setting in a huge arts complex incorporating a library, art gallery, roof-top arboretum, cinema, and concert-hall, it seated 1,166 people in the large auditorium and had flexible seating for up to 200 people in its studio theatre, the Pit. Its large-auditorium design was revolutionary (although that word had become suspect in the context of new theatres since the opening of the National); its two upper tiers were cantilevered inwards, so that those highest from the stage were as close to it as those in the stalls. Just as the Olivier had been, it was touted as a new theatre of astonishing intimacy, with perfect sight-lines, exemplary acoustics and so on, all claims with a sadly familiar sound. It was undeniably beautiful; it afforded the company equipment, workshops, rehearsal rooms and backstage facilities of apparent excellence, and as its opening in 1982 came closer, general company interest and excitement in it began to rise. Yet only a year before there had been the sensation that the RSC was more excited by its plans for a third Stratford theatre, to be constructed in the shell of the old Memorial's walls (a project which, to date, has not found funding) than it was by the move to the long awaited purpose-built auditorium within the confines of the City of London.

The potential danger of the Barbican was undoubtedly connected with its location. As Trevor Nunn put it, it was 'a jewel – set in a concrete sea'.[16] But the problem was not simply that the theatre was situated outside the traditional theatre district in the middle of an island of post-war planned development that lacked the vitality of, say, the Covent Garden area around the Aldwych. It was that it was inside the City of London boundaries, and would represent the City's first venture into subsidy for the arts in that authority's long, and singularly philistine history. That the City had decided to embark on the whole venture was praiseworthy in the extreme, but the potential for tension between paymasters such as the City fathers and an organization as radical as the RSC was considerable, and any sceptics had only to look at the fraught relationship between, say, the National Theatre and the GLC in the 1980–1 period.[17] The RSC, of course, unlike the National, had never received subsidy from local authorities either in London or the Midlands prior to the move to the Barbican. This parsimony had caused bitterness in the past, and it was ironic that the first signs that major local authority aid could have unwelcome drawbacks should come just as the RSC was about to receive indirect subsidy from the City. The most worrying aspect of the move to the Barbican was that it might alter the RSC's identity; that the RSC would, in effect, be smoothed and tamed by its association with, and partial dependence on, City financial interests. That danger, as it happened, was exacerbated by the extremely weak financial position of the RSC as the move grew imminent.

The history of the RSC's financial troubles stretched back to 1962–3 and the Treasury's warning then that, although the RSC might choose to operate on a National Theatre level, that would not guarantee the company a similar level of government aid. From that time onwards the RSC had been underfunded. The degree of its underfunding had become, year by year, more acute. The company had, indeed, chosen to operate on a National Theatre level, but that term applied to its standards as well as its output. By the end of the Seventies it was tacitly acknowledged by the Arts Council that the country possessed two major theatre companies, and that their co-existence and friendly rivalry had been to the great benefit of British theatre and had had few of the dire consequences foreseen either by the Arts Council in the early Sixties, or by critics of the National in the mid Seventies. What was equally clear was that, because of the circumstances surrounding its birth, the National Theatre received funding of a quite different order from the RSC. During the Seventies the Arts Council avoided this issue with its contention that compara-tive studies of recipients of its grants were misleading. Their coyness was understandable: the work of the National and the RSC *was* clearly directly comparable, in terms of quality, number of auditoria, output, and staffing; yet the financial disparities between the two companies were extraordinary. For example: in 1979–80, the NT added 16 new productions to its repertoire; it gave 909 perform-ances; its box-office revenue was £1,611,913; its subsidy from the Arts Council alone (it also received over half a million pounds from the GLC) was £4,125,652. Compare these figures for the RSC: the company added 20 new productions to its repertoire; it gave 1,209 performances; its box-office revenue was £2,785,655, and its Arts Council grant totalled £1,900,000. This meant that the NT received a state subsidy of £8.69 per paid admission, and the RSC £2.30. Not surprisingly, the RSC had to raise its seat prices more swiftly than the NT; by January 1981 the NT's top price seat was £6.90; the RSC's was £10 at Stratford, and £7.50 in London – a level which embarrassed the company and which led, predictably, to price resistance. There was an equivalent disparity in salaries right across the board, from directors, designers, and actors through manage-ment to technicians and workshop staff.

By 1981 the figures revealed that the gap was gradually widening. In the financial year 1981–2 the NT received total funding of £6,030,000 to the RSC's £2,550,000.[18] These sums, cited by David Brierley in a memo to the RSC executive committee in 1981, clearly demonstrate a disparity which had its origins in Treasury and Arts Council policy in the early Sixties and which, by the time the RSC moved into the Barbican, needed urgent reappraisal. It was true that the RSC's own financial canniness had to some extent softened the effect of low grants; in its ability to find a succession of hit productions – *Wild Oats, Piaf, Nicholas Nickleby, Educating Rita* – the RSC had shown a commercial instinct for generating its own sources of revenue that was unrivalled by any other subsidized British theatre. But although the company had ingeniously earned money from transfers, from the sale of television rights in its productions, and from commercial sponsorship (a field pioneered by the RSC for theatre), although it could claim to earn £1 for every 72p of subsidy it received (a claim none of the other 'big three' com-panies, Covent Garden, the English National Opera, and the NT, could match) its financial position deteriorated sharply. This was made worse because during the late Seventies the company's grant did not even increase at the same rate as those of the other 'big three'. In 1979–80, for instance, when Arts Council grants to Covent Garden, the ENO, and the NT, all rose by over 20 per cent, the

RSC's grant rose by only 7.46 per cent against an annual rate of inflation of 15 per cent. As in the past, the grant was supplemented later in the year, bringing the percentage increase on the previous year to 13.4 per cent – an improvement, but still below the rate of inflation, and still below the increase to the other major companies. For the following year, 1980–1, the imbalance was somewhat redressed and the RSC was given a 21 per cent increase on the previous year's allocation. Unfortunately the damage had been done and the RSC ended the financial year 1979–80 with a deficit of £61,000, and began the Eighties, with the move to the Barbican imminent, with an accumulated deficit of some £300,000. As the RSC's financial controller, William Wilkinson, pointed out, it was technically possible to prove on a day-to-day basis that the RSC was insolvent; it survived by adept manipulation of cash-flow, and by borrowing at increasingly high interest rates.

To launch the Barbican from a position of such financial weakness was a prospect no one in the company relished; companies with large deficits tend to be in a weak position when artistic compromises are suggested. It was already clear, in 1981, as the RSC began renegotiating the terms of its lease from the City preparatory to the move into the new theatre the following year, that the City's indirect subsidy to the RSC was going to have to be very substantial indeed. A 'rent' of 3½ per cent of the final capital costs of the Barbican theatre was, in 1982, not the viable proposition it had been in 1965; the RSC had foreseen paying a rent equivalent to a market rent for a West End theatre of similar size. However, that would leave the onus of repaying the major part of the building's capital costs with the City. Short of turning the Barbican into a conference centre, or finding another theatre company, the City had little choice but to suffer it, and the RSC seemed set to retain a theatre at a bargain price. But the long-term prospects of such an alliance were, to say the least, unpredictable, and future contention more than probable: were City interests, for instance, going to be happy supporting at the Pit the kind of plays that had been performed at the Warehouse?

Meanwhile there were already signs that under financial pressure the RSC was prepared to allow subtle shifts in its own identity in order to attract funding. At the Aldwych in 1980, in preparation for the Barbican where the same system would operate, the company introduced a Patrons' Subscription Scheme. Patrons, those individuals or companies prepared to donate £500 to the RSC (it rose to

£1,000 in 1981) were eligible for certain privileges. They could name a seat in the new theatre – a fairly harmless and traditional perk in this kind of fund-raising. Less innocuously, however, they became entitled to join an RSC priority booking scheme in which patrons undertook to buy a minimum of four top-price seats, usually at fortnightly intervals, for a year, for which they paid an additional 'premium' of 25 per cent. In return they had access to a private 'patrons' bar and priority booking over everyone else including the RSC Club members, by whom in the past this privilege had been enjoyed. By 1981, when the scheme was just beginning and had some twenty-one patrons on its list, its advantages were already clear. It would give the RSC quite substantial amounts of money in advance, a valuable asset for a company with a continual cash-flow problem, and it had side benefits in that it strengthened the RSC's connections with companies who might also sponsor productions, or aid the RSC in other ways; the Rank Organization, for instance, an early patron, was providing a small computerized switchboard for the Pit theatre.[19] Nevertheless the scheme was frankly modelled on one already operating successfully at Covent Garden (where the 'premium' is 60 per cent) and while the specific granting of privileges to the affluent might not seem unusual at an opera-house, it chimed oddly in an organization like the RSC.

The Patrons' Scheme, however, was only part of a much larger project that had considerable implications for the company. A three-year fund-raising push had been launched on Shakespeare's birthday in 1978, designed to raise £1,000,000 for the RSC, £900,000 of which would be invested as an endowment fund to provide the RSC with an independent annual income of some £75,000 a year, a scheme exactly similar to the one instigated by Archie Flower in the late 1920s. Response to the appeal had been slow; after two years only £175,000 had been covenanted or donated, and it was to this fund that the 25 per cent premium on seats to patrons was channelled. These moves, while they unquestionably helped the RSC financially, had an unfortunate backlash; the more energetically the RSC raised private funds the less inclined the Arts Council and Treasury appeared to increase government funding. If the RSC really wanted its Arts Council subvention greatly increased it might have done better to drop all fund-raising activities and wait.

These moves to independent financing strongly reflected the influence of the present chairman of the RSC, Sir Kenneth Cork,

Official Receiver and former Lord Mayor of London. It was he who encouraged the company to pursue commercial sponsorship, and certain RSC governors considered that Sir Kenneth would like to see the RSC in the Eighties becoming increasingly independent of state aid, although Sir Kenneth himself has always stated publicly that Arts Council assistance was indispensable. Zealous promotion of such schemes as the new endowment fund and the Patrons' Subscription Scheme was not incompatible with such an attitude. It was a mixed economy approach that had radical implications for the RSC. Was the company increasingly to look for enlightened patronage, not from the state, but from commerce in the future? And if it did so, what effect would that have on the company's identity? It was a question that only time could answer.

Postscript

At the end of his life, when he was dictating his autobiography and looking back at his work with the English Stage Company at the Royal Court, George Devine attempted to sum up what, for him, a theatre should be. The manuscript includes a famous passage which, as his biographer Irving Wardle puts it, 'has been echoing through the English theatre ever since'. 'A theatre must have a recognizable attitude,' it ends. 'It will have one, whether it likes it or not.'[1]

It is and always has been very difficult to define the RSC in the light of that shrewd assertion. The Stratford theatre, and the companies that have sprung up from it, have evolved over a period unique in British theatre for its longevity. All the major changes that have affected the macrocosm of British theatre over the past hundred years can be seen in microcosm in the development of Stratford and its companies: the demise of the actor-manager and the rise of the director; the restitution of Shakespeare to the centre of the classical repertoire; greater respect for the text; the creation of permanent acting companies; the fight to establish the principle of subsidy; the new understanding of the importance of cross-fertilization between classical and modern work; the investigation of new theatre spaces — all these changes have been reflected, and some have been pioneered, at Stratford. Yet in the past hundred years there has also been constancy. The Stratford theatre, like the English Stage Company, was created with a credo and a vision to which it has remained remarkably true in the course of a century. Charles Flower believed in two things: the central and continuing importance of Shakespeare's plays, and the need for a semi-permanent group of artists dedicated to their investigation and performance. However much the company has altered and diversified in the past hundred years, those two beliefs endure. Indeed, they are at the core of the present RSC's identity. However difficult it is to define the RSC in terms of artistic aims, political attitudes, or social role they are the one certain answer the company could make to Devine's challenge. They constitute the RSC's 'recognizable attitude'.

To purists this might seem inadequate. The RSC has had critics who would have preferred a company that was easier to categorize, either because it had a stated and determining political viewpoint like the Berliner Ensemble, or because it was dedicated to one pure artistic approach like, for instance, Grotowski's Theatre Laboratory in Wroclaw, a theatre so convinced of the veracity of its own approach that it can brand all others 'artistic kleptomania'. The RSC has obstinately avoided such identification. Its directors and its actors are sharply differentiated; it would be impossible now to speak of an 'RSC style'. The aggressive, expressionistic Shakespeare productions of Terry Hands (now joint artistic director of the company with Trevor Nunn) are worlds away from those of John Barton which are essentially naturalistic, highly detailed, often sharply specific as to period or social custom (areas that interest Hands not at all). Yet both men have been happily contained within the same organization, often working with the same actors, for many years. Trevor Nunn has always contended that in this avoidance of the doctrinaire lies the RSC's continuing strength. Certainly it is impressive that with little contractual obligation, and without the institutionalized structure that preserves permanent companies in, say, Eastern Europe, the RSC has contrived to keep all its essential staff and a pool of artists over a period of time unrivalled by any other British theatre.[2] The RSC alone among the big four subsidized companies reached the Eighties without major strikes or industrial action – in itself a major achievement.

Such continuity, of course, carries inherent dangers, chief among them complacency and artistic atrophy; there had been 'continuity' at Stratford in the Thirties, and it had been disastrous. Now it seemed to indicate real well-being, a foundation of shared ideals and a common tradition on which individuals could build. By the end of the Seventies the sternest critics of the RSC would be hard put to deny that it had become a great theatre company, consistently willing to take risks, consistently stretching and regenerating itself. It did this, moreover, not in the context of an ivory-tower group of artists, highly subsidized and playing to a tiny group of devotees, but in the context of popular theatre, playing to live audiences that, by the end of the decade, were close to one million a year. It had become the kind of company that many men and women in its history had envisaged, striven for, and in some cases sacrificed themselves to. Yet despite all its achievements, and despite its international acclaim, there were still those within the company who continued to question its future. Demonstrable excellence and appeal to a growing audience had always been the company's only ultimate defence against the kind of philistinism that begrudged subsidy and increased it unwillingly; the same defence now had to be used against a new species of philistinism which saw in classical theatre the perpetuation of an élite, and in Shakespeare a defunct art form. Trevor Nunn could even envisage a society, at the end of the century, in which Shakespeare's plays would not be performed:

For all our good work, for all our discoveries, our insistence on continuity, for all our present audience response, and for all our earnestness, I do not think we have – yet – ensured a future for Shakespeare. We have not yet put that issue beyond doubt.[3]

Notes

ABBREVIATIONS

B-AP   Bridges-Adams Papers, Special Collections Division, University of Calgary Libraries (numbers in brackets give the location of MSS)

BTL   Shakespeare Birthplace Trust Library, Shakespeare Centre, Stratford-upon-Avon

FFP   Flower family papers, in the possession of Lady Flower

RST   Royal Shakespeare Theatre

SMT   Shakespeare Memorial Theatre

PRELUDE

1 The council also offered to display a portrait of Garrick in the town hall, in order to perpetuate not just Shakespeare's name but also that of his greatest interpreter, provided Garrick paid for the privilege. The portrait was painted by Gainsborough, Garrick contrived to make the council pay for it, and it hung in the town hall until 5 December 1946, when it was destroyed in a fire.

2 Quoted by Christian Deelman, *The Great Shakespeare Jubilee* (1964), p. 195. For this brief summary of Garrick's Jubilee I have drawn extensively on Mr Deelman's brilliantly funny account.

3 An account of this festival is given in *An Account of the Second Commemoration of Shakespeare, celebrated at Stratford-upon-Avon, 1830.* Shakespearian pamphlets, BTL.

4 In some cases the committee wrote directly, in others they used intermediaries who claimed to be intimates of the actors involved. This added to the confusion. See Robert E. Hunter, *Shakespeare and Stratford-upon-Avon . . . together with A Full Record of the Tercentenary Celebration* (1864). BTL.

5 21 January 1864, Edward Fordham Flower, *Tercentenary Scrapbook.* BTL.

6 Quoted by Robert E. Hunter, op. cit.

7 *The Times,* October 1864. *Tercentenary Scrapbook.* BTL.

8 *The Times,* 1 June 1864.

1 MONUMENTAL MOCKERY

1 Autobiographical notes by Charles Flower appended to his wife's diary, *Great-Aunt Sarah's Diary, 1846–1892,* by Sarah Flower (privately printed, 1964). BTL.

2 In 1870 the *Illustrated Midland News* referred to Flower & Sons Brewery as 'the chief and only manufactory of the district'. The company employed over 200 men.

3 Sarah Flower, op. cit.

4 *A History of the Shakespeare Memorial Theatre, published for the Council of the Shakespeare Memorial Association* (1878). BTL.

5 Sarah Flower, op. cit.

6 *A History of the Shakespeare Memorial Theatre,* op. cit.

7 Ibid.

8 Verbatim report, *Stratford-upon-Avon Herald,* 10 November 1876.

9 Shaw, reviewing Irving's production of *King Arthur,* for the *Saturday Review* January 1895. Quoted in Laurence Irving, *Henry Irving* (1951), p. 570.

10 *Stratford-upon-Avon Herald,* op. cit.

11 *A History of the Shakespeare Memorial Theatre, op. cit.*

12 Charles Flower seems to have wished to obscure the scale of his donation, for it was never announced *in toto,* and contemporary press assessments of it vary. By April 1877, when building work on the theatre began, only £6,000 of the necessary £11,000 had been raised, £1,000 of which came from him. He guaranteed the contractors the additional £5,000 required for the theatre section of the building in the hope that this sum would subsequently be raised by subscription, in which case his £5,000 guarantee would become the basis for an endowment fund. There is no indication from the subscription accounts that this £5,000 *was* raised, and as the theatre opened without endowment, it seems clear that Flower's guarantee was called upon. His contribution of £6,000 towards the cost of the tower, library, and gallery sections is documented more fully, both in the press reports of the period in the *Stratford-upon-Avon Herald,* and in the published lists of subscribers (included in *A History of the Shakespeare Memorial Association,* 1878 and 1882, op. cit.) This would bring his total contribution to £12,000, plus the donation of the site. He and his wife gave and bequeathed to the theatre numerous other properties in Stratford, and shareholdings.

13 The term seems to have been coined first by *Aris's Birmingham Gazette,* 4 May 1872, at the time when the previous Stratford theatre in New Place gardens had just been demolished and rumours of a new theatre were rife. It was taken up widely by local papers later to refer to the SMT.

14 Shaw championed Sullivan frequently, and considered that 'Irving was a dwarf beside him'. (Letter to Donald Wolfit, quoted in his autobiography, *First Interval* 1954.) But his judgement seems to have been coloured by his lifelong animosity to Irving.

15 Robert M. Sillard, *Barry Sullivan and his Contemporaries* (1901).

16 Ibid.

17 Frank Benson, *I Want to Go On the Stage* (1931).

18 *The Lady of Lyons* was first performed in 1838; then, ironically, the part Ellen Terry was now to play, of Pauline Deschappelles, had been created by Helen Faucit.

19 Sarah Flower, op. cit.

20 *The Theatre,* 1 May 1879. For Irving's ownership, see Laurence Irving, *Henry Irving,* pp. 349–50. Irving acquired the periodical in August 1878 and sold it to Clement Scott for £1,000 in December 1879, although Scott never paid him the money.

21 Sarah Flower, op. cit.

22 Ibid.

2 A RASH YOUNG GENTLEMAN

1 Frank Benson, *My Memoirs* (1930).
2 Quoted by J. C. Trewin, *Benson and the Bensonians* (1960), p. 47.
3 Frank Benson, op. cit.
4 Constance Benson, *Mainly Players* (1926).
5 Ibid.
6 Frank Benson, op. cit.
7 Many of the SMT's early sets were designed and painted by John O'Connor, a well-known London scenic artist who had also designed parts of the Tercentenary pavilion in 1864. A collection of his Stratford designs, including those for *Macbeth* which drew on the scenery at Glencassley, Charles Flower's Sutherland estate, is in the BTL.
8 James Agate, 'Stars in their Courses', broadcast for the BBC, 1935; quoted by J. C. Trewin, *Benson and the Bensonians*, p. 267.
9 Constance Benson, op. cit.
10 Compiled by Benson's then stage-manager, F. Randle Ayrton, later to be associated with the SMT for many years as an actor. BTL.
11 See Benson's Stratford prompt-book for *Othello*, undated but *c.* 1904, and probably used for several productions, BTL. For the nickname 'Notta' scene, see J. C. Trewin, *Benson and the Bensonians*, p. 137.
12 A typically Bensonian description of stock-company actors is included in his essay 'The National Theatre', in *The Nineteenth Century* (1901).
13 Quoted by Ellen Terry in *The Story of My Life* (1908), p. 132.
14 Gordon Crosse, *Shakespearean Playgoing 1890–1952* (1953).
15 Montague's review appeared in the *Manchester Guardian*, 4 December 1899.
16 See Granville-Barker to John Gielgud, quoted in C. B. Purdom, *Granville-Barker* (1955).
17 Frank Benson, op. cit.
18 Quoted by J. C. Trewin, op. cit.
19 *Observer*, 12 July 1931.
20 *Observer*, 11 August 1929.
21 In a series of articles for the *Empire News*, 1929.
22 Quoted in J. C. Trewin, op. cit., p. 115.
23 FFP.
24 A full account of this débâcle is given by J. C. Trewin in *The Night has been Unruly* (1957).
25 Hannam-Clark's recollections are quoted in J. C. Trewin, *Benson and the Bensonians*.

3 THE NEW CHAIRMAN

1 The play was given in Charles Flower's edited version. It was one of the few occasions during the Benson years when he did not play at Stratford, the others being 1895 (Ben Greet); spring 1914 (Patrick Kirwan); summer 1916 (Ben Greet); and summer 1919 (when Benson made minor appearances).
2 According to Tyrone Guthrie (*A Life in the Theatre*, 1960) Charles Laughton considered Baylis 'a scheming, small-minded, mean-spirited old shrew, whose

one idea was to keep the reins of power in her incompetent hands'. Laughton and Baylis disliked one another cordially, and Guthrie's tone frequently suggests that he sympathized with Laughton, even if he did not entirely share his views.

3 Agnes Kingscote, *Family Memoirs*, FFP. Mrs Kingscote was Archie Flower's sister, and recalled these visitors to the family home in her memoirs. The names are confirmed by The Hill's visitors' books for the period.

4 Archie Flower, speech to the Plays and Book Club, New York, 1927. FFP.

5 Donald Wolfit, *First Interval* (1954).

6 Quoted by J. C. Trewin in *Benson and the Bensonians*, p. 148. Corelli was frequently biased against the SMT and seems to have been so here; Irving died at Bradford only a few months later, on 13 October 1905, so the plea of ill health seems to have been accurate.

7 Annual Reports of the Governors, 1907. SMT.

8 Constance Collier, *Harlequinade* (1929).

9 Constance Benson, *Mainly Players* (1926).

10 The spring festival was cut short by the death of Edward VII, after which the theatre closed.

11 Quoted by J. C. Trewin, *Benson and the Bensonians*, p. 180.

12 Archie Flower, memorandum to the executive council of the governors, 1910. FFP.

13 A. Justins to Archie Flower, 16 March 1911. FFP.

14 Archie Flower, memorandum, 1910, ibid.

15 Frank Benson to Archie Flower, 21 September 1910. FFP.

16 See J. C. Trewin, *Benson and the Bensonians*, p. 190, for a fuller account of this season and production.

17 Quoted by C. B. Purdom, *Granville-Barker* (1955), who gives a fine account of both productions.

18 Robert Speaight, *William Poel and the Elizabethan Revival* (1954), gives a detailed account of the Trocadero dinner, including a guest list.

19 At the Trocadero dinner. Quoted by Speaight, op. cit.

20 Ibid.

21 Ibid.

22 Photographs of the cast, in costume, were taken outside the Memorial Theatre. They are now in the collection of the BTL.

23 See Veronica Turleigh's recollections of working with Poel. Collection of MS material relating to William Poel, collected by Sir Barry Jackson, 1948. BTL.

24 A detailed account of the text of Poel's production of *Troilus* is given in Speaight, op. cit.

25 Annual Reports of the Governors, 1913. SMT.

26 Quoted by M. C. Day and J. C. Trewin, *The Shakespeare Memorial Theatre* (1932), p. 125.

27 Avis Lobdell of the *Oregon Journal*, to Archie Flower. FFP.

28 J. C. Trewin, *Benson and the Bensonians*, p. 209.

29 Nigel Playfair, *The Story of the Lyric Theatre, Hammersmith* (1925).

30 Some of Lovat Fraser's original designs for this production are in the collection of the BTL.

31 Playfair, op. cit.

32 Ibid.

33 Constance Benson, op. cit.

34 Playfair, op. cit.

35 After Stratford the production played at Brighton and then at the Lyric, Hammersmith. Bailey was reviewing it in London. His sentiments were endorsed by the local Stratford critics. The *Herald* lamented the loss of Benson's 'faultlessly good and picturesque' sets, with their 'nooks and crannies made charming with flowers and plants', and boasted that Playfair's kind of innovation would never find a footing in Stratford.

4 THE FIRST DIRECTOR

1 Quoted by John Elsom and Nicholas Tomalin, *The History of the National Theatre* (1978), p. 40.

2 Bridges-Adams to William Archer, 13 November 1918. B-AP (5.2.2.)

3 26 May 1919. B-AP (5.2.5.)

4 Ibid.

5 *Daily Telegraph*, 21 April 1921.

6 In his Foreword to M. C. Day and J. C. Trewin, *The Shakespeare Memorial Theatre*, (1932), p. xiii.

7 Ibid.

8 Robert Speaight (ed.), *A Memoir. A Bridges-Adams Letter Book* (The Society for Theatre Research, 1971).

9 Archie Flower, speech to the Play and Book Club, New York, 1927. FFP.

10 In a letter to the author, 1979.

11 W. Bridges-Adams, *The Irresistible Theatre* (1957).

12 Letter to A. C. Sprague, 25 March 1949, Robert Speaight, op. cit.

13 Letter to Laurence Irving, 1 January 1953, ibid.

14 Letter to A. C. Sprague, 28 February 1953, ibid.

15 20 August 1919. B–AP (5.2.7.)

16 11 October 1922. Ibid. (5.3.12.)

17 2 December 1922. Ibid. (5.3.16.)

18 This report exists in two forms, each similar. I have quoted from what appears to be a first draft, dated October 1924. B-AP (5.5.18.)

19 W. A. Darlington, *Six Thousand and One Nights: Forty Years a Dramatic Critic* (1960).

20 Letter to A. C. Sprague, 15 January 1952, Robert Speaight, op. cit.

21 Recollections of J. C. Trewin, in an interview with the author, 1979.

22 In an interview with the author, 1978. Shaw worked with Ayrton at the SMT in 1926.

23 Ibid.

24 Recalled by J. C. Trewin in an interview with the author, 1979.

25 26 May 1919. B-AP (5.2.5.)

26 Letter to A. C. Sprague, 16 December 1953, Robert Speaight, op. cit.

27 The cuts and transpositions Bridges-Adams made for *Coriolanus* are remarkable given his reputation as a champion of full texts. By comparing the set designs and photographs of his productions of the play with the prompt-books, some of the reasons for the cuts and transpositions become clear: they were necessitated by the staging he adopted. Too numerous to detail here, the cuts and adaptations can be seen in B-A's prompt-books for 1926 and 1933, both of which, together with production pictures, are in the collection of the BTL.

5 AFTER THE FIRE

1 This is the form of the telegram which was subsequently often quoted by Archie Flower, and remembered by his family. The original is now lost.

2 *The Times,* 10 March 1926.

3 Interview in the *Sunday Times,* 14 March 1926.

4 An account of their travels and fund-raising activities is contained in Florence Flower's extensive diaries, now in the possession of her daughter, Mrs David Lloyd.

5 *Birmingham Mail,* 23 April 1927.

6 FFP.

7 Bridges-Adams was concerned that the new theatre should be able to cope with repertoire playing, i.e. the rotation of several productions during the course of one week. Backstage and in the flies he wanted swift set changes to be possible, and maximum storage space to be provided.

8 6 November 1927. B-AP (5.9.4.) The recommendations were made before Elizabeth Scott's designs were publicly announced as the winning entry.

9 3 April 1928. FFP.

10 *The Times,* 30 April 1929. In the letter Barker stated his belief that a National Theatre need in fact cost no more than half a million pounds. He conveniently revised his estimate to a million, however, in his book the following year.

11 11 May 1929. FFP.

12 FFP.

13 6 November 1931. FFP.

14 29 December 1925. B-AP. (5.6.41.)

15 The final contract and the correspondence that led up to it are held with the B-AP.

16 See Robert Speaight, op. cit., and B-A to A. C. Sprague, 13 January 1960, after receiving a CBE – a letter which implies he had earlier hoped for a knighthood: 'I have given up every thought of an honour for a quarter of a century. My first impulse was to decline, because it carried nothing for beloved Peg [his wife] . . . '

17 *Stratford-upon-Avon Herald,* 21 August 1931.

18 Annual Report of the Governors, 1929. SMT. These reports were drafted by Archie Flower.

6 OPENINGS

1 This account of the meeting with Elgar and his reactions is taken detail by detail, including Elgar's comments, from Archie Flower's recounting of it to Bridges-Adams, 15 February 1932. FFP.

5 8 January 1928.

6 Letter to the *Architects' Journal*, conveyed via Maurice Chesterton, 24 February 1951. B-AP (5.25.7)

7 See AF to WB-A, 15 February 1932: 'Some [free-]masons say that Granville-Barker's letter to *The Times* prevented the Duke of Connaught from laying the foundation stone, but I have my doubts about that.' FFP.

8 9 February 1932, FFP. This correspondence indicates that Archie was far less opposed to the idea of visiting 'stars' than later critics made out, particularly W. A. Darlington who frequently reiterated the story that Archie had told him stars would go to the SMT only 'over his dead body'. See Darlington, *Daily Telegraph,* 12 November 1955.

9 Cf. recollections of (Sir) Gyles Isham, *Birmingham Dispatch,* 23 April 1953, and Fabia Drake, in a letter to the author, 1979, in which she recalled that everyone in the company was becoming 'extremely rattled and temperamental' as the opening approached.

10 7 January 1932. FFP.

11 *Everyman,* 28 April 1932. Purdom was mistaken; the rolling stage was risked only once in the two productions, for the coronation procession of the newly crowned Henry V at the end of *Part II.*

12 *Era,* 27 April 1932. Although Baughan was right about the lack of rehearsal time, his estimate of the 1932 productions is not wholly reliable. He stayed to review only the opening productions, and did not, that year, review the *Dream,* for instance.

13 FFP. Dame Edith and Archie Flower had been friends for many years; in 1934 Archie's eldest son, Fordham, married Dame Edith's niece, Hersey Balfour.

14 January 1932. FFP.

15 FFP. Although Wilkinson generally supported B-A in Council, he was capable of playing a double game. On this occasion he was swiftly converted again into an ally when he discovered he was going to lose the job of designing *The Winter's Tale.* He then lobbied Archie energetically on B-A's behalf.

16 6 June 1932. B-AP (5.17.4.)

17 18 June 1932. FFP and B-AP (5.17.6)

18 18 June 1932. FFP.

19 John Gielgud, *Early Stages* (1952), p. 95.

20 The rehearsal period is frequently remembered as briefer still by those still alive who appeared in the production. But ten days is the period Komisarjevsky claimed he had, see *Birmingham Mail,* 7 July 1932.

21 It is clear from the correspondence for this period that Bridges-Adams was given his head for 1933 only because he threatened Archie with resignation. (At a luncheon on 16 June 1932, at which Dame Edith Lyttelton was also present.) He informed Bill Savery of this on 21 June 1932, by letter, B-AP (5.17.12.) In 1934, when his contract was due to expire, he could no longer use the threat of resignation effectively.

22 6 January 1933. FFP.

23 Annual Reports of the Governors, 1934. SMT.

24 Ibid, 1933 and 1934.

25 Ibid, 1934.

26 Salary lists. FFP.

27 See Richard Findlater, *Lilian Baylis* (1975), p. 265.

28 Theodore Komisarjevsky, *The Theatre and a Changing Civilisation* (1935).

29 Fabia Drake, letter to the author, 1979.

30 Rachel Kempson, interview with the author, 1979.

31 He later maintained, oddly, that he had hoped to be succeeded by C. B. Cochran; see letter to Bill Savery, 13 January 1938, B-AP (5.23.3.)

32 Undated, but about August–September 1934. B-AP (5.22.4.)

33 8 September 1934. B-AP (5.22.5.) Shaw continued to press him, and Bridges-Adams did finally agree to become a governor in May 1935. He never attended a meeting.

34 Letter to John Moore, Robert Speaight, op. cit.

7 VEERING TO CHARYBDIS

1 Ben Iden Payne, *A Life in a Wooden O* (1977). Iden Payne gives the summer of 1934 for his Poel visit, which must be a confusion, given that his appointment was announced in July 1934, and was preceded by months of negotiations. He made a *second* visit in 1934; the first was the previous year.

2 Archie Flower, visitors' book, 1933. FFP.

3 See Annual Reports of the Governors, 1935 (SMT). The money was, and is, administered by the Charity Commissioners and not by the theatre's governors direct. Only the interest is available for the theatre's use; the value of the capital has, of course, depreciated hugely.

4 13 January 1938. B-AP (5.23.3). Bridges-Adams's files were – and are – formidably complete.

5 Ben Iden Payne, op. cit.

6 28 September 1934. B-AP (5.22.12.)

7 Recalled by Gwynne Whitby, in an interview with the author, 1979. Miss Whitby was in the company at the SMT in 1934–5.

8 21 February 1935. B-AP (5.22.13.)

9 Ibid.

10 Ben Iden Payne, op. cit.

11 See prompt-books and photographs of Iden Payne productions, in the collection of the BTL. One of his 'page-boys' in 1935 was his daughter, Rosalind Iden, later to become Lady Wolfit.

12 Annual Report of the Governors, 1936. SMT.

13 13 January 1938. B-AP (5.23.3.)

14 Recalled by Luise Randle Ayrton (Mrs John Hitching) in an interview with the author, 1979.

15 *Birmingham Mail*, 23 April 1936.

16 Donald Wolfit, *First Interval* (1954).

17 Ibid.

18 Ronald Harwood, *Sir Donald Wolfit, His Life and Work in the Unfashionable Theatre* (1971).

19 Annual Report of the Governors, 1926. SMT.

20 Donald Wolfit, op. cit.

21 Annual Reports of the Governors for the years cited. SMT.

22 19 September 1937. FFP.

23 Darlington gave his version of this meeting in his book, *Six Thousand and One Nights* (1960). Archie Flower's version of it (in his correspondence) differed considerably.

24 This figure was not announced: the exact state of the SMT's assets (as opposed to annual surplus/deficit) was confidential, but is contained in the written governors' reports. Periodic lists of the theatre's liquid assets, in the form of shareholdings, are among the FFP.

25 In a speech at the Birthday luncheon in Stratford. Guthrie stated that 'the governors of the Old Vic would in future welcome the closest co-operation between their theatre and the Shakespeare Memorial Theatre'.

26 31 October 1939. FFP.

27 Undated. FFP.

28 In an interview with the author, 1979.

29 Both Bridges-Adams and Iden Payne had followed Benson in introducing some non-Shakespeare plays to the repertoire. *The School for Scandal* and *She Stoops to Conquer* were revived from time to time; Iden Payne even tackled Jonson, directing *Every Man in His Humour* in 1937.

30 See A. C. Bradley, *Coriolanus,* British Academy Lecture, 1912. Reprinted in *A Miscellany,* 1929.

31 Annual Reports of the Governors for the years cited. SMT.

32 Interview with the author, 1979.

33 At the Annual Governors' Meeting, 23 April 1944, reported in the *Stratford-upon-Avon Herald.*

34 Recalled in an interview with the author, 1979.

35 Fordham Flower's recollection of the event, as recalled by Lady Flower and Patrick Donnell in interviews with the author, 1979.

8 DECAY AND CHANGE

1 Peter Brook, interview with the author, 1979.

2 Nancy Burman, interview with the author, 1979.

3 Peter Brook, interview with the author, 1979.

4 The two other Reps, Glasgow and Miss Horniman's Gaiety in Manchester, closed in 1914 and 1921 respectively.

5 See T. C. Kemp, *The Birmingham Repertory Theatre* (1948).

6 FFP. Fordham Flower was ill, and the speech was read by his sister, Mrs David Lloyd.

7 He was called up as a reservist in 1939, serving in the Middle East and North West Europe.

8 Lady Flower, interview with the author, 1979.

9 Peter Brook, *The Empty Space* (1972), p. 51.

10 Production photographs and the prompt-book for this production are in the collection of the BTL.

11 Annual Report of the Governors, 1947. SMT.

12 SMT Investment List, 1946. FFP.

13 Now among the FFP for the year 1947.

14 Peter Brook, interview with the author, 1979.

15 Peter Brook, interview in *Girls' Own Paper,* June 1947.

16 Simple elements were introduced further to define location, such as a flown-in canopy for Capulet's house, and a somewhat awkward tomb. Photographs and the prompt-book for this production are in the collection of the BTL.

17 Quoted by J. C. Trewin in *Peter Brook* (1971).

18 Peter Brook, interview with the author, 1979.

19 Ibid.

20 Anthony Quayle, interview with the author, 1979.

21 Now among the FFP.

22 In November 1947, for instance, Quayle invited Fordham Flower to dinner in London; his senior partner, Benthall, was not invited to the meal, but for drinks afterwards.

23 Lord Iliffe to Fordham Flower, 30 April 1948; Fordham's reply, 6 May 1948. FFP.

24 Peter Brook, interview with the author, 1979.

25 Anthony Quayle, interview with the author, 1979.

26 Peter Brook, interview with the author, 1979.

27 Anthony Quayle, interview with the author, 1979.

28 FFP.

29 Anthony Quayle, interview with the author, 1979.

30 Sir Barry Jackson bequeathed the portrait to the theatre on his death. It is now in the theatre's picture-gallery.

31 Peter Brook, interview with the author, 1979.

9 THE TRIUMVIRATE

1 Peter Brook, interview with the author, 1979.

2 Anthony Quayle, interview with the author, 1979.

3 Sir John Gielgud, interview with the author, 1980.

4 Anthony Quayle, interview with the author, 1979.

5 Ibid.

6 David Brierley, general manager of the RSC, in an interview with the author, 1979.

7 Annual Reports of the Governors for the years cited. SMT.

8 *Tribune,* 25 November 1949.

9 Quoted by Irving Wardle, *The Theatres of George Devine* (1978), p. 152.

10 Annual Report of the Governors, 1951. SMT.

11 J. Dover Wilson and T. C. Worsley, *Shakespeare's Histories at Stratford 1951* (1952).

12 Ibid.

13 Anthony Quayle, interview with the author, 1979.

14 *The Tablet,* 8 September 1951.

15 Kenneth Tynan, *A View of the English Stage, 1944–63* (1975), p. 152. This

was written when Tynan was reviewing the 1954–5 Old Vic productions of *Henry IV*.

16 Ibid., pp. 114–15.

17 Sir Ralph Richardson, interview in *Great Acting,* ed. H. Burton (1967).

18 A full account of Devine's involvement with these two projects is given by Irving Wardle, *The Theatres of George Devine*, pp. 161–4.

19 Recalled by Patrick Donnell and Anthony Quayle, in separate interviews with the author, 1979.

20 Sir Michael Redgrave, letter to Fordham Flower, 5 June 1954. FFP.

21 Quayle, interview with the author, 1979.

22 Photographs and the prompt-book for this production are in the collection of the BTL.

23 Tynan, op. cit. pp. 157–8.

24 Ibid. Introduction, p. 10.

25 Peter Brook, programme note, *Titus Andronicus* (1955). SMT.

26 Peter Brook, interview with the author, 1979.

27 Tynan, op. cit. p. 163.

28 Ibid., p. 176.

29 Ibid., p. 199.

30 See correspondence, September 1955, FFP. Quayle's contract was not due to expire until 1957.

31 Glen Byam Shaw, interview with the author, 1979.

32 Ibid.

33 Peter Hall to Fordham Flower, 12 July 1958. FFP.

34 Sir Peter Hall, interview with the author, 1979.

35 Ibid. Also Lady Flower (who was present in Leningrad), interview with the author, 1979.

10 THE PETER HALL YEARS: I

1 John Barton, interview with the author, 1979.

2 The contracts gave the RSC management first call on an actor's services for three years but did not preclude his working elsewhere. During non-playing periods (when the actor was neither playing nor rehearsing for the RSC, and those periods could not exceed nine months of the three years) the actor was paid 75 per cent of his salary, unless he accepted other work, in which case the salary ceased for its duration. Though laudable in theory the contracts were easily abused, particularly if the RSC could not come up with enough parts for its companies (often a problem when transferring to London). In some cases it was more profitable for an actor to live on 75 per cent of his RSC salary than to find other work; this led to the nickname 'the Ibiza charter' for the contracts, and to rumours that out-of-work RSC players were more likely to be found adorning the beaches of the Mediterranean than the lobby of the Lisson Grove Employment Exchange.

3 15 March 1960. FFP.

4 Sir Peter Hall, interview with the author, 1979; see also David Addenbrooke, *The Royal Shakespeare Company: The Peter Hall Years* (1974), p. 231.

5 A fuller account of this meeting is given in John Elsom and Nicholas Tomalin, *The History of the National Theatre* (1978), p. 121–2.

6 In an interview with the author, 1979, and elsewhere.

7 Peter Hall, 'Shakespeare and the Modern Director', in *Royal Shakespeare Theatre Company 1960–1963* (1964), p. 43.

8 Peter Brook, interview with the author, 1979.

9 Peter Hall, 'Shakespeare and the Modern Director', op. cit., p. 44. In fact neither Scofield nor Harrison nor Kendall worked at Stratford that first season. The leading actors in a strong company were Max Adrian, Peggy Ashcroft, Geraldine McEwan, Peter O'Toole, Eric Porter, and Dorothy Tutin; important parts were played by two of the company's most promising younger actors, Ian Holm and Ian Richardson.

10 Recalled by Sir John Gielgud and Dame Peggy Ashcroft in interviews with the author, 1979.

11 The prompt-book for this production, and photographs of it, are in the collection of the BTL.

12 Sir Peter Hall, interview with the author, 1979. John Barton had encountered problems on his first RSC production, the *Shrew* in 1960, on which Hall – at the cast's request – had had to undertake last-minute rescue work. Hall had then told him he did not think he could offer him another production. According to RSC legend Barton had not then departed, as expected, but had remained, saying he would one day be needed. He retreated with sage-like dignity to a small office in a remote corridor to await, like a theatrical de Gaulle, the summons to return. It came in 1963.

13 The Stratford season included two revivals; the Aldwych season included one double-bill, four revivals, and one Stratford transfer.

14 Kenneth Tynan, *Observer,* 16 September 1962.

15 30 December 1959. FFP.

16 21 March 1960. FFP.

17 According to Sir Fordham Flower, who quoted him as saying this in a letter to John Profumo, 22 December 1961. FFP.

18 Minutes of the National Theatre executive committee, 2 September 1960; and minutes of the 34th meeting of the Joint Council of the National Theatre, 22 December 1960.

19 27 March 1961. FFP.

20 13 April 1961. Copies of these figures and the statement from Peter Hall were supplied to Sir Fordham Flower (FFP). The amphitheatre was to be designed by Sean Kenny. The figures were drawn up in April; they reached the Arts Council in May.

21 23 June 1961. FFP.

22 Sir Fordham Flower to John Profumo, 22 December 1961. FFP.

23 31 July 1961. FFP.

24 16 August 1961. A temporizing letter giving no specific answer but couched in soothing tones had been sent by Cottesloe in the interim, on 2 August.

25 The RSC was perfectly justified in this expectation: it had been promised subsidy in Selwyn Lloyd's statement in the House of 21 March 1961, and although he had since changed his mind it had also been established at the discussions of the

executive committee of the National Theatre that both Stratford an
would receive interim grants to build up company strength in the
for the NT going ahead.

26 Quoted by John Elsom and Nicholas Tomalin, op. cit., p. 123–4

27 21 August 1961. FFP.

28 30 August 1961. FFP.

29 Sir Fordham Flower, memorandum to the executive council, RST, 25 September 1961. FFP.

30 4 January 1961. FFP.

31 Outline scheme to be presented to the Chancellor and the LCC, unanimously adopted at the 35th meeting of the Joint Council of the National Theatre, 18 December 1961 (FFP). As Chandos acknowledged at that meeting, many of the proposals contained in this document had originated from Sir Fordham Flower.

32 Letter to John Profumo, 25 July 1962. FFP.

33 In a letter to Sir Fordham Flower, 7 February 1962. FFP.

34 22 October 1962. FFP.

35 23 October 1962. FFP.

36 11 May 1962.

11 THE PETER HALL YEARS: II

1 John Barton, Peter Brook, and Sir Peter Hall in separate interviews with the author, 1979.

2 Sir Peter Hall, interview with the author, 1979.

3 Ibid.

4 Annual Reports of the Governors, 1963 and 1964. RST.

5 See John Barton and Peter Hall, *The Wars of the Roses* (1970).

6 John Barton and Peter Hall, op. cit., introduction, pp. x–xi.

7 There were two Theatre of Cruelty seasons at LAMDA, the first in March 1963, the second in 1964. As part of the same work-in-progress Genet's *The Screens* was also performed at the Donmar Rehearsal Rooms in Covent Garden, in May 1964.

8 Antonin Artaud, *The Theatre and its Double* (1970), pp. 59–60.

9 Maurice Colbourne to Emile Littler, 30 May 1964; Emile Littler to Fordham Flower, 22 June 1964. FFP.

10 Peter Brook, interview in the *Daily Mail*, 26 August 1964.

11 FFP.

12 Recalled by Dame Peggy Ashcroft and others, in interviews with the author, 1979.

13 Annual Reports of the Governors, 1965. RST.

14 In 1965–6 the company eventually received grants totalling £95,000.

15 Report by George Farmer to Fordham Flower on a meeting held at the Arts Council, 6 April 1965. FFP.

16 The RSC had been searching for a more permanent London base than the Aldwych for some time before the advent of the Barbican theatre. After lengthy negotiations the company had come to agreement with the Ballet Rambert to share a new theatre to be built in the Notting Hill Gate area of London. In July

1963 it was announced that Sir Basil Spence would be the architect of this theatre, and the same year a million pound building fund had been launched; only £100,000 had been raised, however, by early 1965. The RSC's somewhat abrupt withdrawal from this scheme once the possibility of the Barbican arose caused some ill feeling with their partners in the Ballet Rambert.

17 Interview with the author, 1979.

18 Jan Kott, *Shakespeare Our Contemporary* (1964), pp. 54–7. The phrase 'poor boy with a book in his hands' was a quote from Stanislaw Wyspiański, the Polish painter, dramatist, and designer.

19 See Fordham Flower to Arnold Goodman, 7 July 1965, and his reply, 17 July. FFP.

20 Peter Brook, interview with the author, 1979.

21 Patrick Donnell ceased to be general manager of the RSC in 1967, and became responsible for the development of the Barbican theatre.

22 Patrick Donnell, interview with the author, 1979.

12 A CLEAN SHEET

1 Trevor Nunn, interview with the author, 1979.

2 Some changes were made to the extant text: there was some re-ordering of scenes, cutting, etc; there were also short inserted speeches, written by John Barton. See prompt-book for the 1966 production, BTL. The production was a late addition to the planned five-play 1966 repertoire.

3 *Observer,* 9 October 1966.

4 Terry Hands, Trevor Nunn, and John Barton, in separate interviews with the author, 1979.

5 Sir Peter Hall, interview with the author, 1979.

6 Brook founded his Centre International de Créations Théâtrales in Paris in 1971.

7 Recalled by Ian Richardson, interview with the author, 1979.

8 Trevor Nunn, interview with the author, 1979.

9 Annual Reports of the Governors, 1970–1. RST.

10 Peter Brook, *MSND at the Drama Desk,* a press conference held in New York on 25 January 1971, quoted in full in *Peter Brook's production of William Shakespeare's A Midsummer Night's Dream,* ed. Glenn Loney (1974), pp. 29–30.

11 Ibid.

12 Ibid., p.26.

13 Ibid., p. 25.

14 Trevor Nunn, interview with the author, 1979.

15 John Elsom and Nicholas Tomalin, *The History of the National Theatre* (1978), p. 246.

16 Quoted in Catherine Itzin, *Stages in the Revolution – Political Theatre in Britain since 1968* (1980), p. 268.

17 Quoted by David Addenbrooke, *The Royal Shakespeare Company: The Peter Hall Years* (1974), p. 258.

13 TOWARDS A NEW THEATRE

1 Figures supplied by Trevor Nunn, interview with the author, 1980. The allegation that the new staging cost £250,000 was particularly long-lived: it was, for example, quoted as late as 1980, by Catherine Itzin in *Stages in the Revolution,* p. 184.

2 The controversy over the *Romans* company was, and remains, a vexed one. Nunn maintains a) that he felt the introduction of new blood was necessary; b) that several members of the Aldwych company were invited to play in the *Romans,* and declined; c) that the Aldwych company lacked the actors he needed for such key roles in the *Romans* season as Cleopatra, Antony, Titus. (Interview with the author, 1980.) There are counter-arguments to this, some put forward at the time; chief among them is the difficult question of whether a company like the RSC should endeavour to plan its repertoire around its actors, or pick its actors to suit its repertoire.

3 Nunn's description of the staging for the 1969 Stratford productions. Interview with the author, 1979.

4 Eileen Atkins appeared in *Suzanna Andler* at the Aldwych before going to Stratford to play Rosalind. Neither she, Bates, Dalton, nor directors Peter Gill and Keith Hack worked with the RSC again that decade.

5 Jean Moore was succeeded by Bronwyn Robertson in 1980.

6 Trevor Nunn, interview with the author, 1980.

7 *Guardian,* November 1974; quoted by Catherine Itzin, *Stages in the Revolution* (1980).

8 Statement from Michael Blakemore to a meeting of the associate directors of the National Theatre, 17 March 1976; quoted in John Elsom and Nicholas Tomalin, *The History of the National Theatre* (1978), p. 313. (Blakemore was criticizing the pay differentials between various levels of NT actors. His remarks did not relate to differentials between the NT and the RSC.)

9 Terry Hands, 'An Introduction to the Play', in *The RSC's Production of Henry V for the Centenary Season,* ed. Sally Beauman (1976), p. 16. The book gives a detailed account of the 1975 production.

10 Henry V alters the standard procedures of medieval warfare in two respects, both generally lost on a modern audience, and both emphasized in this production. He rejects that privilege of the nobly born, ransom, and forbids the privilege of the ordinary soldier, plunder. See *The RSC's Production of Henry V,* op. cit. note to p. 164.

11 Trevor Nunn, interview with the author, 1980.

12 'Stock-take at the Warehouse', article by, and interview with, Howard Davies, *Platform* 2, Summer 1980.

13 For a full account of these productions, and of textual alterations and adaptations made on the few previous occasions when the trilogy had been mounted, see David Daniell, 'Opening the text: Shakespeare's Henry VI plays in performance' in *Drama and Society* ed. James Redmond (1979).

14 A detailed account of this production of *Coriolanus* and of its European tour is given by David Daniell, *Coriolanus in Europe* (1980).

15 Trevor Nunn, interview with the author, 1980.

16 Ibid.

17 After protesting, in 1980, at the inclusion of Howard Brenton's play *The*

Romans in Britain in the National's repertoire, the GLC under Sir Horace Cutler took the unprecedented step of reducing, or failing to increase, its £600,000 annual grant to the NT, thus – despite its energetic denials – attempting to use financial leverage to influence the NT's artistic work.

18 Memorandum from David Brierley to the executive council of the RST governors, 19 January 1981, based on figures included in the NT's annual report, 1979–80.

19 The RSC estimated that in the first year of operation at the Barbican there would be thirty-nine patrons bringing in £32,000 in ticket sales and £8,000 to the endowment fund. The company introduced restrictions on numbers so that if the Patrons' Scheme proved increasingly popular it would be impossible to reserve too many seats on any one night in advance. It also attempted to promote the scheme as 'perks' for middle management rather than for client entertaining, though clearly the RSC could have no say in how patrons chose to use tickets.

POSTSCRIPT

1 Irving Wardle, *The Theatres of George Devine* (1978), p. 279.

2 For example: in 1980 John Barton had been with the RSC for twenty years; Nunn, fifteen; Hands, fourteen; Brierley, nineteen; Wilkinson, twelve; Ron Daniels and Howard Davies, six. The continuity among other administrators, workshop staff, technicians, stage-hands and non-staff workers such as actors, designers, and musicians has been equally remarkable.

3 Trevor Nunn, interview with the author, 1980.

Index